Constitutional Revolutions

Constitutional
REVOLUTIONS

Pragmatism and the Role of Judicial

Review in American Constitutionalism

ROBERT JUSTIN LIPKIN

Duke University Press   Durham and London   2000

©2000 Duke University Press
All rights reserved
Printed in the United States of America on acid-free paper ∞
Designed by Rebecca Filene Broun
Typeset in Carter and Cone Galliard by Keystone Typesetting, Inc.
Library of Congress Cataloging-in-Publication Data
appear on the last printed page of this book.

To Sarah Lipkin,
and to her grandparents, Herb Lipkin and the memory of Libby Lipkin,
and Lila Dunphy and the memory of Freeman Dunphy

CONTENTS

PREFACE

    This book examines the practice of judicial review and the jurisprudential framework within which it operates. The book's thesis is that American constitutional law is driven by "constitutional revolutions," constitutional judgments that translate political and cultural attitudes into formal judicial decisions, which themselves do not follow from — and may even contradict — previous decisions. The theory of constitutional revolutions includes a dualist structure of constitutional change that gives new meaning to the idea of a "living" constitution. The constitution "lives" when judges transmogrify ethical and cultural factors into the formal province of constitutional law through revolutionary adjudication. Without this theory we cannot explain how American constitutional law changes.

    The theory maintains that in order to justify judicial review, we must first *describe* and *explain* constitutional change in conceptually and historically accurate terms. Only when such description and explanation are complete can we pose the normative question of justification. In my view the theory of constitutional revolutions is *the* theory of American constitutional change because it correctly depicts American constitutional practice, and because without it American constitutional practice lacks a persuasive explanation. If such an explanation is available, it deserves our respect just because it is *our* practice, unless there exist compelling reasons to the contrary. Thus, the correct explanatory description of constitutional practice provides a prima facie justification of that practice. The cultural setting in which the practice resides provides a framework for criticizing and correcting any unacceptable features the practice exhibits. However, a deeper normative account of revolutionary judicial review is possible. According to this type of justification, revolutionary judicial review is warranted because it contributes to the just and efficient operation of American democracy. Consequently, two kinds of normative factors justify revolutionary adjudication. The first kind derives from the justificatory impact of an accurate description and explanation. A practice is justified if it can be sustained historically and conceptually. Such a justification is conservative because it takes actual practice to be presumptively correct. A justification of this sort gains plausibility because it depicts the unique character of American constitutional development better than alternatives. The second kind of normative factor requires showing how revolutionary adjudication (under a description of a certain kind) is more conducive to (or necessary for) the just and efficient operation of American democratic institutions than are alternative accounts. Such a method of justification does not *entail* progressive politics, but it does encourage a commitment to criticizing and correcting political and judicial mistakes, and therefore it lends itself to an ideology of change for excluded or dominated groups.

The standard view of constitutional change rejects the existence or the independent significance of constitutional revolutions. Standard theories of constitutional change all have a *monist* structure, a structure that insists that constitutional interpretation involves one and only one jurisprudential paradigm. According to standard theories, constitutional law is exclusively conventionalist, coherentist, pragmatist, or naturalist. By contrast the theory of constitutional revolutions rejects the idea that any one jurisprudential paradigm exclusively characterizes American constitutional practice. Instead, the theory demonstrates how these different jurisprudential models are structured and integrated into a syncretic conception of systematically different, but related, movements in constitutional law.

The theory also rejects the standard jurisprudential paradigm, which maintains that constitutional change occurs only as extensions or transformations of prior law. Although it is true that some forms of adjudication are predicated upon a jurisprudence of prior law, the so-called seminal or landmark cases generally are not. These terms, "seminal" and "landmark," are misleading in the extreme because they conflate prior law with present and future law. The standard view of constitutional change regards seminal or landmark decisions to be sterling examples of important, sometimes brilliant, decisions that provide new directions in constitutional law. But, in my view, if they provide new directions, it is because they are revolutionary, that is, they provide new directions just because they cannot be generated from prior law. If they could be so generated, they would not provide new directions at all.

In embracing the position that seminal or landmark decisions are somehow grounded in prior law, the standard view rejects the possibility of

constitutional revolutions. Because constitutional revolutions are by definition external solutions to constitutional practice, they raise the question of
their own legitimacy. It is, of course, true that mainstream theorists sometimes use the phrase "constitutional revolution" in order to lavishly praise
their favorite constitutional case, but typically they deny that the decision in
the case is genuinely revolutionary. Instead, they embrace reductionism of
one sort or another, insisting that if we attend to the correct jurisprudence,
all seemingly revolutionary decisions can be seen to be extensions of prior
law, legal precedent, or the principles that underlie constitutional practice.

In my view a jurisprudence of prior law will never succeed because American judicial review is replete with, and driven by, constitutional revolutions
that cannot be explained by prior law without introducing highly contestable arguments purporting to establish that these decisions are somehow
already a part of the law. Because constitutional revolutions are the modus
operandi of American constitutional law, any jurisprudence unable to explain constitutional revolutions as *revolutions* fails to account for American
constitutional practice. By emphasizing the term "revolutionary," the theory of constitutional revolutions explicitly recognizes the importance of
how political culture and constitutional interpretation interact and insists
that the standard jurisprudential account for explaining this phenomenon is
erroneous. According to the theory of constitutional revolutions, the great
shifts in constitutional law are extraconstitutional. Without properly taking
into account these revolutionary shifts, American constitutional judicial
practice loses its unique character.

Failure to recognize the importance of constitutional revolutions has
created a deep crisis of legitimacy in constitutional law. The institutional
practice of judicial review has been challenged by critics from across the
political spectrum. Constitutional conservatives argue that "judge-made"
law is appropriate, if ever, only when a judicial decision follows directly
from the Constitution, or from the narrowest interpretation of bona fide
constitutional conventions such as the text, intent, or the structure of the
Constitution. Constitutional liberals believe that moral and political values
exist that inform these conventions. Thus, judges are permitted (even required) to identify these values to understand the Constitution properly.
Both conservatives and liberals, however, agree that constitutional law is at
best *evolutionary*, not *revolutionary;* in order to be legitimate, constitutional
law must be anchored somehow in the Constitution or in constitutional
practice. The question naturally arises whether such revolutionary decisions

are constitutionally legitimate. This book offers a functionalist answer to this question, namely, that a branch of government, institution, or practice is democratic and therefore legitimate if, and only if, it contributes in the appropriate manner to the just and efficient operation of American democracy.[1] Formal conceptions of legitimacy such as Framers' intent or judicial precedent play only a limited role in constitutional change. In the final analysis the justification of judicial review rests in its place as the best theory of American democracy.

What is the appropriate role of revolutionary judicial review in American democracy? According to the theory of constitutional revolutions, judicial review functions as a mechanism that gives the deliberative process the capacity of reflection or "second-thought." In the case of an individual's practical reasoning, we distinguish between first-order practical judgments, which motivate conduct and decision, and second-order judgments, which evaluate the propriety of the first-order judgment. So, too, a democratic system needs an institutional device to provide principled reflection on the results of majoritarian processes. Only by having such an institution can we reasonably expect the American conception of deliberative democracy to discover the community's real values and considered judgments. In short, what makes a system *un-* or *antidemocratic* is not whether one of its branches or agencies is countermajoritarian. Rather, the important inquiry involves determining whether the countermajoritarian element is sanctioned by the best conception of American democracy. Judicial review or its replacement is democratic or not as it contributes to the conversational rules, constraints, and goals of a deliberative democracy, despite its majoritarian or countermajoritarian status.

Activist and revolutionary judicial review is designed to create a mechanism, through the judiciary, of providing the community with a capacity for second-thoughts, that is, for criticizing and revising its first-order judgments. Passive judicial review fails to fulfill this reflective, corrective role of the Court. Consequently, passive review contributes insufficiently to American democracy and thus is disqualified as the central form of judicial review in American constitutionalism.

However important judicial review is in a deliberative democracy, it is not sacrosanct. Institutions other than courts in principle can serve this function. The objection to judicial review should be that alternative institutions exist that do a better job of reflecting upon and criticizing the first-order judgments of the community, not that judicial review is countermajoritarian. If that were the real problem with judicial review, it could be resolved simply by electing federal judges. Because few believe that this would be desirable, the real problem may be something entirely different from the countermajoritarian character of judicial review.[2] Instead, critics of judicial review might reject the direct influx of political theory into the affairs of political organization.[3] A truly remarkable rejection since it flies in the face of American constitutional practice and, more important, because rejecting this influx itself requires a *political* justification.

The normative dimension of any theory of judicial review, therefore, must be ultimately evaluated by how well it contributes to American democracy. Democracy seeks to represent the will of the people, which may or may not be equivalent to the will of a current majority. The theory of constitutional revolutions is an attempt to interpret and describe American constitutional judicial practice. Once achieved, the normative dimension of the theory depends on how well it ties judicial review to a preferred theory of constitutional democracy. Constitutional theory is, therefore, political in the sense of political *philosophy,* because the touchstone of constitutional interpretation is how well it contributes to the political philosophy of democracy.

Before turning to the task at hand, let me express my appreciation to several people and institutions for their continued support of my exploration of constitutional revolutions. In 1993 I presented parts of this manuscript to an Association of American Law Schools Workshop in constitutional law in Ann Arbor, and the Ohio Legal Workshop in Columbus, and in 1995 I presented chapter 2 at Millersville University. At these presentations I learned how powerful is the standard theory of constitutional change. I am indebted to the participants at these and other presentations for their constructive critical comments. Widener University School of Law deserves my gratitude for providing me with summer research stipends and sabbatical leaves. I am also grateful to the Widener University School of Law and the H. Albert Young Foundation for awarding me the first H. Albert Young Fellowship in Constitutional Law. My deep gratitude goes to the Widener University law librarians, who provided me with expert professional help, and to Eileen Cooper, the law library director, for her steadfast commitment to legal scholarship. Several excellent research assistants contributed to the completion of this project. Three reviewers for Duke University Press improved this book both stylistically and substantively.

I also wish to thank those scholars who commented on all or parts of the original manuscript in various contexts. Among these are Bruce Ackerman, Erin Daly, Ronald Dworkin, Robert L. Hayman Jr., Ken Kress, Sandy Levinson, Edward T. Sankowski, Steven Shiffrin, Fred Schauer, and Rodney Smith. I have learned much from these authors as well as from Mark Tushnet, Frank Michelman, Michael Perry, Robin West, Kent Greenawalt, Jack Balkin, and John Rawls. My legal education has also been enriched, albeit indirectly, by Richard Rorty, Donald Davidson, Thomas Kuhn, W. V. O. Quine, Wilfrid Sellars, and Ludwig Wittgenstein. The bibliography contains the works of the writers cited in this book. I am grateful to all of them. Philip Johnson contributed to the manuscript's completion by suggesting ways to improve both its style and substance. I have not always taken his advice, but where I do, he alone is responsible for the remaining mistakes. Julia Fischel, Jack Fischel, and Stevie Dunphy deserve special recognition for their supportive words during those inevitable times when this project foundered. Several years ago Rod Smith's friendship and his astute constitutional analyses helped me daily to formulate and reformulate the "theory of constitutional revolutions," and he has supported this project throughout. Rod is one of several wise, loving, and intelligent friends, including Edward T. Sankowski, Christine M. Funk, and Carolyn H. Magid, who have greatly influenced my views on political philosophy as well as on living a meaningful life. Among my debts I thank Ed for sharing with me his perceptive analyses of contemporary American democracy, Chris for her courageous frontline battles against discrimination and intolerance, and Carolyn for both. This project has been greatly influenced, as has much else in my life, by the life and death of my oldest childhood friend, Mike Cotler, who would have been especially pleased at its completion. Finally, and most importantly, my love and appreciation to Carolyn Marie Dunphy, my wife, for making this and all other projects possible. I thank her for her sustaining love and support and for sacrificing more to the completion of this book than anyone is entitled to expect. In gratitude, let me say that turnabout is fair play, and payback can be delightful.

Parts of this book are extensively rewritten portions of the following law review articles: "Can American Constitutional Law Be Postmodern?" 42 *Buff. L. Rev.* 317 (1994); "Beyond Skepticism, Foundationalism and the New Fuzziness: The Role of Wide Reflective Equilibrium in Legal Theory," 75 *Cornell L. Rev* 811 (1990); "Conventionalism, Pragmatism, and Constitutional Revolutions," 21 *U.C. Davis L. Rev.* 645 (1988); "Indeterminacy,

Justification and Truth in Constitutional Theory," 60 *Fordham L. Rev.* 595 (1992); "The Anatomy of Constitutional Revolutions," 68 *Neb. L. Rev.* 701 (1989); "Pragmatism — The Unfinished Revolution: Doctrinaire and Reflective Pragmatism in Rorty's Social Thought," 67 *Tul. L. Rev.* 1561 (1993). I wish to thank the editors of these reviews for permission to reprint those portions in this book.

INTRODUCTION

The Crisis of American Constitutionalism

American constitutional law and theory have been in a state of acute crisis for over a generation, challenging the very foundations of American constitutional government.[1] This crisis manifests itself in widespread disagreement over the proper interpretation of the United States Constitution and its role in American life.[2] Ultimately, the crisis affects every person subject to the laws of the United States, jeopardizing nothing less than the rights, liberties, and responsibilities enjoyed in the oldest and most resilient of the world's constitutional democracies. It also implicates the authority of state and federal governments as well as the general question of the government's role in solving the nation's social and economic problems. Because the very idea of constitutional government is at stake, we must determine whether this crisis in American constitutionalism can be dispelled using traditional methods, or whether we should instead seek new ways of understanding our most cherished political text.[3]

This way of framing the problem is susceptible to the objection that talk of "crisis" and the admonition that "the very idea of constitutional government is at stake" overstates the problems in constitutional theory. After all, the future stability of American constitutionalism does not depend on the resolutions of conceptual controversies. In reply I believe that American constitutionalism is presently in a precarious position of inactivity and fruitless debates over methodology. In short, American constitutional law risks becoming irrelevant to the resolution of political and social issues. More importantly, when the present Court does act, it often adopts revolutionary decisions without admitting it, especially in the areas of religious liberty, federalism, and criminal procedure. The revolutionary dimension of these decisions must be recognized before we can determine whether they are justified. Additionally, American constitutional law is at the heart of American politics and culture.[4] When constitutional law bleeds, so bleeds political culture. Consequently, the term "crisis" appropriately characterizes American constitutionalism, and this crisis threatens democracy. Doubtless, no theorist's conception of constitutionalism alone will lead to a constitutional nirvana; nevertheless, deliberative theoretical clashes are vital to political stability and change. These clashes help clarify the conceptual and intellectual *content* of political practice. Consequently, understanding these debates better is critical to assessing the best proposals for political change. True, in the grand scheme of things, perhaps, the intellectual content is less important than modernist theorists have suggested. Nevertheless, it occupies an important role in practice and must be seriously regarded. Because the conceptual or intellectual content of stability or change depends upon scholarly debates, so too does the future stability of American government. Thus, the future stability of American government *will* depend in part on the debates between Ackerman and Dworkin, as well as on the debates between Rawls and Sandel, Mill and Stephens, Hart and Fuller, Dworkin and Fish, among others. To be sure, more than conceptual or intellectual content is needed for successful political change. However, we should not overlook the fact that political practice is intertwined with conceptual or intellectual content, and, therefore, what scholars say and do in part contributes to producing events that shape the world in certain ways rather than others.

The crisis of American constitutionalism forces us to ask a question as old as the American Republic, namely: How is it possible for a constitutional democracy to serve two masters, one of orthodoxy and the other of change—especially, if desired, progressive change?[5] This question can be stated in alternative ways. Is it possible for constitutional law to maintain its integrity as a historical process while simultaneously being responsive to novel circumstances? Given that the Constitution is at least in part a historical document, should it be reduced to the particular age in which it was formulated? Or can a constitutional democracy stand for something—historically determined—yet apply to the contemporary problems a society faces?[6]

These questions go to the heart of constitutionalism and its role in our culture wars.[7] The central problem here is to determine whether our constitutional democracy can survive, and in what form, when large-scale vituperative disagreement about central values threatens the well of public life. Though this question has roots in our nation's founding, it has special importance now that America is undergoing diverse and radical demographic changes. Shortly, the majority of Americans will not be mostly Caucasian or European. The problem of deciding which traditions to maintain, which to jettison, and which to create in the midst of diversity thus becomes a critical problem affecting both American constitutionalism and American culture.

One presupposition of this book is that American culture is unrecognizable without American constitutionalism, and American constitutionalism cannot be explained independently of the cultural forces that create and are created by constitutional law. American constitutionalism is first of all a cultural phenomenon; it permeates American society. The American experiment has created a culture of constitutionalism whenever Americans take constitutional adjudication seriously and press for inchoate cultural changes to be recognized by constitutional law. In doing so, the courts effectively create the constitutionalization of culture whereby constitutional adjudication in principle applies to cultural development and change. This interweaving of culture and constitutionalism provides a constitutional democracy with a dimension not possible for a purely majoritarian democracy.[8] This dimension consists of the possibility of producing considered judgments about the society's future. This principle of considered judgments has been made possible by a deliberative culture that creates judgments both permanent and subject to refinement, revision, and change.[9]

The contemporary crisis exists because today the disagreement is so basic and apparently irresolvable, revealing pellucidly the great divisions in our constitutional culture. No longer do we take seriously what our opponents have to say. No longer do we seek bridges between polarized extremes. These divisions also suggest a breakdown in America's conception of republican democracy.[10] Our civic republican tradition insists on taking the ideas of self-government and citizenship seriously. In this view American democracy is a "republic of reasons."[11] Minimally, such a republic is committed to intersubjective dialogue, reasoning, and persuasion as alternatives to the coercion that typify nondemocratic societies. In a republic of reasons, citizens expect to be able to convince other citizens of the rightness of their views or, if not, are ready to be convinced by them to relinquish their own views. Consensus, reasoned consensus, through institutional structures is a primary value of such a republic. Yet in America today such institutional structures are fragmented and attenuated.

In American constitutional practice this fragmentation is illustrated by the emergence of a plethora of incompatible constitutional theories, theories that entail incompatible substantive results as well as incompatible constitutional visions.[12] Although it is an avowed article of faith that American democracy means agreeing to disagree, the nature and extent of dissensus in American society is alarming. Constitutional theorists and legal philosophers should take seriously the apparently irreconcilable differences over such pressing moral and political issues as church and state, abortion, gender equality, gay and lesbian rights, free speech, pornography, racism, the role of the government, capital punishment, property rights, the propriety of ordinances against hate speech, and poverty, among others. These theorists should pay greater attention to explaining why these controversies resist resolution than to valorizing the modest, albeit real, consensus that renders political organization possible in the first place. They must attempt to explain why, despite this minimal agreement,[13] the best minds of our era have failed to resolve the controversies that divide American society. What does this failure reveal about the American national character and the American conception of self-government? Does it even make sense to speak of an "American national character" or "the American conception of self-government"? Or are we merely romanticizing American constitutionalism by insisting that there are unified conceptions of these matters?

The present crisis of American constitutionalism is more than just disagreement over constitutional values or constitutional methodologies. Americans have always been thus divided. Indeed, in one such era American constitutionalism faced its most serious crisis in the form of civil war. The current crisis is the most critical since the Civil War, because our differences, even after being refined through cautious reflection, critical confrontation, and rational argument, remain intractable and divisive. Typically, periods of crisis are followed by periods of strong and weak consensus. Strong consensus, differing significantly from unanimity, offers the best chance for stable democratic change. Weak consensus avoids civil strife but renders precarious democratic progress. Yet, after all our juridical and social upheavals, strong consensus still eludes us. This suggests that the goal of democratic constitutionalism — that is, to construct a constitutionally based and effective form of political discourse — is impossible.[14]

The dream of a deeply shared American constitutional character, spirit, or consciousness now appears illusory. In fact, it now seems that such notions are incoherent.[15] But consider the possibility that the U.S. Constitution may turn out to be not one determinate document, but rather a symbol for diverse, competing ways to live politically. What if self-government represents the epitome of constitutional government for some, whereas individual rights, unrelated to and sometimes incompatible with self-government, are the symbol of constitutional government for others? What if different conceptions of self-government and different visions of individual rights capture the imaginations of different voices in the American story? Indeed, a careful excursion through American constitutional history and political reality reveals conservative, moderate, and progressive voices, all vying for dominion over our constitutional culture.[16] American constitutionalism might then be the result of a culture permitting, even encouraging, systematically different worldviews. This essential contestability of the political similarly applies to the concept of a person. On a deep psychological level, human beings may develop as fundamentally different political, social, and personal beings. In fact, that's just what we would expect to happen in a society committed to freedom and equality. If rationality is relative to one's perspective, at some point competing perspectives must have nothing left to say to one another. Unless some novel conception of one of the existing perspectives becomes plausible to a consensus of the citizens, or some novel perspective is devised, mere advocacy and imposition of one's perspective is likely. In this event the crisis could be fatal.

The crisis in American constitutionalism reflects a broader crisis in intellectual inquiry. The landscape of intellectual inquiry, once ensconced securely in modernity, is now emerging into a postmodern era.[17] Postmodernity typically rejects totalizing grand schemes of discourse. It challenges any intellectual or practical domain to reconstruct itself without the assistance of formalistic or rationalistic metaphysics and epistemology. Constitutional theory, traditionally understood as championing reason, objectivity, legitimacy, and truth, is now confronted with the possibility that such notions are illusory. If so, constitutional theory must find new structures in a postmodern age, or continue to founder and abdicate its unique role in American culture.

Accordingly, the crisis of American constitutionalism in general is a crisis of Western civilization and the epistemology and metaphysics Western civilization defends. Western intellectual inquiry is experiencing a sea change away from grand narratives canonizing and legitimizing primary discourses, discourses through which we experience and act upon the world. This move away from foundationalist epistemology and metaphysics is an indictment of the Enlightenment and the modernist, scientific spirit that created it. Antifoundationalism challenges the role of reason in intellectual inquiry; it further challenges foundationalist conceptual schemes and the prominence of the notions of truth and objectivity endemic to such schemes. Essentially, this challenge denigrates the viability of key foundationalist dichotomies such as the objective and the subjective; the real and the ideal; truth and justification; mind and body; altruism and egoism; the public and the private; the descriptive and the prescriptive; abstraction and contextualism; and so forth.

In the context of constitutional inquiry, this challenge denigrates the dichotomy between creating and discovering law, as well as the role of reason, normativity, and methodology in constitutional adjudication.[18] It rejects any attempt to fashion one, and only one, "correct" conception of American constitutionalism as an atavistic attempt to reclaim the security of foundationalism. To meet this challenge, we must rethink constitutional law and theory and steel ourselves to the possibility of discovering that American constitutionalism is a very different beast from what it is conventionally thought to be. This book takes the challenge of postmodernity seriously and understands this challenge to be at the heart of the crisis in American constitutionalism. Moreover, the challenge of postmodernity prompts us to look for easy solutions concerning constitutional theory, when possible, and when impossible to integrate the various contenders for the best theoretical approach to constitutional law.[19]

The point here is that American constitutionalism, like any field of inquiry, depends on methods for discovering and validating its claims. These methods are either unique to American constitutionalism or apply equally across several fields of inquiry. American constitutionalism depends upon several disparate levels of meaning, and therefore discoveries in constitutional theory may have unexpected effects. The methods of constitutional reasoning may be applicable to other fields of law, as well as to other practical domains. Consequently, a theory of American constitutionalism may contribute to a general theory of human intellectual and practical inquiry, typically conceived of as a modernist enterprise, but one that can be reborn in postmodernist or at least pragmatist terms.[20]

Constitutional theory, traditionally understood as championing objectivity and legitimacy, should now seek new structures in postmodernity in order to preserve its role in American culture. The uniqueness of this role is illustrated by the earnestness with which most Americans take constitutional decisions. Many Americans have firm convictions about what is and what is not constitutional. They believe that unethical policies are also unconstitutional, even though, technically, it might be impossible for that objection to stick due to the absence of state action or some other triggering device. For the average concerned American citizen "constitutional" and "unconstitutional" function as strongly evaluative terms, reflecting deep commitments concerning the meaning of life and the proper organization of American society.[21] In such cases, to say that it is unconstitutional to ban smoking or to implement drug testing means that it violates principles of conduct that have a deep hold on the American consciousness. This spiritual, and indeed visionary, interpretation of American constitutionalism pervades the American character. Instead of there being one right interpretation of American constitutionalism, there may be several, though not indefinite, conceptions of democratic personality underlying the Constitution. The Constitution speaks to the idea that American constitutional practice includes conservative, moderate, and progressive ideals, as well as libertarian, republican, and egalitarian interpretations of these ideals. The constitutional battles that now rage in American society are attempts at least in the public forum to remake others in one's own constitutional image. These conflicts and attempts at world — and personality — making have a salutary effect on the constitutionalization of American culture and on the culture of American constitutionalism.[22] They enable Americans to include greater and more diverse perspectives in the constitutional community, and by so doing enable the community to maintain, transform, and re-create itself by the maintenance, transformation, and re-creation of American law. The question is whether there exists a theory that can explain how these "jurisgeneris" processes operate.[23]

Constitutional Legitimacy and the Countermajoritarian Problem

Before examining this question directly, it will be valuable to describe the crisis in greater detail. The crisis in constitutional theory arises from a concern with constitutional or political legitimacy.[24] The problem of legitimacy is a general problem in political theory, especially in democratic political theory. Any society committed to liberty and independence as fundamental values must regard coercion as presumptively invalid.[25] Consequently, democratic political theory must explain how state coercion is justified in the first place. In the judicial context the problem of legitimacy focuses on the Court's authority to strike down legislative acts by the majoritarian branches of government.[26] What justifies the Court in striking down legislation by creating constitutional rights or powers not explicitly mentioned in the Constitution? Constitutional lawyers, sensitive to the problem of legitimacy, are vigilant in their defense of what law actually is, not what some maverick judges think it should be. These traditionalists point out that our political system is a democracy, and in it judges are to follow the dictates of the majority; when judges reject the products of majoritarian democracy, they engage in countermajoritarian lawmaking and are justified in doing so only when the Constitution warrants it.

This countermajoritarian problem is the foundation of contemporary constitutional jurisprudence. How can a democracy countenance nine unelected and virtually unaccountable justices striking down statutes that are the fruits of the majoritarian branches? Some of the most important works in constitutional jurisprudence are attempts to resolve or dissipate the countermajoritarian problem.[27] However, few theorists attempt to explain why a countermajoritarian problem arises simply because one institution of government is not wholly majoritarian.[28] The existence of one (or more) institutions that *are* countermajoritarian does not render the entire political system countermajoritarian, let alone undemocratic.[29] The entire system of government can remain democratic, despite unelected justices playing a role in lawmaking.[30] The majoritarian process is not helpless against the Court. The majoritarian branches select and confirm federal judges, and federal judges can be impeached. Moreover, the people can reverse a Supreme Court decision by amending the Constitution. Accordingly, several majoritarian or democratic factors exist to nullify the untoward effects of undesirable Supreme Court decisions, thereby resolving the countermajoritarian problem.[31]

Yet theorists who believe that judicial review presents a countermajoritarian problem point out justifiably that, practically speaking, the people are virtually helpless against the Court, since the constraints just mentioned are all ineffectual in directly constraining the Court from taking errant countermajoritarian stands. If this really is a problem, the solution is obvious: Call for the election of federal judges, including the justices of the U.S. Supreme Court, or to seriously implement the Framers' plan to permit Congress appellate jurisdiction over the Court. The standard answer is that electing the justices of the Supreme Court, or some other majoritarian control over the Court, destroys the independence of the Court, and judicial independence has proved to be a good thing.[32] To the extent that this is so, one should be less concerned about the countermajoritarian dimension associated with judicial review, for it is that very factor that permits judicial independence. Further, the precise nature of judicial independence used in this objection is not obvious. If democratic controls over maverick courts or activist judges are desirable, then complete judicial independence is not desirable. Consequently, if the countermajoritarian problem is really a problem of *majoritarianism,* it can be resolved. If majoritarian resolutions to the countermajoritarian problem are possible and desirable, reluctance to accept them might reveal some other unstated concern or hidden agenda.

The "countermajoritarian" problem is a great rallying point for criticizing the Court, or at least certain conceptions of constitutional adjudication, as an alien element in the American constitutional scheme.[33] In fact, the "countermajoritarian" problem might be a misnomer. It might have nothing to do with democracy but, rather, reveal an epistemic skepticism about ethics, politics, and law. One might believe that no official, unelected or even elected, can know what rights and liberties we have beyond those explicitly stated in the Constitution. Or it might express a cynicism about trusting others, elected or not, to decide matters of political morality. But the countermajoritarian difficulty, as Bickel expresses it, is neither a skeptical issue nor a cynical complaint. Can it be that in following Bickel we have gotten this problem wrong for all these years?[34] If the countermajoritarian complaint derives from a deep mistrust of theory or intellectual strategies for understanding law, and not from the democratic temperament, Bickel's approach might have been a misdirection in constitutional law.

Skepticism arises in this context regarding a Supreme Court justice's capacity for deciding issues of individual rights and governmental powers. The skeptical argument insists that no one has any rights or liberties, or that no one knows what rights and liberties we have, and therefore the Founders or the present legislature should decide what rights or liberties we have. However, in that case the skeptic's connection with the majoritarian point is mysterious. If we have no rights and liberties other than those explicitly stated in the Constitution, or no one knows what our rights and liberties are other than these, then why should the Founders or the present legislature decide this, and even if they should, how do we know that they should? How can the Founders' decisions or the present legislature's decisions be superior to anyone else's? Of course the skeptic might reply that in the context of a democratic society, when in doubt let the legislature decide. This assumes the existence and desirability of a particular conception of "democracy" that is precisely the issue in dispute. The question is whether an arguably countermajoritarian institution like judicial review is compatible with the appropriate conception of American democracy. The skeptic cannot then just assume or argue by default that the legislature should decide which rights and liberties people have on the ground that democracy requires it. She must first describe her conception of democracy and show why it is the appropriate conception. Similarly, the majoritarian point might not be precisely skeptical, but rather a point about consensus. The majoritarian might argue that because we cannot agree in advance on what our rights and liberties are, it is fairer and provides a more stable government for the legislature to decide the matter rather than the courts. But if we cannot agree about our rights and liberties, how can we agree on the appropriate notion of "fairness" and the desirability of stability required to make this last argument work?[35] Our putative agreement that dissensus about justice is best dealt with by democracy needs an independent defense.

Strict or complete majority control has never been the primary goal of American democracy. Neither the "checks and balances" of liberal constitutionalism, canceling the excesses of interest-group pluralism, nor the republican constraints designed to ensure a deliberative democratic process, nor the doctrines of separation of powers and federalism are troubled by countermajoritarian features. American constitutional republicanism was an attempt to distinguish between the statistical will of the people and the people's true will or considered judgment. That is why American constitutionalism forges countermajoritarian constraints on unmodified majoritarian control. Structural protections and individual rights are both designed to formulate the community's will. They permit the formulation of the people's considered judgments. This notion of "the people's considered judgments" is behind the Founders' republican conception of American democracy. Only when the mechanisms of government produce the people's considered judgments can we have a true democracy. Thus unconstrained majoritarianism is anathema to a true democracy. This is the genius of American constitutionalism, that the Founders understood the difference between a democracy concerned with mere numbers and a republican democracy seeking truth or at least reflective consensus. They also understood indirection; sometimes placing certain antithetical constraints on a system produces the best systemic results. The Founding combined liberal features of political theory as well as republican ones. The republican dimension of the Founding is predicated upon the conviction that democratic consent filtered through the appropriate set of constraints yields truth or, alternatively, produces a reflective consensus controlling raw majority opinion.

After all, the fact that prior majorities control present majorities is itself a countermajoritarian process. If it is justifiable for a prior majority to control all subsequent majorities until a present supermajority changes it, then it is not untoward to represent the will of prior majority in a permanent branch of government such as the judiciary. Accordingly, one way for prior majorities to control subsequent ones is through judicial review. Consequently, judicial review is not countermajoritarian regarding prior majorities, although perhaps it is countermajoritarian regarding present majorities. Having a constitution or any written law in the first place is countermajoritarian with respect to present majorities; that is one of the salient features of law. Even in a direct, participatory democracy, a "new" majority must wait for elections to give its voice effect. Thus, countermajoritarianism is an ineluctable feature of democratic constitutionalism.

Present or subsequent majorities are controlled by prior majorities just as long as the present majority refrains from acting pursuant to article 5, according to which it needs a supermajority, thereby freeing itself from the prior majority control. As previously indicated, the standard reply here is that action through article 5 is impracticable.[36] Modernist or foundationalist sensibilities would consider this reply disingenuous. The Constitution does not guarantee convenience, just the rule of law. Postmodern sensibilities, on the other hand, take seriously the charge of impracticability. If constitutional change is required more readily than article 5 permits, then informal procedures for constitutional change outside of article 5 are likely to develop. Constitutional necessity is mother to constitutional invention. This is not merely a descriptive claim concerning what is likely to occur. Rather, it is an interpretive claim that endorses the informal procedure of constitutional amendments barring a compelling justification against it. The postmodern pragmatic point here is that no one abhors informal constitutional change completely. Every American constitutionalist, no matter how restrained, embraces at least one constitutional revolution outside the confines of article 5: Chief Justice John Marshall's creation of judicial review. Of course, many argue that *Marbury* is not revolutionary. Instead, it is argued that *Marbury* is an exemplar of judicial creativity, or that it is transformative, or in some other fashion coherent with American constitutional practice at the time. Indeed, conventional wisdom in constitutional theory embraces this position. This conclusion, of course, can be drawn, given a sufficiently expansive conception of "coherence." But all the creative literature and ingenious conceptions of coherence will not put our constitutional house back together again.

Pragmatist adjudication helps bring about the ordered benefits associated with pragmatism and conventionalism. Permitting justices to make pragmatist choices, such as in *Marbury,* enables the emergence of the federal judiciary as a viable institution in our constitutional democracy. Without the inclination to make such choices, that coequal branch must atrophy. Just as stagnating capitalist enterprises do not survive, so too vital, democratically based political institutions require the ability to develop and grow. This must be an internal capacity, that is, a capacity that derives from the institution itself. Consequently, any vital judicial enterprise must have the internal capacity for growth and self-criticism.

Reflective pragmatism realizes the conventionalist benefits of predictability and coordination. Consequently, once a revolution occurs and is refined, perfected, and stabilized, normal adjudication takes on a conventionalist dimension, thereby permitting us to make economic and personal decisions in a stable environment. An additional virtue of the theory of constitutional revolutions is that these revolutions have a tendency to avoid violent political revolutions.[37] Further, even if revolutionary adjudication were absolutely illegitimate, it is difficult to know how to return to the past.[38] Returning to the past itself requires constitutional revolution.

The crisis of American constitutionalism is unlikely to be resolved on its own terms. What is needed in part is a rededication to answering some old questions as well as introducing a set of new questions. First, we must seriously address the question of whether traditional conceptions of legitimacy are plausible. In doing so we may come to discover that legitimacy is no more than a functionalist concept justifying a practice if that practice supports a desirable form of democracy. Second, which conception of democracy underlies American constitutional change? Third, what theory accurately describes how courts actually decide constitutional cases? Are there existent models of theory construction in other domains that will contribute to a new, illuminating characterization of judicial reasoning and transformation? Finally, what is the relationship between cultural norms and constitutional adjudication?

One step in the direction of achieving this goal is to abandon the modernist commitment to theoretical simplicity or conceptual elegance at all costs. The lawyer's creed seeks the obvious and eschews elaborate explanations and justifications for legal propositions, as well as obvious candidates for the correct constitutional methodology. The metatheoretical virtue of simplicity derives from the commitment that the greater complexity attributed to reality, the less reason we have to rely on the attribution when other less complex attributions are available. I do not wish to dispute the wisdom of this commitment. All things being equal, simplicity is an important virtue. It can, however, become an obsession leading us astray.

Originalism and Constitutional Meaning

Originalism is such an obsession. Originalism contends that constitutional meaning is derived from the original intentions of the authors or the ratifiers of the Constitution and its amendments. Therefore, constitutional meaning is authoritative because of a past act of constitutional creation. But how do we identify the appropriate intentions? No one has succeeded in creating a methodology translating particular intentions into a collective one. If so, the locution "the Framers' intention" is indeterminate, having no identifiable referent. Furthermore, one must distinguish here between subjective and objective intentions. Subjective intentions are those motivational factors that actually prompt a Framer to vote for a constitutional provision. Objective intentions refer to what the provision meant at the time of ratification. When known, subjective intentions provide a groundwork for future constitutional meaning. A novel interpretation of the Constitution is legitimate if it follows in some way from the Framers' subjective (actual) intentions. If the Framers actually intended that X means Y, then X means Y. If affirmative action follows from the Framers' intention, then affirmative action, surprisingly, is constitutionally warranted.[39] Similarly, if the Framers intended free speech to include speech critical of the government, then that's what the provision means.

This approach fails to recognize that an inquiry into the actual subjective intentions of the Framers is always problematic. Moreover, even if possible, the actual intentions need not be relevant to the discussion at hand. A Framer might have intended to vote for provision A in exchange for a colleague's vote for provision B. Whatever the Framers' subjective intention, the meaning of a provision cannot be explicated in terms of private states of mind. Consequently, intentions must be objective. They must derive from the objective meaning—what the reasonable citizen would understand the provision to mean. However, problems loom here also. If the objective meaning is sought, why not adopt textualism, the view that the Constitution is to be understood in terms of its own language, what it does and does not say. This restricts constitutional interpretation to the language of the Founding period. But it appears impossible to understand the language of the Founding in terms of contemporary American discourse. In this case the primacy of the present precludes truly appreciating the particular meaning of a past constitutional provision. Even if we can provide a complete historical account of the language used to frame the provision, this historical account is always given through our linguistic framework. Of course, the more abstract the provision, the easier it is to regard our contemporary principles as being part of the Constitution's general meaning. The First Amendment's free exercise of religion clause can be understood as protecting "free exercise" of religion. But it will not serve as an arbiter of particular controversies involving a particular conception of free exercise in contemporary society without providing a comprehensive history of American political and cultural language. Even if such an account is possible (and I doubt it), judicial acumen concerning the Constitution would require judges to engage in forms of inquiry beyond their expertise.

Besides these objections, the originalist must face a challenge not easily overcome.[40] An originalist must suggest a noncircular mode for deriving originalism. What authorizes originalism's conception of constitutional meaning? It cannot derive from the Constitution directly, because the document contains no obvious provision on methodology. In this formal sense every constitutional methodology is nonoriginalist, because its authority necessarily depends on constitutionally extrinsic factors. No self-executing methodological provisions exist revealing their own meaning. Even if the Constitution included a provision on methodology, however, that could not be dispositive because one could always raise the question of the proper interpretation of that provision. An answer to that question must then be extrinsic to the Constitution. Consequently, any methodology attempting to answer the question of how to interpret the Constitution must appeal to an extrinsic conception of constitutional methodology and theory, or of political philosophy. Some methodologies, to be sure, might be more obvious than others, but that does not establish their authority. Ultimately, the most plausible methodology follows from the best available political theory of American constitutional democracy. In my view the best political theory of American democracy must be faithful to actual constitutional practice, and vice versa. If it turns out that some theory accurately depicts this practice, then, barring objection, it should be considered the chief candidate for the correct theory. Because American constitutional practice is a richly textured mosaic of interrelated approaches to constitutional adjudication, we can expect the best theory to be so structured. Accordingly, the most comprehensive theory will very likely be one that integrates the major approaches to constitutional interpretation.

The Primacy of Constitutional Change

The key to unlocking the complexity of American constitutional methodology is the problem of constitutional change: How is it possible for constitutional practice to be bound by the Constitution, yet still change significantly over the course of American history? Can we detect any systematic trends or structural phases of constitutional change that contribute to our understanding of this problem? In my estimation there exists such an account that focuses on constitutional revolutions. I use the word "revolution" and its cognates to emphasize the abrupt, precipitous transformations of American constitutional law. Stressing revolution indicates the creative vibrancy and interaction of law, morality, politics, and culture. Some may wish to reject characterizing this creative vibrancy as revolutionary. They, instead, although not denying the creative force of American constitutional law, wish to characterize it as transformatory or evolutionary. This suggests that every creative change is tied to prior law. Of course, in a trivial sense this is true. However, it is far from true once we examine the concept of "tying" constitutional revolutions to prior law. No non-question-begging, uncontroversial argument exists demonstrating the connection between constitutional revolutions and prior law. Further, the prior law thesis is implausible because it doesn't take into consideration America's constitutionalization of culture. Constitutional law serves as a public form of treating individuals and groups fairly and justly. To achieve this, constitutional adjudication integrates critical features of our cultural horizon into constitutional law. This process of "culturizing" constitutional law is a conspicuous feature of American constitutional practice. The point is that certain principles of American constitutional law have been informally repealed or changed fundamentally.[41] Other branches besides the judiciary also engage in constitutional revolutions. Thus, radical alteration in the operations of the executive, legislature, *and* judiciary renders contemporary constitutional law different from anything we can attribute to the Founders.[42]

According to the prior law thesis, the avowed virtue of judicial review is that it maintains fidelity to the Constitution. In an elementary sense this is true. Certain forms of government are precluded by constitutional design. For example, monarchies, theocracies, or dictatorships are not even in the running. However, once we specify who is in the running, for example, libertarianism, communitarianism, liberalism, socialism, and so forth, it becomes apparent that fidelity to the Constitution is in the eye of the beholder.[43] A stricter sense of fidelity is unavailable. Moreover, fidelity is only one constitutional virtue, and in the great seminal cases of constitutional law it is not the operative one.[44]

My goal is to provide a theory whose centerpiece is constitutional change. In order to accomplish this, we must stress *actual* practice. We must avoid ideological commitments to a priori conceptions of constitutional methodology, such as textualism, originalism, structuralism, or normativism. The best way to understand constitutional adjudication is to view it from an engaged but uncommitted perspective. Should a persuasive conception of constitutional adjudication emerge from that perspective, it can then be used to resolve constitutional crises.[45] If not, we must identify the reasons for failure. Finally, in trying to understand the nature of constitutional adjudication, concentrating on the question of constitutional change is indispensable. It is only by appreciating the interrelationships between and among the different levels of change that one can draw an informed opinion concerning what American constitutional practice entails in a given case. The dynamic process of constitutionalism, resulting in useful, provisional judgments, needs identification.

The Fallacy of Monist Constitutional Adjudication

Traditional constitutional jurisprudence rests upon the mistaken assumption that judicial decision making is a monistic activity. This mistaken assumption is usefully called "the fallacy of monist adjudication," or to coin a phrase, "the monistic fallacy."[46] Monism, in my view, characterizes a practice such as adjudication or politics by invoking a single explanatory factor. A monistic explanation of voting, for instance, occurs when one argues that wealth can explain American voting habits. My use of "monism" differs from Bruce Ackerman's.[47] Ackerman uses the term to refer to a certain kind of majoritarian politics, whereas in my view monism is an explanatory framework for understanding adjudication and judicial review. My view is that monism is impossible as an explanation of American constitutional practice, because it fails to appreciate the complexity of constitutional law.

Traditional constitutional theory and scholarship are committed to the monistic fallacy, offering exclusive jurisprudential models of constitutional decisions, models that treat all kinds of constitutional adjudication in a single jurisprudential manner. Although both enterprises are concerned with constitutional change, both have failed to identify the role of constitutional revolutions in constitutional transformation. A failure to identify constitutional revolutions precludes understanding the development of constitutional law. Taking constitutional revolutions seriously helps us to appreciate the role of legal pragmatism in constitutional theory. Though constitutional law and theory are not alone in assuming the monist or singular character of adjudication, its consequences in constitutional adjudication are disastrous, concealing the structured and multileveled character of constitutional adjudication and the pragmatic forces that drive it.[48] One of this book's principal goals is to show that there are at least two different kinds of constitutional adjudication, and therefore the proper model of constitutional adjudication cannot be monist.

One commits the monistic fallacy when one maintains that either conventionalism, pragmatism, naturalism, or coherentism alone is the sole paradigm through which to explain and justify constitutional change. Furthermore, the monistic fallacy occurs when a midlevel theoretical methodology such as textualism is regarded to be the sole explanation of constitutional meaning. The reason for rejecting this view is that it fails to explain constitutional practice. If constitutional practice embodies textualism as the sole explanatory factor, then too many constitutional decisions must be rejected as mistakes. What remains of a practice once a conception of mistakes invalidates its central features? American constitutional practice consists of the integrating of many diverse historical and contemporary voices, methodologies, and ideals. If that practice is desirable, then we must formulate an unbiased depiction of how it operates. A complex, thickly textured practice is likely to combine elements of more than one jurisprudential model. Providing a jurisprudentially integrated account of American constitutional law is this book's aspiration.

Constitutional conventionalists, traditional pragmatists, and coherence theorists are all committed to this mistaken assumption, inevitably resulting in a serious failure to understand the nature of constitutional change. The result of this failure is catastrophic. If we cannot recognize constitutional *change,* we cannot identify the current state of constitutional law. Consequently, we cannot know what the law *is* in a given case.

Constitutional conventionalists commit the monistic fallacy by insisting that judicial decisions are based solely upon explicit legal conventions about which there is a consensus in the constitutional community. Such theorists usually point to some well-accepted convention as the basis for constitutional interpretation. The conventionalist believes that because everyone agrees that the text, the Framers' intent, the history, structure, and logic of the Constitution, are relevant to interpretation, these conventions should exhaust constitutional methodology. An underlying presupposition of this view is that constitutional interpretation should be objective and not depend upon the particular moral or political convictions of particular judges. Appealing to explicit constitutional conventions in judicial interpretation is designed to achieve objectivity, or at least intersubjective validity, in constitutional adjudication.[49] More importantly, conventionalist constitutional jurisprudence usually depends on some form of democratic theory as the ultimate justification of the preferred methodology.

Mainstream constitutional pragmatists commit the monistic fallacy by exhorting judges to always make the best moral or political decision they can in a given case. Consequently, the pragmatist's vision does not include consistency with the past for its own sake. A concern for the past should be a factor in deliberation if it contributes to the best future; if not, it should be abandoned. The monistic fallacy also is evident in the coherence theorist's contention that correct judicial decisions can always be explained in terms of moral or political principles inherent in constitutional practice. According to this view, a judge's duty is to ferret out these principles from the prior cases, statutes, constitutions, and administrative rules, formulate them clearly, and apply them to the present case. Coherence theorists believe that the sine qua non of constitutional *law* is its consistency and the extension of the past's essential vision to the present case. Each jurisprudential theory offers its preferred model as the *sole* basis of judicial decisions. Conventionalist theories, however, cannot explain the pragmatic choices that result in constitutional change, whereas traditional pragmatist theories cannot explain slower, incremental, or organic change.

Metaphysical Realism and Modern Constitutionalism

The monistic fallacy results from a commitment to the conceptual fruit of modernity, namely, foundationalism. Foundationalism insists on uniquely right answers to perplexing questions, answers grounded in principles that are unassailable.[50] To achieve clarity and certainty, modernity worships simplicity and elegance as metatheoretical values; the more complex an explanation, the less reason for relying on it to understand the world. This modernistic conception of constitutional interpretation eschews dualism, because dualism always risks a commensurability problem. If an explanatory theory consists of several irreducible factors, one must determine which factor is dominant. Moreover, how do we understand the interdependence of these factors? These issues are exactly the type that the modern mind seeks to avoid. Postmodernism, by contrast, does not oppose complexity and seeks to understand how plausible conceptions of methodology, for example, can be integrated to form a more comprehensive picture of the domain under investigation.

The monistic fallacy also derives from an additional modernist assumption that reality—in this case, constitutional transformative reality—is a single, uniform phenomenon. If a nonmonistic theory of constitutional transformation is acceptable, then the phenomena involved might be multi-faceted. For the modern constitutionalist such a complex reality presents enormous metaphysical and epistemological problems. How does one identify and individuate different instances of the phenomena? How do we recognize whether the dominant form of the phenomena is X or Y, or some combination of X and Y? Although this modernist assumption does not reject dualist or nonmonistic conceptions outright, it seeks to avoid them as much as possible. The monistic fallacy precludes our understanding constitutional change. What is needed, consequently, is some dualist or nonmonistic conception of the transformation of constitutional law and theory. Which type of dualist account is appropriate?

The appropriate kind of constitutional dualism or nonmonism must achieve two ends. First, it must provide an interpretive history of the ways that American courts have altered constitutional reality. Second, constitutional dualism must explain jurisprudentially the structure of judicial reasoning that makes such alterations possible. The first goal requires formulating a theory of constitutional moments, one that explains the predictable structure of radical shifts in constitutional meaning and law. The second goal requires an account of judicial reasoning, how judges integrate history and political theory in ways that create novel constitutional meaning. Although interpretive history is a conspicuous feature of these theories, the appropriate kind of constitutionalism requires the priority of the jurisprudential over the historical.

History is prior to the jurisprudential only if translating history and culture into constitutional law is relative to one's particular historical conception. Making jurisprudence relative to historical accounts of American constitutionalism, however, has devastating implications. For example, one has no way to compare and integrate the different jurisprudential conceptions in different epochs. Moreover, how do judges translate the jurisprudential questions of one epoch into another? Additionally, the question of how judges transform history and culture into constitutional structures as an independent problem would effectively drop out of the picture. Whatever the historical account of the translation process, no matter how intuitively impoverished or insignificant the judicial role, that account prevails; there is no independent conception of adjudication. In this regard, as modernists would tell us, jurisprudence must have priority over history for it to be significant at all. The priority of the jurisprudential permits us to identify constitutional revolutions as the prime mover behind changes in American constitutional law. The theory of constitutional revolutions is committed to the priority of the jurisprudential over the historical. No purely historical characterization of American constitutional reality is possible. Ackerman seeks a historical explanation of extrajudicial change without showing how courts incorporate those changes into new law. History depends upon a jurisprudential account of how judges reason in order to identify the processes with which judges historically decide cases. Although a historical account seeks to identify critical historical trends that can provide explanations of different constitutional moments, the Court's role in history can be determined only by identifying the relevant jurisprudence of constitutional law. Thus, the problem of adjudication is the central jurisprudential question upon which a historical account depends. Without the jurisprudential account, historical explanation remains radically incomplete. The jurisprudence of American constitutional law will reveal a dualist conception of adjudication.

Once we discover the nonmonist dimension of constitutional law, we can discern that conventionalism, pragmatism, and coherentism each reflect different moments in the unified structure of constitutional adjudication.

A candid, unbiased look at the way constitutional adjudication actually operates reveals a jurisprudential theory that integrates these models, revealing each model's appropriate place in the constitutional landscape. Such candor enables us to formulate a dualistic theory of constitutional adjudication, recognizing two conceptually distinct, though related, movements: revolutionary adjudication and normal adjudication. The name of this dualistic theory of constitutional adjudication is "the theory of constitutional revolutions."

The theory of constitutional revolutions rejects all normative constitutional theories prescribing one exclusive method of constitutional interpretation as unfaithful to actual constitutional practice as well as antithetical to the most compelling conception of democracy. If the theory of constitutional revolutions is correct in its nonmonistic commitment, other theories of constitutional interpretation are wrong or at best incomplete. However, the theory does include a role for such methodologies as textualism, originalism, structuralism, or nonoriginalism, or any other midlevel theoretical device. In fact, it integrates these devices while explaining their appropriate place in constitutional change. The normative dimension of the theory of constitutional revolutions consists in historical fidelity, pragmatic efficacy, and compatibility with democracy. The theory of constitutional revolutions maintains that if a theory faithfully depicts American constitutional practice, then that in itself is a strong normative reason, absent the existence of dispositive normative reasons to the contrary, for supporting the theory. In addition, the political ideals of predictability, flexibility, and equality provide normative support for the theory.

Constitutional Revolutions

Constitutional revolutions are at once the most exalted, yet the most ignored, phenomena in American constitutional jurisprudence. Everyone has something to say about how important constitutional cases should be decided, yet few recognize that these cases are revolutionary and therefore cannot be conceptualized by traditional methods. Traditional methodologies of constitutional law overlook the importance of constitutional revolutions. Instead, these methods are committed to the well-entrenched article of faith that judges must apply or interpret law, not create or change it. This myth compels us to explain the revolutionary features of American transformative adjudication with a Herculean effort designed to keep the faith.

We should abandon this myth and acknowledge what we already know, namely, American constitutional practice is replete with constitutional revolutions. Constitutional revolutions support the American constitutional faith in a community that considers deliberation, participation, and pragmatic fallibilism and revisionism as the hallmark of secular values. This faith treats "the people" as the normative foundation of government. Here the people thrive as sovereign, as subjects, and most importantly as citizens. American citizens are supposed to live according to a constitutional faith in which only deliberatively designed values of the full democratic community have authority in political and social life. No monarchs, priests, or mullahs as such are part of the justificatory framework of this society. In this way a proper constitutional theory depicts the novelty of the American constitutional experiment. Because American constitutionalism is an experiment, it needs the flexibility of revolutionary adjudication.

Constitutional revolutions transform constitutional practice. These revolutions determine the development of constitutional theory and law.[51] They cause shifts in the meaning of foundational constitutional provisions, provisions that determine the meaning of such concepts as commerce, federalism, due process, and equal protection throughout the legal system. These shifts in meaning create rights or prerogatives that could not be asserted prior to the revolutionary decision without raising the contentious question of whether the shift reflects what law is or what it should be. The Constitution and case law are insufficient to explain revolutionary decisions without appeal to controversial normative premises. Constitutional meaning derives from the Constitution's background context, and this background context itself rarely expresses univocal meaning. Though according to some readings of the Constitution, the Constitution contains anything or everything that constitutional practice says it contains, this is a trivial result. It nullifies the Constitution's role as precedent and constraint. Understood as precedent and constraint, the Constitution cannot explain constitutional revolutions. That's why they are revolutionary.

Though constitutional revolutions come in different shapes and sizes, the common feature of this phenomenon consists of replacing one constitutional paradigm with another. Constitutional paradigms are judicial models—or sets of instructions—that govern unified areas of constitutional law. These instructions include definitions of types of cases, the appropriate standard of review, the kind of analysis dictated by that standard, and theoretical factors justifying the preferred approach to that type of case.

Constitutional revolutions create or change these paradigms and cannot be explained merely by appealing to the preceding constitutional paradigms. Instead, constitutional revolutions depend upon factors extrinsic to constitutional practice for their explanation. What counts as "extrinsic to constitutional practice" is itself a controversial issue. If one believes that constitutional practice is not limited to the ordinary or typical constitutional conventions, but instead includes moral, political, or economic factors, one will have a narrow conception of what counts as extrinsic to constitutional practice. On the other hand, if one believes that constitutional practice is restricted to what is uncontroversially legal, one will seek a broad conception of extrinsicality. This makes the question of extrinsicality merely verbal, and not very interesting if not for the fact that the question of extrinsicality dominates constitutional jurisprudence at almost every stage. In traditional monist theories extrinsicality serves as a mode of delegitimation. If a constitutional decision is based on extrinsic factors, it is illegitimate; if it rests on intrinsic factors, it is legitimate. I will deploy the notion of extrinsicality in articulating the theory of constitutional revolutions. However, I am more concerned with what factors may be taken into account in constitutional adjudication, and less in whether they are extrinsic or intrinsic to constitutional practice. Moreover, I do not believe that factors that make the law morally better are *eo ipso* intrinsic to the law. Whether this means that these factors are already included in the governing law or *should* be included is an important question only to those who have a distorted view of both legitimacy and democracy. I am perfectly content to characterize such great constitutional revolutions as *Marbury, McCulloch,* and *Brown* as based on factors extrinsic to the law and still insist that they are legitimate decisions if they have pragmatic benefits concerning the implementation and viability of the most plausible conception of democracy, which, of course, will be contestable.

The American Communitarian Republic

The guiding conception in this book — though for the most part it remains in the background — is the idea of the American communitarian republic. This idea includes the integration of pragmatist, communitarian, and republican ideals. Constitutional revolutions are an essential feature of these ideals embedded in American constitutionalism and politics. These revolutions are deliberative vehicles through which a republic re-creates itself.

Consider the changes informally occurring in the executive, legislative, and judicial branches, and also the advent of the administrative state as a "fourth branch" of government. Consider also the informal ratification of the independent prosecutor act, which, had it been renewed, would have represented the "fourth and half" branch of government. The implications for weakening the presidency and/or tying up government are staggering. Consequently, revolutions in a republic may not always be good.[52] The value of a revolution is that it seeks to remedy a constitutional problem. Whether the remedy is worse than the problem depends on how it contributes to the effective operation of American democracy.

My view of revolutionary judicial review applies to any conception of the American democratic republic. I should add, however, that I am committed to a particular conception of this republic. In my view, and briefly, America's democratic republic ideally creates a communitarian democracy. This communitarian democracy represents a particular kind of polity as well as the fundamental attitude about the ideals of civic life shared by individuals in a democratic and just society. The communitarian democratic attitude is a commitment to civic righteousness in every aspect of one's conduct; it is a way of realizing oneself and simultaneously being sensitive to the individual and collective interests of others. For those who take self-determination and self-government seriously, the communitarian democratic attitude promises to define the purpose and meaning of human existence and social life. For such individuals the communitarian republican attitude will function in a committed person's life similar to the way religion functions in the life of the theist, as art may function in the life of the artist, and as science may function in the life of the scientist. It is a comprehensive conception of the good life for individuals who conceive of existence as finite and value as contingent. Consequently, the communitarian democratic attitude deserves to be described and explained in such a way as to bring out its role in defining both the individual's as well as the community's good.

As a fundamental attitude the communitarian republic has the capacity for representing different kinds of political ideals. This attitude can be cast in conservative as well as progressive terms. For me the pragmatic republic represents a synoptic vision of conservative and progressive commitments, namely, the conservative commitment to liberty, and the progressive commitments to equality and fraternity. Less abstractly, this synoptic vision shows how these conservative and progressive values center on participation and deliberation, and above all on having a stake in self-determination and self-government.

In theoretical terms the communitarian republic joins the conversationalism of contemporary pragmatism with the deliberative ideals of contemporary civic republicanism to provide a comprehensive conceptualization of how individuals in such a society should regard each other. The communitarian republic stresses the importance of the individual as she thrives in myriad important communal interactions with others. What is necessary or beneficial to these interactions becomes a standard according to which we can criticize and correct contemporary social relations. Communitarian democracy differs from totalitarian and authoritarian conceptions of the state and society by emphasizing the centrality of the individual; it differs from libertarianism by conceiving of what is central about the individual to be her development in a community of similar individuals. Through self-government and self-determination pragmatic republicans seek to transform social reality in more authentic and humane ways.

Judicial review encourages just the sort of attitude toward change in constitutional meaning and in constitutional reality that pragmatist communitarianism embraces in a republic like ours. In other words, judicial review is a process supported by communitarian democracy. American judicial review, understood in terms of the theory of constitutional revolutions, is both historically accurate and normatively attractive. A complete explanation of the pragmatist communitarian ideal will examine the constitutional, political, and cultural tensions associated with multiculturalism. It attempts to show how deliberative democracy structures constitutional adjudication, and how this conception of deliberative democracy provides a model for creating a civic discourse to help mediate the conflicting demands of different political and cultural groups. Formal constitutional theory, therefore, can be credited with explaining how pragmatist republican discourse is possible.

American constitutionalism is an attempt to create a dialogic, pragmatist, communitarian republic in which the evolving function of citizenship plays a central role as the standard for evaluating constitutional change.[53] American citizens were committed to certain values such as equality, liberty, fairness, self-reliance, independence, and progress. These values were both fixed at any given time, and subject to deliberative democratic change. The design of the American government was to encourage sustaining fixed values while subjecting them to pragmatic change. A sense of politics that encourages tradition in the context of transformation is central to this pragmatist republican ideal. The theory defended in this book—the theory of constitutional revolutions—is a theory of adjudication that attempts to capture the role of the Court in sustaining traditions of constitutional transformation. This theory depicts the jurisprudential framework of constitutional change and gives new meaning to the idea of a "living" constitution.

The idea of a living constitution need not be understood in a sociological manner. Generally, I am skeptical of sociological studies that purport to show that the Court merely reflects changes in the greater society and that the majoritarian branches are better able to reflect and direct such changes.[54] Even if courts reflect changes already made in the broader culture (and sometimes they most certainly do), the question of who leads and who follows does not exhaust the importance of the judicial role in a communitarian democracy. The Court functions, in principle, as an expression of the community's reflective, second-order judgments or principles. As such, these principles are deeper, more permanent, and more expressive of the ideals of American constitutionalism—or a particular conception of these ideals—than any ordinary majority decisions. Thus, without Court ratification, without this systematic, reflective, second-thought about a majoritarian change, ordinary majoritarian change is unstable in a way detrimental to constitutionalism. Pure majoritarianism means unchecked first-order political judgments. For constitutionalism to be distinguishable from majoritarianism there must exist an institution, not necessarily the courts, that functions as a second-thought or second-look after majoritarian change has occurred: a more reflective evaluation of what is truly, though controversially, expressive of American ideals than the operations of the majority branches. Rather than countermajoritarian, this second-thought permits the majority to carry forth American constitutional ideals in a progressive, if controversial, manner. Without a process of second-thought, or second-look, the majority carries on blindly.[55]

An Overview

This book, an essay in constitutional jurisprudence, has two salient aims. First, it examines the nature of judicial review as it has developed in American constitutionalism. Second, it attempts to locate this kind of judicial review in a comprehensive conception of American democracy. In chapters 1 and 2 I examine the two most influential theories of constitutional change: Ackerman's dualism and Dworkin's coherentism. Both theories are interesting in their own right, and I examine them in detail in order to determine what we may learn from them. If nothing else, these chapters can help us appreciate the problems in providing a comprehensive theory of constitutional jurisprudence. I conclude that although both theories have value, neither theory is adequate as it stands. Ackerman's theory provides at best a theory of judicial moments, that is, a theory about how courts ratify political revolutions in constitutional law. However, Ackerman omits a theory of judicial reasoning, that is, a theory about how judges reason. By so doing Ackerman fails to explain the judicial methods for translating politics into law. By contrast Dworkin's theory provides an important theory of judicial reasoning but fails to provide a theory of judicial moments. Neither Ackerman's nor Dworkin's theory can explain paradigm shifts in constitutional law. My theory of constitutional jurisprudence, the theory of constitutional revolutions, provides an integrated account of how a theory of judicial moments and a theory of judicial reasoning function in a certain kind of democracy.

In chapter 3 I present "the theory of constitutional revolutions," a novel theory of constitutional change. Relying on a distinction popularized by Thomas Kuhn in the philosophy of science, and Richard Rorty in philosophy generally, I argue that constitutional adjudication consists broadly of at least two general kinds of adjudication: normal adjudication and revolutionary adjudication. Normal adjudication occurs when the Court decides a case in terms of a settled judicial paradigm. Revolutionary adjudication occurs when the Court integrates features of our politics and culture into a novel constitutional paradigm that instructs the courts on how to deal with cases in that area of constitutional law. The notion of a paradigm is critical to articulating the theory of constitutional revolutions. For constitutional purposes a paradigm is a set of instructions for resolving or examining constitutional problems. For example, the judicial paradigm for equal-protection cases involves a three-tier approach for judicial review, as well as instructions on when to adopt a particular tier. Constitutional revolutions occur when one set of instructions supersedes another.

The theory of constitutional revolutions provides an integrated account of constitutional change. Because constitutional law seeks normalcy, after a revolution the Court seeks to normalize constitutional practice. There is irony here. For when a constitutional revolution is normalized or stabilized, decisions that appeal to it do so through normal adjudication, despite the fact that the origination of the new paradigm was derived through revolutionary adjudication. For example, a constitutional revolution such as *Brown v. Board of Education* becomes a reigning paradigm for the judicial review of statutes containing racial classifications. Though revolutionary in its inception, the paradigm in *Brown* has been stabilized and perfected through a process exhibiting both revolutionary and normal features. Future appeals to the paradigm in *Brown* will occur in purely normal adjudication. Consequently, a revolution such as *Brown permanently* enriches constitutional law through normal adjudication.

In chapter 4 I present the historical evidence for the theory of constitutional revolutions. Because this work is primarily jurisprudential, I do not show how the theory of constitutional revolutions can explain all of constitutional epochs. Although I believe that can be done, I instead selectively argue that such major periods of constitutional change as the Marshall Court and the Warren Court can be understood only as periods of revolutionary adjudication. The important parallels between two significant constitutional eras, one early and one late, help to confirm the theory. In chapter 5 I defend the theory against interesting conceptual objections. I then sketch the theory of communitarian democracy that underlies this account of judicial review. This theory supplies the theory's normative basis, which conceives of judicial review as a reflective check on the majority's wishes in order to ascertain the community's considered judgments. In this view various processes of voting, deliberation and reflection, and review are necessary to determine what the community's true interests are. A process that helps discover the community's true interests is clearly democratic even if it is not exclusively majoritarian.

1   Constitutionalism and Dualist Politics

If constitutional law is driven by constitutional revolutions, it is necessary to determine what kind of revolutions there are and how they find expression in law. According to the theory of constitutional revolutions, revolutionary judicial decisions exemplify American constitutional practice from its inception. Bruce Ackerman maintains, to the contrary, that constitutional revolutions are for the most part political, not judicial decisions at all.[1] The Court's role is to ratify political revolutions already created by other actors. The central feature of Ackerman's theory is that American constitutional history reveals an informal method of amending the Constitution outside the Constitution's amending power set out in article 5. In itself this claim is unremarkable. Informal changes in the meaning of constitutional provisions occur frequently, caused by overt governmental acts and even newly developing cultural contexts. However, Ackerman's process of informal change creates a "structural amendment," which changes the meaning of constitutional text, and whose derivation is equally as authoritative and lawful as those deriving from the formal method of amending the Constitution. If Ackerman is right, "structural amendments" and amendments based on article 5 exhaustively describe American constitutional change. Like conservative theorists, Ackerman excludes Court-derived changes as illegitimate unless they reflect the most recently created constitutional paradigm or regime, though sometimes in surprising ways. If Ackerman is right, then the theory of constitutional revolutions is erroneous.

Ackerman's dualism should be contrasted with the standard conception of constitutional development, which, according to Ackerman, regards constitutional law as a single process that follows, departs from, and then rediscovers the meaning of the United States Constitution. According to this account legitimate constitutional change comes about by following the Constitution's amending power set out in article 5. In this view American constitutional law began by creating a federal republic decidedly more centralized than the Articles of Confederation. In its early stage this centralization of power created the relations between the central government and the states. Later the Civil War amendments revised the original federal framework, further protecting individual rights from state interference. Subsequently, the courts retreated from centralization and returned power back to the states mostly through the Fourteenth Amendment's due process clause and the commerce clause. Finally, the New Deal judicial revolution rediscovered the nation's original conception of federalism, or more specifically, a new conception of federalism firmly anchored in the constitutional past. In this sketch there is one constitution, one constitutional means of amending it, and one institution, the courts, to interpret it.

Ackerman rejects this picture. Instead, he contends that we must distinguish between two kinds of political lawmaking: normal politics and constitutional politics. Normal politics leaves most decisions to the elected representatives of the people. Constitutional politics enables the citizenry to mobilize to bring forth new constitutional directions. According to Ackerman there are three constitutions, or three constitutional regimes, namely, the Founding, the Civil War, and the New Deal. He further contends that constitutional politics represent moments (revolutions) of higher lawmaking, which democratically legitimizes these informal changes without using the sanctioned methods in article 5. In Ackerman's dualism the Court's role is preservative, merely reflecting the wishes of a majority's deliberative mobilization for change. By contrast the theory of constitutional revolutions maintains the supremacy of the judicial role in constitutional change.

Ackerman takes seriously the countermajoritarian problem and implicitly seeks to resolve it. Courts, in a given constitutional regime, are entitled to define new rights or powers if such rights or powers follow from the present regime's paradigm, despite their being incompatible with the original constitution. The progressive development of the three regimes toward centralization and individual rights is due to democratic participation in certain crucial periods of American constitutional history. The progressive nature of Ackerman's theory is due to the fact that American majorities throughout history have become more and more progressive. Of course, this need not have been the case. Given the appropriate conditions, the Reagan revolution might be a democratic shift toward more conservative politics. Unsurprisingly, for Ackerman the Reagan "revolution" was a failed revolution.

Ackerman's implicit motivation in fashioning his interpretive history is to reconcile democracy and judicial review. Like modernists generally, Ackerman is concerned with the legitimacy of judicial review. Hence, his theory is designed to resolve, or perhaps to dissolve, the problems created by judicial scrutiny of the majoritarian branches of government without having to embrace any of the traditional methods of constitutional interpretation and adjudication.[2] Ackerman seeks a detour around the contemporary debates in constitutional theory purporting to establish one method of interpretation as binding on judges. Instead, Ackerman's interpretive history attempts to explain how judicial review is possible in a democracy. How can a democratic polity permit the judiciary to trump the will of the majority? At first glance, at least, democratic legitimacy would seem to require showing the democratic credentials of each branch of government.

Ackerman's goal is to show also that liberal or progressive features of American constitutionalism and politics are the result of a mobilized and reflective majority of citizens, not the imperial decisions of judges. According to Ackerman's interpretive history, American constitutionalism rests on a unique form of dualistic politics that effectively dissolve the countermajoritarian problem.[3] Once we appreciate how American dualist constitutionalism actually works, the countermajoritarian problem no longer threatens the legitimacy of judicial review. In short, Ackerman promises that American constitutional practice, once understood as the dualistic system it is, creates no greater countermajoritarian problem than democratic law does generally, and, therefore, is no less legitimate.

In this chapter I first suggest a characterization of Ackerman's theory as postmodernist and pragmatist. I do not suggest that Ackerman is self-consciously a postmodern pragmatist. My contention is that his theory can be characterized plausibly in postmodern, pragmatist terms. I further contend that the theory's persuasiveness might be greater in a postmodern, pragmatist framework than in a modern one. Before I launch into an examination of his theory, in the next section I redescribe Ackerman's theory as postmodern pragmatist for the purpose of making it more plausible in general, or at least more plausible to members of those camps.

I then examine in detail the salient features of Ackerman's theory. My ultimate conclusion is that Ackerman's theory is inadequate because he fails to identify correctly the role of judicial revolutions. Instead, in Ackerman's view the Court's role is merely to follow the new constitutional paradigm created by constitutional politics. In pressing this preservative judicial function, Ackerman stresses the democratic legitimacy of judicial review without giving sufficient attention to the problem of identifying the nature of judicial reasoning required to carry out this project. By doing so he overlooks the question of whether courts can follow a constitutional paradigm noncreatively or nonrevolutionarily, or, instead, whether the same problems of interpreting the Constitution reappear in Ackerman's regime conception of constitutional law.

My conclusion is that Ackerman's account fails in this important project, and thus he must engage the same jurisprudential troubles affecting the standard conception of constitutional change. This is the reason for insisting on the priority of the jurisprudential over the historical. Ackerman needs a theory of judicial interpretation, like the theory of constitutional revolutions, for his theory to explain how courts and judges interpret constitutional paradigms, whether the paradigm is a single Constitution or several related ones. Without such an account Ackerman's theory cannot ultimately succeed. Despite its shortcomings, Ackerman's theory surely deserves careful examination. It is a complex, interesting, and ingenious theory; we have much to learn from Ackerman's dualism even if it is unable to explain judicial revolutions. Specifically, Ackerman recognizes the importance of constitutional revolutions in generating American constitutional practice, as well as the importance of democratic theory to justify judicial review.

Ackerman's Dualism and Postmodern Pragmatism

Ackerman's theory can be interpreted as a postmodern constitutional theory.[4] From the postmodernist perspective Ackerman's theory attempts to stretch the limits of our constitutional imagination, to reprogram not only our answers to constitutional questions, but the very questions and methods themselves. From this perspective Ackerman attempts to replace a traditional constitutional paradigm with a novel, more complex paradigm of American constitutional practice. Conceiving Ackerman's theory in postmodern terms generates an intriguing interpretive history of American constitutional change, one that emphasizes both the perspective of the political actors as well as the more detached perspective of observers and judges. Ackerman's theory exemplifies a postmodern concern for context, detail, and perspective. Understood in this fashion, Ackerman's theory rejects implicitly the existence of an Archimedean perspective for understanding American constitutional development. Instead, it can be characterized as committed to one of the salient tenets of postmodernism, namely, perspectivalism. In constitutional theory perspectivalism requires understanding constitutional development first from the point of view of the actual actors and circumstances of times past. It eschews embracing any a priori conception of constitutional change and does not attempt to combine different perspectives into one superperspective; in fact, to the contrary, Ackerman insists against attempting such a task. Perspectivalism countenances no overall combinations of historical or constitutional perspectives or singular grand theories of constitutional evolution.

Thus Ackerman's implicit turn toward postmodernity is discernible in his regime analysis of constitutional law. The division of constitutional regimes suggests a concern for complexity and multiplicity in understanding diverse phenomena. Further, a postmodern constitutional theorist seeks novel constitutional stories to explain our constitutional practice. Of course, with such innovation comes difficulty. For example, Ackerman recognizes only vaguely the problems of individuation and identity. How does one determine that American constitutional history consists of three regimes? Why not two? Or four? Additionally, if American constitutional practice consists of three different regimes, in what sense, then, are these regimes part of the *same* constitutional system? Would not the better view be that such practice includes three different constitutions? Indeed, these three regimes may be incommensurate. If not, how can we integrate the paradigms from these different regimes? Should we even try? Ackerman fails to explore these problems in sufficient detail. Problems of this sort, typically raised by modernist sensibilities, threaten to topple Ackerman's project ab initio.

To reject Ackerman's theory for these failures is to overlook the postmodern dimension of his theory. Before we trouble ourselves over these and other problems, we must learn a new constitutional language, the language of constitutional dualism and Ackerman's theory of constitutional moments.[5] Once this language is learned, we should revisit these questions and answer them in terms of the new language, or perhaps the new language will render these questions otiose. Nevertheless, Ackerman's attraction to postmodernity is implicit only, given his reliance on such startling historically close calls. For example, the ultimate legitimizing factor in the New Deal was Justice Roberts's change of heart in deciding to support New Deal legislation. This "switch in time" becomes the ultimate basis for the New Deal's revision of article 5's amending power. One marvels at Ackerman's acumen in arguing for the legitimacy of a non-article 5 structural amend-

ment on the basis of such sparse historical evidence.[6] Had Justice Roberts
stood firm, we might still be back in the Lochner period of constitutional
adjudication. Moreover, for Ackerman's dualism to work, it must distinguish between the Court acting prudentially on the basis of popular
mobilization and deliberation, on the one hand, and the Court's commitment to a reasoned reexamination of constitutional values. If the Court acts
prudentially, it is not obvious that its action is legitimate. If it acts in a
reasoned fashion, it is not clear why popular mobilization is required to
trigger its decision. The Court might know the reasoned response to the
New Deal prior to the 1936 election.

Similarly, Ackerman never publicly characterizes his constitutional theory as pragmatist, although he does call his political theoretic conception of
neutral dialogue "the supreme pragmatic imperative" for settling political
disagreement.[7] Ackerman's pragmatism concentrates on the actual social
practices upon which American constitutionalism depends. Interpreting
these historical social practices depends on interpreting the concrete features of a particular historical period or periods; it rejects, as pragmatism
should, descriptive or normative theories that have insufficient currency in
the American experience.[8] For the pragmatist the most plausible theories of
constitutional moments and judicial reasoning are ones that reflect actual
constitutional practice. For Ackerman the mechanism of "synthetic interpretation" is a pragmatic device for salvaging the remains of fallen regimes
and integrating them with a contemporary one.

Ackerman, like constitutional pragmatists generally, eschews abstract
theories of American constitutional transformation, though he is more tol-
erant of theories than some pragmatists. In this dispute I side with Ackerman against the pragmatists. The pragmatist rejection of theories is unfortunate because it fails to distinguish between two kinds of theories. The first
type of theory, or "white collar" theory, is demonstrative and exclusive,
rejecting the importance and relevance of other such theories. White collar
theories promise to ground our judgments in unassailable foundations.
Such theories may be deductive, algorithmic, or may in some other rigorous fashion provide a decision procedure for settling constitutional conflicts. If a white collar theory exists, it can be proved true, and hence it can
be used to prove the truth of particular constitutional judgments. The
second kind of theory, a blue collar theory, maintains that theory-talk is
better understood as a social practice that must be evaluated pragmatically.[9]
Because pragmatists generally resist a firm commitment to understanding

truth in terms of correspondence with reality, for them the sine qua non of pragmatic reliability is a theory's overall potential for generating illuminating explanations of the phenomena in question. Consequently, pragmatist theories generally embrace a plurality of theoretical factors in explaining and justifying particular judgments. Accordingly, if formalist or rationalist paradigms represent elements in the most useful account of constitutional change, then such elements can be combined in a blue collar theory of American constitutionalism.

Blue collar theories contain illuminating paradigms, pictures, and contexts within which the particular problem can be better understood. Blue collar theories guide the practitioner to ask the right (according to the theory) questions; they set the order to these questions and determine the relevance of various factors in resolving them. In doing this a blue collar theory often will forge a new lexicon, or at least create certain new terms that express the theory's paradigm(s) and determines the new way old problems are to be conceived. Blue collar theories are designed to specify the details of social and political change and attempt to recontextualize successful theories from other domains to the political and constitutional arenas.[10] Ackerman's depiction of the tripartite division of the New Deal resting on the Reconstruction and Founding is such a recontextualization. Recontextualizations may suffer formalistic and rationalistic imperfections but provide instead a deeper, more illuminating account of constitutional change. In this regard Ackerman's intriguing interpretive history is a sophisticated blue collar theory of American constitutional law.

Ackerman's modernist commitments, however, exist in an uneasy tension with his postmodern pragmatism. For example, Ackerman's theory seems to embrace a correspondence theory of truth. The standard view is false, according to Ackerman, because it is based on the myth of rediscovery, the myth that the New Deal was genuinely uncreative constitutionally, but instead returned American society back toward its original plan. In Ackerman's view his dualism is closer to constitutional reality than the standard view because it recognizes the truly creative features of the New Deal. Here Ackerman seems to step outside the parameters of his interpretive history to some more realist conception of history. Ackerman does not even contemplate the possibility that his dualism complements the standard account in many ways. Instead, modernist inclinations prompt Ackerman to insist that dualism is true and the standard account false.

There is no way to evaluate the final theory independently of its modernist commitments. Ackerman must be aware of the danger that at present his theory is an unholy alliance of modernist and postmodernist features. Ackerman must decide whether he intends his theory to be modern or postmodern, foundationalist or antifoundationalist, pragmatic or nonpragmatic. Combining features of each unwittingly leads Ackerman to distort American constitutional practice. One example of such distortion occurs by conflating a description of the practice of structural amendments with a statement supporting the legitimacy of such a practice.

Ackerman's modernist commitments, the countermajoritarian problem, and the role of consent in American constitutionalism determine his approach to dualistic politics. Indeed, these commitments appear to lead Ackerman toward some form of originalism as an interpretive theory. Although Ackerman never explicitly states what his theory of constitutional interpretation is, his commitment to consent and his characterization of the Court's role as preservative suggest that the Court should follow the intent of the Framers of the latest paradigm. Indeed, that is precisely what the "preservative" role means.

If Ackerman's theory of interpretation is originalist, it is difficult to see how he can succeed in overcoming the countermajoritarian problem without a theory of interpretation that clearly reveals the intent of the mobilized citizenry.[11] No originalist theory has ever succeeded in achieving this, and nothing in Ackerman's presentation suggests that it can be done. The problem is that Ackerman's postmodernist aspirations outstrip his modernist constraints. Ackerman's theory of constitutional moments seems much more closely tied to nonoriginalist theories of constitutional interpretation than originalist ones. However, these theories would grant the Court a larger role than Ackerman envisions.

Ackerman's belief in the legitimacy of dualist constitutionalism will be difficult for modernists to accept. At best the modern constitutional mind will regard events such as the Founding, the Civil War, and the Great Depression as atypical and faulty role models just because they were so cataclysmic. Great paradigms of constitutional politics cannot be modeled after periods of radical instability, war, and depression without an account of how this is possible. For example, the Civil War was a great test of the nation's power of survival. The modernists will argue that nothing should be made of improprieties in constitutional change except the constitutional text, which was indeed revolutionary and monumentally important. Should we follow Ackerman's lead in looking to factors other than text, we have absolutely no parameters to guide us here.

Consequently, modernist constitutionalists will bristle at Ackerman's conviction that constitutional amendments can arise legitimately outside of article 5.[12] Ackerman, in fact, believes that the rule of recognition in American constitutionalism is more complicated than the procedure delineated in article 5.[13] Moreover, the rule of recognition itself changes as constitutional revolutions change its structure. All this happens, presumably, according to some vague superrule of recognition based on the sovereignty of the people. Despite the argument that the purpose of article 5 is to set out clearly the procedure for amending the Constitution, Ackerman believes that the Framers in three different constitutional moments actually intended a more general process. The legitimacy of these "structural" or "transformative" amendments arises from the will of the people. However, the modern constitutional theorist has no problem challenging these notions.

What is less obvious is that what modernists scoff at might actually be Ackerman's ingenuity in depicting the practical genius of American constitutionalism. In this view the regime framework of constitutional law is a better explanatory device than the standard view. Ackerman's account shows, it could be argued, that pragmatism, finding attractive solutions to constitutional crises that fit particular contexts, is the motivating force behind constitutional practice.

At every stage of this process the modernist/postmodernist specter appears. In modernist terms Ackerman can sustain the foregoing argument only by formulating a metatheory or pragmatic conception rendering these pragmatic solutions permanent and canonical features of American constitutionalism. What Ackerman needs is a pragmatic principle to justify elevating what occurs as a practical necessity to a structural feature of American constitutionalism.[14] This would go a long way toward showing that the essence of American constitutionalism, or at least higher lawmaking, is the ability to devise a mechanism for resolving crises. This mechanism shows the Framers' willingness not merely to cope, but to cope by extraordinary means. By contrast the postmodern, pragmatist turn enables Ackerman to obviate the necessity of a metatheory by insisting that dualism provides the best interpretive account of constitutional practice, including the elevation of description to prescription.

Interpretive History and the Countermajoritarian Problem

The centerpiece of Ackerman's postmodernism is an interpretive history of constitutional change, because it is designed to reconstruct the practice of American constitutional transformation and to determine which of its features should be retained. Ackerman's approach is not designed to render American constitutional practice normatively flawless. Indeed, as a political philosopher Ackerman contends that America's Constitution is not the best of all possible constitutions, because it does not entrench certain rights.[15] Nevertheless, interpretive history is designed to discern coherent and important conceptions of the past and how the past must be understood today.

Like modernists generally, Ackerman is concerned with the legitimacy of judicial review. Hence, his interpretive theory is designed to deal with the problems of judicial legitimacy without having to embrace any of the traditional methods of constitutional interpretation and adjudication.[16] Ackerman seeks to preempt contemporary debates about constitutional methodology by demonstrating how dualism is majoritarian and how it can produce liberal or progressive results. Constitutional revolutions are created by a mobilized and reflective majority of citizens, not the imperial decisions of judges. In his view this mobilization effectively dissolves the countermajoritarian problem.[17] Once we appreciate how American dualist constitutionalism actually works, the countermajoritarian problem no longer threatens the legitimacy of judicial review.[18]

One problem with Ackerman's interpretive history is its failure to explain why historical constitutional facts have normative weight. Even if Ackerman's history is in some sense compelling, why should it inform our present constitutional worries? Ackerman here faces the kinds of problems originalists generally face, but threefold. Not only must he appeal to what the Framers (understood as a mobilized citizenry) intended concerning the development of American constitutional law, he must explain this in three different regimes, and across regimes, as well.

A second problem with Ackerman's interpretive history is that it distorts the historical evidence. This is the force behind Michael McConnell's criticism of Ackerman's interpretive history.[19] McConnell challenges elevating the New Deal to a constitutional moment and, in effect, rejects Ackerman's penchant for making too much of the switch in time. In addition, McConnell contends that Ackerman's interpretive history says too little by omitting the end of Reconstruction as a constitutional moment. Ackerman can accept the latter objection and still retain his theory, though as McConnell points out, this might require abandoning his position on the New Deal. The issue between Ackerman and McConnell depends on the parameters of distinguishing different regimes in constitutional history. I do not intend to settle this issue, except to say that Ackerman's tripartite division of constitutional history into the Founding, the Reconstruction, and the New Deal is not novel. Other scholars have identified these three phases of American constitutional history as central structural features of constitutional law.

Monism and Rights Foundationalism in Constitutional Theory

Constitutional democracies can be monistic or rights foundationalist. A monist democracy "requires the grant of plenary lawmaking authority to the winners of the last general election — so long, at least, as the election was conducted under free and fair ground rules, and the winners don't try to prevent the next scheduled round of electoral challenges."[20] The British parliamentary system is an example of a monist democracy. American monists such as Robert Bork insist that in a democracy the majority has the right to rule simply because it is the majority.[21] Consequently, "when the Supreme Court, or anybody else, invalidates a statute, it suffers from a 'countermajoritarian difficulty' which must be overcome before a good democrat can profess satisfaction with this extraordinary action."[22] Ackerman appears to take this argument very seriously, perhaps too seriously. The powerful arguments of scholars for a restrained judiciary, such as Robert Bork's, have caught Ackerman's ear. However, historically, the underlying republican foundation of American constitutionalism never equates democracy with majoritarianism. Rather, it seeks to filter majoritarian decisions through a process of steps (obstacles?) in order to ascertain the community's real interests, or at least the community's considered judgments about its real interests. Consequently, Bork's argument is a nonstarter.

The republican foundation renders it a mistake to identify majoritarianism with the most plausible conception of democracy. This foundation insists on distinguishing between the will of the people as the aggregation of individual preferences, and the considered judgments of citizens concerned with the common good. There are different institutional arrangements for ascertaining the people's considered judgments. One need not give courts the honor of discovering the community's real interests, but the Court is one possible institution for doing this. That there is a coun-ter*majoritarian* element in American government does not necessarily en-tail the existence of a counter*democratic* element. Rather, the most plau-sible conception of democracy may insist upon a republican constraint on majoritarianism.

The distinction between democracy and majoritarianism, together with the fact that the federal government is designed as a limited government, refutes Bork's claim that the majority is entitled to prevail simply because it is a majority. Such a majoritarian view is rejected by republican values ab initio. Republican principles insist on a dichotomy between the majority's initial or intuitive judgments and its considered judgments. The republican structure of American constitutionalism and government is designed to institutionalize this dichotomy. Of course, it does not follow that this in-stitutional design is necessarily better than other possibilities, or that no modification is possible or desirable, which better instantiates contempo-rary republican principles. If judicial review is illegitimate, however, it is because it fails to fulfill the polity's republican ideals, not simply because it is countermajoritarian. The point here is that American constitutionalism rejects decisively the equation between democracy and majoritarianism.

Ackerman argues that, in the American context, monistic constitutional-ism contrasts with rights foundationalism, because rights foundationalists contend that rights trump majority decisions.[23] Rights foundationalists believe that the Constitution's authority is grounded in human rights, whereas monists believe its authority derives from the will of the people.[24] According to Ackerman, monists are suspicious of judicial intervention. By contrast, rights foundationalists see a more expansive role for the Constitu-tion and the courts. In their view the Constitution protects, among other things, fundamental rights. A rights foundationalist may adopt substantive rights, such as the right to religious freedom, as well as processual rights, such as the right to self-government. Though rights foundationalists differ concerning which rights are fundamental, all agree that "[w]hatever rights are Right, . . . the American constitution is concerned, first and foremost, with their protection. Indeed, the whole point of having rights is to trump decisions rendered by democratic institutions that may otherwise legislate for the collective welfare."[25]

For the rights foundationalist the countermajoritarian nature of judicial review is not as great an obstacle as it is for the monist. For the rights foundationalist the countermajoritarian problem casts its shadow only when the Court finds rights not contained in the Constitution. When a majority violates a favored right, the rights foundationalist has no reluctance to exhort the Court to remedy the violation. More strongly, "[w]hen such violations occur, the foundationalist demands judicial intervention despite the breach of democratic principle."[26] For rights foundationalists "[r]ights trump democracy—provided, of course, that they're the Right rights."[27] Majoritarian rule is acceptable, according to rights foundationalists, only when the majority is constrained by the preferred rights.

Ackerman paves the way for introducing a third type of theory by insisting that neither monism nor rights foundationalism adequately explains American constitutionalism. Monism cannot explain those abrupt constitutional transformations that mark our higher-law constitutional tradition. If monism is correct, then the Founding, the Reconstruction, and the New Deal are just instances of normal politics. If so, their constitutional legitimacy is suspect. Which normal paradigms can one invoke to explain these constitutional transformations? Monism provides no insight into how American citizens create these seminal episodes in our constitutional history. If rights foundationalism is an accurate account of American democratic constitutionalism, then these constitutional moments may be legitimate—because foundationalist rights justify constitutional transformations—but then our constitutional system is fundamentally countermajoritarian. Either choice yields an undesirable account of American constitutionalism. Either our constitutional system can be explained by the appeal to rights (but then it is not democratic), or it is democratic (but higher lawmaking is inexplicable). Is there a way out of this dilemma?

One possible answer is the canonical answer. According to the canonical answer, article 5 provides a "normal" route to constitutional politics. If monism is correct, then monism explains both normal politics and constitutional politics. Normal politics insist on following well-recognized paradigms or sets of rules for deciding legal issues. In normal politics laws are legitimized by following the rules (authorities) laid down. In constitutional politics the normal process of amendment yields changes in higher law. In this view normal politics explain everything, in part, as following the rules laid down. This answer needs further exploration. Suffice it to say that Ackerman's reply would no doubt be to challenge whether the rules laid down can determine when a constitutional amendment passes. In fact Ackerman would argue that even when article 5 is invoked as the mechanism of change, constitutional politics—revolutionary constitutional politics — can radically alter the implementation of the article 5 process. Acker-man marshals many interesting facts to support his contention. Before we evaluate this theory, however, he must provide a metatheory for determin-ing legitimacy generally. Without such a theory we have no way of distin-guishing between tumultuous events that amount to constitutional politics and ones that do not. After all is said and done, Ackerman's theory fails to provide the most plausible explanation of American constitutional history, or a useful predictive theory for identifying future constitutional moments.

One possible objection to Ackerman's characterization of monistic de-mocracy indicates that no American constitutionalist can embrace it.[28] No American constitutionalist believes that the winners of the last election have plenary lawmaking power.[29] Everyone believes that the Constitution, espe-cially the Bill of Rights, constrains this power. Ackerman rejects this crit-icism. Instead Ackerman distinguishes between the symbolic Constitution and the effective Constitution.[30] Although no one is a constitutional monist regarding the symbolic Constitution, several important scholars such as Alexander Bickel, John Ely, Jesse Choper, and Robert Bork are indeed mo-nists regarding the effective Constitution. This distinction permits Acker-man to discount textual evidence from these writers, demonstrating that they are far from monists.[31]

It is not clear that this distinction can do the work Ackerman intends it to do.[32] Ackerman's monist cannot truly be a monist if she concedes, as she must, that the symbolic Constitution is committed to the judicial protec-tion of rights in normal politics, and to the supermajoritarian process of amendment through article 5. Ackerman's argument should then be recast to emphasize that this limited conception of dualism fails to fit constitu-tional practice or is unacceptable on normative grounds. He should avoid a dichotomy between monism and dualism as exhaustively describing possi-ble constitutional theories. Instead he should point out that limited dualism is inadequate. Ackerman's reluctance to embrace this conclusion is under-standable. Once we distinguish between weaker conceptions of dualism in contradistinction to dualism and something qualitatively different, Acker-man's method for setting up the problem in the first place is undercut.

Because even monists concede that the Constitution constrains majority will, Ackerman's conception of constitutional monism is radically distorted. Ackerman should concede that calling American constitutionalism "monis-tic" is hyperbole. Instead he should simply say that American constitutional monism insists on majoritarian supremacy in all cases not proscribed by the text. The U.S. Constitution precludes judging that every majoritarian decision is constitutional whether one is a monist or a rights foundationalist. True monism, as in England, is not so qualified, "because the Parliament of the United Kingdom is truly a continuously functioning constitutional convention."[33] The contrast between American majoritarians and English monism should demonstrate that monism fails to apply to the American scene. Given Ackerman's penchant for explaining American constitutionalism in local terms, it should have occurred to him that no serious American constitutionalist can embrace monism.

Consequently, the Constitution itself creates and sustains a dualistic democracy, because the Constitution itself sets out the distinction between normal politics, laws passed by the elected branches of government, and constitutional or supernormal politics as specified by the amendment process in article 5.[34] (Indeed, article 5 collapses the distinction between normal and constitutional change.) Ackerman's point should not be that constitutional monism is inadequate. Of course monism is inadequate, because it is inadequate to the explicit text. Rather, Ackerman's position should be that monism and the article 5 amendment process fail to explain fully constitutional change. Instead there is a third track of constitutional lawmaking that permits amending the Constitution outside the constraints of article 5. Such an explanation needs Ackerman's informal amendment process. It is this third track of constitutional politics that we must address. The distinction between constitutional monism and dualism obscures this issue.

Similarly, Ackerman's characterization of rights foundationalism is distorted. In his view rights foundationalism appears antithetical to democratic rights. However, there is nothing anomalous in recognizing indirection as a useful conceptual tool. Indirection sanctions constraining some value in order to provide that value with a longer, better life. Most American rights foundationalists hold such a view. For most rights foundationalists the importance of rights plays a substantial part in satisfying the requirements of a truly effective democracy.[35] In order for democracy to flourish, people must have certain rights, such as freedom of speech to protect against distorted majorities as well as overreaching minorities. Consequently, Ackerman's description of monism and rights foundationalism triggers the response that neither position has ever been held by any American constitutionalist. If that charge can be sustained, the foundation of Ackerman's argument is flawed.

Ackerman has been taken to task by some rights foundationalists. Miriam

and William Galston argue that rights foundationalism is required to explain when constitutional moments arise and why they are attractive.[36]
Without such an independent standard we have no way of distinguishing
between normal and constitutional politics. To put this differently, constitutional politics no longer have any normative attractiveness if they are
described independently of the notion of fundamental rights. Don Herzog
puts the point more strongly. According to Herzog, "whether it is sensible
to talk about people acting in constitutionally binding ways depends on
background criteria of various kinds."[37] For Herzog rights may well be
included among these criteria.[38] Consequently, "the project of distinguishing the merely formal requirements of democratic action from the substance of rights will collapse: calling the Constitution 'democratic first,
rights-protecting second' will be confounding, not illuminating."[39]

Ackerman bristles at the suggestion that dualistic politics cannot be made
sense of without independent fundamental rights. Referring to Lincoln and
Dworkin, Ackerman insists that "[t]he modern Constitution does not express a timeless philosophy of right revealed in the Declaration of Independence or some Herculean labor of philosophical reflection."[40] American
constitutionalism, instead, "is the product of ongoing political struggle —
generation after generation mobilizing itself to critique and reconstruct
large chunks of the received constitutional understanding."[41] Ackerman
does not sense the need for some independent standard for directing the
critique. We should, rather, be guided by the image of "Neurath's Boat, not
Kant's *Critique.*"[42] Ackerman's tone expresses a pragmatic urgency as well
as an impatience with rights foundationalism when he insists that the
"question was whether the ship would keep sailing during a shattering
reconstruction, not whether its overall desirability would survive a philosophy seminar."[43]

Conceivably, room exists for rapprochement between Ackerman and
rights foundationalists. The Galstons are correct that constitutional transformation depends on extrinsic factors such as the wider culture, including
abstract or utopian statements of moral theory. In order to identify the
concerns of different generations of Americans in higher lawmaking, we
must provide more than a superficial description of the conflict. We need to
understand the conflict in terms of the great moral and political controversies of the day, and this, indeed, requires an appeal to an independent
domain of political and moral theory. Yet to understand how this independent domain played itself out, that is, how it was expressed in American

constitutionalism, and the form of its expression, one must look to the actual ongoing political struggle over different ideals at least during the Founding, the Reconstruction, and the New Deal, if not during other periods as well.

Dualism in Constitutional Theory: Normal Politics and Constitutional Politics

Ackerman contends that American democracy might be illegitimate if its foundations are either solely monist or solely rights foundationalist. In response to this dilemma Ackerman notes that our democracy is dualist, combining the best of monism and rights foundationalism.[44] A dualist democracy, as earlier mentioned, evinces both normal politics and constitutional politics. Normal politics, in the American context, is government *by the politicians.* The *private* citizen need not pay more than casual attention to the vicissitudes of normal politics. There are, however, higher lawmaking moments when the private *citizen* must band together with other concerned citizens as well as with political and social leaders to change the constitutional politics of the American nation. This extraordinary involvement on the part of the citizenry in constitutional politics, according to Ackerman, determines the structure of American constitutionalism. The result is constitutional dualism, a two-track system of American democracy.[45]

The linchpin of Ackerman's dualism is the notion of a "private citizen." Ackerman contrasts the private citizen with the "public citizen" and the perfect privatist. The public citizen regards political involvement as an intrinsic value, whereas the perfect privatist regards political involvement skeptically at best. The personality of the private citizen reflects Ackerman's dualism in that it instantiates normal and constitutional politics. The *private* citizen attends to her private life during normal politics. However, the private *citizen* is ready for political involvement during those higher lawmaking periods associated with constitutional politics.

Ackerman's dualism and his idea of the private citizen enable him to attempt a rapprochement between liberalism and republicanism. Ackerman endorses liberalism, the principle that people are rational, autonomous, and morally independent individuals who have rights that government should protect. For the liberal, government and political involvement is a necessary evil at best. However, Ackerman also endorses republicanism, which holds that people are essentially political creatures capable of the inherently valuable activity of deliberating about the common good. Ackerman's dualism promises to achieve both liberal and republican visions. First, normal politics allows people freely to pursue independent ends, whereas constitutional politics permits dualists to engage the higher lawmaking that is at the heart of our constitutional democracy.[46] More importantly, Ackerman's liberal republicanism "insists that the foundation of personal liberty is a certain kind of political life, one requiring the ongoing exertions of a special kind of citizenry. Rather than grounding personal freedom on some putatively prepolitical 'state of nature,' this kind of liberalism makes the cultivation of *liberal citizenship* central to its enterprise. Since this is the view of people like John Stuart Mill and John Dewey and John Rawls, it seems odd to define liberalism in a way that makes the very possibility of liberal republicanism seem a contradiction in terms."[47]

Ackerman's grand integration of monism and rights foundationalism has several benefits.[48] Monism contributes the majoritarianism of normal politics, which is necessary to the ordinary operation of a complex liberal democracy, whereas rights foundationalism contributes the higher lawmaking of constitutional politics. Ackerman's dualism tries to integrate monism and rights foundationalism into one comprehensive conception of democracy by "offering a framework which allows both sides to accommodate some—if not all—of their concerns."[49] According to Ackerman, "[t]he basic mediating device is the dualist's two-track system of democratic lawmaking."[50] This two-track system "allows an important place for the foundationalist's view of 'rights as trumps' without violating the monist's deeper commitment to the primacy of democracy."[51]

Although dualism combines central features of monism and rights foundationalism, it is conceptually equivalent to neither, even when dualism's judgment corresponds to one or the other theory. The dualist is never only a monistic democrat nor only a rights foundationalist. Instead the dualist is a majoritarian democrat only during normal politics. When dualists and monists each engage in normal politics, the convergence is an extensional, not a conceptual, equivalence. The conceptual difference remains because monism, in Ackerman's conception, countenances only normal politics, whereas dualism countenances normal and constitutional politics. Similarly, the dualist embraces "rights as trumps" when doing so protects prior higher lawmaking. When no such democratic processes exist, the dualist cannot embrace rights unless they can be explicated in terms of democratic values. She cannot, in short, embrace rights for the sake of justice alone. A rights foundationalist, on the other hand, can embrace such rights, and, therefore, the convergence of dualism and rights foundationalism in embracing "rights as trumps" is similarly only an extensional equivalence.

Constitutional politics or higher lawmaking must follow the rule of law as enacted *by the people*. Consequently, the regime framework for constitutional change must show how constitutional changes follow the rule of law. If the Founding is understood in terms of monism, its legitimacy is questionable because no existing law sanctioned the creation of the new charter. In other words, if monism prevails, then it would seem that only normal politics is possible. If normal politics is all there is, then the transition from the Articles of Confederation to the Constitution is inexplicable and illegitimate because the Constitution failed to follow the prescribed procedure for amending the Articles of Confederation. Whereas the Articles of Confederation required a unanimous vote to amend it, the Constitution requires only a three-fourths vote of the states for ratification. In reality, then, the Constitution never amended the Articles of Confederation, and, therefore, the Constitution is illegal.[52] The question monists seem unable to answer is, How did we ever legally get from the Articles of Confederation to the Constitution? If politics were only normal politics, there is no way to make the transition.

Monists have at least two possible replies. First, like any true revolution, the Founding was illegal. Whenever one model of government replaces another, the transition cannot be explained in terms of the first. For if it could, the second model would be merely an extension of the first, except in the rare case when the first provides for its own termination. However, this argument might explain the conceptual transition, but not the political or constitutional one.[53] Political and constitutional change must be carried out legally according to the rule of law. Talk of the nature of conceptual change and political revolutions doesn't address this issue. A second reply is simply that foundings necessarily alter the normal processes of government, and nothing more should be made of it. This commonsensical reply has merit, but nevertheless risks begging the question against Ackerman, because Ackerman insists that there is more constitutional meaning to be derived from *our* Founding, and therefore we blind ourselves to our constitutional past by adopting this commonsensical reply. For Ackerman to make good on this point, he must demonstrate a convincing conception of constitutional legitimacy, that is, why should one accept his conception of constitutional structural amendments? What metatheory permits him to inspect constitutional history with the goal of formulating an informal process of constitutional amendment?

Rights foundationalism explains the adoption of the Constitution as the failure to recognize certain rights. When a regime fails to protect such fundamental rights as the right to private property, or free speech, or the free exercise of religion, then a new constitutional order is warranted. Yet the rights foundationalist cannot explain such a transition when no foundational rights are implicated, as was surely the case in the transition from the Articles of Confederation to the Constitution. Like the original United States Constitution, the Articles of Confederation contained no Bill of Rights. However, the absence of a Bill of Rights was not the raison d'être of the Founding. The Articles of Confederation failed primarily because the fledgling nation had no effective central control over commerce and political factions. Rights foundationalism cannot explain or justify such a transition in terms of such substantive rights as freedom of speech and religion.[54] In this instance the rights foundationalist must appeal to a general right of the people to abolish existing law and create law anew. But what justifies such a right? Does this right permit revolution now? And is such a right an individual right, or a collective right? If it is an individual right of revolution, it potentially subverts the right of the majority to make and enforce law. If it is a collective right, how can we make such a right intelligible? And what can possibly justify it? More important, if constitutional politics were driven by rights foundationalism, then it is difficult to explain the primary role of the people in determining the character of the American government. What happens when majority values conflict with individual rights? According to rights foundationalism, rights trump majority will. It is then difficult to appreciate the democratic character associated with our nation's Founding.

If politics were exclusively normal politics, the legality of the Civil War amendments is also questionable. In this situation the normal process of amending the Constitution set out in article 5 was abrogated. Article 5 delineates the partnership and relationship between the federal government and the states in bringing about constitutional change. Typically, the federal government proposes amendments while the states ratify them. The ratification process must be voluntary. The southern states were permitted to reenter the Union only after first ratifying the Fourteenth Amendment. Consequently, the Framers forged a new conception of amending the Constitution. Article 5 is essentially a state-driven process, whereas the Civil War amendments were proposed and ratified by a congressionally driven process. Finally, the New Deal revolution, which changed the constitutionality of government regulations over the economy, also occurred outside of article 5. Of course, in one sense the New Deal is the least problematic, since its constitutional implications are due to a judicial reinterpretation of the Constitution. There is nothing illegal or unusual about that. In another sense the New Deal is the most problematic, because arguably its judicial decisions amended the Constitution without the benefit of new constitutional text.

According to Ackerman, neither monism nor rights foundationalism explains any of these transitions. Only by positing the existence of a two-track system of normal and higher lawmaking can we understand these constitutional revolutions and both the substantive and procedural changes they created. At the time of the Founding a critical economic crisis over commerce struck the fledgling nation. Instead of a normal, legal transition from the Articles of Confederation, the Founding was an instance of abrupt higher lawmaking that ignored legal formalities. Moreover, the Founders meant to indicate their approval of mobilizing people for revolutionary changes through constitutional politics. Similarly, this higher lawmaking capacity enabled the Reconstruction Congress to procure the ratification of constitutional amendments outside the usual process of article 5. Again, the Framers looked to extraconstitutional means of altering the Constitution in critical circumstances. Ackerman, however, never explains why a simpler explanation is inappropriate here. Why not say that the aftermath of the Civil War marked an extraordinary period, which should not be taken as a paradigm of informal constitution making? Thus, though the Fourteenth Amendment was ratified in an atypical manner, it would be foolish to canonize this event by making it an exemplar of future informal amendments. One hopes that no civil war will ever again devastate the American landscape. Nothing should follow from these extraordinary circumstances — certainly not a change in the procedure for amending the Constitution. Ackerman's reply would be to insist that we fail to identify the novel features of American constitutionalism if we overlook the revolutionary dimension of constitutional moments. Such a failure results in an inability to explain how so much constitutional change occurs in noncanonical ways.

Before adopting Ackerman's approach, we should first search for alternative explanations. For example, it could be argued that the Reconstruction did not represent an alternative procedure for amending the Constitution outside article 5. Rather, the guaranty clause enabled Congress to make ratification of the Fourteenth Amendment a condition of reentering the Union, not for the purpose of ratifying the amendment, but for the purpose of making certain that the secessionists did not seize permanent control of the state government, thereby reinstituting the disenfranchisement of African Americans.[55] Ackerman needs to address alternative historical explanations of this sort.

Perhaps more radically, the New Deal revolutionaries thought it unnecessary for a new constitutional text to be an integral feature of constitutional politics. Instead, New Deal legislation was declared constitutional after a series of events, including a presidential election and a Court-packing challenge, which ultimately forced the Court to reverse its hostility toward the New Deal. This "switch in time," according to Ackerman, was the functional equivalent of a formal constitutional amendment.[56] The constitutional moments associated with the Founding and the Reconstruction created new constitutional text. At least in that respect article 5, in part, explains these moments. Thus, even one sympathetic to Ackerman's theory might be reluctant to embrace the New Deal as an instance of higher lawmaking because new constitutional text is required for constitutional politics. In this view the New Deal might simply be an especially dramatic instance of normal politics.[57]

Ackerman considers the New Deal to be paradigmatic of higher lawmaking in the modern republic. In his view constitutional moments such as the New Deal provide subtext in the form of transformative statutes, and that sufficiently meets the requirement of new constitutional text, if such a requirement exists.[58] Surely Ackerman is right in insisting that the New Deal gave new constitutional meaning to American politics. In general, the argument for these extraordinary changes goes like this: In exceptional moments we need not be tied to business as usual, the orderly, strictly legal method of constitutional transformation. Rather, American government needs an alternative method to express the deliberative will of a mobilized majority in creating new constitutional structures for the benefit of the American democracy. Constitutional politics are an example of higher lawmaking in order to adapt our government and our political lives to the exigent circumstances that will inevitably occur in a vibrant democracy. In any such democracy a mobilized majority cannot be prohibited from informally amending the Constitution when necessary without giving up essential features of democratic self-government. When a constitutional democracy restricts itself from engaging in informal change in the name of majoritarianism or "the rule of law," law ceases to be a vehicle of social change and plays a much less significant force in the culture of the democracy. Thus, *We the People* and *We the Politicians* will find a way to express necessary alterations in constitutional meaning outside of article 5 when the Republic's survival depends upon it.[59]

Conceding this, it still does not follow that we should institutionalize constitutional politics except insofar as its engine is article 5. Instead, it might be more prudent to restrict these forays into informal constitutional politics to only these circumstances. Historically, many more instances of higher lawmaking outside of article 5 are required before we can begin to claim that this informal process of amending the Constitution is even remotely legitimate. In other words, why shouldn't we ignore such atypical instances of constitutional change, or at least reject making these changes paradigmatic of higher lawmaking? Ackerman must provide an independent argument demonstrating why he takes the alternative route. Moreover, even if we grant that these constitutional moments should be institutionalized, Ackerman has not shown that they should be institutionalized as higher lawmaking on the same level as article 5 amendments. Perhaps lawmakers and judges should recognize periods in constitutional development that are more significant than others and should be reluctant to alter the influence of these periods without careful deliberation. It is a non sequitur to infer that judges should feel *constrained* by these developments to the same extent that they feel constrained by constitutional politics resulting in changes pursuant to article 5.[60]

The Role of the Supreme Court in Dualist Lawmaking

Dualistic constitutionalism requires a reconceptualization of the role of the Supreme Court. In contrast to the standard view that the Supreme Court is, at times, forward looking or prophetic, Ackerman depicts the Court as preservationist, protecting the higher lawmaking processes from erosion during normal politics. If normal politics could overturn the results of higher lawmaking, there would be no incentive for the people to engage in the onerous process of higher lawmaking.[61] In order to "maintain the integrity of higher lawmaking, all dualist constitutions must provide for one or more institutions to discharge a preservationist function."[62] Dualist democracy explains the role of the Supreme Court in ways unavailable to demo-cratic monism.[63] Similarly, although rights foundationalism can more read-ily embrace judicial intervention in a democracy when rights are violated, it cannot justify judicial review by appealing to democratic factors. The dual-ist, however, can embrace judicial review because it is needed to protect the democratic results of constitutional politics from the intrusion of normal politics. The chief difference between monism and dualism is that monists always regard the Supreme Court suspiciously as a potential threat to de-mocracy, whereas "the dualist sees the discharge of the preservationist func-tion by the courts as an essential part of a well-ordered democratic re-gime."[64] Without some institution performing this potent preservationist role, the hard-fought gains of constitutional politics could be lost through normal politics. Ackerman argues that the monist is wrong to presume that the Court's invalidation of normal statutes is antidemocratic. The Court's "ongoing judicial effort to look backward and interpret the meaning of the great achievements of the past is an indispensable part of the larger project of distinguishing the will of *We the People* from the acts of *We the Politi-cians.*"[65] The problem here is that no interpretive methodology exists that focuses exclusively on past events. Further, no one has ever specified a methodology that obviously reveals the meaning of past events. To inter-pret the past, one must interpret it in terms of the present and the future. Failure to do so results in a totally skewed vision of history. Even if such a methodology were possible, Ackerman must explain how the Court uses it in the Court's preservative role.

Unlike recent constitutional jurisprudence, Ackerman intends an impor-tant, but relatively minor, role for the judiciary. In Ackerman's view judges are not truly lawmakers. Instead, Ackerman insists, "The critical higher lawmaking precedents were established during moments of crisis by leaders like Madison, Lincoln, and Roosevelt—who, in complex interaction with other institutions and the people at large, finally gain democratic authority to make fundamental changes in our higher law. While courts play a sec-ondary role in the evolving higher lawmaking process, we cannot narrowly focus on judges if we hope to describe, and reflect upon, the constitutional practice of popular sovereignty in American history."[66]

If Ackerman is right, the internecine struggles within the judiciary and the academy are pointless. One need not decide whether textualism, orig-inalism, or the other standard methodologies should prevail. A dualist judge should simply look to the last constitutional moment, synthesize it with other moments, and decide the case before her. In short, we need not ask the following questions within the experience of the dualist framework: Should a judge interpret the law or just apply it? Must a judge be faithful to the text of the Constitution? What is the role of the Framers' intentions in constructing the Constitution? Must a judge's opinion be stated in terms of general and neutral principles? Is there a significant difference between legislating and adjudicating? What is the role of ethics and politics in constitutional interpretation? Is judicial supremacy countermajoritarian? Ackerman implies that the traditional interpretive questions disappear within the dualist, tripartite regime. In fact, Ackerman's project aims at making traditional jurisprudential questions of constitutional methodology superfluous.

However, these questions reappear in different form in Ackerman's dualism. For example, should a judge interpret the paradigm in the constitutional moment, or just apply it? What does it mean to say the constitutional moment has a univocal paradigm? Who are the relevant Framers concerning constitutional moments, and how does a judge discern their intent? If a judge believes one element in the paradigm contradicts another, may she excise that element? Is doing so countermajoritarian or majoritarian? Ackerman never explains how his dualist constitutionalism answers these questions or how it does away with a need to answer them.

Ackerman appears to reject activist constitutionalism by rejecting the Court's prophetic role.[67] Once great constitutional moments occur, the Court's role "is [to] preserve the achievements of popular sovereignty during the long periods of our public existence when the citizenry is not mobilized for great constitutional achievements."[68] Doubtless, it "sometimes happens that a preservationist Court may help spark a new forward-looking movement."[69] However, this "top-down" constitutional transformation is atypical and undesirable, because courts are ill equipped to lead the people to better constitutional values. American constitutionalism, according to Ackerman, derives its power and authority from the people, and "although judges are in a unique position to preserve the past constitutional achievements of the American people, many other citizens are in better positions to lead the people onward to a better constitutional future."[70]

However, one might wonder why the Court should always try to preserve the higher lawmaking of past generations from all attempts — normal or otherwise — to reverse it. It seems that Ackerman's dualism compels the Court to take a conservative position in the face of incipient mass mobilization. Because the Court's role is to preserve, the Court was right to forestall New Deal legislation. But, then, whenever a court perceives an attempt at constitutional politics, it should do everything it can to quash it. Isn't this an anomalous result? It is anomalous because it means that justices should always be on the side of the present paradigm, which ultimately will be deemed unconstitutional relative to the new paradigm. Why shouldn't judges take the lead if doing so can be seen as advancing at least in spirit the basic values that inform constitutional law? In fact, Ackerman's conception of intergenerational synthesis seems to be such a forward method of interpretation. If *Brown* and *Griswold* are remarkable cases of intergenerational synthesis, that's because, without the judicial role, we might never have detected what *We the People* in the Revolution of 1937 really intended.[71]

The preservationist function is rife with internal tension. The Court must simultaneously try to preserve yesterday's constitutional moment and prevent tomorrow's constitutional moment. In short, until the people speak through constitutional politics, today's constitutional moment is sacrosanct, and tomorrow's constitutional moment is blasphemous. The Court must be hostile to what will, hypothetically, become a remarkable constitutional revolution in American society, creating more rights and liberties that result in a better expression of American democracy than the constitutional law that the Court preserves.[72] In other words, in Ackerman's conception, the Supreme Court should never make an independent judgment in terms of democratic factors concerning a budding movement of constitutional politics that ultimately achieves better democratic results than the present system. There should be a more flexible means of responding to mass movements. Mustn't the Court's role be more forward looking than this? Moreover, should the Court reverse itself even when the present mass mobilization has antidemocratic implications?

Ackerman's position is troubling, inter alia, because it assumes that judges can readily identify the precise moment when the people have spoken. According to Ackerman the people speak constitutionally only after a complex period of national debate, including the processes through which a political majority signals, proposes, deliberates, and codifies a redirection in constitutional law.[73] Note the difference between this process and amending the Constitution through article 5. In the latter process it is fairly obvious when the Constitution is amended, though problematic issues can arise,[74] whereas in Ackerman's story, trouble is likely over every element in the process. These problems would involve a difficult question for any court or tribunal to settle were a challenge raised. Imagine the arguments over whether a particular process was a bona fide signal, or proposal, or whether deliberation was sufficient, or codification complete. Moreover, we should not welcome a court to tell us whether a movement's support had "depth, breadth and decisiveness." Something more public, more decisive, and more deliberative is required. Article 5 serves these purposes better than Ackerman's conception of a structural amendment.[75]

Ackerman's theory assumes further that the Court can easily distinguish between a normal political attempt to reverse the past constitutional moment from a normal political attempt to articulate more fully, through legislation, the content of the past constitutional paradigm. Within Ackerman's parameters it is difficult for a judge to know when a piece of normal legislation is compatible with the most recent constitutional moment, when it is incompatible per se, or when it is incompatible because it suggests the need for a different constitutional paradigm. Ackerman provides no methodology for making these distinctions. Yet without such a methodology Ackerman cannot dissolve the countermajoritarian problem or the problems associated with judicial activism. Thus, even for dualists, controversies will abound.

Ackerman's preservationist judicial function is also rife with external problems. In Ackerman's view Marshall believed that "the Constitution has a superior status as higher law by virtue of its enactment by the People."[76] What is the source of this injunction? The Constitution itself? If so, the argument is circular. The Constitution is higher law because the Constitution says it is higher law. If not from the Constitution, then from where? Similarly, in Ackerman's view Marshall believed that "[u]ntil a constitutional movement successfully amends our higher law, the Court's task is to preserve the People's judgments against their erosion by normal lawmaking."[77] If Ackerman is correct about Marshall's convictions, then Marshall believed in at least one extraconstitutional injunction, namely, that We the People create higher law independently of the Constitution. It is Marshall's conviction concerning the extrinsic authority of the people or, differently put, concerning the importance of democracy that underlies American constitutionalism. This conviction also shows Marshall's creative reasoning that marks the Founding period as the foundation of pragmatist appeals to independent constitutional factors. When Marshall "used the Madison and Monroe Presidencies to elaborate a preservationist understanding of its mission,"[78] he was going beyond the original paradigm in the Constitution and subsequent case law. Instead, he was initiating American constitutionalism as a pragmatist force culminating in the form of judicial review we have today.

Ackerman might respond that the preservationist role applies only to normal politics, not to constitutional politics. This response presupposes that the Court can identify when an attempt to overturn a prior constitutional moment is a normal political attempt, or when it is the inchoate beginnings of a new movement of constitutional politics. In Ackerman's conception there certainly must come a time when the Court should capitulate. Here Ackerman tells us that the time for capitulation comes when, "[i]n the light of the sustained popular support for President and Congress, a majority of the Justices have concluded that it would be counterproductive to continue the constitutional crisis until the new movement ratifies formal constitutional amendments. Instead, they uphold the last wave of transformative statutes in a series of landmark opinions, which inaugurate the radical revision of pre-existing doctrine."[79] These comments are truly remarkable. Can it be that Justice Roberts's New Deal switch in time is the foundation of this third constitutional moment? What if Justice Roberts had no views on constitutional revolutions or continual constitutional conflict, but instead feared Court packing or congressional control over the Court's appellate jurisdiction? In other words, what if he was concerned about the Court's nonconstitutional prudence? Most theorists assume that there is a canonical method for characterizing the conduct of individual justices as opposed to ordinary human concerns about holding on to a job. When a single player is the basis of a constitutional reconceptualization, there is a need to know more about his motivation. Future justices need to be able to identify when resistance is counterproductive *for constitutional reasons,* not for other kinds of reasons. Is it conceivable that Ackerman can base a theory of constitutional change on so slender a foundation?

Nothing in Ackerman's theory provides future justices with a reliable guide for knowing when higher lawmaking occurs.[80] Ackerman's theory seems to get something right, but whether this constitutes an alternative form of constitutionalism or merely the improprieties of the standard conception is an open question. Unless Ackerman's theory can demonstrate how to distinguish between these alternatives, it cannot provide a determinate alternative.

Ackerman is also silent on the parameters of internal dualist debate. How are two dualists to resolve a conflict over the dualist process? Suppose one dualist, following Ackerman, contends that a presidential election must be a part of a new constitutional moment, while another dualist says it does not. How does dualist theory resolve this conflict? Because Ackerman's theory appears ad hoc, it cannot coherently provide the rules for internal dualist debate. Indeed, there are two problems here, one conceptual and the other epistemic. The conceptual problem questions the meaning of normal politics as contrasted with constitutional politics: What truth conditions must exist for politics to be normal or constitutional? Given Ackerman's description of the road from normal to constitutional politics, it is never clear exactly what "constitutional politics" means.

Even if we can specify the truth conditions of higher lawmaking, there is still an epistemic problem. The epistemic question challenges us to explain how we know when such conditions occur. In short, how do we know when "we the people" have spoken?[81] One is hard-pressed to know when a movement sincerely appeals to constitutional politics, or when it does so merely to win a normal political gain. How does one know when the movement or its adversaries are deliberating in good faith? Abstractly, even if one can draw a semantic distinction between normal and constitutional politics, it may still be practically impossible to detect when this distinction applies to concrete circumstances.

Ackerman also fails to instruct judges on how to deal with the following situation: What should judges do when a recent constitutional moment fails to provide guidance on a contemporary issue that should have been included in the constitutional moment were the people prescient? When such a gap occurs in a new non-article-5 amendment, should judges abstain, or should they decide the case anyway? Ackerman does not answer this question. This problem also occurs with article 5 amendments, but here the answer is clearer. If an article 5 amendment fails to guide, the people through article 5 should revise the amendment. Moreover, in this context standard American constitutional practice often permits the Court to revise, adjust, or modify the scope of the amendment. However, if a dualist court is preservationist, it cannot do so. Moreover, dualist courts should never reverse prior decisions, no matter how erroneous, if their role is to decide according to the present constitutional moment. If the "amendment" is merely the result of a non-article-5 process of extraordinary political activity, subsequent political activity seems to be a perfectly legitimate means of reversing it.

Although Ackerman is aware of these difficulties, he appears not to take them very seriously.[82] Instead, he declares that these skeptical concerns "are quite healthy if they are kept within reasonable bounds."[83] But what constitutes reasonable bounds? Ackerman insists that "[t]here is simply no escaping the fact that the fate of the Constitution is in our hands — as voters, representatives, justices. If we allow ourselves to abuse the tradition of higher lawmaking, the very idea that the Constitution can be viewed as the culminating expression of a mobilized citizenry will disintegrate."[84] This assertion fails to address any of the conceptual or epistemic concerns. Certainly nothing *guarantees* successful higher lawmaking. The formal process in article 5 eliminates any conceptual or epistemic problems in determining when the People intend to engage in higher lawmaking. Higher lawmaking is proposed when article 5 is invoked. In dualist constitutional politics such conceptual and epistemic problems are rampant.

In Ackerman's analysis Madison's admonition against factions gets lost in the wash. By conflating *We the People* and *We the Political Faction,* Ackerman fails to explore whether the constitutional foundations of structural amendments are genuinely the people or, rather, elites and special interests, in "assuring the circulation of governing elites."[85] If structural amendments reflect a populist, democratic process, identifying "the people" is central. With all the diversity and conflict in contemporary America, it's not clear that a descriptive interpretation of "the people" is possible. Wealthy and poor, white and nonwhite, men and women, religious and atheist, politically involved and politically apathetic, are just some of the differences among people. Descriptively, it is more accurate to say that America is populated by we the people*s,* and our common aspiration has been to find a way of uniting these peoples into one people, or at least many harmonious peoples. This problem has its roots in the Founding itself, given the exclusion of Native Americans, African Americans, women, and poor men. Many forms of exclusion presently exist, preventing some from enjoying full citizenship in the American communitarian republic. In the United States a reflective majority of the electorate rarely existed in any given era. How, then, can dualism express the voice of the governed? How can it dissolve the countermajoritarian problem? At best dualism reflects the voice of the most effective political faction, and the acquiescence of the remainder.

Ackerman might defend against these challenges by pointing out that the Founding was unique because for the first time the people — not the King, State, or Church — served as the legitimizing foundation of government.[86]

As such, the Founding represents both virtue and deceit. Its virtue derives from its move to self-government; its deceit lies in its crabbed conception of "the people." Ackerman might seek its virtue and reject its deceit by showing how the scope of "the people" grew progressively, until the contemporary conception of "the people" reflects the most plausible conception of self-government. Ackerman is certainly right to point out the importance of the Founding. It is less obvious that "the people" today are sufficiently less restricted than during the Founding. Today many more avenues of exclusion exist, though perhaps none so pernicious as during the Founding. In contemporary politics Ackerman's view overlooks the worrisome statistic that fewer than one-half of all eligible voters exercise their franchise. More important, dualism doesn't even appear to address such contemporary problems of democracy as campaign finance reforms and the role of the media in forming public values, nor the rights of groups, if any, in collective decision making.

Despite these important, complex *practical* problems, two theoretical constructs are also critically important to the success of Ackerman's analysis: the ideas of "functional equivalence" and "intergenerational synthesis." The former asserts that two texts are functionally equivalent when they play the same role in adjudication. Consequently, functional equivalence means that the relevant constitutional actors regard both texts as having the same kind of consequences.[87] The idea of intergenerational synthesis is Ackerman's answer to the problem of constitutional interpretation. Contemporary judges should integrate the most recent paradigms with what remains of the past paradigms. Let's examine these constructs in order.

The Functional Equivalence Argument

Ackerman relies heavily upon the notion of functional equivalence. He contends that "transformative opinions" such as *Carolene Products* are functionally equivalent to such textual guarantees as free speech and equal protection. Initially, Ackerman's functional equivalence argument appears to be one of his strongest points.[88] If a judicial decision has the same consequences as a formal amendment, then it *is* a formal amendment except in name only. Upon closer inspection, however, this argument is unpersuasive. First, functional equivalence is not the same as equivalence itself. Typically, when X and Y have the same consequences, the implication remains that they are not the same in other important respects. Functional equivalence applies to the end game of constitutional creation; it says nothing about the canonical ways to bring about these changes, nor does it explain their content. One functional difference between article 5 amendments and Ackerman's structural amendment is that the former requires a formal amendment to transform it, whereas the latter can be performed through constitutional politics or even perhaps through normal politics alone. Consequently, there is an important functional difference between overturning the results of actual constitutional text, and overturning Ackerman's informal amendment of the Constitution. A future court would be justified in rejecting the New Deal revolution expressed in footnote 4 of *Carolene Products*. However, it would not be justified had the Court formally amended the Constitution, thereby constitutionalizing the footnote. The former requires constitutional politics, whereas the latter requires only normal politics. In short, functional equivalence involves not merely how a judicial interpretation *becomes* part of the constitutional text, but also how such an interpretation is *overturned*. If a "functionally equivalent" amendment can be overturned in a manner different from an article 5 amendment, then it is not truly a functional equivalent after all.

Further, if functional equivalence is sufficient to effectively amend the Constitution, then all the Court's revolutionary decisions are amendments to the Constitution. Therefore, the decision in *Brown* is the functional equivalent of a formal amendment desegregating the schools. In fact, the standard view accepts diverse ways for generating constitutional meaning. More importantly, the theory of constitutional revolutions regards the major revolutionary cases as canonical text for interpreting the Constitution. In this case the text of the Constitution calls for a subtext, so to speak, recording the development of constitutional meaning. The primary entries on this subtext are the transformative decisions of the Supreme Court. Ackerman, by contrast, resists this view, because dualism cannot permit truly forward-looking or prophetic constitutional adjudication.

The functional equivalence argument raises additional troubles. If the *Carolene Products'* reinterpretation of the Fourteenth Amendment is the functional equivalent of constitutional text, it would seem to follow that nothing can amend this reinterpretation other than formal amendment, or Ackerman's process of informally amending the Constitution. Normal politics should be precluded from reversing a prior constitutional moment. But does anyone doubt that normal politics can override the New Deal? If the Republican revolution of 1994 has yielded legislation reversing well-entrenched social and economic policies, is there any doubt that it would have been upheld by the Supreme Court? In fact the 1937 judicial revolution held that the majoritarian branches should decide economic policy, whatever that is. So in principle Congress can overrule a "structural" amendment through normal politics.[89]

Ackerman's analysis fails to distinguish between two senses of the New Deal revolution: political and judicial. The political sense contends that the federal government has an important and necessary role in social welfare; it expands the federal governmental role throughout law and society. By contrast, the judicial revolution rejects privileging private property by insulating it from majoritarian regulation. The judicial sense merely asserts that the Court should not interfere in majoritarian decisions concerning the economy and social welfare. The judicial revolution was required for the New Deal, but it does not entail an expanded role of government. Thus, if the Republicans deregulate through normal politics, no emendation of the New Deal constitutional moment occurs in the judicial sense, though it does in the political sense. Had Ackerman distinguished between these two senses, he would realize that the New Deal judicial revolution is compatible with regulation or deregulation depending upon majoritarian sentiments.

Suppose the ghost of the *Lochner* revolution appears on the American constitutional scene. Neither the New Deal's political revolution nor its judicial revolution could countenance the reconstitutionalization of *Lochner*. Consider the following hypothetical: Suppose in 1984 Ronald Reagan had pledged, if reelected, to revamp New Deal legislation and to appoint only judges who are sympathetic to this revision.[90] Suppose, by anyone's standard, this election exemplifies the highest form of deliberative mobilization ever engaged in by a presidential election. Due to increased media technology and public interest, the central issues are framed in the most reflective, clear, and relevant manner conceivable. The Republicans capture both houses of Congress, and Richard Epstein is nominated and confirmed as an associate justice of the United States Supreme Court. As a result, President Reagan radically reduces the government's role in regulating the economy, reversing much of the New Deal. Suppose further that Congress passes and President Reagan signs into law a *Lochner*-like statute regarding the role of government in the economy.[91] Justice Epstein then persuades the Court to reject a challenge to this law. Thus, all these branches of government favor change. In effect this process of normal politics amends the Constitution by supporting legislation that is the functional equivalent of

both formal and informal amendments rejecting the New Deal. This constitutional change, it should be noted, comes about without formal amendment and without invoking Ackerman's informal amendment process, but
by normal politics alone. Intuitively, it seems this hypothetical is a bona fide
instance of constitutional change. But because Ackerman must reject it, his
theory fails. If he accepts it, without further explanation, we must conclude
that normal politics is capable of constitutional revolutions. Yet if this is an
example of constitutional change, Ackerman's distinction between normal
and constitutional politics fails.

The dichotomy is the problem. There are all sorts of degrees of constitutional change, as the theory of constitutional revolutions suggests. Imposing a dichotomy between normal politics and constitutional politics distorts the reality of creative constitutional transformation and revolution. In
Ackerman's view the Court acts illegitimately because a dualist Court
should preserve the New Deal revolution against the *Lochner*-like statute,
but he does not explain why this isn't an example of constitutional politics.
Ad hoc quasi-formalist criteria for determining when the people have spoken does nothing to fortify Ackerman's position here. If the test is deliberation, then why can't the appropriate kind of deliberation take place more
(or less) quickly than in Ackerman's regime? To answer that, in all likeli-
hood, more time is needed for sufficiently deep deliberation and consideration, or that much slower process can do the trick, flies in the face of the
spirit of Ackermanian constitutionalism. A mobilized majority might create
higher law whenever deliberation and consideration are sufficiently deep
and connected, and if the people intend that to count as a constitutional
moment. Further, the very rules of higher lawmaking themselves, in dualist
theories, are subject to revision by the people indefinitely.

Ackerman might reply that in such circumstances the Court errs by failing to appreciate the implications of dualism. The presence of only one
presidential election, for instance, is one reason for insisting that this scenario is not an instance of constitutional politics. Whereas article 5 focuses
on assembly-driven constitutional politics, the modern form of amending
the Constitution focuses on presidentially driven informal amendment processes. Consider Ackerman's reasoning here: "While the Article's narrow
focus blinds us to the importance modern Americans attach to presidential
elections as a forum in which we debate our constitutional future, it would
be a mistake to go to the opposite extreme and suppose that *every* presidential election has catalyzed an effort by the victor to use the appointment

power to make a decisive break with the constitutional achievements of the past generation. Instead, transformative nominations have been seriously considered only after a President has won decisive reelection on the basis of a political program advocating fundamental change in reigning constitutional principle."[92] Presumably, two elections are required because Ackerman believes that the will of the people is determined and known only after deliberative mobilization. Is it inconceivable, however, that future constitutional moments will require more than two elections (or fewer or none) in order to ensure the appropriate level of mobilization, reflection, and deliberation? If so, deliberative mobilizations cannot be equated with any determinate number of presidential elections. If deliberative mobilization is the test, the precise number must remain fluid.[93] If the 1994 Republican revolution had produced the election of Robert Dole in 1996, these normal political events (in these circumstances) would be just as effective in overturning the New Deal as Ackerman's dualism. A constitution can be altered in numerous ways. Consequently, Ackerman's contention that only structural amendments alter constitutional meaning is unpersuasive.

According to dualism, the Court should strike down the new *Lochner* legislation. If the Court strikes down the legislation in order to preserve the constitutional politics of the New Deal, we are left with the astonishing conclusion that the Supreme Court may overturn the overwhelming wishes of the majoritarian branches of government without specific constitutional language requiring it to do so. What could be the basis of the Court's decision? The New Deal revolution states that, practically speaking, Congress and state legislatures may regulate social and economic affairs. Accordingly, if these branches of government pass legislation recognizing strong statutory rights to property and contract, the change is permitted though transformative opinions of that era. In this hypothetical why not say that the next presidential election is required to ratify the *Lochner* "structural" amendments? This would enable the people to ratify Reagan's *Lochner* revolution through a process of mobilized deliberation.[94]

The critical point that Ackerman overlooks in this case is that a conservative constitutionalist can argue as persuasively as does Ackerman that, in such circumstances, the party favoring constitutional change has functionally met the conditions of Ackerman's informal amendment process. Hence, Ackerman's criteria of higher lawmaking can occur through normal politics. Alternatively, a conservative constitutionalist can argue that in the preceding hypothetical, normal politics *is* constitutional politics. The conservative contends that when there is overwhelming popular and govern-mental support for change, normal politics becomes constitutional politics. In essence, that is the genius of American constitutionalism. In short, the conservative dualist has a different criterion for distinguishing between normal and constitutional politics. In order to decide between two compet-ing sets of criteria, Ackerman's theory must limit the multiplication of infor-mal conceptions of constitutional amendments ad nauseam. It is difficult to imagine a nonarbitary way to do so.

If the Court, in the hypothetical, upholds the anti–New Deal legislation, then one must conclude that, in the face of an overwhelming majority seeking to overturn the results of past constitutional politics through nor-mal politics, the Court should relinquish its preservationist duties and join the present majority. Ackerman's theory fails to explain this instance of constitutional change. Further, what happened to the Court's preservation-ist function? We must then conclude that constitutional change can occur independently of Ackerman's informal procedures for amending the Con-stitution as well as outside the purview of article 5.

Similarly, what should a judge do when she detects the beginnings of a movement that she predicts will succeed as the genuine expression of the will of a mobilized majority?[95] In Ackerman's view the judge should still preserve the will of a past *We the People*.[96] But why shouldn't the judge, in-stead, encourage the implementation of the present majority's will? Acker-man's model seems to suggest, without explaining why, that the judiciary should preserve only the past instance of higher lawmaking. Perhaps the judge should join the ranks of the new higher lawmaking movement against the past if, on substantive grounds, it is superior. (How is superiority to be determined?) In some circumstances doing so may even be necessary for the new movement's success. This would abandon Ackerman's process of informal amendment outside of article 5. Moreover, in some circumstances preserving the will of the past flies in the face of common sense. More important, perhaps, preservation of past higher lawmaking at the expense of present and future higher lawmaking is extremely countermajoritarian. At best one protects three moments of higher lawmaking against an infinite number of higher lawmaking possibilities. The judiciary should not system-atically permit past higher lawmaking to trump subsequent expressions of *We the People*.[97]

Ackerman overlooks the fact that the meaning of particular provisions of the Constitution changes through judicial interpretation and reinterpretation that rests on a jurisgeneris, creative function. Thus, constitutional revolutions—changes in the meaning of the Constitution—occur more often than Ackerman's constitutional moments. This emphasizes that there exists an underlying jurisprudential process of "amending" the Constitution that has nothing to do with article 5 or with Ackerman's theory of constitutional moments. According to the theory of constitutional revolutions, this jurisprudential process occurs during both normal politics and constitutional politics. Indeed, this jurisprudential form of constitutional politics is ubiquitous. Consequently, identifying this process is central to understanding American constitutional change.

The Problem of Intergenerational Synthesis

For the functional equivalence argument to work, it must provide a theory of intergenerational synthesis, Ackerman's mechanism for integrating old constitutional paradigms with more contemporary ones. Intergenerational synthesis requires a method for defining the content and scope of a new paradigm together with an explanation of how the new and the old can be synthesized. Surprisingly, Ackerman insists that *Brown*, for instance, is not a constitutional moment itself but is derivative of the New Deal because it follows from integrating the Fourteenth Amendment's equal protection clause with the New Deal revolution. In his view *Brown* is in fact the result of a synthetic interpretation of the Middle Republic with the New Deal's protections of self-ownership, including the ownership of one's labor.[98] In other words, an individual should be permitted to sell his labor for his own gain. The New Deal excised the requirement that property rights be preserved against majoritarian decisions but maintained the strong sense of equality introduced by the Middle Republic.

Briefly, here's how this intergenerational synthesis works: *Plessy* controlled equal protection analysis prior to *Brown*.[99] According to Ackerman, *Plessy* distinguished between political rights—rights found in law—and social rights—rights arising through custom and culture. *Plessy* argued that if blacks feel stigmatized by separate but equal treatment, the fault is not the law's.[100] The law permits separate treatment, but it must be equal. Consequently, equal treatment, even if it is separate, cannot stigmatize or in some other way marginalize blacks.[101] According to Ackerman, if *Plessy*'s position was ever correct, it is certainly incorrect after the New Deal.[102] Because the New Deal rejects the distinction between political and social rights, the government can no longer accept American apartheid. If government is now responsible for economic and social reality, how can it avoid responsibility for the social reality of segregation? Because public education is a critical feature of social reality, governmentally segregated schools must be unlawful. It was no longer possible to argue, as did *Plessy*, that social inequality is not a governmental responsibility, not after "the New Deal Court had authorized the state's power to guarantee a retirement pension or a minimum wage."[103] Synthetic interpretation thus alters our understanding of how the Middle Republic and the New Deal can be integrated. Had Ackerman been around in 1937, we could have gotten a head start on desegregating American society.[104]

Intergenerational synthesis rests upon the notion of consent in Ackerman's theory. The legitimacy of a new constitutional moment, and the methods for determining when one comes along, ultimately rest in the reflective consent of the people. For example, Ackerman contends that "a decisive majority of Americans had voted for the New Deal with their eyes open to the practical and constitutional implications of their collective decision."[105] He further notes: "If ever there was a time that the People could be said to have endorsed a sharp break with their constitutional past, it was when Roosevelt and the Senate self-consciously began to make transformative Supreme Court appointments."[106] Hence, intergenerational synthesis requires consent on defining the new paradigm as well as in integrating it in the proper manner with the old. However, we should be skeptical about attributing a novel theory to historical actors especially when complicated reinterpretation is necessary to warrant the attribution. The proponents of the New Deal need not wait for Ackerman's ingenious explanation in order to appreciate the significance of the New Deal revolution. They could not have predicted the Court's decision in *Brown* in 1937 or 1945 or 1954, nor could they have declared privacy to have replaced property rights, as Ackerman's *Griswold* analysis contends.[107] If intergenerational synthesis is part of dualism, Ackerman obscures the relationship between the actual views of a mobilized majority and what might be the conceptual implications of their views. As we shall see in the next chapter, these should not be conflated.

Ackerman deftly provides these and other synthetic interpretations of American constitutional law, but he reveals no explanation of what this means or how it operates. Neither volume 1 nor 2 of *We the People* gives us a clue to the kind of judicial reasoning required by intergenerational synthesis. Ackerman needs to describe the theory of interpretation, which runs the engine of intergenerational synthesis and tells a judge whether (and how) to engage in intergenerational synthesis. We require here some determination of what the amendment means and how it should be integrated with the past constitutional paradigm. Without better criteria we can neither make judicial decisions intelligible, nor decide whether these decisions are preservative or prophetic. Consequently, we cannot know whether the countermajoritarian problem has been overcome or, more generally, whether Ackerman's project succeeds.

Dualism and Originalism

One major problem with Ackerman's dualism is that it fails to specify the methodology dualist judges should deploy in translating the message of the present constitutional moment into constitutional law.[108] Ackerman appears to assume the validity of some form of originalism, yet one cannot be certain. If so, Ackerman seems to create a type of originalism never before contemplated, namely, once a mobilized majority engage in constitutional politics, the new paradigm contained in the resulting higher law, its scope and content, is pellucid. How is this possible? If the new paradigm must be expressed by some form of text — for example, in transformative statutes — then the traditional problems associated with the interpretation of a text arise in this context. Without an examination of which theories of interpretation are appropriate to Ackerman's regime analysis and why, he fails to resolve the basic problem of adjudication, namely, How should judges decide cases before them? If Ackerman's theory obviates the need for a standard theory of interpretation, he must explain how.

Ackerman's dualism is plagued by the problems of interpretation generally. If transformative statutes comprise the text or subtext of a constitutional moment, at least in the modern regime, Ackerman must explain what features a statute must have to achieve this. In the case of several statutes constituting the subtext, Ackerman must explain how these statutes are to be integrated in order to achieve the status of a transformative statute. Moreover, the fundamental text or subtext of the constitutional moment is not merely the transformative statute, but rather a transformative judicial opinion: How do such opinions, when more than one, add up to or constitute the text or subtext of the constitutional moment? The text or subtext of a constitutional moment, in the modern era, becomes a mystery. We not only contest different interpretations of constitutional text as we do in the conventional case, we must also contest what counts as the new constitutional text and how it can be viewed as the synthesis of what remains of past constitutional moments. Who is able to answer these questions clearly and in a way susceptible to popular consent? This is a heady imperative leading straight to an elitism of the Ackermanian few.

In Ackerman's present account it appears that a justice simply needs to "apply" the new paradigm with nothing further said. Ackerman betrays no concern about a need to explain how this originalism works. What is so surprising about this assumption is that Ackerman nowhere defends originalism against other theories of constitutional interpretation. This is even more surprising because Ackerman expects dualist judges to draw conceptually complex conclusions from the new constitutional paradigm. Remember that Ackerman's conception of intergenerational synthesis contends that, for example, *Brown* and *Griswold* are not themselves constitutional revolutions but instead arise from the New Deal, together with the remains of the Reconstruction and the Founding, respectively. He must then describe the mechanism in the theory of intergenerational synthesis explaining how this process works. His theory first and foremost must tell us how to identify or read the content of constitutional subtext. In fact it seems obvious that all the problems that depict contemporary controversies over constitutional interpretation are replicated in Ackerman's dualistic account of American constitutionalism.[109] Unless we can identify, through a theory of interpretation, who speaks for the people and how we determine what the people say, a judge's preservationist role is impossible. Because Ackerman takes the regime as the basic unit of constitutional analysis, he must explain how his originalism operates in such a constitutional universe.[110]

The absence of a theory of interpretation presents further difficulties. Ackerman is never clear on whether the Framers intended the three structural constitutional moments sanctioned by dualism. More specifically, it is not clear whether Ackerman believes that the Framers actually intended (for themselves and others?) to act outside the purview of article 5, and if they did, did they intend these sojourns into "illegality" to constitute models for future constitutional revolutions. Ackerman seems to imply that dualism requires the internal perspective of actual historical actors.[111] There is obvious irony, however, in attributing Ackerman's unique and complex account of constitutional change to the motivational system of people long since dead. Moreover, Ackerman implicitly rejects (though nonetheless depends upon) an external perspective to make his argument work. It could be argued that the best way to understand a constitutional paradigm is from the perspective of the interpreter even if that is some distance from the actual constitutional revolution.[112] Ackerman wants the internal perspective but, in deploying his analyses, requires the interpreter's external perspective, which negates talk about the Framers' intent and consent.[113]

Ackerman needs to determine what the appropriate evidentiary base is upon which to support originalism. What does it mean to say that the Framers intended X or that the new constitutional paradigm "means" X? How do we *know* what the Framers intended or what the new constitutional paradigm means? Ackerman's problem is akin to those who look to the Constitution's text or to the Framers' intentions as a relatively automatic process for discovering a determinate constitutional meaning.[114] The role of intentions in judicial interpretation is both more and less complex than this picture suggests.[115] Of course, Ackerman need not contend that the Framers intended constitutional amendment outside the purview of article 5 if dualist democracy is the best explanatory and justificatory account of what they did, despite their intentions. However, such a methodology exacerbates the countermajoritarian problem.

Ackerman's originalism fails to explain the regime conception of constitutional change. Assuming it could, one is left to wonder if the Framers intended the three regimes Ackerman describes.[116] Further, he fails to explicate the relationship between the Framers of the different regimes in a dualist democracy. Must each set of Framers intend the same series of regimes? If the most we can say about the Framers' intentions is that they intended Americans to engage in non-article-5 higher lawmaking during the Founding, it is a non sequitur to assume this authorizes the particular set of regimes Ackerman describes, or that the Framers intended non-article-5 changes—dictated perhaps by necessity—to represent a permanent method of amending the Constitution. Moreover, what did the different sets of Framers intend concerning the problem of multigenerational synthesis?[117] Ackerman's theory must address these issues before it can be assessed fairly. Lastly, Ackerman must address the issue of justifying originalism in the first place.[118]

Although assigning the courts a preservationist function diminishes the role of the Court in Ackerman's dualistic democracy, nevertheless "the Court continues in its starring role."[119] Ultimately, "responsibility for determining the shape and direction of constitutional law does not rest with the people and surely not with the . . . people and their elected representatives but with the justices."[120] Indeed, justices must find a way to determine the intent of the new regime's Framers and synthesize the new with the old paradigm. In fact, according to Ackerman's theory, normal politics depicts a time when "the Court is the only player on the constitutional stage."[121] The Court must evaluate the constitutionality of legislation throughout normal and constitutional politics. The Court has no way of knowing, however, whether a particular decision is part of normal or constitutional politics without a jurisprudential theory delineating the conditions for this distinction as well as a method for reading judicial paradigms.[122]

The Jurisprudential Problem

The fundamental weakness in Ackerman's theory is jurisprudential. Assuming he is correct in employing the concept of the regime as the basic unit of constitutional analysis, all the problems of constitutional adjudication remain. Whether the Court should go beyond the Constitution's text, the Framers' intentions, the structure, logic, or history of the Constitution, remain unanswered. These issues are merely transposed, substituting the regime's paradigm for the Constitution's. The question of which judicial strategy should be used applies now to the constitutional regime, not to the Constitution. Ackerman implies that by requiring the Court to preserve the results of constitutional politics, these questions become superfluous. They do not. We must still ask which strategy better preserves the higher lawmaking of the most recent constitutional moment. What precisely does "preserve" mean? Does it mean preserve intact? Perhaps it means preserve in the context of changed circumstances. The conflict between judicial activism and restraint replicates itself within Ackerman's notion of a constitutional regime. Moreover, these different styles of judicial reasoning complicate the controversy further. Must the same interpretive strategy be used in each of the three regimes, or can each regime have its own method of interpretation? If so, how do we synthesize the substantive results of the three constitutional regimes when different jurisprudential methodologies are employed to achieve these results? Moreover, what ideally should constitutional interpretation be? Aren't the traditional questions implicating the role of the judges replicated in Ackerman's regime analysis?

These same questions must now be reformulated as to whether the Court should go beyond the regime's paradigm. Ackerman's theory tells us nothing about what following the paradigm entails, or even how to recognize the paradigm, its scope, and content. These problems aside, knowing that a constitutional moment has occurred does not establish the content of the revolutionary paradigm. The question of whether judges should make law or only apply law, as well as the countermajoritarian problem, are not resolved by Ackerman's theory. Judges need to determine how far they can go in interpreting the new constitutional paradigm. If a judge merely interprets the latest constitutional moment, she may still act contrary to the present majority. If she adheres to the wishes of the present majority, she acts contrary to the past majority.

Justices adhering to their preservationist function will give varying answers to those questions. Indeed, Ackerman's use of *Brown* and *Griswold* as articulations of a synthesis of the Founding, the Reconstruction, and the New Deal show these decisions to be only permissible under the New Deal, not required. If so, presumably other decisions are possible.[123] How does a justice know which decision to adopt or what the content and scope of the revolutionary paradigm are?[124] Moreover, what explains and justifies intergenerational synthesis in the first place? Ackerman's regime analysis is not likely to avoid the contestability of Supreme Court decisions.[125] For example, the Reagan Democrats generally supported the economic expansion of the New Deal but rejected some later civil rights legislation. This poses a critical problem for Ackerman, since he contends that *Brown* was an articulation of the New Deal. This failure to determine the precise nature of the New Deal highlights the need for a theory of adjudication to explain constitutional change, a theory that identifies the meaning of a constitutional paradigm. Such a theory must provide a judicially efficient method for deciding such issues. It must also explain how the other political branches, the people, and the constitutional culture combine to bring about change.

Thus, Ackerman's conception of a preservationist Court begs the question against what he calls the prophetic conception of the judiciary. No one has ever specified a methodology that sufficiently defines the scope and content of a constitutional paradigm. Similarly, the distinction between creating and preserving constitutional meaning is less than obvious. Sometimes it is necessary to create in order to preserve. Sometimes preserving means encouraging present constitutional politics. Should the Court preserve the new constitutional paradigm intact? Suppose the new paradigm has a significant, though not fatal, flaw. Should the Court extirpate this flaw without consulting the people? Are individual liberties sufficiently protected without extensive protection of privacy? If so, was privacy contained somewhere in the penumbra of the Bill of Rights as Justice Douglas proclaimed, or did privacy become inseparable from individual liberty only after the New Deal?

Ackerman answers this last question in the affirmative. Privacy became especially important after the New Deal because the New Deal denigrated the Founders' conception of property.[126] Something must take the place of property in protecting individual rights. But why privacy? Why not religion? Why not collective or communitarian rights? What makes the privacy associated with *Griswold* the most effective means to ensure individual rights? Moreover, Ackerman ignores a more familiar explanation of *Griswold* and its progeny that simply appeals to the changes in personal and sexual morality during that period in American history. These were contingent changes that do not logically depend on the New Deal. Consequently, if different changes had developed in the fifties and the sixties, how would Ackerman's judges integrate those changes with the New Deal?[127]

The key to Ackerman's dualism is the concept of intergenerational synthesis. According to Ackerman's conception of interpretation, a Reconstruction justice or a New Deal justice must integrate the results of the latest constitutional moment with the preserved results of the earlier regimes. The problem with Ackerman's argument here is similar to the problem of interpretation discussed earlier. How does a justice know how to synthesize? Ackerman does not explain why a New Deal justice should replace property and contract rights with anything at all. Or if she should replace property and contract rights with something, why it should be privacy. Ackerman assumes that individual rights or governmental powers contain a formal component and substantive value.[128] The substantive value can be changed while the formal component remains. Why should this be the case? How does a justice distinguish between changing the contents of the right, and getting rid of the right entirely? Ackerman needs a metatheoretical account to explain this.

In another context Ackerman tries to prove the distinction between the formal and substantive conception of a right by appealing to abstraction. He suggests that both property and privacy are instances of liberty or noninterference: "The core of both 'privacy' and 'property' involves the same abstract right: the right to exclude unwanted interference by third parties. The only real difference between the two concepts is the kind of relationship that is protected from interference, 'property' principally protects market relationships while 'privacy' protects more spiritual ones. Yet surely this fact should not prevent recognition of 'privacy' as a dimension of constitutional 'property in its widest sense.'"[129] But what constitutionally permits us to replace property with privacy? Perhaps the appropriate conclusion to draw regarding the New Deal is that we read constitutional rights narrowly consistent with the revolution in federal governmental power brought about by the New Deal. Thus, the governmental activism of the New Deal does not extirpate "property" from the Constitution; it merely restricts its content and scope. And why not say privacy and other individual rights are similarly restricted?

Ackerman also needs a metatheoretical account of how to rank or integrate the paradigms of two different constitutional regimes. Suppose the Founding paradigm includes individual rights, and the New Deal paradigm includes a strong majoritarian control over the economy. Which should be ranked higher? Notice that the way this question is resolved has enormous implications, because if the Founding is ranked first, the New Deal might be effectively overturned or modified drastically, and so with ranking the New Deal first. In fact, a proper reading of *Carolene Products,* footnote 4, obviates the necessity to answer this question because the New Deal *judicial* revolution defers to the legislature in economic affairs.[130] It also disallows Ackerman's solution through abstraction. The problem of intergenerational synthesis, therefore, is a problem of interpretation that Ackerman needs to explain in much greater detail. Ackerman may assert that the later paradigm must be ranked first on the grounds that the more recent mobilization of *We the People* entails that the people self-consciously changed the earlier paradigm. Ackerman does not explain how we know this or if this is necessarily so.

It is, then, the preservationist justice's job to reflect on several possibilities of constitutional change and choose the one she thinks best fulfills the intergenerational synthesis of the Founding moment and the New Deal. Her choice cannot be explained by appealing only to factors intrinsic to the Constitution or to the current constitutional regime. A justice must appeal to factors extrinsic to the constitutional regime and, by doing so, will be creating constitutional revolutions within the context of the regime. Consequently, Ackerman must explain why these constitutional revolutions occur independently of his dualistic interpretation of constitutional change. Disagreement will no doubt occur over the meaning of the constitutional paradigm, over what the voice of the people says. Why should one particular interpretation win out as the people's voice simply because one justice, the deciding vote in a five-to-four decision, thinks this is what the people intend?[131]

This point is fatal to Ackerman's attempt to define the democratic foundations of constitutional change. Even if we accept the utility of Ackerman's three-regime conception of constitutional change, the countermajoritarian question is not resolved by appealing to the preservationist function of the Court. As long as more than one answer is possible to the question of what the paradigm means, the countermajoritarian problem is replicated within the regime system. Ackerman's conception of constitutional change, though an interesting and illuminating conception of some of the principal elements in our constitutional culture, fails to come to terms with the countermajoritarian problem any more than it ultimately explains how constitutional change occurs. The explanation of these failures is the same in both cases. Because Ackerman fails to provide an unambiguous answer to the problem of adjudication, the countermajoritarian problem persists unabated, and constitutional change, as a modernistic phenomenon, remains as illusory as ever. Moreover, Ackerman's theory provides little guidance to judges trying to interpret the Constitution fairly and honestly. For such guidance judges must turn elsewhere.

Positivism and Pragmatism in Constitutional Jurisprudence

Ackerman appears to be a troubled positivist. Ackerman rejects rights foundationalism or natural law theory because in his view history cannot sustain the claim that American constitutional law developed through an appeal to rights or to natural law. The standard form of constitutional positivism maintains that constitutional law is a social fact or set of conventions according to which constitutional change can be validated. The traditional positivist view maintains that constitutional change occurs through the ratification of constitutional text pursuant to article 5. The mere recitation of rights, even the correct rights, cannot identify American constitutional law. What is needed is an account of how these rights become legitimated in American constitutional practice. No natural law conception explains Americans' self-conscious attempt to base American constitutional law in consent. The rights' foundationalist can insist that neither the fact of consent nor the content of consent can make any sense without an appeal to a true or justified theory of natural rights. On this view Americans have never been driven merely by consent, but instead they value consent to help solidify true moral and political rights. Ackerman's reply would be that the rights foundationalist argument misses the point. Of course, we must appeal to extraconstitutional values to explain the value of consent as well as the development of constitutional law. Ackerman would insist, however, that we do not understand the legitimacy of those extraconstitutional values until we understand how they become part of American constitutional practice. Invoking the correct human or natural rights does not contribute to this quest. Surprisingly, invoking article 5, in Ackerman's view, is no more helpful in explaining how rights become incorporated into constitutional law.

Ackerman seeks a conception that embraces neither natural law nor traditional positivism. His dualism can be regarded as an attempt to present an alternative rule for recognizing constitutional change. American constitutional law is based on social facts, albeit complex social facts. The traditional positivist's reply is that rights become legitimated in American constitutional practice only after a ratification process that takes place at the Founding or subsequently through article 5 of the Constitution. Ackerman contends that this distorts constitutional practice. It doesn't explain how the Founding, Reconstruction, or the New Deal become part of constitutional law. Moreover, it obscures the complex rule of recognition that is unique to American constitutionalism. Here Ackerman begs the question against traditional positivists. If their traditional positivism is correct, Ackerman gives the wrong account of American constitutional law. For example, the New Deal, though fundamentally significant in redirecting the American Republic, did not redirect it in the way that an actual article 5 amendment would. Moreover, traditional positivists would simply deny that the irregularities Ackerman points to concerning the Founding and Reconstruction can be elevated to constitutional significance on positivist grounds. They are anomalies to be recognized but not sanctified. Although intricate and illuminating, Ackerman's theory is not best described as positivist. In fact, his theory becomes more interesting and persuasive cast as a pragmatist theory of American constitutionalism. The argument of functional equivalence becomes much more persuasive as a pragmatist point, namely: If the relevant cases of the New Deal are functionally equivalent to new constitutional text, then these cases become a subtext of American constitutionalism that has the same effect as an explicit constitutional amendment. Additionally, if the best explanation of American constitutional practice attributes certain intentions concerning dualism to the relevant constitutional actors, then we can as pragmatists accept such an explanation despite its present counterintuitiveness.

Ackerman's dualism fares better as a pragmatist conception of constitutional change than as a complex positivist rule of recognition. This is not to say that there are no pragmatist reasons for rejecting Ackerman's interpretive history of American constitutionalism change. Ackerman's dualism provides one plausible answer to the question of how a pragmatist constitutionalist, regarding consent as the primary constitutional principle, can best explain the evolution of American constitutional practice.

A different kind of dualism has a role to play in constitutional revolutions, but it is a role that distinguishes two types of adjudication, not political change. A theory of constitutional change should not be predicated on sweeping change and unpredictable circumstances. In the case of the Thirteenth and Fourteenth Amendments, for example, the Framers could only improvise an answer of how to get three-fourths of the states necessary for ratification when more than one-quarter of the existent states had just fought a war rejecting the principles of the proposed amendments and had lost their full civic status under a regime of military rule. Conditioning the readmission to full constitutional and political status only upon ratification of the amendments seemed to be a plausible, pragmatic solution.[132] Moreover, Ackerman never tells us why or how this improvisation could be used in the future. Should we plan on amending the Constitution structurally? Ackerman's calculus itself shows that constitutional moments are in fact a combination of the acts of normal political players, extraordinary events, and a response by the people.

Ackerman's dualism is best seen in the context of postmodernity conflating the distinction between improvisation and legitimacy. Admittedly, this distinction is a modernist one. In characterizing a theory as postmodernist, some of the rigor of reasoning is relaxed in order to provide unique, penetrating explanations of constitutional practice, while nevertheless leaving many loose ends. Ackerman's theory has a permanent role to play in postmodern constitutionalism. His interpretive history haunts our pursuit of constitutional meaning. Ackerman's skill in describing the three central constitutional regimes provides an image that is difficult to shake. The idea of the progression of three constitutional regimes as anchoring the present, though in different ways, can be insightful even if dualism fails to explain constitutional revolutions.

Dworkin's Constitutional Coherentism

Constitutional jurisprudence consists of a theory of judicial moments and a theory of judicial change over time. The latter theory, a theory of judicial reasoning, explains how justices of whatever historical period decide cases. For all its defects Ackerman's theory contributes an interesting, if not entirely convincing, theory of constitutional moments. What it fails to address is a theory of judicial reasoning. The other great American constitutionalist, Ronald Dworkin, possesses only an inchoate theory of constitutional moments; in its place stands arguably the most sophisticated theory of judicial reasoning to date. Dworkin's theory is pragmatist, but because he vigorously denies the pragmatist dimension of his theory, in this chapter I will critically examine law as integrity, not for the purpose of rejecting it outright, but rather to reveal its pragmatist content. In brief I argue that Dworkin's theory cannot explain (judicial) constitutional revolutions without reinterpretation as a pragmatist theory. The theory of constitutional revolutions embraces Dworkin's "pragmatism" as contributing to a comprehensive understanding of constitutional adjudication.

Law as Integrity and Constitutional Revolutions

American constitutional development, in Dworkin's view, has been dominated by two kinds of theories. The first kind of theory—positivism—emphasizes stated rules and distinguishes strongly between the law and justice, or the law and what's right. The second kind of theory—pragmatism, including certain natural law theories—argues that judges should interpret law so that it serves justice and contributes to a better future for the community.[1] In this view the law is informed by nonlegal factors that retain a privileged position in adjudication.[2] Dworkin has consistently rejected both types of theories.[3] Instead, he aspires to formulate a third theory of law, one that incorporates the ideals of both positivism and pragmatism.

This third theory, called "law as integrity," is an interpretive account of constitutional practice that takes legal rights seriously and is committed to finding the right answers to constitutional controversies. The reason a third theory is necessary, according to Dworkin, is because positivism takes legal rights seriously but fails to identify the right answer or the correct set of rights. Similarly, though pragmatism is more likely than positivism to identify the morally right answer, it fails to take legal rights seriously. Law as integrity combines positivism's commitment to legal rights with pragmatism's commitment to the right answer.

Positivism encourages the ideal of protected expectations through the notion of constitutional rights, which trump majoritarian interests and on some readings, the good of the community. Pragmatism captures the instrumentalist and contextualist ideal of flexibility and coordination and integrates this ideal with the naturalist ideal of providing the correct answer to constitutional controversies. Each theory takes a particular stand on the notion of constitutional revolutions. Pragmatism may countenance constitutional revolutions; in the standard cases positivism may not.[4] The overriding concern in this chapter is whether law as integrity can countenance constitutional revolutions, and if so, how often and what kind.

The central problem with law as integrity as an interpretive theory of American constitutional practice is its inability to explain and justify constitutional revolutions, especially the paradigmatic constitutional revolution that involves overruling an authoritative precedent.[5] Put another way, there's much to be said for law as integrity interpreted as a pragmatist theory that weighs the relative importance of principle, fidelity, and history in a given case.[6] When the circumstances warrant it, when the need for a novel justificatory principle is minimal, history will prevail. When the need or superiority of the novel justificatory principle is evident, novelty is embraced, or more accurately, history is filtered through the novel justification. Weighing the respective merits of history and justification is a balancing procedure to be decided pragmatically.

Because constitutional revolutions are an integral feature of constitutional practice, any adequate interpretive theory must account for them and their role in constitutional change. Thus, the failure of law as integrity to provide the appropriate explanation of constitutional revolutions is fatal to Dworkin's entire project of providing a third theory of law. A careful examination of Dworkin's account of *Brown v. Board of Education* reveals important ambiguities in his theory.[7] These problems arise especially in his discussion of the explanatory and normative dimensions of constitutional interpretation. According to Dworkin, a proposed interpretive principle must fit constitutional practice and show it in its best light. My conclusion is that in order for law as integrity to provide the appropriate interpretation of *Brown* and other constitutional revolutions, it must renounce the coherentist stance and embrace an eclectic form of legal pragmatism.

The Moral Reading of the Constitution

In its current form Dworkin contends that constitutional interpretation must exhibit the appropriate fidelity to the Founding Fathers, or Framers of the Constitution.[8] Dworkin's moral reading of the Constitution explains constitutional interpretation as the process of explicating the meaning of the Constitution's abstract provisions or, alternatively stated, those provisions containing abstract values.[9] To achieve this, the interpreter must appeal to the appropriate moral principles expressing the content of these abstract provisions; the interpreter must construct principles of moral and political decency and justice. For Dworkin the process of understanding abstract political and moral values is the same whether we seek to understand the values of a text or that of a social practice or of a social group. If the goal is to understand the value of "equality," say, we must ultimately appeal to the moral or political theory of equality that is consistent with the text or practice under investigation. The important rights provisions of the Bill of Rights and the U.S. Constitution, from the moral reading's perspective, "must be understood in the way their language most naturally suggests: they refer to abstract moral principles and incorporate these by reference, as limits on government's power."[10]

According to Dworkin's moral reading of the Constitution, judges must look to the abstract provisions of the Constitution, such as "liberty," "due process," "equal protection," "free speech," and so forth. In interpreting these provisions we have (at least) two choices: The first choice exhorts us to interpret these abstract provisions in terms of the Framers' expectations or intentions of how these provisions should be concretely applied. The second choice is to understand these abstract provisions according to the best interpretation of American constitutional practice. The best interpretation is one that is morally attractive yet consistent with much of the actual history and development of constitutional law. So a normatively superior interpretation of free speech must fail as the interpretation of our

First Amendment if it does not explain any of the actual American First Amendment decisions, or if it explains this history considerably less well than an alternative principle that functions as a second-best normative interpretation.

The first approach fails because often generality or abstraction is superior to particularizing or concreteness. In ratifying the equal protection clause, a Framer has an intention concerning an abstract understanding of equality as well as particular beliefs concerning the constitutional implications of that abstract understanding. Consequently, the Framers of the Fourteenth Amendment embraced equality and believed equality precluded racial discrimination concerning contracts and property but not segregated schools. Now that we know equality precludes school segregation also, we must conclude that the Framers intended it, despite their actual beliefs to the contrary. Abstract intentions exhibit this magical quality of linking generations, or at least of showing the identity of former and later intentions, despite explicit conflicts between them.

According to Dworkin, being faithful to the Framers' intentions means following their abstract intentions or their intentions concerning the abstract value or ideal contained in the words they use. In this case that abstract value is equality per se. Yet, no one holds an abstract intention without supplemental beliefs concerning its constitutional implications. In this case the Framers, collectively, believed that equality and school segregation were compatible; the Framers, however, were wrong; these are not compatible. If they were wrong, we should reject, not follow, their intentions. Dworkin should argue that their views should be revised, not that our revision is faithful to the Framers' original intentions. By revising their concrete beliefs according to the preferred (best) view of racial equality, we are departing, in the ordinary sense, from the intentions of the Framers, despite the abstract identity of their intention concerning equality, and ours. As a pragmatist I believe that Dworkin's approach here is a splendid method of revision and reform. However, this progressive approach does not begin to explain or justify fidelity as an important constitutional virtue. Instead, it self-consciously abandons it.

Dworkin needs a theory of fidelity that captures what is ordinarily meant by following someone's intentions or directives. Ordinarily, to follow another's directive, one must do what that person would do in the given circumstances, with the appropriate qualifications, of course. The ordinary conception might not answer all questions of fidelity, but it most certainly answers the principal question. If you know the precise intentions of the leader, then fidelity requires using that concept understood as the leader understood it. Suppose the Framers explicitly intended the equal protection clause to permit segregated schools as evidenced by the best understanding of the political and cultural circumstances of the time; if so, it is counterintuitive in the extreme to suppose that in this case fidelity permits abandoning this intention for what is now a better one.

Fidelists tie the meaning of constitutional concepts to the political morality of a certain era. They might be wrong to embrace this position because it might be restrictive, impossible, or in some other way undesirable, yet that's their position. In the preceding example Dworkin ought not to suppose that what the Framers really intended was the "correct" conception of constitutional equality from an ideal perspective. Rather, they intended the correct conception as they understood it. Postmodernity tells us that this is all we have anyway. If so, why follow anyone who does not believe in an ideal conception of equality? The answer to this question can be provided only in terms of theories of interpretation and of democracy, not by artificially attempting to show that fidelity means reading back into the Framers' intentions the correct view, or the presently preferred view, nor by embracing a virtually trivialized conception of fidelity.

To keep the faith with the constitutional concept means, in this view, to honor the supplemental beliefs held by the Framers.[11] If we follow fidelists, according to Dworkin, we do so only by jettisoning the abstract value of equality, and this abstract value was certainly more important to the Framers collectively than any of their supplemental beliefs.[12] Consequently, to keep the faith with the Framers, in Dworkin's view, we must honor the abstract value by jettisoning the Framers' supplemental beliefs because *we* cannot *now* say that equality, properly understood, permits segregation in public schools. Particular supplemental beliefs come and go while the abstract value behind the concept remains. If we insist on fidelity to supplemental beliefs, we unjustifiably risk rejecting the concept of equality for an erroneous *conception* of equality.

Dworkin's distinction can be explicated in terms of formal and substantive features of the idea of equality. Formally, equality refers to a principle concerning the appropriate value and treatment accorded to each citizen. Substantively, a conception of equality resolves constitutional controversies in particular ways, especially the value and treatment of citizens. In the Framers' vision the substantive sense of equality is compatible with racial segregation; in our times it is not. According to Dworkin, in order to really give expression to the more fundamental intentions of the Framers, we must always be ready not to confuse the abstract value that was essentially important to them with their less important, incidental supplemental beliefs concerning the constitutional implications of that value. Consequently, we are faithful to the Framers when we endorse the formal features of their conceptions, despite abandoning the substantive ones.

In Dworkin's view the Framers intended a particular conception of equality. Whatever we now believe to be the best interpretation of the constitutional practice of equality becomes the Framers' conception. But this is an illicit move, one that distorts the reasons for fidelity in the first place by reading the "right" conception back into the Framers' intentions. To avoid doing this, Dworkin needs a distinction between formal and substantive dimensions of the concept of equality. Because both we and the Framers embrace the formal dimension of equality, we are necessarily faithful to them if we retain the concept of equality, no matter how different our conception of equality is from theirs. Unfortunately, this trivializes fidelity. More importantly, Dworkin's position vitiates the very reason one would endorse fidelity in the first place. Fidelity has been a favored theory because it attempts to fix constitutional meaning in a document that gains authority from the consent of the governed. If constitutional meaning is fixed, and the consent of the governed is real, disputes over the constitutionality of future statutes can be settled by referring to the intentions of the Framers. To know what the Framers actually intended requires that we know both the formal and substantive beliefs about equality. Only then can they serve as arbiters of contemporary constitutional disputes, if fidelity is what we seek.

The question left unanswered is, Why should we honor the Framers by retaining their abstract values over their supplemental beliefs concerning their implications? Dworkin needs to answer this question but does not. It is not self-evident why abstract values should be preferred over concrete beliefs. Dworkin seems to assume that if a person values the abstract ideal of equality, then he will never give up that ideal even if its implications are inconsistent with particular judgments that he independently embraces. Thus, if I counsel my nephew to be kind, but I believe giving the homeless a handout imprudent, and not truly kind, then my nephew should interpret "kindness" as I do, unless it is now clear communally or at least to my nephew that "kindness" means giving money to the homeless. In that eventuality my nephew is being faithful to me by retaining the concept of kindness and rejecting my particular conception of it. Abstract concepts are invariably superior to concrete conceptions. The only problem is Dworkin fails to explain why we should call this "fidelity."

Consider another example. Suppose I instruct my daughter to strive to be "cool," in the sense of sophisticated or trendy. Included among the background conditions of my conception of "coolness," known to my daughter, is a deep delight in rap music. My daughter wants to grow up to be cool like her father. One day she hears Snoop Doggy Dogg and thinks the music is awful. Ultimately, she rejects all rap music. She knows, however, that Daddy's conception of "coolness" is integrally related to the value of rap music as a paradigmatic case of what is cool. Whatever else "coolness" means to Daddy, it must mean that rap music is good music. She has the following dilemma: She can abandon coolness, leaving her free to reconfirm her aesthetic judgment concerning rap music, or she can decide that Daddy's conception of coolness is defective and redefine coolness in terms Daddy would have rejected. In the first instance she rejects both his abstract and concrete intentions outright. In the second she retains the abstract value of "coolness" but reverses its substantive meaning in ways that Daddy would reject. In either case, because she is not faithful to Daddy or any principle he endorses, how can she be described as *following Daddy* at all?[13] Fidelity doesn't enter into this process.

Dworkin might reply that it is absurd to think someone would embrace a particular judgment that conflicts with a political principle one has embraced instead of retaining the principle and rejecting the particular judgment. Again Dworkin needs to explain why. Suppose I believe that family concerns are my most important political values. Suppose, further, I come to believe that the principle of individualism best captures the rationale for my political intuitions about family concerns. Finally, suppose I discover that this political principle actually inhibits family concerns: Why must I give up my intuitions concerning family concerns as opposed to the principle of individualism? Certainly, a contemporary judge might give up a proposed interpretation because, though more general, it conflicts with her important intuitions concerning the law. Why can't (shouldn't) we do this with the Framers? There are of course practical problems. How do we know what a Framer would do if confronted with a conflict between his abstract values and concrete judgments concerning constitutional rights? This problem might suggest a mistake in attempting fidelity in the first place, rather than an argument for showing the Framers' preference for abstraction. Would the Framers have ratified the equal protection if they believed that it precluded segregated schools? I cannot see how we can avoid this question. Moreover, I am convinced that many Framers would not have been in favor of equal protection had this been one of its important implications. The test to determine whether (and in what way) we follow another person's values when we jettison her concrete beliefs in case of conflict is always counterfactual: What would she have chosen were she to realize the incompatibility of the values and beliefs? When we cannot answer this counterfactually, we cannot know that we are following the person's values; moreover, there is no conceptual reason to suppose that a person would always embrace the abstract value over the particular judgment.

Dworkin's work distinguishing between two kinds of intentions, abstract and concrete, and two kinds of convictions, linguistic and political, rests on his unargued assumption that fidelity to one's intentions requires fidelity to the abstract intention or the linguistic conviction only. Dworkin needs an argument why fidelity should be understood in this manner. Somehow Dworkin believes that "equality," say, is an abstract concept expressed by linguistic intentions, and that such intentions capture more of what the speaker meant, or in some other way is more faithful to the speaker than the other kinds of intention. I cannot begin to imagine an argument on the basis of fidelity that has a chance of demonstrating this point. I do not reject that choosing the first set of intentions is pragmatically better. It is more likely that my conduct is faithful to the speaker when I concentrate on the abstract concept, except when I know his concrete beliefs clearly. In such circumstances I am not being faithful to the speaker to interpret "equality" in such a way as to force the abandonment of his concrete beliefs. I am being faithful to the correct conception of "equality," despite what the speaker or Framer intended. As a pragmatist, I have no qualms about embracing this argument as a structural feature of pragmatic interpretation just so long as I am not understood to be offering a fidelity argument.

This reveals a more general problem with Dworkin's analysis. Why should we follow other people's lead in the first place? There are at least two possible answers to this question. First, we might follow their lead because of the people they are; they represent some sanctified class to which we give special deference in our culture. Or, we might follow someone's lead because we believe that they are intelligent and rational and began the most rationally justified political system. We do not really follow the leaders in the first sense if we ignore their supplemental beliefs; we cannot be faithful to their intentions without appreciating how they would have decided in cases when faced with a conflict between their abstract values and supplemental beliefs. We follow them in the second sense only if we believe generality and abstraction are superior intellectual values to contextual and individualistic values. In neither case is it obvious why we should always regard the Framers' abstract values to be more important than their supplemental beliefs.[14]

Dworkin appears to respond to this argument by insisting that there aren't two different convictions at work here, abstract intentions and concrete intentions, at least not from the perspective of the persons whose convictions are under examination. Rather, there are different levels of abstraction regarding the relevant intention. The problem of discovering a person's intention does not amount to discovering "what [his] 'true' intentions or convictions or beliefs are."[15] Abstract and concrete intentions, according to Dworkin, are both genuine.[16] Moreover, in Dworkin's view it is not "a problem of discovering which is more important to me, which, as someone might put it, I would abandon first. For I do not hold them as even potentially conflicting convictions—I hold the more concrete as part of the more abstract—and any idea of my choosing between them is incoherent."[17]

There are two fundamental problems with these remarks. First, Dworkin's argument for his conception of judicial fidelity—that contemporary interpreters can be faithful to the Framers by embracing their abstract or formal intentions while rejecting their concrete intentions or supplemental beliefs—depends conceptually on the very distinction Dworkin rejects. Dworkin needs to individuate different convictions, to be able to talk about the abstract values and concrete implications as two separate ideas.[18] Presumably, each can be expressed in different sentences or propositions. For example, Dworkin is committed to the abstract value of fairness just in case he embraces a sentence asserting "The abstract value of fairness is good or right." His concrete intention concerning the question of whether bluffing is fair can be expressed in a sentence asserting "Bluffing is fair." The question whether abstractly "Fairness is good or right" conflicts with "Bluffing is fair" is certainly a question that can be asked and whose answer would be interesting and illuminating.

Suppose Dworkin believes fairness is giving each person her due. Then Dworkin believes that we should give everyone her due. This includes presumably giving blacks their due as well as gays and lesbians, philosophers, and so forth. Suppose, however, Dworkin does not believe that it is right to give gays and lesbians their due. If confronted by this (potential) conflict, Dworkin has a choice. He can retain the abstract principle concerning fairness and correct his errant belief concerning gays and lesbians, or, *if the price is right,* he can embrace the belief about gays and lesbians, and repudiate or modify his abstract intention concerning fairness. It is simply question begging to insist that it is the abstract quality that makes a value more fundamental. Fundamentality is determined by the importance of the value, or that interpretation of the value, in the person's life. A value may in some circumstances be more important the wider its scope. However, this is only one consideration concerning fundamentality, and it is a mistake to think that it is always, or must be, dispositive.

Common methods of theory construction in ethics and politics depend upon the interaction of different kinds of judgments and principles in formulating a person's moral perspective.[19] The notion that abstract and concrete, linguistic and political, general and particular beliefs can conflict is the basis for explaining the generation of a coherent view about anything.[20] The idea of choosing between them is not only not incoherent, Dworkin himself insists that the agent or interpreter who sees these convictions as inconsistent must choose between them. If the agent can, so can the Framer. In fact, there is absolutely nothing incoherent in asking the Framer to imagine herself in a hypothetical case where her convictions concerning fairness and bluffing conflict. That is, although she in fact believes in both fairness and bluffing, because she doesn't believe that bluffing is unfair, ask her to imagine herself in a situation where she believes in fairness, but believes correctly that bluffing is unfair. In such circumstances she can retain her conviction concerning fairness but only by altering her belief about bluffing. It is not obvious that she must always automatically reject the more concrete belief in cases of conflict. Again, fundamentality of belief is determined by the role the belief has in one's conceptual scheme and the continued desirability of that sort of conceptual scheme. This is a common process that Dworkin too easily overlooks.

Perhaps Dworkin's view is that a person accepts an abstract principle only under a certain description or having a certain specified content. Consequently, if someone believes that equality means racial and gender equality, then someone else holds a different abstract principle if she believes that equality can be understood only in the context of white race. Whenever anyone says "everyone is equal under the law," that person understands "everyone" in a certain way or under a certain description, and that description determines the nature of the principle. A narrow understanding of that term renders the principle different from a more expansive understanding of "everyone," or gives the principle a different meaning. Consequently, those Framers who believed that equality did not conflict with segregated schools held a different principle (of equality) from ours, but then the resolution of the question of equality is obvious: The contemporary understanding of equality as precluding segregated schools is superior to, and thus different from, the Framers' understanding.

The issue of Framers' intent can be illuminated by regarding American constitutional culture as either a dedicated or a deliberative system.[21] Dedicated systems are fixed by some authoritative individual(s) or text(s) and require fidelity to those authoritative sources, while rejecting fallibilist reform or revision. Deliberative systems typically require individual and collective deliberation and are committed to the continual reexamination of cultural values. Dedicated constitutionalism defends textualism, originalism, and other conceptions of constitutional law.[22] Deliberativism has as its central goal the capacity for resolving constitutional crises and extending the constitutional culture to a new era. Pragmatist constitutionalism is deliberative, because it is designed to solve constitutional crises by interpreting the Constitution and case law in the most promising manner. Dedicatedness or fidelity can be an important pragmatist value but cannot in itself be dispositive of constitutional truth. It may not be obvious why people prefer dedicated values to deliberative values, but failure to appreciate the distinction between dedicated and deliberative values precludes Dworkin from understanding the deep religious significance of some Americans' conception of constitutionalism.

Constitutional pragmatism abandons the importance of fidelity to the Framers' intentions. In general, pragmatists aim to discover the relevant past actors who are accorded special significance for our constitutional scheme.[23] Given the contextuality of linguistic meaning, a two-part process exists for imparting direction to the future or for discerning directions from the past. First, once the relevant actors are determined, we must then ask which constitutional concepts did they *identify* and *declare* central and which did they repudiate. Call this "the identification problem." Second, once we have resolved the identification problem, we then interpret the concept by providing the best available explanation of what it means and how it functions in constitutional law and political theory. The abstract or formal dimension of a concept answers the identification problem, whereas the concrete or substantive meaning contemporaneously resolves the interpretive problem. Notice how pragmatists trivialize the question of fidelity just as Dworkin does. We follow the Framers' intent by adhering to the resolution of the identification problem, although we certainly abandon, or are prepared to abandon, their intent when resolving the interpretive problem. To insist that both the formal and substantive dimensions of meaning must be met precludes the natural operation of pragmatist theory construction and belief formation. It precludes a constitutional culture from developing progressively from era to era; moreover, it restricts the Constitution's role in our broader culture. A pragmatist system is committed to more vibrant and developed answers to the interpretive question even when holding constant the problem of identification. To insist that this meaning can be revised only after an arduous process of article 5 emendation is artificially to restrict change and to fossilize constitutional theory and law. Dworkin would do better to jettison the notion of fidelity and return to his previous idea of "law as integrity" as an example of constitutional coherentism.

The Structure of Law as Integrity

Law as integrity, as a jurisprudential conception, includes a theory of adjudication that counsels judges to identify the correct set of rights or interests embedded in the law "on the assumption that they were all created by a single author—the community personified—expressing a coherent conception of justice and fairness."[24] It is a "thesis about the grounds of law," contending that statements of law "are true if they . . . follow from the principles of justice, fairness, and procedural due process that provide the best constructive interpretation of the community's legal practice."[25] Law as integrity is designed to represent a third conception of law clearly distinguishable from positivism, which as an interpretive theory Dworkin calls "conventionalism," and pragmatism, and, in his view, is superior to both. It aspires to incorporate the virtues of conventionalism and pragmatism into one synoptic vision of adjudication. The virtues of conventionalism are generally oriented toward the past, including a concern for protecting expectations and minimizing surprise as well as for taking rights and constitutional practice seriously.[26] Pragmatist virtues are generally oriented toward the future, including a concern with flexibility, coordination, and doing what is best for the community.[27] By contrast, law as integrity "denies that statements of law are either the backward-looking factual reports of conventionalism or the forward-looking instrumental programs of legal pragmatism."[28] Law as integrity "insists that legal claims are interpretive judgments and therefore combine backward- and forward-looking elements."[29]

Conventionalism takes constitutional practice seriously, but its crabbed conception of judicial reasoning fails to identify the correct rights or interests that are best for the community. Although constitutional pragmatism is more likely than conventionalism to identify the community's best interests, it does so at the expense of not taking constitutional rights seriously.[30] Law as integrity attempts to combine conventionalism's commitment to constitutional rights with pragmatism's commitment to what is best for the community.[31] Each theory takes a particular stand on the possibility of constitutional revolutions. Hart's positivism requires judicial discretion through which judges engage in interstitial lawmaking, and thus presumably precludes constitutional revolutions.[32] Dworkin's conception of (strict) conventionalism permits revolutionary adjudication, but only when law runs out.[33] Pragmatism, on the other hand, permits constitutional revolutions whenever the price is right.[34]

A constitutional revolution occurs when the Supreme Court decides an issue of constitutional law according to a principle not contained in the Constitution or in constitutional practice.[35] Because the idea of a principle being contained in the Constitution is problematic, my characterization must remain provisional. However, we can indicate the following possible senses of "containment." First, a principle is contained in the Constitution if it is required to explain and justify the constitutional practice it claims to authorize. This also suggests a conception of the individuation of constitutional principles. Two principles differ if and only if, in some concrete context and in competition with other relevant principles, appealing to the first principle would result in a different decision from appealing to the second.[36] Second, a new principle replaces an old principle contained in constitutional practice whenever the rules of constitutional inference change the truth value of at least one constitutional judgment. A constitutional revolution depends not only on the number of constitutional judgments whose truth values have changed, but also on the importance of these changes for judges and lawyers, and especially for the lives of citizens who depend upon the law. Third, a principle is contained in constitutional practice when it is a preinterpretive paradigm of constitutional practice, or, alternatively stated, when reasonable members of the constitutional community agree on its status.[37]

Taking constitutional practice seriously means respecting the role of these preinterpretive paradigms in constraining future interpretations.[38] A paradigm is preinterpretive relative to the time of its interpretation. Therefore, a preinterpretive paradigm in the present may be the result of a past interpretation. Something like a reasonable person standard can be adopted to determine whether a principle is a preinterpretive paradigm in a system of law. A principle is a preinterpretive paradigm if reasonable judges, possessing requisite knowledge, ability to reason, and so forth, agree that the principle governs all or part of the legal system.[39]

Dworkin's integrity asks judges to construct a principle of law that fits legal practice and makes that practice the best it can be. My argument against integrity concerns *Brown* and is straightforward: Because any competent constitutional actor should accept the role of precedent in constitutional adjudication, *Plessy v. Ferguson* must have had a presumptive authority in 1954.[40] This case represents a foundational constitutional decision defining "equality" throughout the legal system.[41] How can *Brown* fit it, the original constitutional practice? The dimension of fit causes the trouble here.[42] Suppose, for example, we discover that an early paradigm failed to meet the fit threshold. Suppose, as a foundational case, it misread the Constitution and the scant number of other authoritative sources existing at that time. Now, however, there is an enormous number of cases following from the "wrongly" decided case. The fit dimension overwhelmingly favors the principle in that foundational case. Indeed, on almost any interpretation of Dworkin's views, the threshold of fit is high and should preclude constitutional change.

If we follow Dworkin's admonition that any competent interpretation of constitutional *practice* must explain or fit the practice, then it is difficult, if not impossible, to see how precedent can be overcome in cases like *Brown*.[43] Instead, precedent should control even when there exists an alternative principle that is normatively more attractive than the principle embodied in the foundational decision.[44] If we reject this scenario, and permit an attractive normative principle to prevail despite its poor or nonexistent fit with actual practice, we have embraced constitutional pragmatism.[45] My conclusion is that in order for law as integrity to provide the appropriate explanation and justification of *Brown* and other constitutional revolutions, it must renounce coherentism as a monist theory of constitutional practice, recognizing that abrupt, discontinuous change is a hallmark of constitutional development that can be explained only pragmatically.[46]

Accordingly, the central problem with law as integrity as an interpretive theory of American constitutional practice is its inability to explain and justify constitutional revolutions, especially the paradigmatic constitutional revolution of overruling an authoritative precedent. Because constitutional revolutions are an integral feature of constitutional practice, any adequate interpretive theory must account for them and their role in constitutional change. Thus, the failure of law as integrity to provide the appropriate explanation and justification of constitutional revolutions is fatal to Dworkin's project of providing an alternative to conventionalism and pragmatism. An examination of Dworkin's attempt to explain and justify *Brown* will reveal important ambiguities in his conception of "fit," and in the relationship between fit and justification.

Law as integrity is intended as an interpretation of constitutional practice revealing how present rights flow from past political decisions. Similarly, once operating under integrity, interpretation is necessary to determine what the law is in a given case. The central analytic device in law as integrity includes fit and justification. A proposed constitutional interpretation must fit, or explain the legal practice it interprets as well as justify it. Accordingly, an interpretive principle of law is an explanation and justification of the point or meaning of a series of cases and other relevant constitutional conventions, and ultimately of law as a whole.[47]

In deciding a case a judge formulates a principle that best explains and justifies the relevant practice.[48] An interpretation fully explains a series of decisions when just those decisions would result if a judge, unfamiliar with the actual cases, self-consciously used that principle to decide those cases.[49] A principle or unified scheme of principles explaining freedom of speech, for example, fits or explains past decisions if a judge could appeal successfully to that principle in attempting to replicate sight unseen the actual decisions concerning free speech. A unified scheme of principles is deficient if it leaves a great bulk of the relevant legal conventions unexplained, or if it ignores those foundational decisions constitutive of the constitutional practice of free speech. If no principle with sufficient normative attractiveness provides an adequate explanation of legal practice in a particular area, then (an interpretively justified) skepticism is warranted toward that area of law. In that case no interpretation counts as following the existing law rather than creating new law.[50] Of course, a principle need not explain each and every past decision. To deal with this eventuality, Dworkin's interpretive methodology includes a theory of mistakes.[51] A theory of mistakes tells us when existing law can be discarded in favor of a normatively attractive principle that provides the best interpretation of the legal practice. Ordinarily, a theory of mistakes, in Dworkin's view, will not discredit an entire practice or legal system, unless that system is irredeemably immoral or incoherent.

A justification of a constitutional principle is an argument showing the principle to follow from the best understanding of our constitutional history.[52] To justify constitutional practice, the principle must portray the practice in its best light. In Dworkin's view it is irrational to embrace a scheme of principles that portrays constitutional practice in a poor light when an alternative principle that fits is available portraying it in a better light. When two principles both fit a practice, the principle that shows the practice in a better light is the appropriate interpretation of the practice.[53] Fit is relevant to the justificatory dimension also. Because a constitutional community should not dishonor its own principles, a better fit can make one explanation a better justification, and therefore a better interpretation than one whose fit is not as good.[54] A better fit reveals the greater integrity of the system of law; consequently, fit plays an explanatory and justificatory role.

Integrity is designed to depict the proper relation between fit and justification. It should also tell us how strong a theory of mistakes should be.[55] Understood in this manner, the dimension of fit is a formal virtue of a legal theory. Any constitutional theory must satisfy a fit requirement, and any judge or other member of the legal community must have a conception of fit that she uses in interpreting the practice. The critical question is, How strong should that requirement be, and should it remain constant throughout different kinds of constitutional adjudication?

Dworkin contends that once we take the interpretive turn, it becomes evident that law as integrity is superior to both conventionalism and pragmatism. Law as integrity reveals the existence of a background theory containing a strong explanatory and normative conception of equality, including, for instance, a conception of racial equality, that portrays constitutional practice in its best light. Generally, and especially in hard cases, the appropriate interpretation of a constitutional practice will reveal this background theory. Hence in cases where people seem unable to agree, it still makes sense to say, according to Dworkin, that there is a right answer to a constitutional question.[56] The right answer to the constitutional conflict is determined by the background theory explaining and justifying the law. Judges and other constitutional practitioners may disagree about which background theory best explains and justifies constitutional practice, but disagreement does not preclude the existence of one correct answer. A legal principle is *the* correct answer to a legal conflict when it follows from the background theory that best explains and justifies legal practice.[57]

The role one's theory of mistakes plays in constitutional theory will determine how much and which kind of case law must be preserved by one's interpretation of the law. In order to overturn a foundational constitutional decision, one must embrace a strong theory of mistakes. Such a theory of mistakes permits the acceptance of an attractive normative justification despite the justification's poor fit with a foundational, constitutional decision, a decision that is constitutive of constitutional practice. Pragmatism permits such a justification, but integrity does not, because integrity precludes strong judicial discretion.[58]

Two Conceptions of the Relationship between Fit and Justification

Dworkin's deployment of the relationship between fit and justification can be interpreted in two ways: the lexical interpretation and the holistic interpretation. The lexical interpretation regards fit and justification as independent, though interrelated, dimensions for evaluating a constitutional decision. First, a judge must determine whether her proposed interpretation fits constitutional practice, that is, whether she can use it to replicate the decisions in that area of constitutional practice. When only one interpretation passes the fit requirement, it is the correct interpretation by default. When two or more sets of principles pass the fit requirement, the judge must engage considerations of political morality in determining which principle makes the better justification. Typically, in these circumstances the better justification should be the basis of the judge's decision in the present case.[59] The lexical interpretation thus ranks fit and justification. In order to be considered a justification, a principle must satisfy a significant threshold level of fit. If it fails this threshold, it is not an eligible candidate for the best interpretation of constitutional practice.

Two approaches further qualify the lexical interpretation. A lexical interpretation can be either *strongly* lexical or *weakly* lexical. An interpretation is *strongly* lexical when a principle must satisfy the fit requirement before its justificatory character is assessed. Further, strong lexical interpretations will reach the justificatory level only when more than one principle equally or sufficiently explains constitutional practice. The strongly lexical approach holds that no justification can fail to explain the relevant constitutional paradigms, including foundational decisions constitutive of constitutional practice. If only one principle explains constitutional practice, then that also justifies the practice. Thus, in some cases the strongly lexical approach need not consider justificatory factors at all. The second approach is weakly lexical in that a sufficiently attractive justification compensates for a weak explanation. This conception uses a comparative approach to the relationship of fit and justification. In the weakly lexical approach, justificatory factors are always considered in interpreting constitutional practice.

The holistic interpretation of the relationship between fit and justification differs from the lexical interpretation. The central difference in the holistic interpretation is that fit and justification are not independent dimensions. According to the holistic interpretation, a principle interpreting constitutional practice must follow from the scheme of moral principles necessary to justify the legal system as a whole.[60] In this view one must posit principles of political morality, including considerations of justice, fairness, and procedural due process to determine which posited principle provides the best justification of constitutional practice or of law as a whole. The moral principles that portray constitutional practice in its best light qualify as the best interpretation of the practice. In both lexical and holistic interpretation two processes are involved. They are nonetheless different. The lexical interpretation begins with an explanatory principle, whereas the holistic interpretation begins with a normative one. These two conceptions depict two different judicial attitudes. Starting with an explanatory principle reveals a conventionalist desire for interpretation to remain as close to the actual cases and practice as possible. Beginning with a normative principle reveals the pragmatist or naturalist desire for interpretation to get the normatively right answer, which needs no more than a tangential connection to what the actual cases say.

Depending upon how expansive is one's theory of mistakes, justificatory principles may fail to explain practice, or require only a marginal degree of fit with case law. The greater the possibility of overlooking a poor fit with actual decisions, the greater a holistic approach assumes a pragmatist dimension. In that event very little constrains the positing of normative principles to which one has a great commitment. One constraint that is probably perverse is that our present constitutional culture does not admit that judges posit normative principles all the time. Thus, if one judge admits to positing normative principles, other judges will falsely deny that they are doing the same.

Another problem with the holistic account is its degree of generality. It may be possible to justify the legal system as a whole only by having general principles compatible with a multiplicity of differing concrete principles. Consequently, these general principles will have an attenuated connection to actual decisions. A further problem with the holistic approach is the alleged necessity of these principles in justifying the system as a whole. It is perfectly possible that some principles are sufficient in justifying the legal system, though no moral principles are ever *necessary* for justifying it. We can adopt different principles for justifying a practice depending upon variations in the conception of the practice or changes in other features of our constitutional conceptual scheme. Only if our descriptions of practices or our constitutional conceptual scheme were fixed or necessary would principles for justifying these principles be necessary, and no one has ever demonstrated that there are such fixed descriptions. For example, I will adopt a different principle of free speech depending upon whether I believe that nonpolitical speech is just as essential to constitutional practice as political speech. Only if constitutional practice is fixed as including or excluding nonpolitical speech will one principle of free speech be necessary.

Neither the lexical nor the holistic approach can explain overruling a foundational decision without capitulating to pragmatism. Taking practice seriously means taking foundational decisions seriously, as these decisions are constitutive of constitutional practice. However, because revolutionary adjudication is constitutive of constitutional adjudication, Dworkin's theory must be rejected. Dworkin has two options when faced with a revolutionary case. Either he can articulate an alternative interpretation of fit and justification that explains the decision, or he must contend that foundational decisions are not part of—or not a significant part of—the data or subtext that constitutional interpretations must explain.[61] Dworkin must provide an account of the data of constitutional interpretation, or what an interpretation of constitutional practice is an interpretation *of*. Moreover, he needs to explain the role of foundational decisions in constitutional practice. One standard manner in accounting for the significance of foundational decisions maintains that they define key features of the practice, such as the practice's conception of liberty, equality, free speech, and so forth. Foundational decisions then constrain future interpretations.

Dworkin could reply that the reflective convictions of the citizenry, the evolving standards of society, or considerations of abstract justice are more important than case law. The problem with this approach is that it inevitably turns toward pragmatism (including naturalism) as the best interpretation of constitutional law. It turns toward pragmatism because only pragmatism can accommodate the abrupt revolutionary changes that represent the unique contribution of American constitutionalism and culture to the democratic political theory.[62] The progression from *Plessy* to *Brown* identifies how this pragmatist shift occurs.

Brown v. Board of Education: *Overruling* Plessy v. Ferguson

Dworkin believes that the decision in *Brown* follows from a principle of racial equality latent in American constitutional practice in 1954, one that provides the best constructive interpretation of that practice.[63] Thus, according to Dworkin, *Brown* is not a genuine constitutional revolution as that term is generally used.[64] Dworkin initially describes how *Brown* arose in the following manner:

> After the American Civil War the victorious North amended the Constitution to end slavery and many of its incidents and consequences. One of these amendments, the Fourteenth, declared that no state might deny any person the "equal protection of the laws." After Reconstruction the southern states, once more in control of their own politics, segregated many public facilities by race. Blacks had to ride in the back of the bus and were allowed to attend only segregated schools with other blacks. In the famous case of *Plessy v. Ferguson* the defendant argued, ultimately before the Supreme Court, that these practices of segregation automatically violated the equal protection clause. The Court rejected this claim; it said that the demands of that clause were satisfied if the state provided separate but equal facilities and that the fact of segregation alone did not make the facilities automatically unequal.[65]

Dworkin then describes the circumstances leading up to 1954 and the decision in *Brown*.[66] He insists that the arguments for and against *Brown* "were arguments about the proper grounds of constitutional law, not arguments of morality or repair."[67] Most important, Dworkin insists that "[i]f the Constitution did not as a matter of law prohibit official racial segregation, then the decision in *Brown* was an illicit constitutional amendment, and few who supported the decision thought they were supporting that."[68] As with Ackerman, Dworkin also believes a great judicial decision can be great but never revolutionary. For a judicial decision to be great, for it to be a judicial decision in the first place, it must reflect fundamental standards already in the law.[69] In this view constitutional revolutions do not exist. Judicial decisions must be interpretations of existing practices; revolutionary decisions create new practices and therefore must be rejected.

At the very outset Dworkin's argument against the possibility of genuine constitutional revolutions is circular;[70] it depends on some non-interpretive distinction between following an existing practice and beginning a new practice. This distinction cannot reliably be used to ground a theory of law for the following reasons: First, it is unclear and contestable what counts as continuing the old and creating the new.[71] Second, revolutions are within practices; consequently, the practice might be the same as in *Brown*, namely, equal protection jurisprudence, yet the precise paradigm "separate but equal" or "equal and not separate" may differ. In my view the decision in *Brown* was a paradigmatic interpretive constitutional "amendment." That an unreflective constitutional culture, sometimes including even judges themselves, refuses rhetorically to recognize this process of pragmatic revolutionary change does not mean that it is illusory.[72] Rather, it suggests, if the theory of constitutional revolutions is accurate, that a deeper understanding of judicial practice is needed.[73] *Brown* is a pragmatic interpretive amendment because it, in conjunction with the per curiam cases that follow, in effect overrules the foundational decision in *Plessy*, which was at that time constitutive of American constitutional practice.[74] Unless other foundational features of American constitutional practice can be identified that are compatible with *Brown*, the fit requirement can be met only by following *Plessy*. In other words, law as integrity must account for *Brown* by showing which features of American constitutional practice *Brown* fits better than *Plessy*. If law as integrity takes constitutional practice seriously, it is difficult to see what can warrant overturning fifty-eight years of American constitutional practice from within that practice, especially as *Plessy* was regularly reaffirmed during those years.[75] If *Brown* was the law of racial equality all along, what constitutional paradigms prevented its implementation?

We must keep in mind that such decisions as *Plessy* are "foundational constitutional decisions," and foundational constitutional decisions are constitutive of the institutional history of law in the society. Any theory taking practice seriously should regard foundational decisions as playing an authoritative and presumptive role in any normative account of judicial practice.[76] Accordingly, any interpretation that cannot explain such a decision must be presumptively deficient. No higher paradigm or convention is available to evaluate such a constitutive decision, not even the Constitution itself.[77]

Of course, the Constitution *was* the highest paradigm at the beginning of constitutional practice. In this case, however, institutional history is also relevant. What did the Framers intend the equal protection clause to achieve? If we take the considered convictions of the Framers to be our guide, the best interpretation of the equal protection clause yields inconclusive results concerning the interpretation of equality.[78] I do not rest my case against law as integrity here. Instead, I want to point out that constitutional practice developed through *Plessy,* and once such a Supreme Court decision is made interpreting the Constitution, it is foundational or authoritative, irrespective of what might have been true of the original understanding of the constitutional provision in question. That is the role of a foundational decision, and that is what it means to take *practice* seriously.[79]

Thus, *Brown*'s normative superiority to *Plessy* cannot prevail on the level of fit. Because the principle in *Plessy* is constitutive of actual constitutional practice and the background moral theory associated with that practice, *Brown*'s normative principle of racial equality cannot adequately explain the actual practice of racial inequality in the United States in 1954. Furthermore, the background theory associated with *Brown* cannot be a better interpretation than *Plessy*'s background theory because *Brown*'s background theory cannot *explain* the constitutional practice of racial equality in 1954.

The Lexical and Holistic Interpretations of Brown

Dworkin's treatment of *Brown* is not always clear and at times borders on the mysterious.[80] Throughout *Law's Empire* Dworkin continually stresses the fit requirement, but when he approaches *Brown*, fit appears to be ignored completely. Rather than first explaining how Hercules might even *consider* overruling *Plessy,* he begins his discussion of *Brown* after Hercules has already decided that *Plessy* should be overruled. Dworkin simply asserts that "[i]t seems plain that the Constitution mandates some individual right not to be the victim of official, state-imposed racial discrimination."[81] That leaves an enormous gap in Hercules' reasoning. When an intelligible paradigm, a foundational constitutional decision, governs a particular area of constitutional law such as racial equality, what factors may legitimately prompt a judge to reconsider the continued use of that paradigm? Dworkin needs to specify the factors (legally) motivating and justifying Hercules' decision even to consider overruling *Plessy*.

Dworkin avoids this question of what *triggers* overturning a foundational constitutional decision such as *Plessy*.[82] Additionally, he avoids any discussion of how the principle in *Brown* explains the actual cases that are constitutive of American constitutional practice.[83] Instead, it is apparent that, despite his contention that Hercules is ready to test which conception of equality "fits and justifies," there is in fact no significant discussion of fit and case law at all.[84] This problem is exacerbated by Dworkin's failure to discuss specifically whether the principle in *Plessy* — "separate but equal" — or some alternative principle fits actual judicial practice in 1954.[85] If case law is irrelevant, just what is a proposed justification supposed to fit?[86] In fact, due to *Plessy*, a rule denying "separate but equal" would in 1954 be a disastrous fit with the actual institutional history of equality in American constitutional law.[87] Anytime the court reverses or overrules a foundational constitutional provision, the new principle will not (cannot) fit constitutional practice. This point is a conceptual, not empirical, implication of the concept of overruling a foundational constitutional provision. Moreover, this conceptual point is an essential feature of the actual judicial practice that law as integrity cannot explain.

Dworkin might reply that this begs the question against integrity's explanation of overruling a foundational constitutional interpretation. In integrity's view this means overruling some explicit constitutional principle in favor of an underlying or implicit principle, which explains and justifies constitutional practice better than the explicit one. What does it mean to say that "an implicit principle explains and justifies constitutional practice better than an explicit one"? Surely, it must mean that the implicit principle at least explains the actual decisions in that area of law or explains actual decisions in other areas of law, but the implicit principle expressed in *Brown* cannot explain actual decisions in constitutional practice better than *Plessy* because *Plessy* was constitutive of constitutional practice in this area.

It seems clear that Dworkin's discussion here concerns justification even when it speaks of fit.[88] What Hercules wants to know is what normative conception of equality *fits* the citizenry's "convictions about racial justice."[89] This interpretation of fit differs from an interpretation that is designed to explain the institutional history of a constitutional provision and how this history constrains and guides judges. It is an interpretation of fit that prefers the cultural convictions of the citizenry: This interpretation of fit permits a judge to ignore the institutional history of a constitutional provision in favor of what she considers to be the reflective convictions of the American people. Revolutionary decisions ratify cultural and political norms and codify them as law. Dworkin overlooks this obviously pragmatist process and therefore is forced to say that the decision in *Brown* was somehow always part of American constitutional practice.

Dworkin is *probably* right that the normative principle in *Brown* now "fits" the normative convictions of the American people.[90] It is not obvious that this principle reflected the convictions of most Americans in 1954. However, this conception of fit does not require a normative principle to explain the institutional history of the equal protection clause, and therefore it cannot explain actual constitutional practice. Accordingly, this interpretation of fit does not require an explanation of American constitutional practice where that practice includes foundational decisions such as *Plessy*. Such an interpretation of fit is congenial to a pragmatist conception of adjudication wherein the best explanation of institutional history can be ignored, or can at least satisfy a reduced threshold, when the normative principle under examination is sufficiently attractive. In this regard Dworkin's interpretation of fit does not preclude an even more radical form of pragmatist adjudication that permits a judge to ignore both institutional history and the reflective considerations of the American people when she is convinced that a proposed normative principle is sufficiently attractive to warrant doing so. Thus understood, law as integrity, rather than offering an alternative to legal pragmatism, simply embraces it.

The lexical interpretation of fit and justification in *Brown* can be contrasted with the lexical interpretation of fit and justification in *Bowers v. Hardwick,* the Georgia case upholding a statute prohibiting consensual adult sodomy. The argument in favor of invalidating the law contended that homosexual intimacy is not constitutionally distinguishable from heterosexual intimacy, that both include the value of intimate association. Suppose two principles were considered as interpretations of the *Griswold* line of cases: Principle 1 followed *Griswold* closely in asserting that heterosexual intimacy is an important value that should be free from unnecessary state interference.[91] Principle 2 states that sexual intimacy generally is important and should be free from unnecessary state interference. Arguably, both Principles 1 and 2 explain the *Griswold* and *Eisenstat* line of cases equally well.[92] As mentioned earlier, both provide an equally good fit of the case law in the sense that a judge unfamiliar with the case law could replicate the *Griswold* line of cases sight unseen using either principle.

A strongly lexical interpretation of fit and justification then takes these two principles to the next level, namely, the dimension of justification. Which principle portrays constitutional practice in its best light? Which principle is a better moral justification of constitutional practice? Either principle appears to explain or fit constitutional practice. Either justification is tied directly to the foundational decisions constitutive of constitutional practice in this area. Consequently, both justifications qualify as valid interpretations because both justifications explain constitutional history and practice. Consequently, in *Hardwick* the two principles both explain the case law, though of course in different ways.

In *Brown,* however, the normative principle justifying American constitutional practice has no purchase in the case law. Indeed, it seems that Dworkin's contention is that the principle in *Brown* fits the reflective convictions of the American people and that it need not explain the case law at all. In one case, *Hardwick,* either of two possible justificatory principles explains the case law equally well. In *Brown* the correct normative principle does not. In other words, the lexical interpretation of fit and justification operates differently in constitutional revolutions that create new constitutional paradigms, on the one hand, and in cases specifically designed to spell out the implications of a settled paradigm.[93]

Dworkin might attempt to defeat this objection in the following ways: First, he might argue that an antisegregation principle can be derived from other areas of constitutional law or from the legal system generally. This attempt assumes that there are other constitutional provisions or judicial decisions concerning racial equality and that these other sources provide paradigms concerning racial equality more favorable to *Brown* than to *Plessy.* This approach maintains that constitutional practice concerning racial equality is mixed, with some paradigms favoring *Plessy,* whereas others favor *Brown.* Hercules' decision to repudiate *Plessy* fits these other conventions or paradigms, and thus Dworkin can explain *Brown* by indicating its fit with actual constitutional paradigms. In *Brown,* a constitutional decision to reverse a precedent can be explained by indicating additional constitutional paradigms or features of constitutional practice, which, if existing alone, would require the decision in *Brown*.

If such authoritative factors exist, Dworkin must identify them. In the context of *Plessy* and *Brown* no further paradigms appear to exist.[94] Unless we embrace the highly dubious supposition that the American Constitution itself implicitly or structurally entails an antisegregation principle — dubious because it fails to explain American constitutional history and practice — no additional constitutional provisions or judicial opinions yielding an antisegregation principle exist that conflict with *Plessy*.[95] American constitutional practice concerning equal protection is defined in part by *Plessy*. However, even if such paradigms can be found, their role in authorizing a constitutional revolution is doubtful because the equal protection clause and *Plessy* and its progeny are constitutionally foundational in that they determine the meaning and scope of (racial) equality throughout the entire legal system. Any alternative paradigms concerning racial equality have a lexically inferior role to the equal protection clause and case law interpreting this clause.[96]

Alternatively, Dworkin might argue that the original paradigm in the equal protection clause includes a principle of antisegregation, and if the original understanding did not recognize this principle, it was simply wrong.[97] Similarly, if the *Plessy* Court failed to recognize this principle, it too was wrong. However, it is question begging in the extreme to say that *Brown* fits constitutional practice, because constitutional practice, especially the equal protection clause, always contained a principle of antisegregation. Even if we grant that an antisegregation principle provides the best justification of the equal protection clause as originally written, this does not mean that Hercules can ignore *Plessy* and the constitutional practice that reflects *Plessy*. A pragmatist or naturalist judge can embrace her conception of what makes the equal protection clause *the* best it can be *simpliciter*. In 1875 perhaps a judge following law as integrity could also embrace such a normative conception, but not in 1954. To do so ignores the practice that developed from *Plessy* to *Brown* and *Plessy*'s constitutive role in that practice.[98]

Should Dworkin, nevertheless, insist that the original Constitution, structurally or implicitly, or the equal protection clause contains an antisegregation principle, then *Brown* does fit prior constitutional practice, but in a way that challenges the conventionalist roots of law as integrity and makes it virtually indistinguishable from pragmatism. Moreover, it will render fit arbitrary as a future constraint. Instead of fit functioning as a constraint on what judges decide, fit will follow from whatever decision they wish to make. Fit will no longer *guide* a conscientious judge who seeks to make an unbiased decision. A principle will no longer fit independently of its normative appeal. I do not think these problems are dispositive against constitutional pragmatism; indeed, certain forms of constitutional pragmatism embrace these elements of adjudication. However, law as integrity is designed to be distinguishable from constitutional pragmatism, and in this it fails. Dworkin *seems* to give an alternative characterization of the fit requirement in *Brown*. Rather than interpreting fit lexically, the alternative characterization renders the relationship between fit and justification holistic.

A coherentist justification of constitutional practice succeeds, however, only when it also *explains* the practice. A valid justification of constitutional practice, a principle showing the normative attractiveness of the practice, must show how constitutional practice in fact evolved over time. This type of justification must also show how contemporary judges decide cases before them. It must also provide an explanation of the evolution of constitutional practice and the present case law. If the justificatory principle cannot serve an explanatory function, it cannot be a successful interpretation of the actual practice no matter how attractive a justification it is. Interpretation requires that the correct justificatory principle in a given area of the law also fit or explain the cases in that area. For example, for the antisegregation principle to justify constitutional practice concerning racial equality, it must explain the decisions in these cases, and it cannot do this because it conflicts with *Plessy,* and *Plessy* controls the area.[99] The "separate but equal" principle in *Plessy* provides the best nonnormative explanation of constitutional practice irrespective of what the practice might look like if it were morally improved.[100] To honor the fit requirement, one must take controlling law seriously.[101]

One could imagine an alternative interpretation of the holistic interpretation, distinguishing between the surface structure of constitutional practice and its deep structure. The surface structure consists of the explicit law in the society. Any competent lawyer can, in principle, characterize the surface structure of American equal protection law. However, there also exists a deep structure of principles, which justifies the surface structure.[102] *Plessy* depicts the surface structure of American equal protection law, yet the principle in *Plessy* never became part of the law's deep structure. Instead, the

deep structure of American equal protection law entailed an antisegregation principle concerning racial equality. Dworkin's point might be sup-
portable by showing how the principle in *Brown* was part of, and therefore
fit, the law's deep structure.[103]

Dworkin does not embrace this distinction, and it is not likely that it will
work. If integrity embraces fit, it must explain how we formulate the justificatory principles in the law's deep structure. What must these justificatory
principles fit? If not the surface structure, then what? If the justificatory
principles in the law's deep structure must fit only other justificatory principles, then we jettison explanatory constraints on justification. If the data to
be explained by these justificatory principles are the reflective convictions of
the citizenry or the evolving standards of society, then the deep structure is
clearly pragmatic or naturalist. In this event the distinction between the
law's surface structure and its deep structure is a complex reformulation of
constitutional pragmatism. To argue otherwise leaves us with the unexplained and tendentious claim that the principle in *Brown* was constitutional law all along because it was (always) part of the law's deep structure.
If fit is to be a historical constraint, then the deep structure must reflect, at
least in part, the foundational decisions that make up the surface structure
of constitutional practice. Finally, the notion of "foundational decisions"
reveals an inadequacy in the dichotomy between surface and deep structure.
They do not fit either level but, instead, seem to be deeper than surface
decisions, though not as deep as deep structure.

Under what circumstances would we say that a desegregation decision
follows from *Plessy*?[104] Suppose the Court in *Brown* chose to affirm that
separate but equal facilities were constitutionally protected. Instead, "[i]t
might have put flesh on *Plessy*'s bones and insist that racially separate
schools be truly equal."[105] Call this imaginary case "the *Brown Hypothetical*"
or "*Brown H*" for short. Would *Brown H* be revolutionary, or would it
follow from the paradigm in *Plessy*? One thing we can say for sure, a Dworkinian argument that *Brown H* was already the law would be persuasive.
Still, one can question whether *Plessy* and *Brown H* contain the same paradigm. The argument against this conclusion would be that because *Plessy*
did not have teeth, a *Plessy*-like case having teeth represented a different
judicial paradigm. As a practical matter this is certainly true.[106] However,
the conceptual paradigm in *Plessy* and *Brown H* are the same. *Brown H*
would simply insist on *equality* while simultaneously respecting the associational rights of individuals not prepared to integrate with members of other

races. The revolution in *Brown H,* if there were one, would be in the practical results and the remedy.[107] Conceptually or theoretically, there would be no revolution at all.[108] Consequently, a Dworkinian argument showing that the principle in *Brown H* is, after all, the same principle or judicial paradigm as in *Plessy* could be successful.[109]

Brown H cannot answer the question of how the principle in *Brown* can follow from actual constitutional practice if *Plessy* is to govern the explicit law in the area of equal protection. We cannot take foundational constitutional decisions like *Plessy* seriously, if the decision in that case does not govern future equal protection law. Moreover, if foundational constitutional cases like *Plessy* determine in part what both explicit law is as well as the underlying justificatory principles, then a principle denying *Plessy* cannot be one of these justificatory principles.[110] I am not asserting either that foundational decisions govern absolutely, or that they cannot be overruled. My point is simply that any interpretive theory regarding historical factors as constraining elements on interpretation has a presumptive problem with overruling foundational decisions.[111] Dworkin needs to explain how this problem can be overcome.

Suppose we use Corwin's distinction between a formal and a material constitution. The formal sense of constitution is the document itself, including the amendments.[112] The material sense of constitution refers to "a body of rules in accordance with which a government is organized and operates; and in this sense 'the Constitution of the United States' comprises a vastly extended system of legislation, customs, adjudications, of which the constitutional document is . . . but the nucleus, and into which it tends ever to be absorbed."[113] Dworkin may then argue that the principle in *Brown* inheres in the material constitution, though not in the formal constitution. We must then confront a fundamental conflict between these two senses of "constitution," and determine why in such a conflict the material sense of the term should prevail. Even if we conclude that it should prevail, it must be conceded that such a move involves a radical change in the formal constitution. Such a change can be explained only in pragmatic terms. Nothing in the formal constitution prompts such a change; indeed, the formal constitution is the main opposition to a change of this sort.

Here Dworkin might invoke an unfortunate distinction between a legal *rule* and a legal *principle.* A legal rule has an all-or-nothing characteristic, whereas legal principles are prima facie reasons, which have a certain degree of weight, but which must be balanced against other reasons or values.

With this distinction Dworkin can argue that in *Plessy* the "separate but equal doctrine" is a rule that conflicts with a more fundamental principle of equality, which is embedded in our constitutional scheme and which is the basis for the rule in *Brown*. There are two problems with this reply. First, it is unclear that this distinction is viable. Rules may be regarded as merely unopposed principles. Second, we must justify how a principle of equality embedded in our constitutional system can be opposed to the rule in *Plessy*, and if it can, how we determine its comparative weight. Dworkin cannot say, without begging the question, that such a principle is required to justify actual practice. In fact, what Dworkin really means is that this principle is required to justify the constitutional practice we would like to have. In this view unstated *principles* exist in our system of law that have the force of law in a given situation. Consider Dworkin's words:

> A principle like "no man shall profit from his own wrong" . . . states a reason that argues in one direction, but does not necessitate a particular decision. If a man has or is about to receive something, as a direct result of something illegal he did to get it, then that is a reason which the law will take into account in deciding whether he shall keep it. There may be other principles or policies arguing in the other direction. . . . If so, our principle may not prevail, but that does not mean that it is not a principle in our legal system, because in the next case, when these contravening considerations are absent or less weighty, the principle may be decisive. All that is meant, when we say a particular principle is a principle of our law, is that the principle is one which officials must take into account, if it is relevant, as a consideration inclining in one direction or another.[114]

Hence, the rule, an absolute, self-executing imperative, that Jones not receive the bounty in a given case, is justified by the application of the foregoing principle.[115] In the preceding account of principles, they function something like prima facie duties that presume a result given no other considerations override them.[116] Still, two fundamental problems plague this approach. First, how do we identify unenacted legal principles? Second, how do we calculate the comparative weight of principles, rules, statutes, and judicial decisions?

Dworkin might reply that the principle in *Brown* need not explain actual decisions, since those decisions based on *Plessy* were just plain wrong.[117] The *correct* decision concerning racial equality, according to Dworkin, is one that explains or coheres with fundamental justificatory principles underlying constitutional law. Such principles are required to justify the entire scheme of constitutional law. *Brown* is merely an elaboration of this justificatory scheme, implementing an existing (implicit) justificatory principle as positive law.[118] In other words, Dworkin might argue that there is a *theory* of American constitutional law that entails an antisegregation principle. A justificatory theory of such factors as separation of powers, federalism, judicial review, and the Bill of Rights requires an antisegregation principle. This means that a justificatory theory good for some parts of constitutional practice can override the constitutional provisions and case law specifically concerned with equality.

Again, this fails to take actual practice seriously and is better understood as a form of constitutional pragmatism. This is not, as Dworkin contends, to grant his point but to resist calling it "integrity." He can redefine "integrity" to be consonant with pragmatism, if he chooses. However, in respecting the past itself and not its instrumental value alone, Dworkin marks out a theory that is incompatible with constitutional pragmatism. This point reveals a very different orientation toward constitutional practice and the judicial role in that practice. According to integrity, actual practice should significantly constrain judicial decisions. Pragmatism need not seek such constraints and can focus explicitly on which judicial decision contributes more to the community's future good. Alternatively, law as integrity means one thing when Dworkin presents it, and something rather different when utilized by Hercules in deciding *Brown*. Dworkin presents a theory that tries unsuccessfully to incorporate the ideals of conventionalism and pragmatism. Hercules is, at least in *Brown,* an unabashedly pragmatist judge.

In reply Dworkin could say that the principle in *Brown* derives from the spirit of the Constitution, from the best scheme of principles needed to explain and justify constitutional law. There are two problems with this reply. First, one must show that explicit provisions of the Constitution and explicit judicial decisions require the principle in *Brown* despite a foundational decision, the most authoritative kind, denying *Brown*.[119] This alternative implies that we need not worry whether the principle has any significant fit with actual practice. The reason for this is that when morality and history conflict, morality usually is the natural choice. This is the letter and spirit of pragmatism. Second, if a scheme of principles posited to justify explicit constitutional conventions need not reflect key constitutional provisions as interpreted by the Supreme Court, then there are no conventional constraints on such principles.[120] Taking fit seriously should entail creating a higher threshold of fit.

This argument casts doubt on Dworkin's contention that law as integrity is "more radical in circumstances like those in *Brown,* when the plaintiff succeeds in showing that an important part of what has been thought to be law is inconsistent with more fundamental principles necessary to justify law as a whole."[121] In *Brown* integrity is more radical. However, that is because integrity functions pragmatically in this case. Hercules ignores the fit requirement due to the existence of a morally compelling justificatory principle, but Dworkin leaves unexplained which moral or political principles he has in mind. If, as Dworkin insists, "[t]he integrity of a community's conception of justice demands that the moral principles necessary to justify the substance of its legislature's decision be recognized in the rest of the law," it would seem to follow that integrity requires that the substance of its judicial decisions also be recognized in the rest of law.[122] Consequently, one can fashion an argument in terms of integrity that the principle in *Plessy* be recognized in the rest of the law.

Pragmatism and Law as Integrity

Constitutional culture explicitly denigrates judicial activism as an illegitimate exercise in judicial power.[123] Similarly, Dworkin's explicit position rejects judicial activism partly because "[a]ctivism is a virulent form of legal pragmatism."[124] According to Dworkin's explicit position a pragmatist judge "would ignore the Constitution's text, the history of its enactment, prior decisions of the Supreme Court interpreting it, and long-standing traditions of our political culture."[125] However, it is simply false to insist that pragmatist judges must be oblivious to precedent, legal history, our political traditions, or even to the reflective convictions of our citizens. Pragmatism, like conventionalism and integrity, is concerned about fit and justification. Although Dworkin's explicit position seems to require that fit is always a serious requirement in constitutional interpretation, our discussion has shown that when Hercules decides revolutionary cases, fit may be constructively satisfied or just ignored.[126] For the pragmatist the relative importance of fit is determined by comparing the scope of a principle's fit with its attractiveness as a moral or political justification. Not *any* scheme of justificatory principles is a candidate for the justification of the American constitutional and political order. Our history will, of course, rule out such normative ideals as a theocracy or monarchy. Consequently, there is a minimal threshold that a justificatory scheme must satisfy. However, within the spectrum of principles taken seriously in American political life — from libertarian perspectives to democratic socialist ideals — any plausible normative ideal can become the best justification of our constitutional practice and hence should be the law of the land.[127]

A pragmatist theory of mistakes informs us that when an attractive justification of a constitutional practice declares the practice to be a mistake, the moral significance of the justification outweighs the deficiency in fit. In the presence of an extraordinary justification, the fit dimension of interpretation may have a value of zero. When we have an especially attractive normative principle, one that rectifies an existing constitutional abomination, we may endorse the new principle despite its poor fit with actual judicial practice. The newly decided foundational case then functions as a new paradigm according to which much preexisting law will be considered a mistake.[128] This process avoids the irrational insistence that a poor, but minimally satisfactory, explanation should be ruled out despite the fact that it is the best way to continue into the future, simply because it fails to satisfy some preconceived (and contestable) notion of what constitutes an appropriate fit.

A principle of law must show *some* "fit" or explanatory power if it is to be a candidate for the best justification of the practice, but in some cases this power may be very weak. There is no a priori threshold that must be met. Different conceptions of interpretation will interpret "fit" differently. Further, on pragmatist grounds, the notion of fit cannot be too powerful in precluding certain principles as candidates for best interpretation of constitutional practice. If it is too powerful, we do not take the future seriously enough. If it is too weak we do not take the past seriously. When the principle clearly appears the best way to continue into the future, then its lack of fit should not weigh heavily against it. Hence, the general rule is that fit and justification take on different values in different situations. Sometimes a justificatory principle must fit closely with past practice. Other times we require only a loose fit.[129] A strict lexical ordering of the relationship between fit and justification radically distorts the practice of judicial reasoning operative from almost the inception of the republic.[130]

In *Marbury v. Madison* Marshall conducted a constitutional revolution par excellence. Few of his arguments centered on fit. In 1803 there was little constitutional practice for his decision to fit. Instead, his argument is essentially structural, interpreting the role of the judiciary with regard to the other branches of government. On their face his arguments are not logically compelling. In postulating judicial review Marshall's decision sought to control majoritarian excesses concerning political and constitutional change. Understood in this way, Marshall's decision is pragmatic in the sense that he embraces poor explanatory principles whose normative superiority compensates for its poor fit. But it is difficult to see how law as integrity fits the constitutional practice of the fledgling republic. The U.S. Constitution represents, as far as possible, beginning a new story, not continuing an old one. Dworkin believes law as integrity explains *Marbury;* it does, but only if understood pragmatically.

Dworkin's argument is subject to the following general objection: A principle having a perfect fit will always be a better explanation than one whose fit is imperfect, but whose justification is superior. Consider the following argument. A perfect explanation is one that fits the relevant case decisions *and only those* decisions. An explanation can be a poor fit because its fit is too tight or too loose. A fit is too tight when it fails to explain the relevant cases; it is too loose when it explains the relevant cases but entails an additional judicial decision not yet encountered.[131] This presents Dworkin with the following problem. If a principle P1 explains decisions 1–5, and P2 explains decisions 1–5 but yields a new decision that is either explicitly rejected by the decisions in 1–5 or about which 1–5 are silent, then on the dimension of fit, P2 is a poorer fit than P1. In Dworkin's view P2 is more general than P1 and therefore may be a better justification of 1–5 than is P1. Consequently, anytime a principle is preferable to an alternative principle on moral or political grounds, it follows that it is a poorer fit than that alternative. This objection insists that it is precisely the normative feature of a principle that Dworkin exalts on the justificatory dimension — its greater generality — that renders that principle a poorer fit. Additionally, there are no adequate general rules for determining fit in advance. We do not know how to establish comparative fit. What if P1 explains five cases moderately well, and P2 explains three of those cases precisely, and two poorly? Which principle fits better? Fit by its very nature calls out for exactitude, and by its very nature eludes it. It's no answer to talk about fit in intuitionist terms. Such a conception of fit permits ideology to enter at the very beginning of the adjudicative process.[132] If justifications are fungible and two principles are equally good justifications, then a difference of fit certainly is relevant to our final choice of justificatory principles, but it is not dispositive. Justificatory principles, like good people, are in short supply, and consequently we should not arbitrarily restrict the domain of possible justification by appealing to a strong conception of fit.

Keep in mind that *Brown* not only revolutionized American social and political life, but more dramatically, it permanently changed the role of the federal courts. As a result of *Brown,* the role of judges in supervising deseg-regation decrees was greater both in "scale and detail" than in other cases.[133] How can we explain this significant change in the role of the courts? It seems to be inexplicable on Dworkin's theory, because it fits so poorly with past judicial practice. If Dworkin's explicit goal had not been to provide an alternative to constitutional pragmatism, law as integrity might have been charitably modified and recast as a pragmatist theory. In other words, law as integrity is an attractive theory of constitutional law. However, Dworkin's applications of his theory reveal its pragmatist dimension. Pragmatism takes stability, reliance, and the internalization of constitutional values se-riously. When these concerns are paramount, pragmatism counsels judges to adopt a more conventionalist approach. A pragmatist judge will even adopt a coherentist approach when appropriate. There is nothing duplic-itous in this. The switch occurs when the historical circumstances suggest that the fit-justification relationship should be modified. The only thing pragmatism fails to countenance is an a priori conception of this relation-ship and a requirement of more than a minimal fit.[134] Pragmatism, as an interpretive enterprise, is superior to law as integrity in providing the flex-ibility to deal with important cases pragmatically in a way that law as integ-rity, understood as requiring a strong fit requirement, cannot.

Consequently, constitutional pragmatism can encourage the growth of constitutional law in ways that law as integrity does not. Consider the entitlement cases, the call for economic democracy, and women's equal-ity.[135] Integrity, according to Dworkin, probably will not endorse strong progressive principles concerning these issues, because any interpretation having such progressive consequences would probably fail to fit actual case law and constitutional practice. According to constitutional pragmatism, a judicial decision having progressive consequences may be constitutional, despite its poor fit with constitutional practice.[136] If one believes that politi-cal morality is best understood as evolving toward a progressive principle, its poor fit would not be a reason to automatically disqualify it.[137] Because the constitutional pragmatist's primary concern is with the future develop-ment of law and justice, he will invoke this principle despite its poor fit. The pragmatist's reason for endorsing this principle is that it is the best principle for governing relations between employers and workers. The claim here is that we cannot disqualify a principle just because its fit is poor without first determining how good a justification it is. Only by comparing its poor fit with its justificatory role can we rationally decide whether to accept or to reject the principle.

Let's be clear on just what the argument is. I am saying that two people who agree that principle P is the best principle of justice may still differ on the best interpretation to invoke in a given situation. Someone stressing the fit dimension, as law as integrity is supposed to do, will rule out his own choice as the best principle if it does not adequately fit constitutional practice, whereas if he were a constitutional pragmatist, the fact that P is the best principle of abstract justice may compensate for the poor fit.[138] My point is that when there is a minimally good fit, it is irrational to disqualify your own candidate as the best interpretation simply because it does not provide as good a fit as some other principle. In this regard, law as integrity is irrational, whereas constitutional pragmatism is not.[139]

Right Answers in Hard Cases

The right answer thesis maintains that controversial constitutional questions have uniquely right answers. According to Dworkin, a constitutional proposition is true if "follows from the principles of justice, fairness, and procedural due process that provide the best constructive interpretation of the community's constitutional practice."[140] Dworkin counts as evidence of this thesis the phenomenological experience of being right in arguing about constitutional controversies such as abortion, affirmation, federalism, and so forth. But phenomenological experience is hardly conclusive; instead, this experience better lends itself to interpretation as a postmodern, pragmatist process that precludes collective right answers. The problem here is that law as integrity includes a protestant "conception of law and political obligation according to which each individual must ultimately discover for herself the community's principles" and their implications in novel circumstances.[141] Dworkin fails to realize that his protestantism invites disagreement at every level. If the protestantism associated with constitutional decision making is not mediated by some additional mechanism, a judge will have no way to "prove," or to rationally convince her fellow judges, to adopt her position. Further, Dworkin's protestant attitude is at odds with his own phenomenology of judging, concerning the judge's internal perspective. Dworkin's method may enable any judge to discover what she thinks is right in a particular situation, but it cannot validate this opinion across judges.

The standard response to the question of right answers in hard cases is that there are none, but constitutional reasoning nonetheless is capable of limiting the field by ruling out some solutions. In this view "[i]t [may be] enough to assume that the sets of acceptable answers, given by different rational individuals, will be relevantly similar. . . . [An] interpretation presented by Interpreter 1 is *true* if it is sufficiently similar to the rationally reworked interpretations other persons would present."[142] Hence, constitutional reasoning is valuable not because it determines a uniquely right answer, but rather because it detects implausible ones. Ultimately, we are left with different possible solutions, each having strengths and weaknesses, but none superior to the others. Dworkin inveighs against this view, contending that interpretive methodology yields right answers to most constitutional questions, irrespective of whether proof exists to persuade one's opponent. Truth does not entail proof. Thus, Dworkin denies the intelligibility or possibility of what he calls external skepticism.[143] An external skeptic accepts the reasoning within an enterprise, but then attacks that enterprise from the outside. Dworkin thinks it is silly to seek an external procedure for validating an enterprise. Such an external procedure does not show that the enterprise is objective or rational. Consequently, if you believe that there are some good constitutional arguments, it makes no sense then to question constitutional reasoning in general from an external point of view.[144]

Dworkin's argument against skepticism in law amounts to this: If one argues that there is no right answer, one's argument takes place either within the judicial enterprise or external to it. If the argument is within the enterprise, then it might be right, but that is because it assumes the very legitimacy it seeks to attack. It says, in other words, that there is no right answer in this case, but right answers must be possible in other cases. If the skeptic's argument, however, is external to constitutional practice, then his argument is a second-order claim about the philosophical standing of judicial claims. According to Dworkin, this second-order claim is somehow inappropriate. Often the external skeptic challenge involves questioning whether something is part of the fabric of the universe, or part of an independent existing reality, and so forth. Much of Dworkin's argument against external skepticism rests on his rightly pointing out the difficulty associated with these metaphors. Such metaphors may be unhelpful, but the skeptical challenge does not depend upon them. Instead, the skeptic wants a principle of ratiocination that validates — shows the reliability of — the chief principles of justification in a given domain of human inquiry. Why does Dworkin believe this principle is not required? Dworkin seeks escape from traditional philosophical quandaries. He argues that he doesn't understand what the terms "objective" or "objectively true" mean, other than that some fact exists or that some statement is true. So Dworkin denies that the question of objective truth is a real issue. Presumably, Dworkin would argue that the question of objective values is similarly not a real issue.[145]

How can we reject external skepticism in light of the separation of truth and proof? No doubt universal assent is not required for truth. However, shouldn't reasonable people in epistemically favorable circumstances embrace the same statement as true? Certainly, true statements should bring agreement among reasonable participants in a social practice. However, if qualified participants in a social practice systematically disagree over its implication, we have evidence that there's no single correct answer. It is difficult to see how there can be right answers when there are no principles of proof. Of course, Dworkin can agree with this; he can say the right answer is the one supported by the best argument. However if that's his view, he only replicates the problem of skepticism at the level of justification. If there is no way of determining that one argument is better than another, there is no way of determining in hard cases that one solution is the correct one. In short, if in principle there is no way of generating epistemic agreement over when an argument is better than another, what good is the better argument?[146] There are right answers to hard cases in law only if there are principles of reasoning that would convince an impartial, unbiased participant in epistemically favorable circumstances that one interpretation of constitutional practice is better than another.[147] Dworkin's theory conspicuously fails to achieve these results. Consequently, his theory of interpretation cannot support the claim that there are uniquely right answers to hard cases.[148]

Dworkin walks into the den of epistemological skepticism. If there are no reliable principles for demonstrating the truth of constitutional propositions, we cannot know that they are true, even if they are true. More important, even if Dworkin's contention that constitutional propositions can be true, though not susceptible to proof, is conceptually and epistemologically correct, it leaves constitutional reasoning and interpretation with a conspicuously embarrassing problem. The purpose of settling conflicts of law is to achieve a practical result.[149] It is designed to produce an answer that other constitutional actors endorse, or can be brought to endorse in the appropriate circumstances.[150] That there are true but unprovable constitutional solutions is not much help for a judge, attorney, or either the plaintiff or defendant. Constitutional law is therefore more concerned with praxis than with metaphysics.[151] If there are no principles of proof, then even if we concede that there are right answers, we must also conclude that we cannot discover uncontroversially what these principles are.[152] Or if we can discover them, we cannot persuade, in a principled manner, other citizens to accept them as true.[153] If so, what use is constitutional reasoning in the constitutional community? The concept of true but unprovable constitutional truths fails to fit actual constitutional practice, or to make it the best constitutional practice it can be.[154]

Nevertheless, Dworkin seems right to deny that truth does not entail proof. However, this slogan, like other slogans, is systematically ambiguous. It might refer to psychological persuasion or epistemic validation. Dworkin is certainly right that the former is not a condition of truth. It is unnecessary to *prove* a statement's truth to all challengers. A constraint requiring that the truth of the proposition "The earth is a sphere" (or, more accurately, the earth is an oblique spheroid) depends upon convincing members of the Flat Earth Society is too severe. Even when confronting Truth, there will always be disbelievers. However, Dworkin might also be advancing the curious position that a constitutional proposition is true even if agreement is impossible in principle. Because constitutional truth depends upon interpretation, and interpretation ultimately depends upon the particular judge's interpretive and substantive values, the phenomenological aspect of truth depends upon the judge's set of values. Unless some criterion for correct values exists, judicial decisions will reflect more about the judge than about the truth of the law. Given a diversity of values, intersubjective agreement among judges will be impossible. In this view uniquely right answers are possible only from the perspective of the individual practical reasoner or judge. For those not sharing the judge's particular values, no uniquely correct answer capable of being endorsed by each member of the judicial community is possible.[155]

Dworkin's argument rejects the intelligibility of external skepticism, but intersubjective agreement has little to do with skepticism. Dworkin's theory has nothing to say to judges who follow the strategy of fit and justification yet have incompatible answers because each judge's conception of fit and/ or justification differs from the other. This is not a skeptical challenge; rather, it simply reinstantiates the modernist commitment to foundationalist determinacy as one of the chief elements in rationality. We must, however, conclude that on that commitment Dworkin's conception of interpretation is plausible.[156] Dworkin's postmodernist pragmatism cannot be reconciled with his commitment to modernity.

Dworkin's interpretivism can be used to validate constitutional decisions only if each judge is required to hold the *same* explanatory and justificatory values, or if there are rules or principles to adjudicate between judicial decisions stemming from different explanatory and justificatory values.[157] If not, Dworkin's procedure assists an individual judge in discovering what he *believes* the correct decision to be, not what the correct decision *is* or what the reflective constitutional community is likely to endorse. In other words, Dworkin's theory tells us that the correct decision depends upon certain explanatory and justificatory values, not what the intersubjectively correct decision is. His discussion raises the issue of whether there are uniquely correct explanatory and justificatory values that then determine a uniquely correct judicial decision. Additionally, Dworkin fails to provide a way to take into account what other participants in the practice say.[158]

Dworkin also opposes substituting "reasonable" answer for "true" answer, because the same problems arise with the one reasonable answer thesis. The point of this substitution is at the very outset to make reasonableness an epistemological concept, not a conceptual one. Reasonableness focuses on what a practical reasoner may judge, not which judgment is true. Consequently, Dworkin's argument here is unconvincing. We can now understand better the confusion on the part of Dworkin and his critics in the controversy over the one right answer thesis. This thesis maintains that each judge will conclude her reasoning with one right answer. Assuming that constitutional language is relatively determinate for individual judges, each judge will be able to reason to one conclusion, so most answers are ruled out on every judge's list. Dworkin may correctly insist that one right answer always exists even in hard cases if that means that no judge will say "any answer you give is correct," whatever that means. On the other hand, Dworkin's critics are correct to argue that when we inspect the conclusions on the lists of several judges, each judge maintaining that her answer and her answer alone follows from the given premises, we will discover *different* answers on each list with no further way to adjudicate between or among them. From the perspective of this inspection, when we retreat from arguing the constitutional issue and reflect on the process of argumentation, there will be different answers. If a right answer is defined as one that follows from the given premises, then no right answer can be known collectively by the relevant judges. It is virtually inevitable that there will be more than one right answer across judges. In other words, among equally qualified judges, after they have considered all the evidence, no one answer will achieve consensus, because a judge's prior epistemic and practical commitments — permissible commitments, but ones that are not conditions of judicial rationality — inevitably differ. This reflective dissensus, or dissensus in epistemically favorable test conditions, should suggest that, despite an individual judge's phenomenological sense that only her answer is correct, no uniquely right answer exists.

In the next chapter I describe the theory of constitutional revolutions, which explains and justifies constitutional evolution and change. In this view constitutional revolutions — judicial revolutions nourished by the wider legal culture — drive the evolution and transformation of American constitutional law.

3   The Theory of Constitutional Revolutions

The theory of constitutional revolutions explains and justifies constitutional change by showing how judges, prompted by history and morality, are either faithful to constitutional practice or depart from that practice to begin again. When history prevails, a judge will engage in normal adjudication by appealing to such conventional authorities as constitutional text, intent, and history. However, when a judge perceives a constitutional crisis, she will attempt to resolve it by altering its future direction and even by abandoning it. This conception of adjudication proceeds according to Kuhn's structure of scientific revolutions. Kuhn's theory of science depends upon distinguishing between normal and revolutionary science.[1] However, because constitutional law is not science, my conception of constitutional change revises Kuhn's conception so that its relevance to constitutional adjudication is apparent.

Before I embark on the delineation of the theory of constitutional revolutions, it would be helpful to take stock of the conclusions of the last two chapters. Ackerman's dualism is best interpreted as a pragmatist theory of constitutional moments. His framework for constitutional investigation concentrates on how shifts in politics and culture cause shifts in the court, and vice versa.[2] Ackerman's theory is pragmatist or nonfoundationalist because it seeks the best explanation of constitutional practice. The resulting framework reveals American democracy to consist in normal and revolutionary *politics*. Whether this accurately depicts American political change, it fails to elucidate constitutional *judicial* change. His approach distorts the Court's role in changing American constitutional law. Knowledge of how a Court integrates normal and revolutionary adjudication contributes to its independent role in the American communitarian republic and provides an institutional mechanism through which the majority's first-order judgments can be evaluated in order to derive the community's or people's considered judgments.

Dworkin's coherentism reveals the analytic structure of constitutional adjudication. However, the entire structure sets strict limits on coherentism itself. Rather than constituting a third theory of law, integrity, understood properly, provides a pragmatist basis of constitutional law. By comparing the values of fit and justification, we observe a pragmatic method for understanding the development of constitutional law. Dworkin's pragmatism explains how judicial reasoning evaluates the role of history and morality in a given case. Its most striking postmodern feature is Dworkin's separation of truth and proof, precluding the possibility that creating a collective decision procedure for balancing these values is possible. Different judges will strike the balance in different ways. Dworkin's theory is a protestant conception permitting, at best, each interpreter to formulate her own interpretation of constitutional practice, but it cannot achieve reliable collective assent. If two interpreters agree after deliberation, they agree; if not, they don't. Dworkin concedes that values concerning fit and justification vary, and so, particular interpretations of fit and justification will inevitably vary unless there is a rational way to bring consensus on these values. Consequently, Dworkin fails to explain what a uniquely correct balance would be.[3] For Ackerman's and Dworkin's theories to be plausible, each theorist must take the pragmatist turn. I have suggested that implicitly both authors do so, Ackerman by formulating a theory of constitutional moments, and Dworkin by constructing a theory of judicial reasoning. My overarching goal is to present a theory that combines both types of theory.

American constitutional practice is pragmatist through and through. Although it is fair to say that the pragmatist nature of American constitutional adjudication does not provide a procedure for mechanically achieving collective assent, it does show why certain solutions are attractive and why others ought not to have currency in American constitutional law and culture. The pragmatist theory of constitutional revolutions is an interpretive description of the way courts and judges have actually transformed American constitutional law. It is a theory of what judges and courts actually do, rather than of what judges say they do or what academic lawyers say they should do. As I argue in a later chapter, this theory is a normatively attractive interpretation of the role of judicial review in the American communitarian republic.[4]

The Proper Role of Dualism in Constitutional Jurisprudence

The theory of constitutional revolutions is committed to an important general point concerning constitutional jurisprudence. It condemns all monist descriptive or normative theories — theories prescribing *one* method of constitutional interpretation — as being unfaithful to actual constitutional practice. If the theory of constitutional revolutions is correct, all other theories of constitutional interpretation are wrong. However, the theory does not reject a role for textualism, originalism, structuralism, or any other midlevel theoretical device. In fact it integrates these devices while explaining their appropriate place in constitutional change. What it rejects is the notion that any one of these paradigms or methodologies alone can provide an accurate theoretical account of American constitutional practice. Consequently, this more general feature of the theory remains true, even if my particular conception of judicial dualism is modified.

Judicial dualism depicts the process by which the American constitutional law develops and grows. It refers to the kinds of revisions courts make in constitutional law outside of article 5.[5] In principle these revisions provide not just a check on majoritarian choices but an explication and refinement of such choices. Any democracy concerned with more than a simple majoritarian form of government should embrace this role. Dualism should exist in any society desiring an independent, reflective judiciary, a meaningful constitutional practice, and a viable relationship between constitutionalism and culture. This reflective evaluation or "second-thought" is critical in formulating the community's considered judgments. It provides a deliberative method for filtering majoritarian preferences through a government structure designed to achieve the common good. No doubt such a process removed from majoritarian control risks countermajoritarian or even possibly antidemocratic results. Without such side constraints, however, we have no reason to believe that a given judgment is driven by anything more than the current fashion. Democracy cannot be equated with fashion. Instead, democracy must connect individual autonomy and dignity with collective self-government in a way that preserves both.

The theory of constitutional revolutions is a theory of *judicial* revolutions. It is a mistake to infer that the theory is unconcerned with revolutions that occur in the legislative or executive branches of government.[6] On the contrary, as Ackerman shows, what happens in these branches as well as in the society generally often has implications for constitutional jurisprudence. These implications can sometimes define a constitutional problem for judges, but they cannot resolve the problem. Judges must have a conception of constitutional methodology that translates the revolutionary politics of the greater society into workable judicial paradigms. Consequently, we must ascertain if our constitutional history suggests a uniquely American form of pragmatist constitutionalism, permitting the courts to integrate into the law political and cultural change. The theory of constitutional revolutions is just such a judicial theory. The theory rejects the conventional wisdom concerning constitutional change. According to this view, constitutional law is evolutionary: Each stage of development adds to the previous stage. Some versions of the conventional wisdom regard constitutional law as a coherent representation of an ideal constitutional democracy, which, though unattainable, guides our constitutional development.[7] The conventional view regards constitutional change as continuous; abrupt discontinuous change, in this view, is almost certain to be a mistake. Furthermore, such change is almost certainly illegitimate. According to this view constitutional change is evolutionary, just like history and knowledge generally.[8] In rejecting evolutionary change, the theory of constitutional revolutions is not abandoning theory or coherence. Rather, it seeks to describe how constitutional law abruptly changes, and how this revolutionary process is at the heart of American constitutionalism and the normal adjudication that dominates the everyday world of constitutional law.

The theory of constitutional revolutions is an attempt to interpret American constitutional practice as formulating a constitutional jurisprudence that integrates conventionalism, coherentism, pragmatism, and naturalism into one structured conception of constitutional change. In order to do this, the Court must incorporate the yet unannounced changed constitutional meanings occurring in the wider culture, especially, but not only, in political culture. Far from being formalistic or rule bound, the theory of constitutional revolutions takes seriously the notion that constitutional law is a mixed domain continuously altered by both internal and external factors. The Court has had the unenviable responsibility of recognizing and recording these changes by officially reinterpreting constitutional provisions to reflect this newly acquired meaning. The theory, therefore, rejects the conventional wisdom that law constrains and that final legal knowledge is possible.

The Classical Conception of Constitutional Adjudication

The conventional wisdom informs the classical conception of constitutional change, committed to the view that demonstrably correct judicial procedures exist for uniquely resolving all constitutional conflicts. This conception of constitutionalism typically insists that law is rationally grounded; that constitutional principles are intersubjectively valid; that constitutional conflicts have correct, determinate answers; and that constitutional law represents a domain of human practical reasoning that is sufficiently distinct from ethics and politics to be called autonomous.[9] In this view there exist neutral, objective, and coherent principles that express the meaning of explicit constitutional provisions.[10] The quest for neutrality and objectivity is a motive for seeking constitutional standards that are independent of the judge's personal values.[11] In this view a judge does not decide a case objectively when she reads her personal values into the law.[12] A judge should block out her own constitutional values in order to discover the correct constitutional principles.[13] These principles, according to the classical conception, can be produced by a unique form of reasoning concerning the text, intent, history, structure, or logic of the Constitution.[14] In principle this form of reasoning is capable of establishing *true* constitutional propositions.[15] The classical conception of law maintains that constitutional reasoning is not reducible to other modes of discourse such as politics, ethics, economics, or sociology.[16]

The question of whether there are uniquely correct answers to constitutional problems goes to the heart of the issue of legal objectivism and skepticism. It could be argued that if there are such answers to constitutional questions, constitutional theory avoids skepticism, and therefore shows itself to be an objective domain of inquiry. Here we must make an important distinction between metaphysical and epistemic skepticism. Metaphysical skepticism denies the possibility of providing a coherent definition of truth in law. Epistemic skepticism is weaker, maintaining that although we can provide a coherent definition of truth in law, we can never know whether a constitutional proposition is true. Suppose a constitutional proposition is true if it follows from the best abstract theory of politics. This definition resists metaphysical skepticism because it sanctions a coherent definition of truth. However, unless one can show which is the best abstract theory of politics, as well as in what sense the proposition "follows" from it, this definition of truth in law has little practical effect. In fact, conceptual truth independent of a collective method of establishing truth leaves a constitutional actor just as much in the dark as not possessing a conceptual definition at all. Epistemic skepticism, the belief that no intersubjective principles of argument exist guaranteed to convince, is sufficient to show that from a practical point of view, legal skepticism must be taken seriously.

In this case, although a person may know what it means to say that a constitutional proposition is true, she can never know when, or if, it is true, because she does not know which is the best abstract theory of politics.

The classical view rejects both metaphysical and epistemic skepticism. The classical view informs contemporary theorists and judges who believe that no change in the legal system is legitimate unless that system can explain its genesis. Of course, theorists committed to the classical conception attempt complex arguments showing how explanation works in this context. Often they describe changes as "creative," "discretionary," or the result of judicial brilliance. Rarely do they ever show how these terms differ from revolutionary adjudication. Nevertheless, adopting the classical view does not entail Langdellian formalism any more than repudiating it entails legal realism.[17] The classical view, however, has some of the same deficiencies as formalism. Both views obscure the dualistic dimension of constitutional adjudication. Similarly, both the classical view and formalism obscure the role that interpretation plays in legal theory.

The Interpretive Turn

Mainstream constitutional theory has taken the interpretive turn toward appreciating that meaning does not inhere in a text waiting to be discovered but instead is dependent in part upon the interpreter — her needs, interests, and circumstances and the interpretive community of which she is a member. A text's meaning is a function of the author's intent, its sentences, and the interpretive resources brought to the text by the reader. The reader's goal is to apprehend the text's point or meaning. In the case of a mature constitution, the interpreter must also apprehend the point of the judicial decisions interpreting the document. A clear, well-accepted interpretation of a foundational constitutional provision plays a special role in this process; until overruled, it represents the final word on the meaning of the provision and the relation between that provision and the rest of the legal system.[18]

The interpretive turn takes constitutional change seriously and therefore is conducive to the task of identifying constitutional revolutions. A revolutionary interpretation "is never *just* exposition of an existing principle; it is also a positing of the very principle it reads into the case law through the enunciation of the 'should be' inherent in the justification of principles."[19] Constitutional revolutions are statements of principle that do not, in any obvious manner, flow from the Constitution or Supreme Court decisions.[20] Constitutional revolutions are often (but not always) permissible constitutional results. Sometimes constitutional revolutions overturn past decisions or traditions in constitutional law. These decisions are pragmatic choices that are derived from principles of morality, culture, and politics, and ultimately from some conception of democracy.

As an interpretive theory, the theory of constitutional revolutions maintains that constitutional interpretation occurs in a constitutional interpretive community, consisting of judges, lawyers, scholars, and, most importantly, citizens. The scope and vibrancy of this community depend on what the constitutional culture encourages. The constitutional culture must extend to ordinary citizens who perhaps are unaware of technical constitutional law but who can participate in this community by becoming involved in political and social reform. More importantly, however, ordinary citizens are presently involved in this community when they argue about such great constitutional controversies of the day as affirmative action, abortion, gay and lesbian rights, and so forth.

The Constitution is the primary constitutional symbol in our constitutional scheme and therefore directs members of the constitutional interpretive community to appreciate its significance. Case law is a contemporary elucidation of this symbol. The role of judges, according to this theory, is to determine what the Constitution and constitutional practice imply for the resolution of a present controversy. When these symbols are inconclusive, the Court must interpret them through the wider political culture. Constitutional interpretation includes analyzing constitutional practice in terms of foundational constitutional decisions. A foundational constitutional decision is a Supreme Court decision concerning the meaning of a power-granting or rights-protecting provision of the Constitution, such as the necessary and proper clause, the free speech clause, or the equal protection clause. When interpreted, such a provision is foundational in the sense that it supplies the meaning of the relevant provision throughout constitutional law and beyond to law as a whole. These decisions also constitute the data upon which to test constitutional theories. Constitutional interpretation includes analyzing constitutional practice in terms of foundational constitutional decisions. Both the history and political attractiveness of a given constitutional provision determine its status as foundational, together with an assessment of its consequences throughout the legal system.[21] The great abstract provisions are foundational in two senses. First, their interpretation contributes to formulating the political morality of the Constitution. Second, their interpretations constrain every other relevant area of law. Together with the Constitution, foundational constitutional decisions constitute the key elements of constitutional practice. These decisions make up the Constitution's subtext. Any adequate constitutional theory must explain these elements.

The Pragmatist Turn

Pragmatism and interpretation are mutually supportive enterprises. Interpretation is a process through which pragmatist judges analyze, redefine, and create new constitutional meaning ultimately leading to new constitutional law. New law, however, is not the personal fancy of particular judges. Rather, a judge's decision must be based upon the actual constitutional landscape and an understanding of how her decisions contribute to helping the community reach for an improved, or ideal, future. A judge must look to various theories of this progression, theories that describe and explain prior law and provide a vision of its progression to the ideal, whatever that ideal might be. Her focus is on the Constitution and political and moral culture, not on what she personally values and believes. Yet even so there is no escaping that her decision is hers, even if it is compatible with current mainstream opinion. Nothing in law, if anywhere else, automatically commands assent. Conventionalist theories that implicitly seek not only to limit the discretion of judges, but also to reduce their anxiety, are chimeras. Decisions to assent typically escape our awareness; but they are usually present and retrievable. According to pragmatist constitutionalism, a judge evaluating evidentiary factors must evaluate them from her perspective, including her background beliefs and values, her convictions about political and constitutional meanings, and her abilities to reason successfully, but she focuses on what is true or reasonable. Those contemporary theorists who insist that judges "interpret," not "make," law succeed in taking the judge out of judging. True, some forms of assent may be more probable than others. However, every time a judge decides a case, it is the judge that chooses to make the decision, and to make it a particular way. Denying this is tantamount to autonomy-phobia. In a free society we are destined to be free.

Before further elaborating constitutional pragmatism, we should recognize the distinction between conventionalism and coherence theories of adjudication. Conventionalism maintains that whenever possible, a judge should decide a case by appealing to explicit constitutional paradigms. When there are no such paradigms, a conventionalist judge should use judicial discretion in deciding the case. Coherence theories maintain that judges should decide cases in terms of the explanatory and justificatory principles underlying the constitutional scheme. Nevertheless, constitutional constraints exist informing judicial reasoning, but they are contextual constraints and therefore less durable than conventionalist or logical constraints. Contextual constraints are derived from our participation in a constitutional interpretive community. Constraints on constitutional interpretation flow from this community. As such, an interpretation is precluded only if it has insufficient currency in that cultural interpretive community. It is a truism, of course, to say that the relevant community is the present one, but few, if any, communities are without context, history, and culture. So too in this case. The present constitutional community exists in a context of history and tradition. From our vantage point (the only one we can have) this tradition includes the recognition of the considered judgments of prior communities as relevant not only to the solution of a constitutional controversy, but, more importantly, as conceptual tools for framing the controversy in the first place. Both past and present communities ultimately look to the future of the polity and attempt to formulate principles, rules, decisions, and policies that contribute to the community's ability to cope with, and possibly flourish in, constitutional society.[22]

This turn of constitutional and legal theory toward pragmatism has profound implications. A pragmatist legal or constitutional theory maintains that judges, in deciding cases, should take into account constitutionally extrinsic factors from the wider culture. These factors often derive from a judicious exploration of constitutional history, contemporary constitutional culture, abstract ethics and politics, and social scientific studies.[23] The central element in American constitutional pragmatism requires judges to maintain a lively sense of how judicial decisions and constitutional principles contribute to what's best for the future of democracy. To develop and maintain this judicial sense, judges must have at least an inchoate conception of the kind of democracy that has emerged from American constitutional and political practice. Without this sense judicial decisions, as well as judicial philosophy, are likely to be aberrant.[24] (This does not mean that a judge must ignore precedent or consistency with the past.) In pragmatist constitutional theory, consistency with the past is one factor among others to weigh in the balance of a pragmatist calculus; however, it is never valuable for its own sake. A pragmatist judge is always concerned with the community's best interests. Pragmatism counsels judges to evaluate a constitutional decision in terms of how it contributes to bringing about this goal.[25] This is a striking advantage that pragmatist theories have over conventionalist theories; whereas the latter respect the past for its own sake, pragmatist theories respect the past as one important factor contributing to the future of the democracy.[26] In this regard pragmatist judges have more flexibility and can incorporate eclectically into a comprehensive conception of adjudication those valuable elements in other conceptions. This flexibility and eclecticism encourages judges to resist extremes in adjudication.[27]

Pragmatist judges insist that neither absolutism nor relativism is plausible, and consequently the challenge of postmodernity is to forge new theories of discourse without infecting them with either an absolutist or a relativist core. A pragmatist theory contends that constitutional meaning and value develop within a specific context or cultural tradition. By "cultural" I refer to those norms and attitudes of personal and collective conduct that are imbued in our social environment, and that represent public standards of behavior.

Any meaningful constitutional practice will exhibit or develop ways of dealing with crises, including filtering out those elements in the broader culture that can be co-opted for constitutional use. This process of looking to the broader culture revivifies constitutional text and practice. Although pragmatist judges must act in this manner, they do not necessarily need to apply pragmatism self-consciously to their reasoning and styles of adjudication. Pragmatism, as expressed in the theory of constitutional revolutions, needs to provide the best explanation of constitutional practice from the interpreter's perspective, however particular judges describe their reasoning. The question is whether the theory of constitutional revolutions provides greater understanding of constitutional moments and judicial reasoning than does conventionalist rhetoric, not whether judges self-consciously interpret their role in this fashion. If conventionalist rhetoric is a central feature of constitutional practice, then any description of such practice will be conventionalist in part. It does not follow that conventionalism is the best explanation of constitutional adjudication. Nor is it relevant how a particular judge understands his conduct, especially if important judges throughout American history have used the conventionalist rhetoric in revolutionary adjudication. In short, if we cannot make sense of their conduct without invoking revolutionary adjudication, it does not matter that they chose to use a conventionalist language in explaining constitutional change. In fact, one strength of the theory of constitutional revolutions is its capacity to explain how some uses of conventionalist rhetoric such as text, intent, structure, history, and logic make constitutional revolutions possible. Indeed, pragmatist judges perennially use these ostensibly conventionalist factors such as the Constitution, statutes, and case law to liberate society from the dead hand of the past.[28] Consequently, according to constitutional pragmatism, neither the Constitution nor case law *requires* constitutional revolutions. Instead, these decisions are derived from some source extrinsic to constitutional law.[29] Pragmatist choices are based on many factors. Common knowledge and economic theory are just two examples of such sources. Ordinary language, reason, and the collective conscience of humanity are other examples of factors leading to pragmatic choices. Ultimately, on the appropriate level of abstraction, pragmatist choices are influenced by moral and political considerations that can be systematized in interpretive theories of American constitutionalism.

Surprisingly, pragmatist constitutional theory exhibits a naturalistic dimension, but one that must be understood in pragmatist terms. Typically, naturalism is understood as virtually an absolutist theory that records eternal truths about the world and the universe. A weaker form of naturalism maintains that moral and political truths exist and can be validated by reasoning, though not perhaps in any absolute sense. In either case pragmatic naturalism appears oxymoronic. In my estimation traditional natural law theory had three fatal defects that pragmatism avoids. First, some versions of natural law had questionable ontological commitments. Second, natural law often failed to provide an adequate epistemological basis for legal theory. Finally, natural law theories are typically derived from a legally, morally, and politically conservative ideology. A pragmatist natural law theory claims that *new* "natural" rights emerge as a result of historical evolution, and is neither conservative nor necessarily epistemologically or ontologically inadequate.[30]

There is good reason to attempt the integration of pragmatism and naturalism. The operative theory of the Founding incorporated elements of naturalism.[31] The relevant naturalism involved the political and moral truths that people could discover in a deliberative setting, and that could historically develop over time throughout the culture. Consequently, a particular constitutional system or culture can generate truths that are not true independently of a social system, but are tied to the deep structure of a particular society. The Founders, as political and constitutional actors, were pragmatists, rejecting the notion that absolute truths exist, or if they exist, that they can be known absolutely. This implied the necessity of both reason and tolerance in public discourse.[32] However, because the Framers never conceptualized their theory in terms of pragmatist naturalism, the language or reasoning used to frame their questions differs from the language or reasoning we would now embrace to express their convictions. The important point here is that pragmatic naturalism reflects an American constitutional practice of discovering "natural" rights not yet recognized, or recognized only dimly, and that sometimes these rights should preempt precedent. Pragmatist naturalism insists that there are truths but rejects the claim that they are discoverable once and for all, or that the salience of the truths remains constant. When a pragmatist theory insists upon yet undiscovered natural rights, it represents a theory that is both pragmatist in its concern with the future and naturalistic in its concern with rights, the existence of which is completely dependent upon neither positive law nor moral factors completely removed from positive law. Instead, pragmatic naturalism suggests that, in any vibrant constitutional society, rights develop that are more than positive rights and less than full-blown universal rights.

Pragmatic naturalism acknowledges the possibility of two kinds of "natural" or nonconventional rights: absolute and dependent natural rights. Absolute natural rights exist independently of a particular system of positive law. Dependent natural rights arise through the process of a "living constitution," which integrates absolute natural rights and living political institutions and traditions.[33] Such rights are derived from particular constitutional and cultural circumstances but have not yet been declared to be positive law.[34] Pragmatic naturalism contends that basic dependent rights exist that depend in part on the fundamental principles of a particular political society. Examples of these rights in the American context include privacy or personal autonomy, equality of lifestyles, the importance of dissent, the centrality of religion in civic life and family values, among others. The dignity of the individual to flourish according to her own reflective life plans, in concert with other such individuals in collective self-government, is a basic, evolving, dependent natural right in the American communitarian republic.

A pragmatic naturalist might also endorse the view that once these rights are constructed, they become candidates for more permanent or universal

rights. Alternatively, their importance in reflecting the explanatory and justificatory principles underlying the positive law of a given society permits
them to be considered as part of an abstract moral and political system.
These rights develop contextually, but once they have developed and are
identified, their importance can, if desirable, transcend the particular culture in which the development took place. Pragmatic naturalists reject the
notion that rights always come top-down from universal theory. In denying
this possibility, pragmatic naturalism does not abandon universality entirely. Instead, universal principles might exist, but only after choosing the
best candidate for such a principle from principles arising in the interpretive
experience of given societies. Pragmatic naturalism is naturalistic in yet
another sense. It is concerned with human flourishing; it offers a pragmatist
strategy for understanding the concept of human nature and for applying it
to concrete social circumstances. Finally, pragmatic naturalism takes seriously the background conditions that render American constitutionalism
possible.

In pragmatist fashion the theory of constitutional revolutions rejects the
picture of linguistic or semantic determinacy that words, or their proposi-
tional content, somehow dictate or determine the meaning of a text. Even
when the constitutional text appears to yield just one answer to a specific
constitutional problem, there are other answers possible, given a change in
the needs and circumstances of the interpretive community. For example,
U.S. Constitution, art. 2, sec. 1, cl. 5, says that a president must be thirty-
five years of age. Dworkin argues that this requirement means thirty-five
years of age, and is not a proxy for sufficient maturity.[35] Dworkin's point is
that in this case the text prevails. Unlike abstract provisions, such as equal
protection or freedom of speech, this requirement is fixed and need not be
reconsidered. Unfortunately, this view fails to adhere to Dworkin's own
interpretive view that renders every interpretation relative to a set of historical facts, contemporary facts, and political theory. Given changes in context, a novel interpretation of the age requirement is possible.

Suppose after President Nixon resigned and President Ford assumed
office, it was revealed that President Ford was only thirty-four. President
Ford was an orphan, and perhaps his correct age was omitted through the
adoption process. In this situation must the Court disqualify him as ineligi-
ble for the presidency?[36] Or perhaps Ford should be disqualified and the
then Speaker of the House should be sworn in as president.[37] These are,
however, not the only alternatives. Instead, could one argue that the consti-

tutional provision concerning the age of the president does not apply to these unforeseeable circumstances? Or could one adopt a more general interpretation of the requirement, pace Dworkin, to refer to sufficient maturity at least in these circumstances? Thirty-five years was (roughly) equivalent to maturity then; now thirty might be. Or suppose an epidemic of unknown origins attacks all those thirty-five and over. Is there any doubt that some thirty-four-year-old would constitutionally serve as president at least until a suitable amendment was passed? The simple point is that constitutional provisions have both a constraining and a creative dimension. However, we cannot specify in advance what results these two dimensions will have in any given case.[38] Needs, interests, and circumstances will usually yield results, though perhaps never uniquely correct results.

For constitutional pragmatists embracing the theory of constitutional revolutions, the Constitution symbolizes different, sometimes incompatible, moral and political visions of the best society. Furthermore, it is always the present constitutional community that determines the meaning of a constitutional provision, even if the object of its gaze is the meaning given the provision by a past, even a hallowed past, constitutional community. Thus, even if past meanings are relevant to interpreting a constitutional provision (and such meanings always are), it is always the present interpretive community's interpretation of past meanings that controls. When we interpret the past, everything we identify as a factor, every principle we formulate, and every process required is filtered through our present conceptual scheme. There is no way to get to objective history except through a present filter that provides one possible (and useful?) way of making statements about the past.[39] To achieve a concrete result in interpreting the past, one assumes an epistemic framework whose legitimacy might simply be in its utility in achieving present goals. It is the text, the interpreter, and the interpreter's epistemic framework that determine the meaning of constitutional provisions. Unless critics can formulate one and only one epistemic framework that any rational observer must use in interpreting the past, we are left with a plurality of pasts, though probably a delimited plurality.[40]

The Constitution determines the parameters of the constitutional debate about what makes a good and just constitutional community. Determining the parameters of the debate need not entail determining the debate's content or its conclusions. In fact, the content or conclusions of the debate might need as a matter of logic, to be reconstituted with every passing generation.[41] When the Court chooses one set of principles, it is choosing between different visions of the good society. The Constitution represents a constraint on, or more accurately a guide for, judicial decisions. The Constitution's symbolic function merely rules out certain choices. However, within these loose constraints different theories of interpretation have generated very different conceptions of equality, due process, and liberty. Moreover, the Court's interpretations of the necessary and proper clause, the commerce clause, federalism, and separation of powers have been indispensable to the transformation of American constitutionalism. The Court has therefore emerged as a creative force supplying the Constitution with meaning.[42] In my terms the Court has, from its early beginnings, initiated constitutional revolutions.[43]

A constitutional revolution occurs when the Court pragmatically creates a formal or structural principle, or when it creates a substantive principle of constitutional adjudication.[44] For example, Marshall's foundational decisions concerning the Court's role in reviewing federal legislative acts and state judicial decisions represent articulations of formal constitutional principles.[45] The decision in *Brown v. Board of Education* represents a substantive principle. Both kinds of choices are pragmatic because they are designed to improve or fulfill our constitutional democracy. Pragmatic choices, interpretively understood, are valued for their effect on the polity. Pragmatist constitutional theory, therefore, necessarily includes a comparative or balancing mechanism, though it is neither necessarily utilitarian or consequentialist.

Constitutional pragmatism relies upon both intrinsic and extrinsic constitutional factors, including the text, the Framers' intent, and the history, structure, and logic of the Constitution. Where these conventional factors resolve a problem, the result is derived from something intrinsic to the Constitution, but often the solution of the problem depends upon a factor extrinsic to the Constitution. This factor could be a new cultural context, a further understanding of the concept behind a key constitutional provision, scientific discoveries, or simply the passage of time, whatever that means. Revolutionary adjudication certainly occurs in most cases of first impression. Any decision in such a case is revolutionary in the sense that the historical evidence underdetermines the result. In such circumstances history, morality, and politics integrate extrinsic factors into constitutional practice. These extrinsic factors comprise considerations derived from the wider political culture or from abstract ethical or political theory anchored by the most important extrinsic factor, the concept of democracy.

The Traditional Conception of Scientific Change

The theory of constitutional revolutions models itself after the late Thomas Kuhn's theory of scientific revolutions. Kuhn's theory of science is a theory about how scientific knowledge is transformed, whether it is rational, and what force it should have in the lives of scientists. Kuhn's theory is opposed to a certain traditional conception of scientific change. Similarly, the theory of constitutional revolutions rejects a traditional conception of constitutional law. The traditional conception of scientific change describes the cumulative growth in scientific knowledge. New scientific discoveries add to the prior body of scientific knowledge. In this view a scientific theory explains phenomena and reflects reality. If that theory is then discarded, it is due to its failure to explain all the relevant phenomena. Though discarded, it still supplies part of a story. A theory that replaces the first theory explains both what the first model explained and what it failed to explain. Scientific knowledge is therefore cumulative. Each successive theory provides information that increases scientific knowledge. Consequently, in the traditional view, science develops rationally because each change can be explained by reference to a prior theory. This process enables scientific knowledge to move closer and closer to a unified theory of reality.

Kuhn has argued persuasively that scientific development and change do not occur in this fashion.[46] Scientists, or the scientific community, acquire paradigms or models that determine the concepts, methodologies, and scientific laws in a given area of science. The paradigm functions as *the* model, exemplar, or "master theory," which is part of a "disciplinary matrix" employed by the scientific community in a particular scientific enterprise. In these circumstances scientists agree on the basic concepts and methods of their respective disciplines. As a result of this agreement concerning the scientific paradigm — a period called "normal science" — scientists are able to solve a myriad of problems defined by the paradigm. Within normal science progress *is* cumulative as scientists explore the nature of the paradigm.

Generally, in normal science, dissent over the foundations of the domain is legitimately suppressed. Scientists cannot accumulate knowledge when there is continuous debate as to the nature of the paradigm governing their scientific efforts. As long as normal science succeeds in solving problems within the confines of the paradigm, suppressing dissent is perfectly acceptable. A crisis occurs, however, when scientists are no longer able to make progress within normal science because they detect an unacceptably large number of anomalies between the model and the available data. Consequently, the model loses its explanatory capacity. In these circumstances dissent becomes possible and necessary. If the crisis cannot be overcome, a scientific revolution occurs, and a familiar paradigm is abandoned and replaced by another. According to Kuhn, the second paradigm is revolutionary; it cannot be explained by reference to the prior paradigm. In fact, sometimes the successive paradigms are completely incompatible. Surprisingly, a paradigm may not answer precisely the same question as its predecessor. Because paradigms do not always address the same problems, one paradigm cannot be explained as the rational outgrowth of a former paradigm. Scientific communities change paradigms for pragmatic reasons, that is, because the new paradigm is a better predictor, not necessarily because one paradigm is intrinsically, ideally, or rationally superior to its predecessor.

Constitutional Paradigms

Constitutional revolutions reflect a similar structure.[47] A revolutionary paradigm determines the meaning of a constitutional provision and its implications for adjudication. A constitutional paradigm contained in, for instance, the equal protection clause, encompasses the following features: First, the paradigm indicates the kind of facts capable of triggering adjudication. In equal protection adjudication a statutory classification is required to initiate the analysis. Second, the equal protection paradigm provides the standard of review to be employed — for example, rational basis scrutiny, intermediate level scrutiny, or strict scrutiny. Third, a constitutional paradigm determines the analytic structure, the procedure through which the standard of review translates the facts of the case to reach a conclusion. Fourth, the paradigm expresses the appropriate general rule of law and its application to the case before the court. And, finally, a constitutional paradigm determines the available remedies — for example, desegregation or compensatory hiring.[48] Summarizing, a constitutional paradigm is a complex set of instructions for conceptualizing and adjudicating constitutional controversies under a particular constitutional provision.

Constitutional paradigms are interpretations of foundational constitutional provisions. Like scientific paradigms, constitutional paradigms determine how a particular problem is to be conceptualized as well as what arguments and facts are relevant to disposing of the case. The concept of a constitutional paradigm is a powerful tool of adjudication, but it is nevertheless limited in scope. The more indeterminate the paradigm, the less likely it will achieve a reflective consensus over the applications or scope of the paradigm.[49] The equal protection clause again illustrates the operation of constitutional paradigms. According to the present equal protection paradigm, for example, the Court should engage in heightened scrutiny whenever a piece of legislation burdens a suspect classification or a fundamental right. In cases not involving suspect classifications or fundamental rights, the Court should, according to the present paradigm, defer to the legislature unless the law is irrational in the extreme. Although this basically describes the concept of equal protection, the present paradigm is slightly more complex. When a classification involves certain traits such as gender, an intermediate level of scrutiny is invoked. Some justices would like to see something like this middle level of judicial review replace the fundamental rights strand of the two-tier approach. If successful, this would involve a restructuring of the present constitutional paradigm and require a constitutional revolution.

The Court in *Plessy v. Ferguson* interprets the equal protection clause to contain a particular paradigm of equality. The *Plessy* paradigm first implies that a reasonableness standard will apply to race; no higher standard of review is necessary. It then states that if blacks and whites are physically separated into different train compartments, equality is met when the physical facilities are the same; equal protection can be satisfied even when the races are segregated. In other words, given its best reading, the holding in *Plessy* rested on the conviction that the equal protection clause was satisfied so long as both races were given access to equal physical accommodation on trains. The *Plessy* Court refused to constitutionalize the abstract ideal that separation is inherently unequal or the psychological stigma suffered by blacks as a result of segregation. According to the paradigm in *Plessy,* if the physical environment was the same, psychological stigma was constitutionally irrelevant to the question of equal protection.

Brown v. Board of Education amounted to a constitutional revolution overruling *Plessy.* It implies, though it had the conceptual resources to state, that a higher standard of review in race cases is applicable. The *Brown* paradigm, based on extensive if somewhat dubious social scientific evidence, states that in educational contexts racial segregation precludes equality of education. Under the old paradigm, equality in physical accommodations satisfied constitutional requirements. The new paradigm dispensed with the possibility of such proof in education, holding that segregation itself precludes equality. *Plessy*'s holding is formalistic, stating that equality is protected according to law narrowly conceived, whereas *Brown* repudiates this formalistic conception, at least in education, for a pragmatist change for the future. Together, *Brown* and several subsequent per curiam cases represent a broader constitutional paradigm concerning equality in public facilities. This broader paradigm stated that segregation in public facilities was intolerable. In issuing the decisions perfunctorily, the Court "obviously meant to teach that *Brown* was to be read broadly as a declaration of American policy that race relations will not be solved by apartheid."[50] Rather than formulate a broad antidiscrimination principle in *Brown*, the Court restricted its holding to the special circumstances of modern education. However, the Court subsequently proceeded to invalidate segregation in other public facilities, invoking *Brown* as authority. We have a choice here: Either the Court was duplicitous in the series of cases from *Brown* through the per curiam cases, or the new paradigm began to emerge pragmatically only after *Brown*. This complicates the new paradigm, and we are left with uncertainty concerning which jurisprudential theory adequately explains *Brown* and the new equal protection paradigm. Any adequate theory of constitutional change must explain *Brown*. Yet the facts concerning the development of the new paradigm in *Brown* suggest that a straightforward explanation is impossible.

The Theory of Constitutional Revolutions

The theory of constitutional revolutions provides a comprehensive account of constitutional adjudication.[51] It opposes any monist conception of constitutional change, or ones that deny the revolutionary character of constitutional change. Although the theory of constitutional revolutions distinguishes between the institutional roles of courts and legislatures, it rejects any constraining *dichotomy* between making and applying law. The theory further rejects the notion that constitutional law is objective in any nontrivial sense, or that constitutional adjudication operates with neutral principles. In this regard the theory of constitutional revolutions insists that we have sold ourselves an enormous myth about the operation of constitutional change, and though myths are not necessarily pernicious, this one is. It is pernicious because it blocks our capacity to understand the actual workings of our constitutional system and, instead, forces us to fight battles over methodology and legitimacy that none of the contestants can win.

Though the theory of constitutional revolutions does not reject procedural and institutional arguments out of hand, the theory's salient predilection is toward substantive, moral, and political arguments,[52] designed to win assent or, failing that, to understand why our substantive disagreements are unresolvable.[53]

The theory of constitutional revolutions distinguishes between two kinds of constitutional adjudication: normal and revolutionary adjudication. After this initial division, the theory then distinguishes from within each category different kinds of adjudication and constitutional change.

Normal Adjudication

Normal adjudication occurs when an area of constitutional law contains a well-defined constitutional paradigm, a set of instructions for settling particular kinds of constitutional conflicts. In these cases judicial actors appeal to the paradigm to resolve the conflict.[54] Normal adjudication occurs when a court confronts a minor question of law.[55] Here the Court, at most, fills in a minor gap in the law. In normal adjudication closing the gap does not alter the paradigm's basic character.[56] Normal adjudication also includes mechanical *applications* of constitutional paradigms.[57] When operating mechanically in normal adjudication, the case never gets litigated or, if it does, is treated summarily by the Court.[58]

Normal adjudication, like normal science, takes place within the context of a shared paradigm that members of the legal community use to define relevant facts, constitutional questions, appropriate analytic frameworks, arguments, conclusions, and remedies. The Constitution's text itself serves as a constitutional paradigm of varying degrees of generality. When normal adjudication is based on the text of the Constitution, the authority of the decision is apparent. When a constitutional argument rests on history, the historical account must be uncontroversial. For example, no one can dispute that the Framers of the Fourteenth Amendment intended the equal protection clause to protect blacks. Any interpretation of that clause that did not apply to blacks would be preposterous. When a constitutional provision's historical purpose is controversial, appealing to it is unpersuasive for that reason. One problem with originalism is that it often fails to provide such an unambiguous historical account.[59] Similarly, the structure and logic of the Constitution are useful in deciding constitutional issues when their implications are clear. When the implications are themselves controversial, these devices cannot settle the issue and instead condemn us to eternal controversy.

Normal adjudication functions by appealing to constitutional text, intent, history, structure, and logic. One can, of course, contend that all constitutional decisions are derived from one or more of these conventions. Not only is such a contention erroneous, but more importantly, constitutional scholarship demonstrates just how erroneous it is. Despite the objections to the reasoning in *Marbury v. Madison,* for example, constitutional theorists and scholars still regard it as good law. Surely something other than the decision's logic persuades scholars to endorse it. American constitutionalism looks to revolutionary adjudication to extend or retract the Constitution's reach. Constitutional law also seeks normal adjudication. Judges feel most comfortable when a constitutional paradigm explicitly resolves a problem. I doubt any legal system could operate with only normal adjudication; but American constitutionalism certainly could not. Pragmatist constitutionalism permits us to proceed with an explicit paradigm just until the paradigm can no longer resolve the problems it was designed to resolve.[60]

Revolutionary Adjudication

The context for revolutionary adjudication involves constitutional crises of varying degrees of magnitude. Constitutional revolutions, sometimes together with other factors, drive, determine, and extend the breadth and scope of constitutional meaning. They typically occur in the "context of social, economic, and ideological upheaval."[61] Courts design constitutional revolutions to resolve conflicts and to promote and control social change.[62] Constitutional revolutions occur when the Constitution fails to provide a readily accessible procedure for accommodating such change. More often than not constitutions fail to provide such procedures, creating the need for revolutionary adjudication. If a constitution did include clear and readily effective instructions for resolving conflicts, constitutional adjudication in this case might not be revolutionary. Problems, however, exist in making this the standard of constitutional construction. First, in interpreting a constitutional provision intended to resolve the conflict at hand, judges must embrace a particular conception of interpretation. This cannot preclude revolutionary interpretation without circularity. Second, and more importantly, Marshall's distinction between a constitution and a legal code in itself licenses and directs the areas in which constitutional revolutions should occur. In that sense, though particular constitutional revolutions are not implied by their constitutions, the *idea* of constitutional revolutions is the lifeblood of any morally and politically acceptable constitution. Any society taking morality and politics seriously sets the stage for revolutionary adjudication. Third, once revolutionary adjudication becomes an integral part of constitution practice, two factors make it impossible to abandon. The first factor regards revolutionary adjudication as a sign of the moral vitality of the constitutional scheme and considers it to have a structured, disciplined role in constitutional practice. By "a structured, disciplined role in constitutional practice," I mean a role that shows how revolutionary adjudication contributes to the solution of moral and political problems, as well as to the stability of the constitutional scheme. The theory of constitutional revolutions reveals the structure of revolutionary adjudication and normal adjudication. A constitutional scheme's capacity to select moral and political solutions to its problems from the larger culture, and then incorporate these solutions into conventional law, has obvious survival value for any constitutional system. The second factor indicates the conceptual impossibility of abandoning revolutionary adjudication once in place without engaging in revolutionary adjudication. Consequently, there is something inconsistent in calling for the end of revolutionary adjudication. Of course, it is conceptually possible to call for a revolution to end all future revolutions. However, it is difficult to see what apocalyptic vision could possibly justify this exhortation.[63]

Revolutionary adjudication explicitly embraces the judge's role of translating the wider political culture into constitutional law; these cultural factors are not contained in the law prior to the decision. Hence, prior decisions cannot explain constitutional revolutions. The terms "evolutionary," "transformative," and "landmark" fudge the issue of novelty. Constitutional revolutions break new ground or reverse prior decisions. In any case, a constitutional revolution is revolutionary because it neither follows from the Constitution itself through normal means, nor from the Constitution and any intrinsic constitutional background theory. If a constitutional result is possible only by appealing to such a theory, and if there exist a plurality of such theories, there exists no chance of demonstrating how judicial decisions follow the Constitution. Only by demonstrating the priority of a particular background theory can we succeed in demonstrating this. No such demonstration is available. Perhaps uniquely right answers to controversial questions exist, but it is highly unlikely that they will be discovered in time to save constitutional adjudication. To that end we might construct a reasonableness standard as the criterion for "following from the Constitution."[64] Would a reasonable participant in constitutional practice judge a decision to follow from the Constitution in circumstances epistemically favorable to a reasoned, informed, unbiased decision? However, it is certain that this standard would not yield a uniquely correct result to most constitutional controversies, and, therefore, it could not obviate the need for revolutionary adjudication.

The point is not that dissensus in constitutional arguments entails revolutionary adjudication. However, when the best legal minds throughout American history are unable to describe an incontestable method of adjudication, and when these minds examine and reject the best candidates for "following from the Constitution" or "following from precedent," it is difficult to accept the notion that some workable consensus exists for showing how "revolutionary" decisions really follow from the Constitution or from precedent after all. This does not deny that some adjudication meets these conditions. My point is that once we identify normal adjudication as inhering in a constitutional or judicial text, we discover that it is impossible to explain the entire range of American constitutional law as a result of normal adjudication. The additional explanatory factor required is the idea of constitutional revolutions.

Constitutional revolutions, when justified, are decisions based ultimately on a pragmatic assessment that the decision makes our constitutional democracy better, all things considered. When a constitutional revolution occurs, for example, in free speech cases, adjudication in that area reflects a new model for deciding controversial cases. Once the revolution is completed, constitutional adjudication in that area becomes normal. In normal adjudication the new constitutional paradigm provides the precedental authority for deciding cases in that area. The new paradigm provides answers to such questions as which facts raise relevant constitutional issues, what standard of review is appropriate, upon whom does the burden lie, and which facts will be dispositive. Normal adjudication generates decisions that, although not self-evident, are readily seen by members of the litigating community as flowing from the paradigm. At times the precise nature of the revolutionary paradigm achieves no consensus, and adjudication in that area cannot be stabilized.

In constitutional adjudication revolutions deal mostly in particular conceptions of an abstract concept. In the case of equality, say, the textual provisions and structural features of the Constitution ultimately converge on the equal protection clause. This clause, however, constitutionalizes workable judicial paradigm making and adjudication only trivially. True, equality is the value, and not domination or hierarchy. Yet, within the confines of the abstract value of equality, many different conceptions compete for the title "the Constitution's idea of equality." Because the same abstract conception of equality can accommodate these competing conceptions, when a court changes, revises, or abandons one conception for another, it does so through revolutionary adjudication. This is the paradigm for resolving many equal protection cases and, therefore, a means of fighting injustice in American culture. Justices do not simply make up completely new concepts. Rather, the kinds of concepts they employ are pretty well fixed by constitutional text. However, within that framework justices are free to alter and revise the contemporary meaning of a constitutional provision if doing so has sufficient pragmatic benefits. That's what a careful examination of some of the important periods in American constitutional practice reveals.

Revolutionary adjudication consists of three phases: prerevolutionary, revolutionary proper, and postrevolutionary adjudication. Prerevolutionary adjudication occurs when some member of the constitutional community becomes disenchanted with the reigning constitutional paradigm. This disenchantment may express itself through a social movement, or merely through the efforts of independent judges trying to normalize (or keep normal) a particular area of constitutional law. The revolutionary process often begins through a series of cases that begin to question the prevailing paradigm and sometimes identify replacement norms existing in the wider political culture. These cases are precursors to revolution because, though containing the seeds of change, the Court refrains from departing from precedent. Precursors are cases that try to repair the defect in the current paradigm by delicately altering the paradigm.[65] Sometimes the precursors indirectly quash the crisis and normal adjudication can be revived. Other times only revolutionary adjudication proper can deal with the crisis.[66] The civil rights decisions in the late forties and early fifties illustrate this notion. None of the cases repudiated *Plessy*, though several questioned its legitimacy. Finally, in the fifties, *Brown* and the per curiam decisions in effect overturned *Plessy*. Indeed, the seeds of the revolution in *Brown* were evidenced by two lines of cases. In 1944 the Court adopted the strict scrutiny strand of equal protection analysis, making classifications based on racial characteristics "immediately suspect." If no "pressing public necessity" could justify the classifications, it had to be struck down. The Court finally made it clear that racial antagonism could not justify a statute that classified individuals according to race.[67]

This strict scrutiny strand of equal protection analysis was a precursor to the principle in *Brown;* yet, astonishingly, it is not mentioned in *Brown.* The cases mentioned in *Brown* were cases in which the *Plessy* doctrine was upheld, but integration was ordered due to unequal facilities. These cases indicate the uneasiness the Court felt at this time with the doctrine in *Plessy.* Precursors to revolutionary decisions come in different forms. The difference between *Korematsu v. United States* and the cases upholding *Plessy* consists of this: The cases upholding *Plessy* were not revolutionary in themselves. Instead, they were harbingers of a revolutionary decision. *Korematsu,* on the other hand, was a revolutionary decision in itself, laying the groundwork for an even more significant revolution. The revolution in *Brown,* combined with the revolutionary *Korematsu* decision and the per curiam decisions after *Brown,* represent a total rejection of the separate but equal doctrine. Subsequently, the *Brown* revolution was extended from the segregation of public facilities to public associational values generally.

Revolutionary adjudication proper involves decisions that cannot be explained by reference to ordinary constitutional conventions, such as constitutional text, the intentions of the Framers, the structure, logic, or history of the Constitution. Instead, through revolutionary adjudication, political meaning and value that develop in the wider community are given constitutional significance by the Court. American constitutionalism has always relied upon revolutionary adjudication in interpreting the Constitution.[68] The formative revolutions, *Marbury v. Madison,*[69] *Martin v. Hunter's Lessee,*[70] *McCulloch v. Maryland,*[71] and *Gibbons v. Ogden,*[72] gave content to the structure of the American government.[73] The Civil War amendments, though arguably derived through normal politics, throughout their history were interpreted in revolutionary terms.[74] The New Deal revolution transformed the content of the Fourteenth Amendment's due process and equal protection clauses as applied to economic regulations; it also continued to centralize power and authority in the federal government. The Civil Rights revolution similarly, in fact if not in theory, reversed the apartheid conception of equal protection enunciated in *Plessy v. Ferguson.*[75] Later the privacy cases recognized additional fundamental rights as well as revolutionized our conception of constitutional methodology.

After revolutionary adjudication proper, a postrevolutionary stage occurs with the task of *refining, perfecting,* and *stabilizing* the new constitutional paradigm in order to permit normal adjudication in that area of law. The privacy cases following *Griswold*[76] clearly exemplify the postrevolutionary phase of constitutional adjudication.[77] Revolutions can continue without limitation. They can occur in an orderly fashion or engender incoherence, and the revolutionary paradigm must be spelled out to make its content and scope explicit. In this phase the Court appeals to the newly minted paradigm while deploying contemporary cultural values to explicate the paradigm fully. Of course, this does not entail that *Griswold* was rightly decided. Indeed, an argument against *Griswold,* according to the theory of constitutional revolutions, might be that the privacy paradigm is so amorphous that it cannot be normalized. When the paradigm is inadequate in this way, refining, perfecting, and stabilizing it in order to achieve normal adjudication is thwarted. However, this argument is different from an originalist argument appealing to the countermajoritarian dimension of such review. Countermajoritarianism is not the problem; rather, the problem, if there is one, arises from an inadequate paradigm. This does not, of course, settle the issue of *Griswold.* Instead, it shows how the framework for competing positions arises in the language of the theory of constitutional revolutions.

Constitutional revolutions are integrally related to constitutional crises. Constitutional crises occur for a variety of reasons, among which are: (1) cases of first impression for which no constitutional paradigm exists except the constitutional text; (2) cases such as *Brown,* in which the existing paradigm no longer resolves the social conflict in a fashion congruent with society's cultural values; (3) cases in which the evolution of one paradigm brings it into conflict with another existing paradigm, such as when legislation passed under the commerce clause conflicts with the states' police powers under federalism; (4) cases that render a constitutional provision ineffective, such as the *Slaughterhouse* cases; and (5) cases that define systematically indeterminate provisions.

A society's critical cultural convictions can then be seen as a foundation for, and a test of, the evolution of constitutional doctrine. Indeed, a theory of these convictions represents a background theory that suggests changes in constitutional law. Unfortunately, no method exists to prove which critical cultural background theory, if any, is the substantive theory of American constitutional practice. Instead, different constitutional actors have different critical cultural convictions, which courts will appeal to in crises through revolutionary adjudication. Within the confines of a stabilized paradigm, these convictions may be appealed to only in exceptional circumstances, if at all. One need not ask whether a case, clearly resolvable in terms of the paradigm, is consistent with the society's critical cultural convictions. One asks only whether the case conforms to the constitutional paradigm. However, this is only one possible outcome. When a number of these cases are decided according to the paradigm, but still conflict with common sense or the society's critical cultural theory, it is because the critical cultural perspective has changed. In such circumstances a conscious shift in the paradigm's meaning is appropriate. When a constitutional paradigm no longer resolves the problems and conflicts it was designed to resolve, normal adjudication breaks down. When a crisis brews in constitutional law, the first thing courts try to do is quash or defuse it. This reflects a perfectly natural prudence not to alter the present course unless it is necessary. In constitutional law this prudence often and legitimately succumbs to the necessity of dealing with crisis. In these circumstances judges and practitioners face a crisis, and, consequently, judges should consider engaging in revolutionary adjudication.[78]

American constitutionalism clearly rejects the possibility of constructing a constitution with "the prolixity of a legal code."[79] If it did, the constitution "could scarcely be embraced by the human mind."[80] Instead, American constitutionalism "requires only that [the Constitution's] great outlines [be] marked."[81] Marshall's remarks suggest that the very idea of American constitutionalism entails the necessity of revolutionary adjudication. The more general these great outlines are, the more indeterminate their meaning. In such cases constitutional adjudication favors revolution.

The theory of constitutional revolutions opposes any conception of constitutional change that denies the creative role of judges in making constitutional law. Although the theory of constitutional revolutions distinguishes between the institutional roles of courts and legislatures, it draws the distinction between interpreting and making law very differently from the classical conception. According to the theory of constitutional revolutions, revolutionary adjudication is making law. Typically, judges do not survey the political culture to determine which problems need fixing or when; they do not initiate cases or have comprehensive programs of political change.

Judges must self-consciously interpret the Constitution and apply it to the present case, whereas legislators are concerned with the nation's policy needs and may leave the Constitution to the Court.[82] Most important, judges are concerned with the form of law, whether the required necessary conditions for its validity exist, whereas legislators are more concerned with the law's substantive content. This is a distinction, not a dichotomy exhaustively characterizing the difference between courts and legislatures. Both branches *make* law, one by interpretation, the other by deliberation. The point here is only that the different ways courts and legislatures make law preserves the important distinction between the two different roles.

A constitutional revolution is a judicial decision establishing a paradigm or model for disposing of constitutional cases in that area of law. Once a revolution occurs, the Court must then attempt to refine and perfect the revolution so that the paradigm extends to every similar case. Sometimes the paradigm entails a set of rights conflicting with another set of rights. In such cases the Court must find some criteria to determine whose rights prevail. This does not necessarily entail a simple balancing procedure. It might be that one set of rights, according to the paradigm, is significantly more important than the other. Consequently, the paradigm might explain why and how rights in these circumstances must be lexically ordered.

Sometimes the creation of a paradigm does not settle every problem in that area. In *Brown* the foundational paradigm for equal protection enunciated in *Plessy* was effectively overturned. Racial segregation was no longer consistent with the newly minted equal protection paradigm. Two questions immediately arise. The first question centers on whether invidious discrimination is constitutionally invalid only in cases involving *racial* discrimination. When the Court proceeds beyond racial discrimination, it alters the paradigm and extends the revolutions. In such cases the revolution is not complete until the law becomes settled in the equal protection area. The second question involves remedies. Do certain kinds of remedies, such as affirmative action, follow from the new paradigm, or does such a proposed remedy itself violate the paradigm? Until the appropriate remedies are determined, the revolution is incomplete. A remedy itself might be revolutionary relative to what is thought possible concerning remedies in that area. The central concern during the period in which the paradigm is perfected and refined is coherence with the paradigm. Coherentism does not merely appeal to the paradigm as a precedent. Instead, it attempts to create general principles that adequately state the essential values embodied in the paradigm. The logical limits of a paradigm might not be obvious until the paradigm is perfected and refined. The precise nature of the paradigm's values is not revealed until the logical limits of the paradigm are determined.

Dworkin's theory, law as integrity, contends that a constitutional decision must closely fit the constitutional paradigm. When two possible decisions fit the paradigm, we should choose the one that provides the best interpretation of the constitutional practice from the point of view of the community's moral and political convictions. Cultural, moral, and political considerations enter into this process only insofar as they help identify the legal paradigm decided in the revolutionary moment. Furthermore, these considerations are relevant only when there are two or more possible decisions consistent with the revolutionary paradigm. When only one decision exists that is consistent with the paradigm, normal adjudication becomes routine, adopting a narrowly conventionalist approach to constitutional law. Normal adjudication, including routine applications of the law, is more generously conventionalist, whereas revolutionary adjudication proper is clearly pragmatist, seeking the wider culture for answers to constitutional conflicts.

Postrevolutionary adjudication represents a hybrid jurisprudential basis for adjudication. When courts attempt to refine and perfect a revolution, they typically elucidate the new paradigm in pragmatist terms, keeping a conventionalist eye on whether the newly developing case law is consistent with the recently constructed paradigm and not creating a new one. Once the revolutionary paradigm has been refined and perfected, the Court begins to stabilize the paradigm. Court decisions begin to deny explicitly the extension of the paradigm. Sometimes this occurs when lower courts fail to extend the paradigm and the Supreme Court denies certiorari. Other times the Court will take the case in order to prevent the extension of the paradigm. Once the Court responds in either of these ways, the paradigm is completed and the revolution is stabilized. One example of this process is the stabilization of the right to privacy in *Hardwick*, where the Court stabilized the privacy paradigm by denying the extension of the right to include homosexual sodomy. Describing the Court as establishing a paradigm has two senses. The first sense merely refers to the fact that the Court, right or wrong, refuses to extend the paradigm. The second sense is normative, claiming that the Court should or should not extend the paradigm. The furor over the result in *Hardwick* results from the normative judgment that the right to privacy should not be limited to heterosexual contexts. Stabilizing a revolution requires insight and technique. Conceivably, perfecting the revolution could conflict with the revolution's stabilization. In *Hardwick* the normative instability of the revolutionary paradigm consists in its perceived arbitrariness of the Court's decision in this case. On the other hand, if the citizenry is totally opposed to an extension of the revolutionary paradigm, its extension could also be unstable. For example, in *Casey* the privacy right is stabilized, ending, for now at least, the question of the constitutionality of abortion. Without the public's concurrence, however, it is not obvious that the revolution will remain stable.

Background Theories of Constitutional Change

Judicial decisions in principle appeal to three different kinds of constitutional background theories, according to which the decision follows in both normal and revolutionary adjudication. The first kind of theory, an intrinsic theory, is a moral and political theory of actual constitutional practice—call it "the relativized constitutional background theory," or "the relativized theory," for short. This first type of theory systematizes and generalizes the particular foundational constitutional decisions in *our* constitutional scheme. Consequently, if the equal protection clause rejects segregation, and no other foundational provisions permit segregation, then this constitutional background theory must similarly reject segregation. In that respect the constitutional background theory is relativized to a particular context and constitutional practice.

The other two theories are extrinsic, since they include principles and factors not necessarily contained in constitutional practice. The first such extrinsic theory is a critical cultural theory of American constitutionalism. This theory, or perhaps more accurately, this narrative, contains a critical account of our constitutional culture, a critical account of those deep constitutional values that structure our culture.[83] The critical cultural theory must include much of the constitutional values contained in the Constitution and constitutional practice, but it can, and should, go beyond this practice. Consequently, the critical cultural theory need not be equivalent to the relativized theory. When someone argues for some proposed constitutional right to health care or welfare or education, she appeals to a critical theory of American constitutional culture—of what this culture entails. Such rights may or may not be contained explicitly in the relativized theory.

The second extrinsic background theory is an abstract moral and political theory. This theory ideally explains and justifies the principles contained in constitutional practice, but in practice is more concerned with justification than explanation. Whereas the relativized constitutional background theory, the critical cultural theory, and the abstract moral and political theory each contains a theory of mistakes, the abstract moral and political theory permits the theory of mistakes to have the greatest latitude.[84] This should not be surprising, as the abstract theory more closely approximates the ideal theory than either the critical cultural or relativized theories.

The term "relativized constitutional theory" should be understood as denoting a blue collar theory of principles implied by the Constitution or by foundational constitutional decisions.[85] This theory is narrowly interpreted *relative* to our constitutional practice, not to constitutional practice abstractly conceived. The principle of judicial review in *Marbury v. Madison* is a relativized constitutional principle as that term is defined in this book.[86] Similarly, the general right of privacy created in *Griswold v. Connecticut* is now a principle contained in our relativized constitutional theory. Relativized constitutional theories must reflect the foundational constitutional provisions in the particular constitution they explain. For example, if a constitution includes an implied notion of equality that does not permit segregation, then the relativized constitutional theory explaining that constitution cannot permit segregation. The Supreme Court determines the meaning of foundational constitutional provisions. Consequently, the relativized constitutional theory must explain foundational constitutional decisions. The difference between a relativized constitutional theory and a list of actual constitutional decisions is that the former systematizes the latter, and in some cases its principles are more general than the actual constitutional decisions. Such a relativized theory is committed to a rigorous threshold of fit with constitutional practice. Conventionalist constitutional theories are generally relativized theories because they are more concerned with explaining legal decisions than with constructing justifications of the legal system.

Critical cultural theories include principles that reasonable citizens in a given society would embrace, irrespective of whether such principles have been declared to be law.[87] Identifying these principles may be controversial, but the important point here is that critical cultural principles are those that a reflective citizen believes best explain and justify our political culture, including constitutional law.[88] A critical cultural theory includes a relativized theory, but holds that factors from the former can be integrated with the latter to change constitutional law. For example, most Americans would probably now agree that an individual is entitled to be free from official state-imposed segregation. With a few notable exceptions I believe this principle, or one very much like it, would be accepted by most Americans regardless of political persuasion except perhaps members of white supremacy groups. Furthermore, such a principle must *now* be included in our relativized constitutional theory. It does not follow, of course, that there was a consensus about any such principle prior to *Brown,* or that the relativized constitutional theory at that time contained such a principle. However, Dworkin argues, "It seems plain that the Constitution mandates some individual right not to be the victim of official, state-imposed racial discrimination."[89] But if *Plessy* controlled the meaning of the equal protection clause and therefore the meaning of equal protection in the relativized theory, the Constitution, properly understood as taking practice seriously, cannot mandate such a right.[90] Indeed, the civil rights revolution changed the meaning of the Constitution properly understood.[91]

Political culture is in harmony with the Constitution when the relativized constitutional theory is consistent both with constitutional practice and the critical cultural theory. However, this is not always the case. The civil rights movement was predicated on the conviction that constitutional practice was inconsistent with our critical cultural theory, as well as with abstract moral and political theory. Therefore, constitutional practice had to be altered. Historically, the critical cultural theory may conflict with the relativized constitutional theory. For instance, the relativized constitutional theory permits abortion. Antiabortion advocates contend, probably incorrectly, that most reflective people abhor abortion in most circumstances.[92] If they are right, we can describe this in terms of the different background theories. Abortion foes insist that a sharp break exists between the relativized constitutional theory — protecting abortion — and the critical cultural theory — opposing it. Often a constitutional crisis occurs when critical cultural principles find no obvious place within constitutional practice. Sometimes the relativized theory *and* the critical cultural theory imply one decision, while abstract moral and political theories imply a contrary decision.[93] When this type of conflict occurs between the relativized and critical cultural theories on the one hand, and abstract theories on the other, the citizenry must abandon the conviction that these principles should be law, or the Court must interpret the Constitution to include these controversial principles. When it does so, the relativized constitutional theory then contains the same principle as the critical cultural theory or the abstract theory. The emergence of *Brown v. Board of Education* is a good example of this process.[94] Prior to *Brown, Plessy v. Ferguson* controlled constitutional practice; thus, the *Plessy* interpretation of equal protection was contained in the relativized constitutional theory.[95] Though constitutional practice followed the rule of separate but equal treatment, many people began to question the compatibility of equality and segregation.[96] Ultimately, the Court effected a constitutional and social revolution, which would permanently alter our conception of equality and racial justice. This illustrates how newly acquired cultural values become integrated into constitutional law by radically reforming the judicial paradigms the law contains.

This pragmatic process functions in constitutional theory by eschewing mechanical methods for determining how closely a principle must fit our considered constitutional values. There are no a priori answers to the question of how we decide a case when precedent and normative attractiveness collide. What we must do is evaluate the precedent's comparative value against the value of the novel principle and decide which is more important in a given case. In effect, we seek a fit between a set of moral principles and our considered judgments; but we seek this fit not only with out considered judgments but with the considered constitutional judgments from every quarter of society. In other words, we seek a *wide* reflective equilibrium.[97] Our decisions, in cases of conflict of this type, are influenced by a moral and political theory and by the broadest possible spectrum of evidentiary factors.

The Theory of Judicial Reasoning

The theory of constitutional revolutions integrates external and internal constitutional perspectives. Viewed from an external perspective, the theory of constitutional revolutions is a theory of constitutional moments, an interpretation of how courts transform American constitutional law. Viewed from the internal perspective, the theory of constitutional revolutions is a theory of judicial reasoning, delineating the actual processes judges use when deciding the cases. So far our discussion is limited to a theory of constitutional moments or how courts transform American constitutional law. The second component, a theory of judicial reasoning, describes how judges decide cases. In joining the theory of constitutional moments and the theory of judicial reasoning, the theory of constitutional revolutions becomes a syncretic conception of pragmatist constitutionalism.[98]

Wide Reflective Equilibrium and Constitutional Change

Judicial reasoning is a species of wide reflective equilibrium.[99] Wide reflective equilibrium is a pragmatic process through which we reflect on our considered constitutional values, which function as rudimentary, atheoretical beliefs about constitutional propriety. Reflection enables us to achieve a less idiosyncratic perspective so that we can fully evaluate our beliefs and values. This perspective is more general, enabling us to evaluate our considered constitutional values, which contributes to the fallibilist's goal that is the hallmark of pragmatist constitutionalism. This pragmatic process helps us criticize and correct our constitutional intuitions, retaining those values or principles that have the best pragmatic result.[100] Some people engage in these practices intuitively; other people need to reflect on the process in order to learn how to "engage in these practices intuitively." The goal here is not to discover an "otherworldly" perspective, independent of our own, but rather to create a new perspective for evaluating our constitutional values, *which becomes our own*. Certainly, this new perspective is a perspective *in the world*. However, it is not *just another perspective*. It is a pragmatist perspective that is more likely than other perspectives to result in defensible judgments.[101] When we achieve this perspective, we then consider various principles and theories whose job is to provide a rationale for our considered constitutional values.

When a person holds her considered values and her constitutional theory in wide reflective equilibrium, no further correction exists that will render an alternative theory superior to the one she presently embraces. Hence, she can then use the theory to resolve constitutional conflicts.[102] This perspective helps us achieve a balance between one's constitutional intuitions and more generalized principles or theories. Where no balance is possible, the perspective helps us explain why values in one case, or theory in another, are held so clearly as to preclude achieving equilibrium. Of course, neither one's considered values nor one's theory is ever fixed or closed. Rather, both values and theories can be stabilized only temporarily in order to achieve equilibrium. Wide reflective equilibrium is in part an answer to the question of what to do when one's values and theories collide. When connotational values conflict with theories of constitutional law, the conventionalist rejects the theory. The naturalist resolves such conflicts by embracing theory. The pragmatism associated with the theory of constitutional revolutions admonishes us not to embrace either alternative a priori. Rather, constitutional pragmatism recognizes that in cases of conflict, sometimes values should prevail, whereas at other times, theory should. This flexibility, which distinguishes wide reflective equilibrium, is the underlying condition of constitutional pragmatism.

Imagine a constitutional scheme consisting of concentric circles, each circle representing principles derived from reflective values. The more central a principle is, the less likely we will abandon it in favor of a theory. On the other hand, if a particular theory helps us systematize and order this conceptual scheme, if it has significant explanatory power, even a central principle may be abandoned. Based on this view, no principle is immune from revision; none must be retained at all costs. We can even abandon well-entrenched moral principles, though we cannot do it all at once. On the other hand, principles contained in a constitutional theory must be tested, in part, by determining how well they preserve the plausibility of more central values. Without anchoring constitutional theory (at least temporarily) in more central intuitive principles, the theory loses its connection with its subject matter and loses the right to be called a constitutional theory.

The theory of judicial reasoning applies to constitutional change. When a proposed change contributes little or nothing to constitutional practice, a judge, in conventionalist fashion, should engage in normal adjudication by retaining the well-settled constitutional paradigm. Even when a minor change is warranted in normal adjudication, it should be narrowly drawn to resolve the precise problem that warranted it in the first place. When a paradigm shift is required to mediate a conflict or constitutional crisis, a judge should embrace the change, knowing it will have sweeping ramifications. In this context the judge will choose revolutionary adjudication. Ordinarily, when a judge finds herself in postrevolutionary adjudication, she articulates her values in light of the newly emerging paradigm. There's no escaping this hybrid phase of revolutionary adjudication wherein the judge must balance conventionalist and pragmatist factors in order to determine the scope of the new paradigm, and avoid creating a different one.[103]

Constitutional provisions are foundational in the sense that they determine the meaning and application of critical constitutional concepts throughout the constitutional scheme. If the Court defines equal protection in a certain manner, all other areas of relevant adjudication must reflect that foundational interpretation. Furthermore, if there were two constitutional provisions that bear on the same issue, and one of these provisions is foundational and the other not, the first provision provides constraints on the interpretation of the second provision. One principal question in constitutional law is how foundational constitutional provisions acquire their meaning. The traditional picture of constitutional adjudication postulates the existence of a fairly recognizable neutral methodology. The theory of constitutional revolutions, by contrast, denies the existence of such a methodology and instead maintains that foundational constitutional provisions acquire their meaning through constitutional revolutions.

Summarizing a Supreme Court decision is the final authoritative statement of American constitutional law. Until such a decision is overruled, that decision becomes a controlling constitutional principle. The theory of constitutional revolutions distinguishes between two kinds of adjudication: revolutionary and normal adjudication. Revolutionary adjudication drives constitutional law but always seeks normalcy. Additionally, the theory shows how theories of different domains enter into adjudication to fulfill the promise of constitutional law. The theory of constitutional revolutions contends that American constitutionalism cannot be explained or understood without appealing to the concept of constitutional revolutions. No neutral or formal methodology for deciding constitutional cases explains the actual decisions. This has both explanatory and normative implications. If the concept of revolutionary adjudication is necessary to explain our particular brand of constitutionalism, we ought to deploy it. The theory of constitutional revolutions is designed as a new language of American constitutionalism superior to the language of the classical conception. Its superiority must first be tested by assessing how well it explains key periods in American constitutional history.

4   The Historical Defense of the Theory

The theory of constitutional revolutions requires historical support. Two approaches suggest themselves: The first approach studies each era of judicial constitutional development and shows how the pivotal cases are revolutionary, the rest normal. This would be tedious and require several volumes in its own right. The second approach selects certain key periods of constitutional change and uses them to illustrate how the theory of constitutional revolutions operates. Because this is an essay in constitutional theory and jurisprudence, not constitutional history per se, I have chosen the second approach. If the cases I discuss support the theory of revolution, and the theory is otherwise persuasive, then I have established it as a candidate for the theory of American constitutional change.

The theory of constitutional revolutions interprets most, if not all, of the major Supreme Court decisions as revolutionary; they cannot be explained by normal adjudication. Thus, describing the normal modalities of constitutional adjudication cannot possibly constitute an adequate constitutional theory of these cases, not because such a theory is descriptive; rather, because it is necessarily incomplete. Any theory that conflates normal and revolutionary adjudication will fail as a theory of American constitutionalism. This precludes defining a normal modality as one that permits revolutionary adjudication. The theory of constitutional revolutions is supported by the critical accounts of the defective reasoning in many pivotal constitutional cases. Reasoning is "defective" when the judicial conclusion does not follow from the claimed authorities; *logically,* the rule adopted in the case is a non sequitur. That logically an argument is a non sequitur does not mean that it is a bad informal argument, though it does mean that the conclusion is underdetermined. Most good practical arguments are not logical deductions. Instead, they provide reasons for or against a certain proposition. In ethics, politics, and practical reasoning generally, reasons support certain propositions without logically entailing them or even logically implying them. However, the formalist view of law is that somehow prior law determines a present case. This implies that something stronger than ordinary practical reasoning is at work here.

In constitutional law sometimes the conclusion follows only by presupposing the very issue in dispute.[1] In other circumstances the conclusion is arrived at only by appealing to some factor extrinsic to constitutional practice. Constitutional conservatives and liberals alike appear to realize this, though few are willing to admit it candidly.[2] Nonetheless, a logically flawed decision still may be sound as a piece of political philosophy. That is, even if the practice of judicial review was first formulated through a revolutionary adjudication in *Marbury,* it might still be desirable relative to a particular conception of democracy, nationalism, or both. To call judicial review revolutionary simply means that no normal constitutional or legal argument can establish its legitimacy.

Although there is little point in my replicating the standard objections to the reasoning in *Marbury,* it is necessary to provide some examples of the defects in reasoning contained in some constitutional revolutions. Consequently, I will discuss examples from two periods of constitutional revolutions: the formative revolutions of the Marshall Court, and certain foundational equal protection and due process revolutions from the Warren Court.[3] I choose these periods because the Marshall Court's formative revolutions are not considered to be revolutionary, whereas the Warren Court, considered by many as the chief example of an activist defense of individual rights, is rejected as illegitimately activist. In my view, however, both courts exhibit revolutionary adjudication. I believe that no one created constitutional revolutions better than Marshall.

This selection in no way purports to be an exhaustive account of constitutional revolutions or the process by which constitutional adjudication evolves into normal adjudication. Though there is room for dispute, I would take it as a critical defect in the theory of constitutional revolutions if a good number of the following cases were not considered revolutionary. Demonstrating how some or all of these decisions follow from a preexisting paradigm refutes the theory. Although many such attempts exist, they ultimately fail to provide an intelligible standard for adjudication, or they have counterintuitive results by failing to explain key constitutional decisions such as *Brown v. Board of Education.*[4]

There are, to be sure, different degrees of revolutionary adjudication. Some decisions are revolutionary per se; other decisions are revolutionary within the context of a constitutional paradigm that is itself a revolution. We can, therefore, analytically distinguish between macrorevolutions and microrevolutions. Macrorevolutions are decisions creating new paradigms and are based entirely on pragmatic factors. Microrevolutions are creations of subparadigms within the overall purview of a major paradigm. Subparadigms are constructions designed not just to elaborate the new paradigm further, but also to provide a model consistent with the new paradigm, extending it into circumstances that require the paradigm's refinement. Microrevolutions are generated by an appeal to both extrinsic pragmatic considerations and to the defining features of the paradigm. Whether scientific or constitutional, revolutions come in different sizes. The essential feature of either type of revolution is, in Kuhn's words, "a special sort of change involving a certain sort of reconstruction of group commitments. But it need not be a large change, nor need it seem revolutionary to those outside a single community."[5] Within the constitutional community the change must be seen as adding to or subtracting from constitutional meaning. It must be a change that a reasonable member of this community would have excluded from her prior statement of the content of the constitutional scheme. For example, no reasonable person would say that the Court's present understanding of the equal protection clause protects striking workers from losing their jobs. If the Court subsequently decides to grant this protection, it can be achieved only through constitutional revolution. Indeed, proponents of such a protection recognize that revolutionary conditions do not obtain, and therefore even those endorsing the protection cannot argue that the Constitution presently warrants it.

A critic might object that the introduction of micro- and macrorevolutions, paradigms and subparadigms, is suspect. If there are different degrees of revolutions and paradigms, the difference appears to be evolutionary, not revolutionary. This objection fails, in my opinion, for the following reasons. First, however blurry the line might be between a microrevolution and normal adjudication, it is nevertheless true that macrorevolutions are clearly distinguished from normal adjudication. For example, the revolution in *Brown* includes a paradigm concerning equality, and this process is different from applying *Brown* to a host of racial equality cases. *Brown* is the revolution, whereas a given decision citing *Brown* in the *U.S. Supreme Court Reports* and especially in the lower courts is not revolutionary at all. However, sometimes a revolutionary paradigm does not itself address, or is claimed not to address, a vexing social policy implicating constitutional law.

One such case of a vexing issue is affirmative action. Does the *Brown* paradigm settle affirmative action through normal adjudication, or is a revolution within the *Brown* paradigm needed? If affirmative action is already contained in the *Brown* paradigm, then affirmative action is part of the law through normal adjudication. If it is not contained in *Brown,* then only a microrevolution can achieve it by creating a subparadigm connecting equality with compensatory racial justice.

From *Bakke* to *Adarand* courts have considered various subparadigms within the *Brown* paradigm to determine whether racial quotas, preferences, or goals were consistent with the *Brown* paradigm. Initially, the Court held that racial classifications were warranted in certain specified circumstances, especially for reasons of diversity. For this subparadigm to work it was necessary to distinguish between invidious discrimination and benign discrimination. Accordingly, this subparadigm helps clarify the paradigm in *Brown*. If accepted, this affirmative action subparadigm would have been a microrevolutionary decision. Ultimately, the Court refused to create this subparadigm and instead asserted that *Brown* controls affirmative action with some minor qualification. Consequently, the Court refused to extend the scope of the civil rights revolution by fashioning a subparadigm for affirmative action. After a long flirtation with this subparadigm, the Court ruled that affirmative action statutes are subject to heightened scrutiny just as are other racial classifications. Rather than engage in a microrevolutionary decision, the Court decided the case through the normal reasoning of precedent, which mandates following *Brown*. Both proponents and opponents of this decision can describe the issue in terms of the theory of constitutional revolutions. The proponents contend that *Brown*'s paradigm covers affirmative action, and that affirmative action statutes violate the paradigm. Opponents of the Court's decisions argue that proponents of normal adjudication mistake the nature of the governing paradigm. The governing paradigm maintains that *Brown* precludes *invidious* discrimination predicated on the belief in the inferiority of the burdened race; it speaks little, if at all, to discrimination designed to remedy the shameful institution of American racial apartheid. This issue is substantially one of which kind of adjudication, normal or revolutionary, is appropriate in these circumstances. Ultimately, a judge will choose one or the other position based on her conception of the legitimacy of revolutionary adjudication. For proponents of the Court's decision, despite *Brown* itself being revolutionary in altering the paradigm of equality, further revolutionary adjudication within the confines of *Brown* is not warranted because it would conflict with the governing paradigm. In this view the Court, in the affirmative action cases, should normalize constitutional adjudication so that the reigning paradigm will be stable. Opponents, on the other hand, maintain that the stability of the paradigm in *Brown* requires a subparadigm permitting benign discrimination if the reigning paradigm is to be fully realized.

The theory of constitutional revolutions cannot provide a decision procedure demonstrating formally the distinction between normal and revolutionary adjudication; it is a pragmatist theory and recognizes that no such demonstration is possible. Instead, the theory offers a new language for better conceptualizing disputes in constitutional law. As a result of this conceptualization everyone must admit the following: We are all normal judges, and we are all revolutionary judges. The answer to the question whether a decision follows from the Constitution, therefore, is not dispositive of constitutional legitimacy. We must also ask whether this decision improves our constitutional and political culture in ways not possible without it. Alternatively stated, the question judges should ask is whether a particular case should be treated as normal adjudication or as revolutionary adjudication. This will not eradicate disputes. It will, however, focus on the reasons for and against judicial restraint in a given case. For constitutional pragmatists, no longer will textualism or originalism dominate the discussion of methodology, because these conventions typically apply only to normal adjudication and usually cannot answer the question of whether revolutionary adjudication is appropriate. In short, neither constitutional law nor methodology can itself determine the kind of adjudication warranted. For that, we must follow the theory of constitutional revolutions, appreciating that extrinsic factors affecting the republic may help persuade changes to create new paradigms. In this regard the theory of constitutional revolutions is a language of constitutional change. If it accurately depicts this change, helps us to focus on the reasons for controversy, and prompts us to recognize a resolution already embedded in constitutional practice — then the judicial role encompasses revolutionary adjudication — it moves us closer to resolving *some* controversies, and permits us to appreciate why other controversies will remain. Finally, we should be skeptical of the view contending that wide use of the term "revolutionary adjudication" debases and trivializes the notion of revolution. Instead, it points out that most prominent cases in a constitutional law casebook are revolutionary.[6] That is why we teach and study them.

Occasionally, within a revolutionary paradigm, a subparadigm is required for the original paradigm to succeed. Naturally, a subparadigm is warranted only if the original paradigm is desirable. Furthermore, the subparadigm must not conflict with any other constitutional principles, or with extrinsic moral and political factors. If the subparadigm is objectionable in either of these ways, support for the original paradigm may be withdrawn. The decision whether to retain an original paradigm must be made pragmatically.

As indicated earlier, there are several different types of constitutional revolutions. A constitutional revolution occurs when the Court gives meaning to a vague or indeterminate constitutional provision, such as due process or equal protection. These provisions invite revolutionary adjudication. A constitutional revolution also occurs when the Court creates standards for applying constitutional provisions. Because the theory of constitutional revolutions is concerned with the abstract provisions of American constitutionalism as they have been historically interpreted, changing the levels of review or the analytic structure of a provision can reverse the provision's practical effect and, in that sense, is revolutionary. A critic might object that this unremarkable feature of constitutional revolutions renders revolutions quite ordinary and not extraordinary at all. However, it is not obvious why frequent and even predictable revolutionary decisions negate the importance of revolutionary adjudication.[7]

One particularly surprising revolution occurred regarding art. 4, sec. 3, cl. 1 of the Constitution.[8] The Framers had discussed and rejected the inclusion of a clause stating that new admittees into the Union would be admitted on an equal basis. Their reason for not including the condition was based on a desire not to bind future congresses. Despite the original rejection of this concept, the Court ultimately interpreted the provision to include this condition.[9] The case of the admission clause is interesting because the Constitution's text, in conjunction with the explicit historical omission of the provision, should have bound the Court if it was engaged in normal adjudication. Instead, the Court embraced the previously abandoned condition on pragmatic grounds. Cases of this sort make the theory of constitutional revolutions inevitable, further shoring up the conviction that the central feature of American constitutionalism is not dictated by normal paradigmatic factors such as the Constitution's text, intent, history, structure, or logic. The propriety of this decision must be found elsewhere in cultural or abstract moral and political values.[10]

The theory of constitutional revolutions accurately describes one salient feature of constitutional adjudication, namely, that most landmark decisions are based on constitutionally extrinsic factors. Indeed, the source of law in such cases usually comes from our rich political and moral culture, not from the four corners of the Constitution. Many of the following examples are cases that we could not now imagine repudiating, however dubious their original justification. This suggests that everyone, or almost everyone, supports revolutionary adjudication, even those judges heralding originalism and judicial restraint. The problem is that though most people are aware of how such decisions come about, the myth of normal adjudication persists. The problem here is "not that the Court acts on a myth, but that the talk about it heads the Court in the wrong direction. It backs into questions it ought to face. It's like going up a one way street in reverse."[11] Stated differently, no ordinary, intelligent citizen would spontaneously say that Marshall's decision in *Marbury* was "ordained [by the words of the Constitution] in the beginning."[12] He must go to law school to say that. But "[e]ven a lawyer must strain to extrapolate supporting evidence from the words."[13] Law school teaches students how to dress extrinsic factors in "acceptable" constitutional arguments. This supports the position that constitutional rhetoric is not the same as actual constitutional and judicial reasoning. The decision making cannot be explained by appealing to normal paradigms, despite constitutional rhetoric insisting that normal paradigms are all that matter.

The Countermajoritarian Question and the History of Revolutionary Adjudication

Judicial review is a structural feature of American constitutionalism that implicates two fundamental features of American government: separation of powers and federalism.[14] Yet the legitimacy of judicial review is subject to perennial controversy.[15] Some argue that the kind of judicial review the Marshall Court instituted is very different from the contemporary practice of judicial review.[16] Others argue that Marshall instituted "interpretivist review," whereas contemporary review is "noninterpretivist," and that his arguments are not compelling.[17] Therefore, we should be cautious about extending the Court's power to include "noninterpretivist methodologies."[18] The current furor over activist adjudication is just a modern incarnation of the original uneasiness over the legitimacy of judicial review itself.

If *Marbury* is truly a revolutionary decision, whether or not compelling as a legal argument, then it already includes "noninterpretivist methodologies." Because Marshall's decision in *Marbury* was revolutionary, revolutionary judicial review is central to constitutional practice, and a pragmatic presumption exists in favor of that kind of review. Barring reason to the contrary, such a practice seen in the context of American democracy ought not to be artificially restricted. It is difficult to understand how Marshall's decision in *Marbury* "could be rendered by reference to the text, intent, history and structure of article III."[19] The decision in *Marbury* is undetermined by conventionalist evidentiary factors without an elaborate and highly controversial argument to the contrary. It is useful to emphasize this point. Perhaps *Marbury,* like other constitutional revolutions, can be derived from controversial arguments of political morality or culture. If so, the relativistic constitutional theory does not support it. In other words, a reasonable constitutional interpreter would not judge the principle in *Marbury* to be part of the conventional evidentiary factors prior to deciding the case. Many have attempted ways around this conclusion. For example, one can say that *Marbury* follows *indirectly* from constitutional conventions, or that an *expansive* conception of constitutional conventions supports the decision, or that the *structure* of the Constitution requires it. These, among other attempts, are obfuscations. If the constitutional evidentiary factors do not support *Marbury* unless we appeal to indirection, expansiveness, or structure, then it is likely that this decision is controversial, which shows at most that the decision is permitted, not required. The problem here is that when evidentiary factors suggest revolutionary decisions, other contrary decisions are also possible. In that case, whatever the decision is, it is not determined by the evidence. If one objects that no constitutional decision is determined by the evidence, then no decision is due to normal adjudication. Although I find that view implausible, if it is true, it doesn't defeat the claim that constitutional law is based on revolutionary adjudication. Rather, it confirms it.[20]

This raises the question of the legitimacy of judicial review. Essentially, the challenge here is to reconcile judicial review with democracy. Because judges are not elected by the people, nor directly accountable to them except in rare circumstances, their role in the republic is potentially countermajoritarian.[21] How can such officials justifiably strike down legislation produced by democratically elected leaders? Any careful study of the Constitution and the American communitarian republic shows that majoritarian democracy is only one part of its republican structure. Much of this structure is decidedly countermajoritarian. In fact, the Constitution is itself a thoroughly countermajoritarian document.[22] Federalism is also decidedly countermajoritarian. Congressional legislation representing the majority position on an issue can be struck down by judicial review because it conflicts improperly with state sovereignty, which itself could be countermajoritarian.[23] Moreover, the rights basis of American constitutionalism is countermajoritarian. Finally, there is no escaping the fact that American constitutionalism is countermajoritarian in its political foundations.[24] The recognition of the countermajoritarian features of American constitutionalism generally should quiet the charge of countermajoritarianism when it applies to the Court.[25] Finally, the republican nature of American democracy may help to reduce the force of the countermajoritarian problem.[26] American politics are concerned with consent and the will of the people. Thus, we need a supplementary theory to explicate the locution "the will of the people," which should refer to the will of a community of equal members.[27]

The theory of constitutional revolutions is not an answer to the countermajoritarian problem, although it is part of such an answer. Rather, it is an attempt to describe and explain the dualistic dimensions of constitutional adjudication as they have existed from *Marbury v. Madison* to the present day.

The Formative Revolutions

Before discussing the formative revolutions, let me issue a warning. Historical analysis, though essential to constitutional theory, has its own dangers. One danger is what might be usefully labeled "the present perspective fallacy," which admonishes the historical observer to recognize that sometimes the past appears inevitable or necessary to the present observer. The interpreter, wishing to diminish the effects of this fallacy, tries to locate a point in history when the past, and therefore the present, were undetermined. Thus, the fact that judicial review presently is, as a historical fact, a structural feature of American constitutionalism ought not to suggest that it was inevitable. One commits this fallacy when one reads back into the contingent conditions that formed judicial review the features of necessity or inevitability, which now appear to anchor this practice — specifically, seeing a contingent event such as John Marshall's stewardship of the formative revolutions as merely reflecting what was already there in the Constitution, or the history of the Founding, or some other normal authority. The circularity on which the present perspective fallacy rests should be obvious. Our question is whether judicial review was a constituent feature of constitutional reality, or whether instead it is due to the creative judicial genius of John Marshall.[28] Embracing the former by simply reading back into the history of the Founding is circular and obscures the revolutionary nature of the Marshall Court.[29] One needs only to consult this historical evidence to see that this was untrue. It is not clear why article 3 did not include a provision authorizing judicial review. The reason, perhaps, was that it was too controversial. Some Founders thought it obvious; others thought it tyrannical. Even if some form of judicial review was anticipated by the *Federalist*, why should that be dispositive? The *Federalist* was the political expression of the views of certain Framers, not the considered judgment of the ratifiers who were as much the Founders of the Republic as those who participated in the constitutional convention. The *Federalist* may guide us in understanding one important ideological commitment of the times, but that is a far cry from representing an irrefutable authority.

The Revolution to Launch All Judicial Revolutions: Marbury v. Madison

Judicial review was first asserted as a means of striking down a federal legislative act in *Marbury v. Madison*.[30] This revolutionary case reflects the revolutionary spirit of the Founding, extending beyond what even many Federalists envisioned.[31] In this case Marshall attempted to do several things. First, he tried to establish the legitimacy of *review,* namely, that acts inconsistent with the Constitution are void. This was in itself revolutionary, as the Constitution nowhere states or implies any sort of formal review. Of course, there are many arguments purporting to establish that some sort of review necessarily follows from the notion of a written constitution, or a constitution setting up a limited form of government, or the nature of judicial practice as illustrated by some state courts. However, none of these arguments are dispositive.

Marshall not only established review as a legitimate function, he also established that *judicial* review is the only effective form of review. Moreover, his conception of review was activist, not Thayerian.[32] One could imagine a principle of judicial review that stated that the Court should interfere with acts of other branches of the government only when it is obvious that the Constitution has been clearly violated.[33] If he had fashioned such a rule, our constitutional history would have been different and the Court's role weakened. However, the question of legitimacy would be rendered less vexatious. Thayer talks about such a rule when he argues that the Court can disregard a legislative act "when those who have the right to make laws have not merely made a mistake, but have made a very clear one, so clear that it is not open to rational question."[34] Such a rule would permit judicial review and the invalidation of legislation only in extreme cases. I think such a rule would be a bad rule, but not because the Constitution, its text, intent, history, structure, or logic, entails a stronger one. Rather, on pragmatic grounds a stronger rule is required for the kind of constitutional government we desire.[35] However, whether good or bad, Thayer's conception of judicial review is clearly not the form of judicial review instituted by Chief Justice Marshall.[36]

There is an enormous amount of literature describing the errors in Marshall's decision in *Marbury*. Many critics have challenged Marshall's reasoning in this case,[37] arguing that although the reasoning is defective, the conclusion is still good.[38] Professor Tribe argues: "[On the issue of judicial review] the Constitution is indeterminate. Marshall resolved the indeterminacy, in essence, by *postulating* that federal courts have the power independently to interpret and apply the Constitution; it is no argument against Marshall's postulate to point out (correctly) that it is not a corollary."[39] Tribe is certainly right in arguing that judicial review is not a corollary, but instead a useful postulate. However, he must then concede that constitutional interpretation involves a process of revolution. That is, great constitutional postulates are the results of the Court following prudence, morality, or common sense, *not* the text, intent, history, structure, or logic of the Constitution.

I do not intend to repeat the numerous allegations concerning the impropriety of the reasoning in *Marbury*. My central thesis is that there was no compelling basis for Marshall's decision. Instead, Marshall assumed the power of judicial review. This is not to say that Marshall created the idea of judicial review from whole cloth. Several states assumed the practice of judicial review as part of state constitutional law. However, the evidence for this is usually overstated. The practice did not enjoy widespread acceptance.[40] Furthermore, Marshall's assumption of power in this case was the beginning of a series of constitutional revolutions centralizing power in the federal government.

For Marshall's decision to be the result of normal adjudication, there must be some plausible constitutional paradigm sanctioning the result. In other words, the constitutional paradigm must be obvious and uncontestable. In the republic's early years the paradigm of judicial review certainly was contestable.[41] Commentators have conclusively shown that the decision in arguments against the reasoning in *Marbury* is not entailed by the text, intent, history, structure, or logic of the Constitution. There are two kinds of criticism of Marshall's reasoning in this case: logical or formal deficiencies, on the one hand, and practical deficiencies on the other. Logical deficiencies are mistakes in reasoning, whereas practical deficiencies are the misuse or abuse of commonsense knowledge, precedents, or history. Marshall misused and abused traditional legal conventions to make his point, which was that a certain kind of nationalist government was pragmatically desirable whether or not it was implicit in the Constitution.[42]

Denying that the holding in *Marbury* inextricably follows from the Constitution or from constitutional practice does not, according to the theory of constitutional revolutions, indicate that it is bad law.[43] Indeed, pragmatically one could argue that Marshall's conclusion in *Marbury* is good law. Such an argument consists of demonstrating, morally and historically, that the principle in *Marbury* has been conducive to bringing about a desirable form of polity.[44] However, this means that we must revise our conception of what makes a constitutional decision good law. Good law contributes to the successful operation of the constitutional scheme according to a conception of democracy we share. We may no longer assume that under these circumstances good law can be explicated only in terms of either conventionalist or coherentist conceptions of law. For a conventionalist account of the decision in this case to be illuminating, the argument must entail judicial review, or in some nonlogical sense be inexorably linked to judicial review. I submit that there is no such argument. We cannot base such an argument on general principles required to justify our constitutional scheme.[45] Instead, we must recognize that, as early as *Marbury*, justices were creating revolutionary constitutional decisions that can be explained only pragmatically.

Dworkin is one of the few contemporary commentators who defends Marshall's decision in *Marbury*.[46] Dworkin writes: "He [Marshall] was right to think that the most plausible interpretation of the developing legal practices of the young country, as well as of its colonial and British roots, supposed that an important part of the point of law was to supply standards for the decision of courts. History has vindicated the substantive demands of that interpretation. The United States is a more just society than it would have been had its constitutional rights been left to the conscience of majoritarian institutions."[47] This requires a sophisticated conception of what was "the most plausible interpretation of the developing legal practices of the young country, as well as of its colonial and British roots."[48] This account needs to specify which legal documents, statutes, or judicial decisions tell us what *the* legal practice was.[49] More importantly, it needs to specify how our "colonial and British roots" can be part of the developing judicial practice. Because Dworkin regards the distinction between "continuing the same story" and "beginning a new story" as a constraint of judicial interpretation, wasn't the break with England and the subsequent ratification of the Constitution a paradigmatic example of "beginning a new story"? Consequently, in interpreting prior judicial practice, a judge must have some intuitive conception of what the practice is. Surely, American constitutional practice could not begin prior to the ratification of the Constitution. Or if it could, just what are the parameters for identifying this practice? If American constitutionalism predates the Constitution's ratification, then Dworkin vitiates his own distinction between "continuing the same story" and "beginning a new one."[50] What Dworkin understandably overlooks is the fact that in the beginning there was no discernible structure to our political environment capable of showing *the* way to the future, save for certain explicit constitutional conventions or paradigms such as the Constitution and case law.[51] The fledgling republic did not have a discernible structure other than these conventions. To the eighteenth-century constitutional lawyers, the structure of American government and the structure of constitutional law were yet to be created. Diverse cultural and ideological factors influenced how these lawyers conceptualized the world. The relative absence of a discernible institutional structure meant that courts filled in the structure by incorporating ideas from the critical cultural and abstract theories of politics and morality.

There is an obvious reason for this early lack of structure. Though American constitutional law stems from English law, it also derives from English and French political philosophy.[52] Indeed, American constitutional law stems from multifarious sources. However, the source of law is not the law itself. When a nation truly has a revolutionary beginning, its legal system must itself contain new paradigms, even if these paradigms are also in some sense part of the older tradition. Legally and politically the United States began a new legal tradition with the adoption of the Constitution. Hence, the sort of relativistic moral theory associated with a developing constitutional tradition had little opportunity to develop at the time of *Marbury*. At that time constitutional law could be identified with explicit constitutional conventions. Moreover, general principles, conspicuous of a relativized constitutional theory, had not yet emerged.

No doubt Dworkin could reply that, even at the beginning of the Republic, American law exhibited a structure inherited from colonial life and English common law, but American constitutional law cannot be identified with English common law. Moreover, the fact that American constitutionalism can be traced to inchoate beginnings in English law does not prove that there must have been a well-defined structure in early American constitutional law, operating as a criterion for determining unique answers to hard cases. Nor is it true that if American constitutional law derives causally from English common law, the latter is the normative authority of the former. Finally, it is insufficient to argue that constitutional revolutions must be viewed epistemologically as occurring within the scope of a single coherent intellectual history.[53]

Marbury is a paradigmatic revolutionary decision. Prior to this case, the notion of judicial review had been debated with no clear victory for either side.[54] Not even Hamilton believed that judicial review followed directly from the Constitution.[55] Instead, judicial review follows a priori from the meaning of a limited government. In his view judicial review is an inherent feature of the concept of constitutionally limited government. Hamilton's view is reminiscent of natural law theory and suffers from its definitional and justificatory methodological weaknesses.

The fundamental problem is that we do not know that the United States government is a limited government until we provide an authoritative interpretation of the Constitution, and this requires precisely the process of judicial review whose legitimacy we are examining. We cannot escape the commitment to a theory of interpretation before we can be certain what sort of polity the Constitution creates. This process permits us to formulate provisional interpretations, test them against the text and history, and revise the original interpretation in accord with the political culture. Consequently, it is futile to believe that the uninterpreted Constitution places many constraints on judicial interpretation. This casts the interpretive turn in a different light. Rather than providing the ground for subsequent interpretations, normal constitutional conventions are themselves dependent upon a persuasive interpretation of American constitutional practice.

Besides the language of Marshall's opinion, nothing in the intent, history, structure, or logic of the Constitution makes judicial review inevitable. It is ironic that at the same time that Marshall is extolling the importance of a written constitution, a constitution creating a limited government, he is assuming power for the judiciary neither stated nor arguably implied in the Constitution. Had Marshall not created this judicial power, the United States probably would have survived, though it might have turned out to be more majoritarian than it is today. Essentially, Marshall created judicial review as a pragmatic response to the inevitable crisis over the role of the judiciary in the constitutional scheme.[56] Judicial review is conducive to creating a national republic, and *that* is what Marshall sought.[57] Marshall sought a more nationalistic government, but he also sought a government in which pragmatic decisions and deliberative democracy prevailed. However, even so, the argument that judicial review is a *necessary* feature of a constitutional republic is unpersuasive. In hindsight, what now appears *necessary* appeared at the time of its occurrence merely *useful*. When one interprets the past, a successful means takes on a certain grandeur; it appears conceptually essential. Generally speaking, it is dangerously misleading to identify present historical and legal structures with what is essential, privileged, or necessary when in fact these structures are at best contingent, and at worst fortuitous.[58] Conflating the contingent with the necessary precludes transformation and revolution and severely retards the flexibility of governmental authority and the recognition of individual rights. Judicial review seeks to overcome this problem by making federal judges "the watchdogs of eternal constitutional verities."[59]

Marbury teaches us that pragmatist arguments are perfectly acceptable constitutional arguments in the context of revolutionary adjudication as long as a conscientious attempt is made, successful or not, to connect the new decision to prior law. Ordinary constitutional conventions cannot be cited as a justification of the result in *Marbury*;[60] instead, *Marbury is* a revolutionary decision. Marshall tried to write a great opinion by using normal constitutional conventions. Normal adjudication appeals to the Constitution's text, intent, history, structure, and logic to justify a constitutional decision;[61] revolutionary adjudication does not. If we are to appreciate *Marbury* and the other great constitutional cases, we must unmask the Court's tendency to drape revolutionary adjudication in normal garb.[62] We must instead realize that all the normal conventions and prior law will not put revolutionary adjudication back together again. Revolutionary adjudication can be explained only by appealing to the wider culture and to abstract ethics and politics.

The Federal Judicial Supremacy Revolution: Martin v. Hunter's Lessee

In *Martin v. Hunter's Lessee,* the Court, through Justice Story, held that the Supreme Court may invalidate state supreme court decisions.[63] The case arose in the state courts in Virginia and its facts are complex, including the validity of treaties and property rights. For our purposes we must ask whether the decision follows from constitutional conventions that structure normal adjudication. The arguments that normal adjudication generates the *Martin* decision are familiar. If there was no federal supremacy, insuperable problems would abound.[64] First, there would be no uniformity in state court decisions interpreting the Constitution. Second, the Supreme Court would have a limited purview over state courts. No doubt, from a contemporary perspective, this decision was a sensible one. Assuming the sort of federalism we have today is desirable, *Martin* was instrumental in bringing about a logical balance of power between the states and the national government. Nevertheless, *Martin* is a revolutionary decision because it did not flow from the text, intent, history, structure, or logic of the Constitution. In fact, some states challenged the right of the Supreme Court to issue writs of error to state courts.[65]

The Historical Agreement Argument

Martin was one of the formative revolutions occupying a unique place in constitutional adjudication. Considering that the republicans, a majority at the time of ratification, believed that a more decentralized government would have been good for the republic, the possibility of different state courts interpreting the Constitution in different ways would have been the price one paid for pluralism. Such pluralism might have encouraged different constitutional experiments that might improve both the state and federal systems. Though different from our conception, this is a possible ideal of a just society, and one that would have encouraged a "marketplace of ideas." Consequently, the result in *Martin* is a pragmatic result. It is a decision resulting from the Court's conception of what is proper to a strong nationalist government and a rejection of certain kinds of constitutional diversity. It hardly follows in a normal fashion from the Constitution.[66]

One could argue that because the Constitution does authorize Congress to create federal appellate jurisdiction, section 25 of the Judiciary Act of 1789 created federal jurisdiction over state court decisions. Consequently, it is arguable that the Constitution and congressional discretion warrant federal appellate review of state court decisions. Hence, *Martin* cannot be a revolution, as it merely confirms Congress's legitimate authority under article 3. However, art. 3, sec. 2, cl. 2 of the Constitution gives Congress authority to affect the appellate jurisdiction of *federal* courts. It must surely be revolutionary, though not unwarranted for that reason, to assume that Congress can use this authority to give the federal courts jurisdiction over state courts.

Since no normal paradigms required the Court to have held that section 25 was unconstitutional because it conflicted with state sovereignty, delegitimizing section 25 was a revolutionary Court decision. The Court argued that the language of article 3 and uniformity of federal law require the decision.[67] However, the notion of dual sovereignty, a true separation of national and state sovereigns, suggests that a plausible federalist argument cuts the other way. Federal judicial supremacy tends to destroy the sovereignty of state courts, thus rejecting federalism for something more closely tied to nationalism.

Indeed, one central point of contention between the Federalists and Anti-Federalists was the belief that there was a distinction between national consolidation and true confederation, and that the latter was preferable.[68] Perhaps a true confederation would have been more likely if the federal judiciary had no power to overrule the decisions of state courts.[69]

There is an argument in *Martin* that must be confronted if the theory of constitutional revolutions is to succeed. Basically, the argument is that when proponents and opponents of a constitutional provision endorse it or reject it because of what they both agree that it means, we can conclude that that is the meaning of the provision. Because this is a fundamental point, I quote Justice Story's opinion at some length:

> [It] is an historical fact, that this exposition of the constitution, extending its appellate power to state courts, was, previous to its adop-

tion, uniformly and publicly avowed by its friends and admitted by its enemies, as the basis of their respective reasoning, both in and out of the state conventions. It is an historical fact, that at the time when the judiciary act was submitted to the deliberations of the first congress, composed, as it was, not only of men of great learning and ability, but of men who acted a principal part in framing, supporting or opposing that constitution, the same exposition was explicitly declared and admitted by the friends and opponents of that system. It is an historical fact, that the supreme court [*sic*] of the United States has, from time to time, sustained this appellate jurisdiction, in a great variety of cases, brought from the tribunals of many of the most important states in the Union, and that no state tribunal has ever breathed a judicial doubt on the subject, or declined to obey the mandate of the supreme court [*sic*], until the present occasion.[70]

Consequently, if Federalists desired, and Anti-Federalists feared, that article 3 subjects state court decisions to federal appellate review, then that is precisely what article 3 means. The Federalists believed the Court had the power to review both federal and state court decisions. The Anti-Federalists feared that this would make the central government too strong. However, it simply does not follow that because the Anti-Federalists *feared* such an interpretation, this interpretation was inevitable. The Anti-Federalists feared that the relevant provisions would be interpreted as implying a federal limitation on state courts, not that the relevant provisions *must* be so interpreted. Instead, Marshall himself at one time believed that such an interpretation was absurd. Ironically, Story's decision in *Martin* conflicts with statements Marshall made at the Virginia ratifying convention, to wit: "I hope no gentleman will think that a state will be called at the bar of federal court. . . . It is not rational to suppose that the sovereign power should be dragged before a court."[71] Of course, one can suppose that Marshall merely changed his mind.

The point here is that Story could have followed Marshall's lead, the Chief Justice's views providing ample evidence against the decision, or he could have decided as he did. Either way his decision depends upon factors extrinsic to the Constitution. Indeed, Story's decision is a Federalist argument infused with political theory. The question here is the nature of constitutional meaning. Is constitutional meaning politically neutral, following logically from the Constitution? Is constitutional meaning dependent upon a particular moral and political perspective? The conventional wisdom is that constitutional meaning is, or should be, politically neutral. However, that view is a charade. The Marshall Court contributed to this charade by presenting its arguments as following from the text, intent, history, structure, and logic of the Constitution, when in fact the Court was fashioning a strong central government conducive to those with Federalist sensibilities and beyond.

The Federalism Argument

Many commentators have argued that the decision in *Martin* necessarily follows from the concept of federalism.[72] For example, Charles Black writes that "there is nothing in our entire governmental structure which has a more leak-proof claim to legitimacy than the function of the courts in reviewing state acts for federal constitutionality."[73] After all, how could there be a federal republic if the states need not bow to federal interpretation of the Constitution?[74] Hence, the decision in *Martin* encourages uniformity of federal constitutional law. Of course, this assumes that federalism requires uniformity or that uniformity is desirable. It does not explain *why* uniformity is either required or desirable. Common-law rules are not always uniform across the states. If state sovereignty is sufficiently important and entrenched in American constitutionalism and culture, then the possibility of differing state interpretations of the Constitution may be desirable, or this diversity might be worth the cost.[75] Whether or not desirable, the decision in this case follows from a particular political philosophy or commonsense perspective, not from the Constitution. In short, what is so troubling about the argument is its univocal concept of federalism.[76] Perhaps our current idea of federalism is conceptually tied to the *Martin* decision. However, it is a non sequitur to conclude that *every* type of federalism requires this decision. Even if one specific conception is tied to the decision in *Martin,* it does not follow that it is the only plausible one. It becomes even more troubling when we remind ourselves that in the 1780s the states truly regarded themselves as sovereign.[77] In other words, is it conceivable for the Supreme Court to have authority to declare acts of the coequal branches of the federal government to be unconstitutional, and still resist authority to enforce a judgment against a state court? Such an argument indicates two different kinds of constitutional norms, to wit: those that are fully enforced and those that are not.[78] Following this lead, *Martin* might have held that the federal judiciary was supreme in interpreting the federal constitution, statutes, and treaties, but render this decision a legally valid *underenforced* constitutional norm for institutional reasons. The *Martin* decision follows from a certain conception — perhaps the best and most likely conception — of federalism.[79] Relative to that conception the decision in *Martin* is warranted. This is very different from the conventional view that *Martin* is necessitated by normal constitutional paradigms.

Professor Currie argues persuasively that the principle in *Martin* was permissible, but not required.[80] Even permissible decisions involve constitutional revolutions when more than one plausible resolution of the conflict is possible. Many judicial solutions to national problems are constitutionally permissible. However, the Court chooses only some of these solutions. If among the class of possible constitutional decisions only some are chosen, it follows that there is an independent standard for choosing which possible decisions to pursue. The Court is likely to appeal to moral and political factors, the exigencies of the historical circumstances, or common sense in deciding which constitutional course to follow. The theory of constitutional revolutions reflects this structure. The theory informs us that the Constitution does not determine constitutional law in revolutionary contexts.

Consequently, though the revolution in *Martin* was probably grounded more in the structure of the Constitution than is the decision in *Marbury*, *Martin* is still a constitutional revolution. It required a Court to decide that federal courts are supreme over state courts in interpreting the Constitution. The Court could have decided differently. If this case could have been decided differently, the reasoning does not necessitate the conclusion. To reply that most, if not all, constitutional cases could be decided differently is to concede that revolutionary adjudication is embedded in American constitutional practice. The *Martin* revolution established federal judicial supremacy over state courts. In *Cohens v. Virginia* the Court extended this decision by extending this supremacy to the appellate jurisdiction over state criminal cases, thereby further restricting the sovereignty of the states.[81]

The Court wrote what would become Marshall's conception of judicial review, one that lends itself to interpretation as revolutionary adjudication. Consider: "[A] constitution is framed for ages to come, and is designed to approach immortality, as nearly as human institutions can approach it. Its course cannot always be tranquil. It is exposed to storms and tempests, and its Framers must be unwise statesmen indeed, if they have not provided it, so far as its nature will permit, with the means of self-preservation from the perils it may be destined to encounter."[82]

Keep in mind that state sovereignty at the Founding was deeply enshrined in the political culture. Indeed, allegiance to a federal or national government was an incomplete, undetermined idea. Had the Court engaged in normal adjudication in these cases, the likely result would be to protect the integrity of the states and their judicial systems. *Martin* held that the states had voluntarily surrendered their sovereignty to some degree. This is merely a truism, one that cannot function as a justification for expanding the federal court's role. Normal adjudication would have concluded that nowhere in the document or the Framers' intent does it specify federal judicial control over state courts. What we now see as a logical result Jefferson regarded "as another step in the scheme of the Supreme Court to destroy the federal constitutional system by consolidating all authority in the central government."[83] Normal adjudication would be on the side of Jefferson. The court by engaging in revolutionary adjudication rejected Jefferson's position.

On the view presented in this book, the controversy surrounding the *Martin* paradigm was a political controversy over the nature of the union. One side — the states' rights side — wanted a federal union, that is, a compact among independent and sovereign states. The other side wanted a national union with limited state powers and a supreme central government.[84] *Martin*'s paradigm was extended by the Court in *Cohens* by fashioning a subparadigm concerning state criminal cases.

Indeed, it is possible that America's original compact was libertarian in nature. The national government was to be concerned with defense and other distinctly national issues, whereas the state governments were to be concerned with everything else, including protecting individual liberty. The argument against this form of libertarianism is historical and pragmatic: It did not work. The Marshall Court immediately recognized this fact. On the other hand, the original compact might have expressed a different form of libertarianism, one specifically concerned with protecting property owners from oppressive state governments.[85] Whatever the nature of the original compact — if that is even determinable — time, crisis, and necessity determine how the original compact is instantiated in practice. Beneficial results have typically been the benchmark of constitutional plausibility.

The early constitutional revolutions established structural features of American constitutionalism, which create distributions of power in a governmental system. In *Marbury* the Court established the federal judiciary's power over federal legislative and executive acts. In *Martin* and *Cohens* the Court exercised federal appellate power over state courts. A constitutional system possessing these structural features of government is very different from a constitutional system not having them. Consequently, the Court in these early cases, rather than implementing the structure of the Constitution, in essence created it.[86] Marshall's revolutionary jurisprudence constructed a Federalist conception of nationalism that is the forerunner of contemporary constitutional nationalism.

The Federal General Powers Revolution — Legislative Means: McCulloch v. Maryland

The fledgling republic agonized over the legitimacy of a national bank throughout the first third of the nineteenth century. Federalists supported the idea of a national bank, whereas Anti-Federalists opposed it. In *McCulloch v. Maryland,*[87] Marshall interpreted the necessary and proper clause expansively, permitting the federal government to have broad powers in solving national problems.[88] Marshall's interpretation of the necessary and proper clause was at least as broad as the Federalists' interpretations. Jefferson's conception of the clause differed sharply from Marshall's interpretation. Indeed, Jefferson contended that "the Constitution allows only the means which are 'necessary' not merely 'convenient' for effecting the enumerated powers. If such a latitude of construction be allowed to this phrase as to give any non-enumerated power [to Congress], it will go to every one, for there is no one which ingenuity may not torture into a convenience, in some way or other, to some one of so long a list of enumerated powers. It would swallow up all the delegated powers, and reduce the whole to one phrase as before observed. Therefore, it was that the Constitution restrained them to the necessary means, that is to say, to those means without which the grant of power would be nugatory."[89]

Marshall's decision is clearly a political decision and cannot be explained in terms of the classical conception of constitutionalism or any other neutral account of judicial reasoning.[90] Marshall's decision also deploys nonpolitical forms of analysis. Among these forms of analysis are linguistic analysis, conceptual analysis, common sense, and rationalism. In the end Marshall's argument is political, not judicial in the classical conception's sense. In fact, he was implementing his conception of Federalist political philosophy.[91]

The necessary and proper clause is vague and indeterminate. During ratification its indeterminacy was the cause of much concern.[92] However, the logic of the clause seems to suggest that only those powers that are necessary and not otherwise inconsistent with the Constitution are permissible. The term "necessary" can mean absolutely required or required relative to circumstances as we know them. It is doubtful, however, that on any reasonable interpretation, it can mean useful or expedient. Even at the time of the decision, the implausibility of interpreting "necessary" in this manner was noted.[93] Marshall's interpretation of this clause was controversial even to his contemporary, interpretive community.[94]

Marshall's revolution in this case created another structural feature of American constitutionalism, namely, where the federal or national government has power, it has supreme power. *McCulloch* gives the federal government virtually unlimited power to decide means to adopt in bringing about constitutionally permissible ends. Marshall's constitutional methodology involves reconstructing the consciousness of members of the political community to reinterpret the relationship between state and federal government.[95] His rhetorical genius consisted in his ability to reconstitute judicial culture without giving the appearance of departing from the traditional framework. One might suggest that Marshall's genius camouflaged his pragmatism within the traditional framework. If so, one concedes that the language of revolutionary adjudication is the operative even if it is not the symbolic or ceremonial language. The question naturally arises: If the theory of constitutional revolutions accurately depicts the operative language of constitutional change, why isn't it also the symbolic language? The reasons for this are deep and complex, including invocations of the rule of law, countermajoritarianism, and most importantly, the idea that constitutional reasoning forms an independent, objective sphere, the results of which should be embraced by future generations if they are to keep the faith. This Burkean view denigrates unbridled deliberation and favors the slow, incremental evolution of the law. In this context the Burkean conception is wrong because that's not how American law develops.

In discussing the question whether the Constitution includes unenumerated powers, Marshall's view is strikingly similar to the theory of constitutional revolutions. At times this revolutionary process involves rhetorical methods that help revolutionary decisions become normal.[96]

> A Constitution, to contain an accurate detail of all the subdivisions of which its great powers will admit, and of all the means by which they may be carried into execution, would partake of the prolixity of a legal code, and could scarcely be embraced by the human mind. It would, probably, never be understood by the public. Its nature, therefore, requires, that only its great outlines should be marked, its important objects designated, and the minor ingredients which compose those objects, be deduced from the nature of the objects themselves. That this idea was entertained by the Framers of the American constitution, is not only to be inferred from the nature of the instrument, but from the language. Why else were some of the limitations, found in the ninth section of the first article, introduced? It is also, in some degree, warranted, by their having omitted to use any restrictive term which might prevent its receiving a fair and just interpretation. In considering this question, then, we must never forget that it is a *constitution* we are expounding.[97]

Presumably "*a constitution*" for Marshall is a blueprint for future guidance but does not fix every important feature of the government. There is pragmatic merit to this conclusion, but it far from follows from the Constitution's text, intent, history, structure, or logic.[98] One explanation for the Framers' writing a document establishing a limited government is that they truly wanted it to be limited.[99]

Marshall appears to deal with this point when he concedes the following: "We admit, as all must, that the powers of the government are limited, and that its limits are not to be transcended. But we think the sound construction of the Constitution must allow to the national legislature that discretion, with respect to the means by which the powers it confers are to be carried into execution, which will enable that body to perform the high duties assigned to it, in the manner most beneficial to the people."[100]

Marshall makes this point after providing an argument showing that the place of the necessary and proper clause in the Constitution, and the nature of its terms, support his interpretation of the provision. Yet here he fails to recognize that had the Framers wished Congress to have discretion in selecting means to bring about enumerated constitutional goals, they would have said so. Instead, they restricted this discretion by requiring that the choice of means be limited to those permissible means that are required for achieving the goal. It is then inconceivable how the test in *McCulloch* can be the following: "Let the end be legitimate, let it be within the scope of the constitution, and all means which are appropriate, which are plainly adapted to that end, which are not prohibited, but consist with the letter and spirit of the constitution, are constitutional."[101] With still living Framers, Marshall contends — and his view is supported today — that the intent, language, logic, or structure of the Constitution permits Congress to adopt just about any means it desires, and that that construction is compatible with the intent of the Framers.[102] In my view, Marshall is clearly amending the Constitution in this decision.

Several pages later, in discussing Congress's power, Marshall goes on to say that "[t]his provision [the necessary and proper clause] is made in a constitution, intended to endure for ages to come, and consequently, to be adapted to the various *crises* of human affairs."[103] The republican notion of a constitution intended to endure perennially and apply to different crises charts a revolutionary strategy, in my sense of "revolutionary." I am unpersuaded by the argument that the phrase "adapted to the various crises of human affairs" modifies the necessary and proper clause, not the Constitution.[104] Even if one concedes the possibility of an ambiguity, adapting the necessary and proper clause to future crises is tantamount to adapting the Constitution, and the revolutionary nature of the clause and the Constitution has the same result. After all, we must not forget that, in this case, the necessary and proper clause is the *Constitution* we are expounding.

The formal illegitimacy of Marshall's decision is not diminished by Black's characterization of Marshall's argument as structuralist: "Marshall's reasoning . . . is . . . essentially structural. It has to do in great part with what he conceives to be the warranted relational properties between the national government and the government of the states, with the structural corollaries of national supremacy — and, at one point, of the mode of formation of the Union. [In] this, perhaps the greatest of our constitutional cases, judgment is reached not fundamentally on the basis of the kind of textual exegesis which we tend to regard as normal, but on the basis of reasoning from the total structure which the text has created."[105]

However, talk of constitutional structure is often talismanic in order to provide a rhetorical backdrop for allegedly proving a novel result. A normal adjudicative role for structure would suggest that structure is a clear and determinate concept. However, if this book's thesis is correct, appeals invoking structure are far from clear and unlikely to produce consensus. What finally achieved consensus regarding the Constitution's structure was in part created by the formative Supreme Court decisions, many of which occurred during Marshall's stewardship.[106] Consequently, the decision in *McCulloch* determined the Constitution's structure concerning the necessary and proper clause, rather than being determined by it.

Even if it is conceded that the national government has implied powers to bring about enumerated ends, Marshall's conclusion concerning the unconstitutionality of the Maryland tax requires an independent argument. After all, it is only by assuming that the power to tax is an unlimited power that this power becomes the power to destroy. Had Marshall recognized that such a power is a matter of degree, he could have accepted a state tax just as long as it did not have the tendency to significantly interfere with the existence of the bank. Justice Holmes correctly pointed out that the "Court . . . can defeat an attempt to discriminate or otherwise go too far without wholly abolishing the power to tax."[107] Consequently, in itself the power to tax is not the power to destroy. Rather, it is the power to regulate. State power to regulate does not destroy congressional power, nor does it violate the supremacy clause in an area that is arguably only an enumerated power in the first place. Moreover, permitting a *de minimis* state tax or the regulation of an enumerated power would serve two important purposes jointly. First, it would not significantly interfere with the enumerated power, and second, it would shore up the notion that federalism is a system of *dual* sovereignty. However, to criticize the reasoning in *McCulloch* is not to deny the importance of the principle Marshall established. The best way to understand Marshall's argument is to view it as a pragmatic statement, predicated on the supposition that the best way for the fledgling republic to develop into a strong national government would be by having an appropriately qualified principle of legislative discretion. As such, Marshall's decision found its source in political theory. Marshall's argument in *McCulloch* was not original, "[b]ut he deserves the credit for stamping it with the die of his memorable rhetoric and converting it from a political theory into the master doctrine of American constitutional law."[108]

Constitutional revolutions usually create law out of a vision of government found in moral and political theory. To many contemporary observers history has certainly vindicated Marshall's vision.[109] Conventional wisdom now endorses the view that a strong national government is essential for the United States to function as a constitutional democracy in today's treacherous world. If so, we may conclude that revolutionary adjudication is necessary to the proper development of American constitutionalism, whatever that might be.[110]

One final observation on *McCulloch*: What if Marshall argued that the necessary and proper clause, properly understood, sanctions, even requires, revolutionary adjudication? If so, then we discover through normal adjudication that this clause has revolutionary implications, and hence revolutionary adjudication flows from the Constitution. Consequently, we discover the meaning of the necessary and proper clause — a surprising meaning — through normal adjudication concerning the text itself, the intent, and history. Thus, although the theory of constitutional revolutions depicts adjudication that follows from these earlier cases, the earlier cases themselves were entirely normal. I do not think Marshall's decision in *McCulloch* does this, but even if it does, the theory of constitutional revolutions remains viable. In that event, where revolutionary adjudication is sanctioned by the Constitution or various clauses of the Constitution, we can then describe the Constitution as being a truly revolutionary judicial document, and those who object to judicial activism are simply wrong on the basis of a normal, proper understanding of the Constitution's own revolutionary clauses. Revolutionary adjudication is legitimate and relevant to present circumstances because the best normal interpretation of the Constitution's provisions sanctions revolution.

The Federal General Powers Revolution — Legislative Ends: Gibbons v. Ogden

During his tenure as chief justice, the effect of Marshall's major decisions was to help to create a federal or national government. The early revolutionary decisions established the supremacy of the federal judiciary regarding the proper interpretation of the Constitution. Yet Marshall was not satisfied with this result.[111] His strategy included creating a stronger central government. In one sense Marshall's strident nationalism was the embodiment of Madison's federalism-nationalism. Federalism creates a scheme of dual governments with constitutional constraints. Nationalism creates a strong central government. Madison's conception of nationalism would relegate the states to a type of administrative (nongovernmental) agency.[112] There were others who would render the states impotent at the drop of a hat.[113] It is, however, a mistake to think that these sentiments were universal. The Federalist leaders knew "that a union which abolished the states would never win acceptance."[114] In *McCulloch* Marshall gave the federal government virtually unlimited power in deciding upon the *means* to otherwise constitutionally permissible ends. He now sought a vehicle for granting the federal government power to determine ends not specified by the Constitution. *Gibbons v. Ogden* is one of the most important revolutionary cases because it lays the groundwork for achieving this goal.

The revolutionary decision in this case consists of two elements. First, Marshall defined commerce[115] in terms of intercourse;[116] and second, he insisted that the federal government's legitimate power to regulate commerce among the states was plenary.

Consider Marshall's words: "If, as has always been understood, the sovereignty of congress, though limited to specified objects, is plenary as to those objects, the power over commerce with foreign nations, and among the several states, is vested in congress as absolutely as it would be in a single government, having in its constitution the same restrictions on the exercise of the power as are found in the constitution of the United States."[117] In making this judgment Marshall rejected "the Tenth Amendment as an active principle of limitation."[118] What normal legal conventions could justify Marshall's rejection? Marshall's characterization "of the powers of congress, and of the commerce power in particular, as the possession of the unqualified authority of a monist sovereign" does not justify his apparent objection to the Tenth Amendment.[119] Nowhere in the ratification process was this or any other instruction given concerning the interpretation of the commerce clause.[120] Moreover, "[t]he Constitution itself . . . does not articulate the boundaries of this commerce power vested in Congress, particularly when Congress has not spoken. Whether or not the commerce power is exclusive or to what extent concurrent state regulation may coexist is not textually demonstrable."[121]

The commerce clause invited revolution. It was written of this provision that "[i]t is remarkable . . . that so important a clause should be so briefly expressed, and leave so much to future determination."[122] This alone cannot account for Marshall's decision. If Marshall wanted to create a real balance between the states as semi-independent sovereigns and a strong federal government, there were alternatives to his decision in *Gibbons*. This was not, however, what Marshall wanted. While apparently paying the requisite homage to the distinction between regulating commerce among the states and regulating intrastate commercial activity, Marshall's decision, in essence, destroys this distinction. However, the concept of a federal government presumably not having general police power requires such a distinction. Had Marshall wanted to, he could have interpreted the commerce clause in such a way as to limit intrusion into state sovereignty. The decision in this case no more follows from the commerce clause, its intent, history, structure, or logic, than any other of Marshall's revolutionary decisions, because the original purpose behind the commerce clause was arguably merely to give Congress the power to prevent state trade barriers.[123] In saying that the decision in this case does not follow from any obvious legal authority, I am not asserting that it was a bad decision.[124] In fact, it was vital to this nation's ultimate industrialization.[125] It was a revolutionary decision based on pragmatic considerations; it was a correct decision politically, not constitutionally, that is, it was correct relative to a certain vision of nationhood.[126]

Contract Clause Revolutions

Marshall's approach to contract clause litigation continues to limit state power in order to protect individual rights. This clause states that "[n]o state shall . . . pass any . . . law impairing the Obligation of Contracts."[127] In *Sturges v. Crownshield* the Marshall Court invalidated a New York State insolvency law based on the original understanding of the clause fearing the common practice of legislatively relieving debtors.[128] Portents of change began in *Ogden v. Saunders,* which held that state insolvency laws were invalid only regarding preexisting contracts.[129] However, Marshall's views on contractual obligations are not limited to original understanding. In addition, Marshall invokes principles of right reason or natural law as the clause's primary meaning. A normal interpretation of this clause would apply to debtor-creditor relations, but perhaps not much more. If it applies to other kinds of contracts, a theory of interpretation must be spelled out that warrants its extension. Without such a theory any extension of the clause has few guidelines. Marshall entered into the fray by appealing to a theory of interpretation drawing on the extrinsic resources of natural law.[130] For Marshall the obligatoriness of contracts arose from the foundations of promising contained in principles of right reason or natural law. Therefore, states did not have the power to intervene with contractual relations because doing so violates natural law. Because the contract clause could be understood only in naturalist terms, Marshall rejected the distinction between contracts existing before the allegedly offending law, and those created afterward.[131] For Marshall it was obvious that "[i]ndividuals . . . bring that right [contract] with them into society."[132] Marshall's libertarianism in this context struggles against his Federalist or nationalist interpretations of other constitutional provisions. This is not to say that Marshall's views were bizarre or idiosyncratic. Many people believed the clause to be "the bulwark of American individualism against democratic impatience and socialistic fantasy."[133] However, this was a partisan position not everyone shared. The contract clause was one of the few rights-protecting clauses in the original Constitution before the existence of the Bill of Rights, and perhaps Marshall's valorization of the clause derived from its right-protecting function. If so, this can be explained by the following: First, perhaps Marshall believed that the Framers were libertarian in the classical liberal sense; in this view individual rights, most prominently the right to contractual freedom, was an essential feature of the social will. In libertarian society, beyond obligations concerning law and order, contractual freedom was the only basis of obligation. Marshall might also have taken a stringent position on the clause because he found it desirable for Congress and the federal courts to police state laws. In this regard Marshall's contract clause revolution extends his revolutions regarding the other key constitutional clauses.

Although the records of the Constitutional Convention contain few details concerning the purpose and scope of this clause, the standard view is that the clause was designed to prevent states from intervening on behalf of debtors, a common practice at the time of the Founding. Marshall's position effectively permitted federal policing of state laws, tilting the balance toward the federal government in the federalism controversy. Marshall could have narrowly interpreted this clause, holding it inapplicable to contracts violative of public policy, but he did not. This is a revolutionary use of the clause to help establish national supremacy at the cost of state power. Marshall's interpretation appeals to extrinsic constitutional factors by appealing to a system of law that has independent and supervening validity. Interpretations of this sort lend themselves to revolutionary adjudication.

The problem is that, if natural law is an appropriate vehicle for constitutional adjudication, whose version should we invoke?[134] Given the limits of human knowledge, natural law plays right into a revolutionary judicial temperament. During his Court's tenure, Marshall's expansive view of the scope of the clause prevailed. Arguably, Marshall's use of the clause was merely an appeal to normal conventions such as text and historical intent. Understood in this fashion, the early contract clause cases were not revolutionary but rather followed from constitutional practice itself. The reason I am not persuaded by this argument is that although the text recognizes the obligatoriness of contracts generally, the historical intent was very specific. We take it as an article of faith that general language applies generally, though no one really believes this completely. Consider, for example, the equal protection clause. No one takes seriously a constitutional argument that the common law of theft is invalid because "theft" assumes legal ownership, and that violates equal protection of the laws. Similarly, Marshall read the contract clause in a more expansive manner than history warrants because he believed natural law, not history, settled the matter.

Marshall's revolutionary stance toward the contract clause is evidence for the theory of constitutional revolutions, because the subsequent development of litigation in this area is strikingly revolutionary. Despite the initial indeterminacy of the clause, and Marshall's expansive interpretation, the post-Marshall Court began to restrict the clause's reach,[135] and ultimately, in *Home Building and Loan Association v. Blaisdell,* the Court virtually reverses the standard interpretation of the clause, rendering it in effect a dead letter in regulating state laws.[136] In this case the Court upheld a Minnesota law regarding foreclosure, specifically permitting states, in times of emergency, to relieve temporarily mortgagees from paying their debt. What is remarkable about this case is that its facts are almost exactly like the facts the contract clause was designed to cover, and the law in question almost exactly like the law the contract clause was intended to strike down. Despite these potentially constraining facts, Chief Justice Hughes upheld the law as consistent with the contract clause. The chief justice argued that a permanent law of this sort might be invalid. However, as a temporary measure, nothing in the Constitution precludes it. His views of the history and jurisprudence of the clause ring out in true revolutionary fashion. Here he introduced the topic:

> [I]n the construction of the contract clause, the debates in the Constitutional Convention are of little aid. But the reasons which led to the

adoption of that clause, and of the other prohibitions of Section 10 of Article I, are not left in doubt and have frequently been described with eloquent emphasis. The widespread distress following the revolutionary period, and the plight of debtors, had called forth in the States an ignoble army of legislative schemes for the defeat of creditors and the invasion of contractual obligations. Legislative interferences had been so numerous and extreme that the confidence essential to prosperous trade had been so undermined and the utter destruction of credit was threatened.

The first part of the chief justice's opinion concerns delineating reasons for the constitutional protection of the contract clause. The chief justice then turns and bargains away the contract clause, in good revolutionary fashion, by finding that states must have the capacity to place reasonable regulations on contractual freedom. The state cannot relinquish its police powers authority by permitting contracts contrary to public health, welfare, and safety. If "legislative action is addressed to a legitimate end and the measures taken are reasonable and appropriate to that end," the statute is valid.[137] Thus, if the state's interference with contractual freedom is designed to achieve the general good, and does not invidiously burden creditors, then the clause is inapplicable. Chief Justice Hughes admits that the state's police powers and the contract clause must be read coherently. According to Hughes the state could not "adopt as its policy the repudiation of debts or the destruction of contracts or the denial of the means to enforce them."[138] However, temporary restraints of enforcement are constitutionally valid.

The natural reply here is to be perplexed. The circumstances in *Blaisdell* are precisely the same as those for which the clause was originally constructed. Yet Hughes has little patience for this complaint:

> It is no answer to say that this public need was not apprehended a century ago, or to insist that what the provision of the Constitution meant to the vision of that day it must mean to the vision of our time. If by the statement that what the Constitution meant at the time of its adoption it means to-day, it is intended to say that the great clause of the Constitution must be confined to the interpretation which the framers, with the conditions and outlook of their time, would have placed upon them, the statement carries its own refutation. It was to guard against such a narrow conception that Chief Justice Marshall

uttered the memorable warning—"We must never forget that it is *a constitution* we are expounding."[139]

For Hughes the Minnesota law must be evaluated through the entire practice of American constitutionalism, and not merely the concrete expectations of individuals who lived in the past. Justice Sutherland's dissent included these observations: "The defense of the Minnesota law is made upon grounds which were discounted by the makers of the Constitution. [That] defense should not now succeed, because it constitutes an effort to overthrow the constitutional provision by an appeal to facts and circumstances identical with those which brought it into existence. With due regard for the processes of logical thinking, it legitimately cannot be urged that conditions which produced the rule may now be invoked to destroy it."[140]

Justice Sutherland eloquently warns that "[i]f the provisions of the Constitution be not upheld when they pinch as well as when they comfort, they may as well be abandoned."[141] Two points require mention. First, the split between Hughes and Sutherland can be understood in terms of the theory of constitutional revolutions. The chief justice believes extrinsic factors such as economic depression *can* temporarily suspend a constitutional provision, whereas Justice Sutherland believes discretion defeats constitutional protection. The former advocates revolutionary adjudication in this case, whereas the latter sticks to normal adjudication. Second, the theory does not show why one side or the other is more plausible. If one agrees with the result in *Blaisdell,* one must endorse revolutionary adjudication. If so, one is ready to embrace the theory of constitutional revolutions.

Marshall's critics have argued that his decisions, in effect, destroyed a system of two governments and transformed a government of limited powers into one of unlimited powers.[142] It is difficult to believe that Marshall embraced a serious role for the states in American constitutionalism.[143] Instead Marshall was, among other things, the architect-in-chief of American constitutional nationalism.

The Failure of the Individual Rights Revolution: Barron v. Mayor of Baltimore

In *Barron v. Mayor of Baltimore* Marshall ended the series of revolutions he began in *Marbury.*[144] In this case Marshall found that the Fifth Amendment's prohibition on confiscating private property for public use without just compensation did not apply to state governments. Marshall went further in his decision in concluding that none of the first eight amendments applied to the states.[145]

Although Marshall, in the revolutionary decisions discussed previously, reached out to secure sufficient power for the national government to offset the power of the states, his aspirations dwindled when it came to protecting individuals from the excesses of state government. Only in the area of human rights did Marshall's belief in the effectiveness of central power wane. Now, it is an article of faith that the Bill of Rights was designed to limit only the powers of the national government. With certain notable exceptions, the historical evidence, so the argument goes, supports Marshall's decision in *Barron*. However, not every commentator shares this faith. Indeed, one writer contends that the historical evidence goes against Marshall's decision in *Barron*.[146]

Admittedly, there is no explicit textual evidence that the Bill of Rights applies to the states. However, this means only that if the Bill of Rights can restrict the states, its authority to do so is implied. Because many of Marshall's revolutionary decisions involve finding implied powers, why did he hesitate to find implied rights? If the Bill of Rights consists of such fundamentally important constitutional values, it is implausible to argue that the Founders intended to restrict its application to the national government only. The Bill of Rights expresses the people's desire to protect their fundamental interests. They wanted protection from government, not just from federal government. The point here is that amendments one through eight of the Constitution proscribe conduct that was anathema to these interests. Consequently, "[i]t is . . . utterly impossible to suppose that, as to a single one of the matters the amendments cover, the true intention of the First Congress was to create sole and exclusive state powers to do the things forbidden."[147] Of course, the argument restricting the application of the Bill of Rights to the federal government does not sanction state governments in violating the substance of these amendments. It merely says that a different vehicle for restricting the states must be found, such as state constitutional law. Although Marshall had grounds, there was also creditable evidence to support the view that the Bill of Rights applied to the states, especially in light of the earlier formative revolutions concerning federalism and nationalism.

Seen in this light, *Barron v. Baltimore* represents one part of the conclusion of the most revolutionary judicial revolutions in American history. Consider the following clear statement of the principle:

I am inclined, however, to the opinion, that the article in question [the Fifth Amendment's proscription of double jeopardy] does extend to all judicial tribunals in the United States, whether constituted by the Congress of the United States, or the states individually. The provision is general in its nature, and unrestricted in its terms; and the sixth article of the constitution declares, that the constitution shall be the supreme law of the land; and that the judges in every state shall be bound thereby, anything in the constitution or laws of any state to the contrary notwithstanding. These general and comprehensive expressions extend the provisions of the constitution of the United States to every article which is not confined, by the subject matter, to the national government, and is equally applicable to the states.[148]

One early commentator argued that some amendments other than the first "apply to the state legislatures as well as that of the Union. The important principles contained in them are now incorporated by adoption into the instrument itself; they form parts of the declared rights of the people, of which neither the state powers nor those of the Union can ever deprive them."[149] In such circumstances, when normal adjudication — that is, adjudication based on traditional authoritative devices — does not settle the issue either way, Marshall could have effected a revolution concerning individual rights, which would have been no more revolutionary than his other revolutionary decisions. Instead, he mysteriously chose to stabilize his own revolutionary efforts. The republic was forced to wait for both new constitutional text and the interpretation of a future Court for the view that the Constitution's notion of due process clause incorporated portions of the Bill of Rights to state government. What makes this odd is the fact that one could argue that the Constitution does not adequately protect due process and equal protection of its citizens unless the Bill of Rights applies to all governments within the purview of the Constitution. Federal supremacy would have been extended by finding that the Bill of Rights applies to the states. Why Marshall chose not to continue his revolutionary federalism is unclear.

The Marshall Court

We have examined some of the Marshall Court's formative revolutions by inspecting them through the lens of the theory of constitutional revolutions. Each decision is revolutionary because it does not follow from the Constitution's text, intent, history, structure, or logic in a way conducive to reasonable agreement. Moreover, each case could have easily been decided differently. Few, if any, controversial constitutional decisions could not have been decided differently, because these decisions that engage constitutional scholars, lawyers, judges, and citizens typically are underdetermined by normal conventions.[150] When a decision is underdetermined, constitutional revolutions of different degrees of magnitude usually occur. In these circumstances, for the decision to be generated, a judge must appeal to cultural or moral factors not explicitly stated in the law.

The postmodern pragmatist position is committed to resolving—and more importantly, to understanding—controversy. The argument is not that dissensus in itself entails revolution, but, rather, that when highly competent reasoners choose sides of a controversial issue, and when their arguments are refined and coherent, it is difficult to appreciate how one side is right and the other wrong. Admittedly, not even this sophisticated dissensus entails that neither view is true. Dissensus of whatever kind cannot entail falsity any more than reflective consensus can entail truth. Practically speaking, though, when a person gives a compelling argument for one side of a controversy, met by an arguably equally compelling argument from the other side, it is impossible for a third party, or even the two participants themselves, to know with any assurance who is right. In constitutional law when this situation occurs, the natural tendency is to seek the result that follows from the Constitution. From a God's-eye perspective maybe there is such a result. Yet because we can never have assurance that we've identified the true result in controversial cases, revolutionary adjudication will occur perennially.

Genuine disagreements exist in constitutional law "which, although not resolvable by argument of any kind are nevertheless sustained by perfectly respectable arguments and evidence."[151] These disputes involve essentially contested practical concepts, "concepts the proper use of which inevitably involves endless disputes" about their application.[152] The idea of essentially contested concepts in constitutional adjudication explains, on one level, why revolutionary adjudication occurs. A Court applies a constitutional provision using an essentially contested concept to resolve some constitutional crisis. Within that provision adjudication becomes normal, but the governing paradigm is in principle open to dispute, depending upon how well it did its job as well as how palatable it is to the citizenry on other grounds. We see here that a normal paradigm typically is a provisional fixed point in constitutional law. Without such fixed points adjudication could not occur successfully, which is why constitutional law seeks normalcy. In normal cases reflective agreement is typically abundant. The postmodern pragmatist seeks such consensus, but when it is not forthcoming, she tries to understand why competent reasoners systematically disagree.

In the Marshall Court decisions each seminal decision was revolutionary because it read into the Constitution a particular substantive political philosophy, not a neutral or objective principle of constitutional law. Under the guise of constitutionalism Marshall implicitly or explicitly appealed to extrinsic political factors on which to base his decisions.[153] In these cases the Marshall Court blended a certain conception of federalism with formal constitutional provisions.[154] The meaning of the Constitution regarding these provisions did not reside inherently in its language. Rather, the Marshall Court placed it there in order to advance a particular conception of a constitutional democracy. No doubt Marshall claimed to be fulfilling the intentions of the Framers.[155] Despite this, Marshall "consciously furthered the political goals of the Federalist party, by stretching the Constitution's meaning to increase national power at the expense of state power,"[156] while insisting that he was distinguishing constitutional law from politics.[157] Even if the distinction between law and politics were a defensible distinction, drawing the distinction in the first place is itself determined by one's political philosophy. Moreover, where one draws the distinction in any given case is again determined by one's political philosophy.

Neither Marshall's interpretations, nor anyone else's, can permanently disguise the political elements in constitutional law. These elements are political in the sense of political *philosophy,* not necessarily in the sense of partisan politics or disputes over policy. Marshall's "rules of interpretation," for the most part, were rhetorical devices for ensuring the legitimacy of his revolutionary decisions. These rhetorical devices helped Marshall conceal the pragmatic dimension of his decisions. Whether disguised as a rhetorical device or an explicit appeal to extrinsic factors, Marshall's decisions embodied a pragmatic strategy for achieving certain meritorious political goals. Marshall's brand of revolutionary adjudication may indeed be unique. Its uniqueness may be attributed to Marshall himself. Perhaps a modicum of Marshall's success rests in the fact that American constitutionalism, as any fledgling practice, needed to be created, and Marshall reserved that job for himself. One thing we can say with certainty is that the kind of revolutions occurring during this period is not surprising. Anytime a freshly minted written document is to function as positive law, revolutionary decisions are likely to occur. Such decisions define the way constitutional law develops. In short, a written constitution, rather than seriously constraining constitutional practice, sets the major concerns of the practice and invites radically different interpretations of these terms.[158]

Contemporary Revolutions

The Civil Rights Revolution: Brown v. Board of Education

We have already seen how *Brown* in our own era is paradigmatic of a revolutionary decision overturning precedent.[159] At this point one should realize that two things are true of *Brown*. First, everyone, or almost everyone, believes that the result in *Brown* is correct. No one, however, has yet demonstrated the normal reasoning that generates this result. *Brown* was not merely the reversal of any precedent,[160] it was the overruling of a foundational constitutional interpretation, an interpretation that determined the meaning of the relevant provision throughout the legal system.[161] Given the centrality of a foundational provision, we must determine how it is possible to overturn its current interpretation. If the decision to be overturned is law, what then is the constitutional basis of the new decision?[162] As indicated in our earlier discussion of Dworkin's theory, law as integrity, there is no constitutional basis for such a decision, because the new decision is a constitutional revolution.[163] This does not mean that the revolutionary decision cannot be causally explained by reference to the wider culture or to abstract moral theory. Indeed, the seeds of the revolution might exist in the distant past.[164] However, it is always a judge or a court that constitutionalizes the fruits of this seed so that it might become law.

Both conventionalist and pragmatic theories of law allow for the possibility of constitutional revolutions such as *Brown*. According to conventionalist theories, judges must decide cases according to well-accepted legal paradigms. When such paradigms run out, a judge is permitted to use his discretion.[165] Pragmatism counsels judges to decide cases in accordance with the best overall moral and political interpretation of the relevant practice. With respect to both conventionalism and pragmatism, the decision in *Brown* was new law.[166] In such cases judges are clearly making, not merely applying already existent, law.

The Personal Autonomy Revolution: Griswold to Hardwick

The decision in *Griswold v. Connecticut* to invalidate a law forbidding the use of birth control devices was one of the most important and controversial constitutional revolutions in the twentieth century.[167] Its importance lies in both the substantive right created and in the methodology instituted to find such a right. The magnitude of the *Griswold* revolution lies in formulating a general principle implying "a constitutional right of privacy divorced from the specific privacy-oriented guarantees of the Bill of Rights."[168] Nowhere in the Constitution's text, intent, history, structure, or logic does the word "privacy" appear; yet the Court in this case began a revolution that has now captured the imagination of the American people.[169] In *Griswold* Justice Douglas's methodology indicates that "specific guarantees in the Bill of Rights have penumbras, formed by emanations from those guarantees that help give them life and substance."[170] These explicit constitutional provisions "create zones of privacy," or a general constitutional principle for justifying decisions invalidating laws that intrude on this salient right,[171] "a right older than the Bill of Rights — older than our political parties, older than our social system. Marriage is a coming together for better or worse, hopefully enduring, and intimate to the degree of being sacred. It is an association that promotes a way of life, not causes; a harmony in living, not political faiths; a bilateral loyalty, not commercial or social projects. Yet it is an association for as noble a purpose as any involved in our prior decisions."[172] Despite the normal judicial reluctance expressed in the dissent to create constitutional principle, the majority began a revolution by fashioning a particular paradigm, never before held in that form, at least in constitutional thinking. The paradigm in this context tells us what kinds of facts generate issues of privacy as well as the sort of methodology to use for discovering implicit constitutional rights generally. Thus, *Griswold* is a paradigm for disposing of issues of constitutional privacy, as well as a paradigm or general methodology for discovering rights.

Both the substantive and methodological paradigms in *Griswold* had an immediate precursor in *Poe v. Ullman,*[173] where Harlan in dissent characterized the right of privacy as emanating "from the totality of the constitutional scheme under which we live."[174] Harlan thought the Connecticut statute was constitutionally invalid because " 'liberty' is not a series of isolated points pricked out in terms [the relevant provisions of the Bill of Rights]. It is a rational continuum, which, broadly speaking, includes a

freedom from all substantial arbitrary impositions and purposeless restraints, and which also recognizes, what a reasonable and sensitive judgment must, that certain interests require a particularly careful scrutiny of the
state needs asserted to justify their abridgement."[175] Consequently, Justice
Harlan could not separate the specific grants of privacy from their moral
justification in terms of personal autonomy. To accept one requires accept-
ing the other. Harlan's rationale ultimately prevailed in *Griswold*. In *Griswold* the Court appealed to a general principle of privacy or personal autonomy, which it thought grounded the particular privacy values contained in
the Bill of Rights. It was necessary to postulate this general right of privacy
in order to formulate a coherent conception of personal autonomy found in
American constitutionalism.

The Court's unfortunate use of language has been one reason that *Griswold* is still used as an example of "unprincipled adjudication." Many theorists and jurists find it difficult to regard the metaphorical language of
"penumbras" and "emanations" as useful judicial guides. Without instructions for interpreting and applying the metaphor, we have no way of determining precisely what the methodology is. We know from the opinion that
the right of privacy is derived, in some manner, from some of the first eight
amendments and not "independently on an interpretation of the due process clause."[176] How this right derives from the particular amendments is
still a mystery. Constitutional revolutions giving rise to innovative adjudicative strategies for creating new substantive constitutional meaning
must be based on more than metaphor.[177]

No one denies that the Constitution contains specific grants of privacy,
for example, in the First, Third, Fourth, and Fifth Amendments. The question arises whether these specific grants are constitutionally sufficient to
generate a general right of privacy.[178] Because we can easily imagine a society that values only certain kinds of privacy, or certain aspects of a univocal
sense of privacy, the Constitution cannot be said to include a generalized
right to privacy over and above the particular grants of privacy, unless
normal adjudication says it does. It is incumbent, of course, upon those
asserting that the Constitution implies a general right to privacy to present
a clear and demonstrable theory of implication sufficient to justify such a
conclusion. The notion of implication employed here is one of pragmatic
inference, not logical proof. Logical proof is deductive and presumably
yields determinate answers, whereas pragmatic inference is interpretive and
contestable. Because no one pragmatic result necessarily will force itself

upon us, whichever result is chosen will be a revolutionary choice. Consequently, the substantive result as well as the methodology adopted in *Griswold* are both revolutionary.

One might object that decisions like *Griswold* are simply wrong. If *Griswold* does not follow from the Constitution through the normal methods of adjudication, it is unjustified and should be abandoned. If constitutional decisions, generally, cannot be explained by normal adjudication, then they are not just revolutionary, they are illegitimate. However, revolutionary cases produce pragmatic benefits, which few are likely to give up. Many revolutionary cases appear retrospectively to be essential to American constitutionalism. Moreover, if we take *actual* constitutional practice seriously, courts have been engaging in revolutionary adjudication from the beginning of the Republic. To say these decisions are wrong and should be abandoned would mean invalidating large pieces of two hundred years of American constitutional practice. A basic reason for not considering the decision in *Griswold* wrong is that it is absurd to think that American constitutionalism and democracy would permit a state government to enter into the intimate details of an individual's life to prescribe proper conduct. Our contemporary culture, partly due to *Griswold,* recoils at that intrusion, in part explaining the failure of the Bork nomination. Privacy, now a culturally entrenched value, simply renders talk of retrenching this right as "politically incorrect" in the best sense of that term.

Nevertheless, the methodology implicit in this process needs to be articulated. Suppose a document protects a person's car, her house, and her boat. One possible justification of these protections appeals to a principle citing the importance of an individual's capacity to control her property. If this principle best conveys the justificatory force of the individual protections, that is, if these protections require the principle of private property for their justification, then that principle becomes just as lawful as specific provisions in the document. If, in novel circumstances, the question arises whether the document protects a person's horse, the new generalized justificatory principle should apply here also unless conclusive argument excludes horses from the category of property; it should apply with equal force as the specific provisions in the document. Without this generalized justification for owning certain artifacts, the specific protections have no justificatory force. Similarly, the argument for privacy in *Griswold* is that specific privacy protections in the Bill of Rights require a general right to privacy for their justification. Consequently, this generalized right is as much a part of the

Constitution as the specific provisions concerning privacy. This argument is a good one. Specific examples of privacy are meaningless without invoking a general principle to provide the context and to determine what is attractive about a range of privacy activities. The standard response is that constitutionally we need no general justification of privacy to justify specific privacy provisions; we merely need normal conventions to justify them. After all, we are engaged in constitutional, not moral, reasoning.

Although a defender of *Griswold* might defend the decision in different ways, my purpose here is not to continue this argument, but rather to indicate that the controversy itself suggests that *Griswold* was revolutionarily decided.[179] For our purposes *Griswold's* importance lies in providing an excellent example of both revolutionary and postrevolutionary adjudication. The revolutionary decision in *Griswold* determines the scope of the general right to privacy. The period following *Griswold* illustrates postrevolutionary activity in all its splendor. Subsequent cases extended privacy in marriage to privacy more generally, including to the postrevolutionary abortion decisions.[180] During this period courts attempted to determine whether and to what extent other constitutional problems — for example, contraception among unmarried couples, family living arrangements, parental rights, the right to marry, personal appearance, the right to die, and so forth — should be solved according to the paradigm in *Griswold*.[181] This postrevolutionary period seeks to perfect, refine, and stabilize the privacy paradigm in order to generate normal adjudication.[182] Stabilizing the paradigm involves ending the revolution.

In carrying out normal adjudication the precise nature and desirability of the paradigm might be questioned. *Bowers v. Hardwick* is a good example of such a challenge to the paradigm.[183] In *Hardwick* the Court refused to invalidate a Georgia statute prohibiting consensual homosexual sodomy. In this case the Court took a narrow view of *Griswold* and its progeny, ending the extension of the *Griswold* revolution. The question of when to end a revolution is as controversial as revolutionary adjudication itself. Typically, coherentists argue against the legitimacy of failing to extend a revolutionary paradigm in cases to which it reasonably applies. Here the basic argument is that *Hardwick* distorts *Griswold* because no reasonable distinction exists between the privacy rights in these cases. The privacy right in *Griswold* cannot be restricted to heterosexual contexts.[184] Thus, on coherentist grounds, so the argument goes, *Griswold* and *Hardwick* are incompatible.

Coherence theorists typically argue against normal adjudication in this context. The constitutional question can be resolved by appealing to general principles embedded in constitutional practice. According to such theories, a judge should decide to seek explanatory and justificatory principles in order to determine the decision these principles imply for the present case. Coherence theories favor decisions that follow from and extend past decisions. In the limiting context, a coherence theory dictates simple consistency with prior opinions. A more complex conception of coherence requires us to derive our decision from the scheme of explanatory and justificatory principles underlying that area of law. One adopts a coherence theory when one insists that apparently different cases can be subsumed under a general principle, thereby requiring equal treatment. Because arguably there is no relevant difference between homosexuality and heterosexuality, for example, advocates of coherence theory insist on constitutionally protecting both. In their view *Griswold* and its progeny are sufficient ground for Justice Blackmun's dissent in *Hardwick*. Hence, in this view the Court in *Hardwick* erred by not including consensual homosexual sodomy under the constitutional protection of the general right to privacy.[185]

Notice that the coherentist's enthusiasm for extending *Griswold* to *Hardwick* is not diminished despite the privacy cases' explicit recognition of privacy in the context of marriage, family, and procreation. Moreover, this enthusiasm does not wane even in the face of the Court's explicit exclusion of homosexual privacy from the privacy paradigm.[186] The coherentist argument insists upon a more general principle of independence from state interference, or a constitutional value of the freedom of intimate association that protects consenting adult homosexual relations.[187] The functionalist dimension of coherentist arguments contends that a constitutionally protected activity, valued because of the role it plays in an individual's life, entails that other activities playing the same role in someone else's life must be afforded the same protection. In this view homosexuality between consenting adults should be (is?) protected because homosexuality is a form of intimacy, self-definition, or a central feature of being a person. Consequently, barring some compelling justification, the principle of privacy or personal autonomy in the privacy cases already extends to homosexual privacy.

Professor Tribe eloquently states the functionalist argument.[188] Tribe faults the *Hardwick* majority for misidentifying what the law is in this case. Tribe's first reason for this objection is:

The *Hardwick* majority's decision to cut off constitutional protection "at the first convenient, if arbitrary boundary" drawn by prior cases is not only antithetical to the genius of the common law, it also ignored the warning in *Moore v. East Cleveland,* against "clos[ing] our eyes to the basic reasons *why* certain rights . . . have been accorded shelter under the fourteenth amendment's due process clause." As the dissenters pointed out, "we protect the decision whether to marry precisely because marriage 'is an association that promotes a way of life, not cause; a harmony in living, not political faiths; a bilateral loyalty, not commercial social projects.'" And we protect the family because it contributes so powerfully to the happiness of individuals, not because of a preference for stereotypical households. The underlying value in those contexts, as in the *Hardwick* case, is protection for intimate human associations.[189]

This passage raises important conceptual questions about the relationship between a constitutional result and its justification. It is not obvious that the Court's job is to extend a justification intended to apply to certain specific circumstances of unintended cases. Marriage is valued for many reasons, such as, religious, utilitarian, or even egoistic or narcissistic reasons.[190] The problem is that the degree of generality of the principle in *Griswold* is difficult to determine. Apparently, Tribe believes that a constitutional principle's level of generality is determined mechanically. On the contrary, not only is there no mechanical procedure for determining the appropriate level of generality, there is no reliable procedure at all. Presently, the law is indeterminate regarding the level of generality of the right to privacy. The law must "embrace" a decision to settle the matter. This shows a revolutionary element is the process of refining and stabilizing a revolution. Tribe believes that a more general principle than marriage, procreation, and family is the appropriate principle in the privacy cases.[191] The majority in *Hardwick* also believes in a general principle but one that restricts the issues to heterosexual contexts. We will never appreciate the nature of the majority's view unless we recognize that insisting upon greater generality will not always work. The majority's view represents seeing the world differently; it is tied to incommensurable conceptions of society.

In *Hardwick* the dissent's argument is that this case implicates a general right to privacy, not specifically the particular right to engage in homosexual sodomy. For the dissent a general principle or fundamental value exists, the right of intimate associations. This general right is constitutionally protected, which means that concrete applications of this right are also protected. Generality is the key to the argument in *Hardwick*. However, the acceptable degree of generality in constitutional reasoning is largely indeterminate. The dissent and Tribe must describe and defend such a methodology.[192] The question of relevantly similar conduct and circumstances arises here; unfortunately, relevance is often deeply contested. If the justification of a portion of one's moral values required a principle P to justify them, and the individual wants to retain these values, then the justification should apply to cases unintended. To say that logically this point is correct is not tantamount to saying that it is constitutionally correct. One important feature of common-law systems is that there can be an agreement on result without an agreement on justification. Thus, everyone might agree that marriage is a fundamentally important human institution without agreeing on what makes it so. Consequently, the reason certain rights are accorded protection under the Fourteenth Amendment's due process clause may differ from social group to social group; yet all may agree on the result. This distinction between result and justification is one salient difference between law and morality.[193] If we agree on the propriety of a particular law, we need not agree on the law's justification. However, sharing an ethical system requires agreeing on the result *and* the justification. A legal system can be understood as those promulgated dictates, endorsed by diverse moral systems, that are necessary for social life to be stable and to flourish.[194] Opponents of this distinction overlook the fact that the *source* of law derives from many quarters, morality being a principal one. In such circumstances it makes no sense to say that the moral principle is already in the law, because in revolutionary adjudication a new constitutional paradigm is being created.

Fundamental rights are always balanced against social interest. To make the right of privacy general as applying to intimacy or moral independence gives almost any activity a presumptive correctness against state intervention. On the other hand, most violent or otherwise obviously harmful activities will easily rebut the presumption. Other offensive but not harmful activities will be protected, as perhaps they should. Further, even if one agrees with Tribe's reasons for valuing marriage, why does this make Tribe's conception the constitutional paradigm in the privacy cases? Tribe's model may be the appropriate moral paradigm without being the paradigm referred to in the privacy cases.

Constitutional or legal paradigms indicate the appropriateness of certain relations among individuals in a political society.[195] These paradigms involve recognized procedures for determining how to resolve legal conflicts.[196] Finally, legal theory itself involves a "morality of the law," but this is not the same as abstract moral theory. No doubt, a legal paradigm must be explicated in terms of its logical implications, but it is misleading to describe what we do when we look for these logical implications as "the imaginative extension of the significations of laws and other relevant social phenomena to situations and areas in which no plaintiff in a given contemporary society has perhaps yet brought suit or about which possibly no member of a past society that is being studied is ever known to have complained."[197] The process is a pragmatic, interpretive process, a process that gives new meaning to old laws. It is one principal way the law changes and evolves toward a nobler moral vision. What we can't say of such a process is that it tells us what the law is; instead, it tells us what the law should be and is becoming.

The question here is whether this pragmatist process is a change in the law or whether "the life of the law is a permanent striving to fulfil the practical moral imperatives implicit in legal institutions and legal rules."[198] If every constitutional decision follows from imperatives implicit in the law, constitutional change is trivialized; it virtually never occurs. More strikingly, the terms "implicit" and "direct" and their kind can be dangerous devices for camouflaging constitutional change.[199] If constitutional rules are already "implicit" in the law, or follow "indirectly" from the law, this methodology must be described and defended. According to the theory of constitutional revolutions, no one has yet successfully done so. Of course, one can insist that because the best moral paradigm is so important, we simply identify the moral paradigm with the constitutional one. In that event we abandon the need for justifying our present decision in terms of how well it fits prior case law. In other words, we have given up entirely a commitment to coherence as a condition of adequacy for judicial decisions.

Suppose the best justifying paradigm of privacy included the right of homosexuals to marry. Would we say that they had that right all along? Would we say this right was originally included in the sexual privacy paradigm? Or would we instead say that the sexual privacy paradigm needed to be perfected and refined through adjudication before it included this right? One ought not to interpret this dispute as merely verbal. It matters greatly how we characterize the evolution of constitutional paradigm, because it tells us what is methodologically proper for future cases. Indeed, how we characterize this issue is one way of distinguishing between coherentist and pragmatist constitutional theory. Coherentism insists that "new" law be derived from old law by a specifiable method of derivation. Pragmatist adjudication requires only that the price of new law is worth the cost of the departure.

Pragmatist constitutional theory looks to the actual constitutional para-digm — as it is at the time of decision. A pragmatist judge then determines how closely the constitutional paradigm conforms to the moral paradigm. If these paradigms are sufficiently close, pragmatist theory interprets the constitutional paradigm to be identical to the moral paradigm, thereby implying a new constitutional right. If the moral paradigm fits the constitu-tional paradigm poorly, the moral paradigm is rejected unless its attractive-ness as a justification compensates for its poor fit. In such circumstances pragmatist theory contends that the constitutional paradigm *should* be transformed into a morally acceptable model. Coherence theorists contend that coherence explains both normal and revolutionary adjudication. How-ever, only a minimal consistency can explain normal adjudication, and a more full-blooded coherence cannot explain revolutionary adjudication. Even when coherence contributes to a good explanation of a change in the law, it usually does so through an appeal to values in the wider culture.

Dworkin believes that the structure of constitutional principles requires invalidating the law in *Hardwick* because it violates the principle in *Griswold* and its progeny. Dworkin argues that "[i]f the nation's history generally endorses the idea of moral independence but denies independence to ho-mosexuals, though the distinction cannot even plausibly be justified in principle, fairness is not offended by insisting on a coherent enforcement of that idea."[200] His argument is not merely that it is morally wrong to dis-criminate against homosexuals; we shouldn't discriminate against them because the right of personal sovereignty or intimate associations commits us (through generality) to constitutionally protect homosexuals as well. If we are truly averse to protecting homosexuals, we can give up the principle of privacy and fashion a more crabbed conception of personal autonomy. "Privacy," "autonomy," "personal dignity," and so forth are open-textured terms that necessarily include and exclude different classifications. Some conception of moral independence is endorsed by the nation's history, to be sure, but precisely which conception is controversial. The case law protect-ing private sexual morality arguably involves sexual conduct that in principle is tied to marriage and procreation.[201] Is there a good moral reason to make this connection? I think not, but that requires a moral argument, not a constitutional one. Those opposing homosexual privacy on constitutional grounds contend that it is easily distinguishable from the paradigm for privacy in the case law.[202] Because they do not see homosexuality as having anything to do with the sexuality associated with marriage and procreation, in their view homosexuality is not constitutionally protected. Dworkin's "generality" argument in itself does not work, because other values qualify the principle of independence; just what those values are, and their respective weight, is subject to controversy.

Suppose we formulate the Kantian attitude of concern and respect for individuals as persons as the basis for extending to *Hardwick* the decision in *Griswold*. This attitude involves coming to see the moral legitimacy of the nonharmful expression of individual sexuality. Thus, consensual adult sexuality deserves respect, regardless of whether it is marital or not, heterosexual or homosexual. Suppose further that this is abstractly or ideally the correct moral view of adult consensual sexuality. Is it also a constitutional principle? Dworkin must explain how moral principles become constitutional ones. Without such an explanation his contention that there are moral principles embedded in the law is no more than ipse dixit.[203]

Dworkin argues that "liberty is secured only when the government leaves citizens alone to decide the most intimate or personal questions about their own lives for themselves, except when urgent social policies make that impossible."[204] However, this view is both under- and overinclusive in anyone's interpretation, because it leaves undecided the question of what counts as intimate. The point here is not that Dworkin's position is morally wrong, but that given the different meanings of this perspective, the answer can be reached only through revolutionary adjudication. When viewed as a moral or political principle contained in our cultural traditions or in abstract theory, Dworkin's principle is correct, but this does not mean this is a *constitutional* principle. The actual cases on sexual privacy tie that privacy right to marriage, family, and procreation. Thus, it could be argued that *Hardwick* was decided correctly through the stabilizing dimension of postrevolutionary adjudication while for the dissent's view to have prevailed would require further refinement of the *Griswold* paradigm. Thus, either position in *Hardwick* is postrevolutionary all the way down.

There appear to be two reasons for Dworkin's conviction that the preceding principle is the correct *constitutional* principle. First, it is more general than alternative principles.[205] In favorably commenting on Blackmun's dissenting opinion in *Hardwick*, Dworkin writes that "Justice Blackmun's opinion . . . insisted on treating those cases [*Griswold* et al.] as decided on a more general principle that future judges should try to identify and respect, and therefore as extending to other groups, including homosexuals, beyond their immediate beneficiaries of the decisions,"[206] but this does not explain why a more *general* principle is a better *constitutional* principle. Second, it is contained in a theory of constitutional practice. However, he fails to tell us how to construct that theory or what kind of theory it is. He leaves undetermined whether "constitutional practice" is tied closely to the actual Supreme Court interpretations of the text or instead includes aspirations of how to live the good life and form the good society. If it is the former, then the theory explains the *Hardwick* majority opinion. If it is the latter, then principles in the theory may indeed approach moral principles, but it is difficult to see how they fit actual practice.

Dworkin's view, and the coherentist view generally, is that the principle in *Griswold* entails constitutionally protecting homosexuality, not that homosexuality deserves constitutional protection in itself. Although I do not doubt that Dworkin's own views embrace the moral justifiability of homosexuality, his constitutional argument appears to be based on the existence of the privacy principle in *Griswold*. Thus, if that principle was repudiated, homosexuals would not have a constitutional leg to stand on. The pragmatist is not restricted in this way. For pragmatist constitutionalism homosexual acts between consenting adults should be constitutionally protected even if no one else's right to sexual privacy is.[207] Morally, homosexuals may have rights because consensual sexual expression is a good in itself, whether that self-expression is heterosexual or homosexual — but not legally, if we read the privacy cases straightforwardly to apply to marriage, family, and procreation.

It can be argued that the degree of a principle's generality determines whether it should be extended to new and arguably different circumstances.[208] This "generality" argument fails as a formal argument because it does not take into account a Burkean factor that many conservatives endorse, which counsels gradual incremental changes in constitutional doctrine — changes that meet the test of history.[209] According to this principle, we should not extend privacy — or formulate a more general rule — because legal change should be studied, gradually and incrementally.[210] Such a view may be erroneous — and I believe it is — but we need an argument why more abrupt change is preferable or permissible in particular circumstances, not an argument merely stating that constitutional principles must be general. The generality argument must be a conclusion of the argument, not one of its premises.

We just cannot say that judicial decisions protecting privacy in matters of marriage and procreation logically extend to sexual relations having nothing to do with even the possibility of procreation, without circularity.[211] The emphasis on procreation in *Griswold* suggests that a more general principle of sexual freedom was not intended.[212] For a principle of privacy to include homosexuality, something more is needed. There are at least two possible principles concerning sexual privacy. Principle 1 states sexual privacy is a right in the context of marriage and procreation. The second possibility says sexual privacy is a right in any context involving consenting adults. (Moreover, an even more general principle regarding sexuality is that sexual relations are constitutionally protected under any circumstances, but no one accepts that.) We cannot derive the second constitutional principle from the first one. It is perfectly possible to have a society endorsing the first and not the second, though it might not be morally desirable. If constitutional adjudication is to be distinguished from moral theorizing, its historical dimension must be taken seriously, and principles of the first kind must be possible. If not, we must accept the conclusion that law is not an independent realm of practical reasoning, and pragmatist solutions may be fundamentally moral despite not finding optimal support in the case law.

If the general principle in the privacy cases protected either intimate associations or a person's private life, it would require constitutionally protecting private consensual homosexual relations. However, the statement that these principles are morally superior to the more narrow principles prompts the query: To whom? and in what manner?[213] Unless we are willing to argue that sexual expression is simply good, we must find in a nonarbitrary fashion a point beyond which we are unwilling to extend the right of privacy. It is not impossible that such a nonarbitrary principle can be found, but it might require revising our convictions on many activities such as prostitution, adult incest, adultery, and so forth.[214]

If we take fit seriously, we cannot include homosexuality under the constitutional privacy cases without begging the question against the Court's majority opinion in *Hardwick* that sexual privacy excludes homosexuality. Arguably, such a view fits the privacy cases. The principle that private, nonharmful sexuality of any kind is permissible also fits the privacy cases, though not as well as the first principle. (This second principle is explicitly denied in some of the cases.) There is no reason to insist that this second principle is the principle of privacy because it is more general. It is a morally superior principle, to be sure, but in choosing it as the principle in the privacy cases, we are going beyond what those cases said. Dworkin's point here is that if you believe that the second principle is morally superior and that both principles fit the cases reasonably well, then you must accept the second principle as the principle of privacy. This is not true if one believes that the moral principle involved in privacy is one more narrowly tailored to fit the constitutional principle. Hence, if the privacy cases concern family privacy, then the constitutional and moral principle states that family privacy should be protected. In such matters I might believe that the moral principle implied by the Constitution and Supreme Court decisions must satisfy the same or nearly the same degree of generality as the actual principle in the cases.[215]

Endorsing a principle that homosexuality between consenting adults is good because it follows from the more general principle that sexual expression among consenting adults is good—even though we must include sexual relations more generally considered aberrant—is more candid than trying to smuggle homosexuality in under the privacy cases on the grounds of the generality argument. Similarly, a principle stating that people are independent in their homes doesn't do the trick either without begging the question against the *Hardwick* majority. The constitutional theory emanating from *Hardwick* is that constitutional principles are inextricably linked to the facts of a case. Hence, the sexual privacy cases are tied to the context of sexual privacy in matters of marriage and procreation. That's the difference between constitutional principles and moral principles. This raises the possibility that there is something defective in a constitutional scheme that must weave autonomy and privacy bit by bit into the constitutional tapestry. Arguing directly that a person has a moral right to engage in private adult consensual homosexual relations entails that such a right exists even if the Court had not found it in the actual privacy cases. Dworkin's argument is not merely that it is morally wrong to discriminate against homosexuals. Rather, we shouldn't discriminate against them because the principle of sexual privacy for heterosexuals commits us (through generality) to protect homosexuals constitutionally as well, and if we are truly averse to protecting homosexuals, we can give up the principle of privacy under that generalized description.

This discussion shows that revolutionary adjudication is required in the postrevolutionary stage of perfecting, refining, and stabilizing the revolutionary paradigm. Political and cultural factors are relevant to both extending and stabilizing the paradigm. Most important cases, therefore, can be seen as revolutionary because they are either precursors to a revolutionary paradigm, the creation of the revolutionary paradigm itself, or the perfection, refinement, and stabilization of the paradigm. Coherence theories have an especially important application in postrevolutionary adjudication. However, in this context narrow coherence alone will not always work. Typically, a broader conception of coherence is required, one whose results will be contestable and require the appeal to moral and cultural factors in the wider society as the source of their values.

Taking Stock of the Argument

This chapter has shown that certain critical Supreme Court decisions cannot be explained satisfactorily by any monist theory of constitutional change, especially conventionalism and coherentism. Instead, these cases can be understood by seeing the incorporation into judicial reasoning of extrinsic factors drawn from political or moral philosophy, which indicates that these decisions were products of revolutionary, rather than normal, adjudication. Although these cases do not typify the majority of cases that appear before the Court, they do apply to an overwhelming majority of the cases that most interest us, such as cases in any constitutional law casebook. Indeed, our interest in them is due to their power in revolutionizing law. Any theory of constitutional adjudication must accommodate this historical information and the principle of adjudication underlying it.

5   The Conceptual and Political Defenses
of the Theory

The theory of constitutional revolutions distinguishes between revolutionary and normal adjudication and then explains the richness of the former. Controversial cases typically arise when normal adjudication fails to resolve an impending constitutional crisis. If normal adjudication cannot dissipate the crisis, prerevolutionary adjudication occurs, chipping away at the existing paradigm. The scene is now set for revolutionary adjudication, which involves replacing one constitutional paradigm with another and then refining and perfecting the new paradigm until that area of law is stabilized. Some areas of law might resist stability and present continual problems (perhaps) incapable of constitutional solution.

The Conceptual Defense

One way of evaluating this theory is to examine its coherence and intelligibility. In this chapter I consider and reject several important conceptual objections to the theory of constitutional revolutions. According to this theory, descriptive accuracy provides one kind of justification of a practice. The practice is justified, on this level, when it describes and explains constitutional practice better than alternative theories. My method abandons a totem of analytic ethics that "ought" cannot be derived from "is" by deliberatively conflating ab initio these two allegedly different modes of discourse. What turns out to be American constitutional practice should have a presumptive hold on any reasonable constitutional actor. Although the precise contents of this practice are contestable, the important point here is that, if the theory describes and explains American constitutional practice and this practice is not otherwise normatively unattractive, all things being equal, we ought to follow that practice.[1] When a particular practice is challenged, one must show how it is a vital part of a larger, more inclusive practice. If it is part of that practice, normative reasons associated with the larger practice apply to the practice now challenged. Consequently, even if the theory is descriptively accurate and intelligible, and in part normatively attractive for that reason, the full normative dimension of the theory must be sketched in greater detail. This will be only a sketch, for it ultimately involves describing and defending a theory of democracy that supports revolutionary adjudication. The legitimacy of revolutionary adjudication, therefore, ultimately depends upon whether the theory accurately depicts American constitutional practice and whether communitarian democracy or some other democratic conception sustains the theory.

How Do Judges Identify the Need for Revolutionary Adjudication?

Revolutionary adjudication is necessary to resolve different types of constitutional crisis. One type occurs when the Constitution and existing constitutional practice fail to resolve a social or political conflict. Systemic, prolonged controversy is sufficient evidence of crisis. A second type of constitutional crisis occurs when a conflict exists between different provisions of the Constitution, or when one or more judicial decisions conflict with other decisions or the Constitution itself. Usually, in these cases, there also must be some sort of extrinsic problem forcing the resolution of the constitutional crisis. A third type of constitutional crisis exists when a constitutional paradigm is *practically* indeterminate, that is, when a provision is abstractly determinate — for example, the equal protection clause refers to equality — but when applying equality to concrete cases defies simple categorization.[2] This list is necessarily not exhaustive because future courts may extend the kinds of crises beyond our contemporary conception of "crisis." This suggests that no determinate procedure exists for identifying in advance the existence of a crisis. Thus, initiating revolutionary adjudication always will be contestable.

Some might object that if the type of adjudication is contestable, then the theory of constitutional revolutions has limited value. In response, the theory of constitutional revolution provides a means of identifying the need for revolutionary adjudication. When a constitutional crisis occurs, a judge, sensitive to its implications, will be alerted and will get ready for the possibility of revolutionary adjudication. She will decide that the relative merits of staying the course and embracing novelty augur in favor of novelty.[3] This objection insists further that without some intersubjective and consensus-building method for identifying crises, different judges will identify different crises and, subsequently, will not all prepare for revolutionary adjudication at the same time in the same circumstances. These observations are correct, but they do not constitute an objection to the theory. Judges, for the most part, will achieve a consensus on how to identify crises, but it will be a contestable consensus. Postmodern pragmatist constitutionalism doesn't pretend to provide a modernist answer to the crisis of American constitutionalism. Instead, it seeks a conceptualization of constitutional practice that contributes to our understanding of how that practice actually works, and whether it can be defended by an attractive theory of democracy. Moreover, shorn of modernist pretensions, it is not obvious that a lack of uniformity in judges' predispositions is bad. If we believe in deliberative democracy throughout the government's structure, we would avoid a decision procedure for determining when a crisis exists, because this, again, takes the judge out of judging.[4]

As a postmodern constitutional theory, the theory of constitutional revolutions makes no pretense at being algorithmic, nor does it pretend to guarantee a method for achieving consensus in hard cases. However, the theory does provide a conceptualization, an aesthetic so to speak, a postmodern vision of American constitutionalism. This conceptualization enables us to understand the perennially competing constitutional positions better than alternative theories. Achieving this understanding is crucial to achieving consensus when possible, and to better understand our disagreements when consensus is not likely.

Even If the Theory Accurately Depicts What Judges Do,
How Does It Inform Judges What They Should Do?

A related objection to the theory of constitutional revolutions is that it confuses normative imperatives with descriptive generalizations.[5] If the theory is only descriptively accurate, then it is an open question whether it has any normative value.[6] This argument has been the centerpiece of analytic ethics for much of this century, admonishing us not to confuse an "ought" with an "is."[7] Perhaps the theory does capture how in fact constitutional adjudication develops, so the argument goes, but that descriptive fact has no normative implications for how judges *should* behave. If the theory has descriptive implications only, an additional premise stating its norma-

tive attractiveness elements is required. Without such an additional premise, the objection contends, the theory of constitutional revolutions is irrelevant to the controversy over the correct constitutional methodology.

Several responses are in order here. First, the theory of constitutional revolutions rejects this distinction between two qualitatively different modes of
discourse. If the theory of constitutional revolutions captures constitutional
practice, it is difficult to see how the critic can argue that a theory that
adequately describes current constitutional practice is lacking in normative
force, for various reasons. First, a practice that has survived for over two
hundred years has provided, by the fact of its existence alone, an adequate
measure of stability and predictability that enable both constitutional actors
and normal citizens to satisfy their expectations, conform their actions to
the constitutional regime, and, in general, resolve social and political crises
without violence.[8] Second, the theory itself contains background values,
such as limited government, deliberative judgment, fairness, and respon-
siveness to felt needs that are preconditions for the generally accepted notion of American democracy. Third, regardless of the end point of normative
discussion, its starting point must be the moral and political scheme in
which we currently act, if for no other reason than that scheme constrains
the language and the imaginative interpretations for change.[9]

Only if there is a conclusive moral argument against actual practice would
it be plausible to argue that actual practice has no normative relevance to the
present case. Such an argument might appeal to the actual practice itself, but
then the normative element is already a feature of the practice. If such an
appeal involves factors extrinsic to the practice, the critic must justify her
argument on pragmatist grounds. If she does so, she will be prescribing a
revolutionary change away from, or reversing, actual practice. In this case
the argument denying the normative force of the theory of constitutional
revolutions depends upon an external normative justification that confirms
the theory. The theory states that external factors can count as justifications
for future decisions when overriding the normative force of existing practice. Second, the notions of progress, truth, and so forth are defined in
terms of actual constitutional practice. If the theory of constitutional revolutions adequately describes actual constitutional practice, these epistemic
notions are conceptually tied to that practice, explicable only in terms of the
theory of constitutional revolutions. Upon closer inspection we see that
there is nothing wrong with regarding so-called "descriptive" discourse
(which, after all, contains at least yesterday's norms) as presumptively

worthy of belief, unless a compelling moral or political reason exists for disregarding it. The fact that it is descriptively accurate should count strongly in its favor.

This position does not entail a pernicious relativism; it simply maintains, on pragmatic grounds, that moral evaluation must begin with one's own community. In lieu of transcendent ideals, the starting point must subsequently begin with the legal and moral conceptual scheme into which one is born. No matter how much we later depart from this scheme ultimately, it is necessarily our starting point. Consequently, barring a reason otherwise, our social practices are prima facie good.[10] Of course, American history is replete with practices that should be criticized and abandoned, such as racism and sexism, among others. Yet we are lucky that the cultural background theories in which our constitutional scheme resides, with all its defects, are sufficiently rich and complex to permit redescriptions or recontextualizations that permit radical critique of current constitutional practice. The Marshall and Warren courts engaged in such redescriptions and recontextualization of American constitutional practice, as did the New Deal Court. For example, in rejecting *Lochner v. New York,* the New Deal Court reconceived and redescribed the appropriate paradigm for dealing with economic crises.[11] The new paradigm redescribed the roles of Congress and the Court in the new and worrisome context of the Great Depression. The Court was influenced by the harsh facts of depression to alter the government's prerogatives in regulating the economy.

Pragmatist evaluation rejects this modernist dichotomy between descriptive and normative discourse. Modes of discourse do not determine an evaluative argument; purposes and contexts do. In different contexts language functions in different ways. Permanently labeling certain types of discourse as descriptive or normative based on their logical or syntactical structures cannot be persuasive on pragmatic grounds, because the relationship between facts and values are too interwoven to make this dichotomy plausible. For example, the statement "There's a Mack truck" is descriptive when one wants to identify the vehicle, but exhortative when one wants to warn someone crossing the street about an oncoming truck. Similarly, the sentence "The market is falling" might produce an embarrassed chuckle from an embittered socialist, while at the same time prompting significant activity on the part of an interested capitalist. A normative context is determined by the facts that constitute it and the types of reasons relevant to decision making in that context. Sometimes, for example, as in the case of constitutionalism, the facts are themselves so imbued with normative value that a complete description of the practice will contain within itself a significant normative justification.

The issue of the relationship between descriptive and normative discourse implicates a much broader issue of the proper method of philosophical inquiry. There are at least three ways to approach philosophically and theoretically interesting controversies. The first, "the Platonic approach," denigrates practice with all its infirmities. Instead, it continually asks the normative question, What is the ideal nature of the practice? The second approach, "the Humean approach," seeks empirically to understand human society and its conventions. The first approach valorizes the normative dimension and denigrates the descriptive dimension, though not entirely. The second embraces the descriptive and the explanatory dimensions of discourse and seeks to eliminate the normative, though not completely. Neither approach is compelling. A third view, "the Wittgensteinian approach," seeks to integrate the normative and the descriptive. Normative evaluation is possible, but not by invoking transcendental principles. This does not mean that we are all restricted to our own idiosyncratic or solipsistic perspectives. If we were, human communication would be impossible. In the appropriate circumstances we can and should achieve a more general, self-critical perspective from which to make decisions. However, we must realize that the more general vantage point is still a perspective in the world. In short, it is a view from somewhere. Indeed, we achieve a more general perspective not by going somewhere else but, rather, by reasoning with certain critical constraints while remaining in the same place. This vantage point is simply a pragmatist method of reasoning, which seems to be less vulnerable to criticism than alternative modes of reasoning.

The Platonic approach, however, like so many philosophical conceptions of normativity, contrasts both a person's idiosyncratic perspective and her self-critical perspective with a perspective located neither in space nor time, nor arguably occupied by any human reasoner. This approach is tantamount to embracing the possibility that all human practices are normatively defective, because they fail to reflect the correct ideal, a view that pragmatism finds incoherent. Pragmatism denies the possibility of such an identifiable, neutral perspective.[12] For the pragmatist social practices are explained and justified by some element in the practice or by a related practice. No ideal perspective is possible. Instead, normative pragmatist evaluation is a human, cultural practice, used to present other practices in as favorable a light as possible. When a practice is significantly defective, we must change it; but when no compelling pragmatic reason for abandoning a practice exists, what is ought to be. Alternatively, the level of description captures, for the most part, past attempts at justification, past attempts at normative world construction. Consequently, the descriptive should prevail normatively unless there is a reason for it to be reformed in a particular situation. Pragmatists reject the possibility of a noncircular, ultimate justification of social practices. If one does not think the present practices of justification useful, one may demonstrate how they might be improved. But no inescapable foundation exists grounding the practice of justification.

By contrast, the Wittgensteinian approach suggests that normativity is internal to social practices. Normative questions can arise only within a language community. Consequently, we cannot ask normative questions about an ultimate description of human society. Within that description we will discover normative arguments that have force within a language game or social practice. To ask if the total description is normatively attractive is to ask an unanswerable question. As Wittgenstein remarked: "The danger here . . . is one of giving a justification of our procedure where there is no such thing as a justification and we ought simply to have said: *that's how we do it.*"[13] This is why descriptive accuracy has normative force; it defines our practices at their most fundamental level. True, Wittgenstein was concerned ultimately with the description or justification of human reasoning generally, in which justification is internal. In constitutional law, however, justifications can arise either internally to the practice through norms already contained in the practice, or externally in terms of some other social practice like politics, culture, or ethics. That is why a double justification exists for the theory of constitutional revolutions. It depicts central features of constitutional practice yet is also supported by an attractive theory of democratic practice.

In constitutional law a proponent of change must convince the constitutional community that an internal or external crisis exists, one that should be examined and resolved. Conservative constitutionalists might then grant the centrality of revolutionary adjudication but insist that it is unattractive and, therefore, should be abandoned. In their view the ultimate justification of this reaction is that revolutionary adjudication is anathema to the most defensible theory of democratic practice. Notice that this democratic theory needs to apply not to ideal contexts, but rather to the context of a society that depends upon revolutionary adjudication. It is difficult to see how any theory of democracy applying to the United States could propose abandoning judicial review without causing a total revolution of our constitutional system. Moreover, a call for overturning revolutionary practice ironically requires embracing the theory of constitutional revolutions. If the theory accurately depicts revolutionary practice, then it can be abandoned only by legitimizing the theory of constitutional revolutions. If it is legitimate to use the theory in one kind of circumstance, it must also be justified to use it in relevantly similar circumstances. Hence, the critic establishes the legitimacy of revolutionary adjudication and the necessity of the theory. If the theory of constitutional revolutions accurately describes practice, then abandoning the practice calls for a constitutional revolution of monumental proportions.

In reply the critic might argue that calling for a rejection of the theory of constitutional revolutions might be a call for a return to the "correct" jurisprudence. In what sense is it the correct jurisprudence, if practice doesn't embody it? The theory of constitutional revolutions rejects the notion that there could be a correct "original jurisprudence" outside of actual practice. Pragmatism cannot tolerate divorcing correctness from actual practice in this manner. A critic might charge nonetheless that because actual constitutional practice is normatively invalid, altering the practice may require revolution. In this situation such a revolution is limited simply to rectifying the normative invalidity of actual practice. Once we return constitutional adjudication to its conventionalist, coherentist, naturalist, or pragmatic essence, we are done with revolution and thus do not tacitly embrace the theory of constitutional revolutions. Two responses are in order here. First, the rejoinder begs the question in favor of the normative dimension of practice. However, it is unclear why the normative should take precedence over the descriptive.[14] Second, this criticism relies on metaphysical essentialism. It seeks to identify those features of a practice that are necessary for the practice's existence.[15] It is also unclear why the normative reflects the essential nature of a practice better than the descriptive, or why we should bother about the dichotomy between descriptive and normative discourse in the first place. As a practical matter we need to go about our business giving reasons for or against social practices and worry less about the descriptive, normative, explanatory, or motivational status of these reasons.

Lastly, a more direct justification of revolutionary adjudication points out that it is necessary to ensure that law is a vibrant discourse adaptable to various contexts through the force of its own spirit. Otherwise, law becomes mechanical and encrusted, more suitable to tyrannical regimes than to constitutional democracies. The theory suggests that the revolutionary dimension of conceptual and constitutional change may be impossible to stamp out without adversely affecting the deliberative benefits of intrajudicial and interbranch dialogue. By emphasizing this deliberative element concerning the common good, the theory of constitutional revolutions establishes itself as a contemporary republican theory.[16]

Most conventionalist conceptions of constitutional law, such as textualism and originalism, are normative theories of constitutionalism; they describe and justify a certain mode of constitutional interpretation. But adherents to these theories seldom ask why the constitutional text or the Framers' intentions should control constitutional interpretation. To answer that the Constitution's text or intent says or implies so is inadequate because it is circular. It assumes the truth of the precise issue under discussion. One could argue erroneously that these conceptions are normatively based on other constitutional and nonconstitutional practices, but why these practices should be imported into constitutional law remains an unanswered question, especially when actual practice is driven by something other than authorial meaning. Once opening the floodgates to external reasons or reasons that transcend a given practice, the theory of constitutional revolutions explains how judges and courts translate that data into constitutional law through revolutionary adjudication. Second, if the critic is calling for a return to the correct jurisprudence, it is doubtful that this can occur without establishing a precedent for future use. If it is right to return constitutional practice to its essential nature by revolutionary adjudication, it is unclear why the same cannot be done in the future. In other words, engaging in revolutionary adjudication for remedial or corrective purposes legitimizes it. Theories must assume some degree of generality; if it is right to engage in revolutionary adjudication to correct misinterpretations, then the judicial argument will continually be that a given set of present circumstances is sufficiently like the paradigm case as to warrant remediation. Thus, a theory of *corrective* constitutional revolutions will drive constitutional change and depends upon the theory of constitutional revolutions for its legitimacy.

This descriptive basis of the theory provides a place for familiar constitutional paradigms. Textualism and originalism are two constitutional paradigms that play a significant role in normal adjudication. Structuralism and normativism, or nonoriginalism, are clearly more appropriate to revolutionary adjudication.[17]

Doesn't the Existence of Macro- and Microrevolutions Collapse the Distinction between Normal and Revolutionary Adjudication?

One feature of the theory of constitutional revolutions is its distinction between macro and micro constitutional revolutions. Macrorevolutions are changes of paradigms in constitutional law, whereas microrevolutions are changes within an existing paradigm. *Brown* is an example of a macrorevolution reversing a normal paradigm of equality, whereas *Bakke* and now *Adarand* are microrevolutions because they determine the law of affirmative action, which comes under the paradigm *Brown* first formulated.

One might raise the objection that if there are macro- and microrevolutions, there is really no qualitative distinction between revolutionary and normal adjudication.[18] Revolutions and abrupt change occur in all sorts of judicial circumstances; they cannot be limited only to one type of case. However, this objection fails for the following reasons: First, it overlooks the fact that the existence of macro- and microrevolutions, or even the fact that many important constitutional decisions have revolutionary and normal aspects, does not vitiate the overall explanatory usefulness of this distinction.[19] We can still identify cases that are more heavily revolutionary despite having some normal features. Second, it ignores the fact that both macro- and microrevolutions occur within the purview of revolutionary adjudication alone. Recall that revolutionary adjudication has three elements: prerevolutionary, revolutionary per se, and postrevolutionary adjudication. These are all examples of revolutionary adjudication because each type depends on the creation and/or explication of a novel constitutional paradigm. Third, the objection obscures the fact that despite the existence of different degrees of revolutionary adjudication, there are also forms of adjudication that have no revolutionary components. Many decisions in federal appellate court are decisions that do not create law at all in any interesting way.[20] During normal adjudication, after a revolution has been stabilized, the paradigm alone determines the results of adjudication; neither macro- nor microrevolutions occur. Fourth, the notions of revolutionary and normal adjudication are employed to explain the source of a constitutional principle. If the principle has a revolutionary source, it is based on factors extrinsic to constitutional law. If its source is normal, then it is based on a present paradigm internal to the constitutional scheme. The distinction between macro- and microrevolutions is useful precisely because it refines our conception of the source of constitutional principles. In macrorevolutions the source of constitutional principles is extrinsic, whereas in microrevolutions the further articulation of the new paradigm requires an integration of both intrinsic and extrinsic features that lends itself to interpretation according to coherentist legal theory. Consequently, in microrevolutions we must identify two different sources of principle. Only if it were impossible to separate these two different sources would the distinction between macro- and microrevolutions jeopardize the distinction between normal and revolutionary adjudication.

Though the distinction between normal and revolutionary adjudication is more complex than it first appears, the underlying difference between appealing to intrinsic factors to settle a controversy, and appealing to extrinsic factors, survives. However, the interlocutor can pursue this objection. If one concedes that there are different degrees of revolutionary adjudication, one faces the problem of how we are to determine when a case involves revolutionary rather than normal adjudication. Without a plausible answer it seems that the theory is monist after all. If neither the features of normal adjudication nor the features of revolutionary adjudication are completely distinct, normal adjudication will blend into revolutionary adjudication. However, this is far from an objection to the theory. When a court attempts to deal with a case through normal adjudication but cannot, it will begin to engage in prerevolutionary adjudication. The shift from normal to revolutionary adjudication in such a case is not always obvious. However, I do not see that this counts against the theory. If the theory provides illuminating descriptions of these complexities, that is in the theory's favor, and not to its detriment. Although it adds complexity to the distinction between normal and revolutionary adjudication, the distinction between macro- and microrevolutions permits us to give a more fully nuanced explanation of constitutional change. In the final analysis we can tell the difference between normal and revolutionary adjudication by attempting to explain the decision in a new case by appealing to an existing paradigm. If we fail in such an attempt, the decision's legitimacy must rest on extrinsic factors. Certainly it will be controversial whether and to what extent a decision is either normal or revolutionary, but controversy breathes vigor into the law and does not obviate the usefulness of the distinction.

Does the Theory Confuse the Legislative and Adjudicative Dimensions of Law?

The theory of constitutional revolutions might be criticized for confusing the legislative and adjudicative dimensions of law. According to this objection the appropriate place for "revolutionary" change is the legislature, not the courts.[21] Judicial tinkering with the Constitution should be gradual and incremental. Consequently, the theory of constitutional revolutions founders by prescribing a form of judicial review that usurps the legislative role. In reply we must determine in which sense, if any, this dichotomy is true. The theory of constitutional revolutions revises the distinction between legislative and adjudicative features of law. It recognizes the United States Supreme Court to be in part a constitutional court; and a constitutional court must be a "superlegislature." The dichotomy between legislation and adjudication is a modernist dichotomy that should be revised rather than embraced as a constraint on adjudication. However, this dichotomy is not merely an expression of the separation of powers, it conceptually distinguishes between two kinds of reasoning. Rejecting this dichotomy does not entail denying these two kinds of reasoning nor all differences between legislatures and courts but simply recognizes that these activities are not mutually exclusive. Judges unavoidably function as political actors when they decide constitutional questions, in that they are participating in the dialogic process of ruling and being ruled. This process is crucial to the republican dimension of the American communitarian republic.

This objection also fails because it conflates two kinds of change: change in policy and change in principle. A change in policy is a change from one constitutionally permissible course of governmental action to another. A change in principle alters the meaning of existing constitutional provisions, affording greater or lesser structural protections, or protection of constitutional rights and liberties. According to the theory of constitutional revolutions, courts change principles, not policies, when engaging in constitutional interpretation. A change in principle often results in policy changes, and in theory policy changes can result in a change of principle. Although judicial alterations of constitutional principles might be held illegitimate on other grounds, the theory of constitutional revolutions cannot be faulted for abolishing the distinction between legislative and adjudicative changes. The former are changes in policy, whereas the latter are changes in principle or governmental prerogatives. The distinction between policy and principle cannot be applied mechanically, because determining whether a change is one in a policy or in a principle is itself an interpretive problem and, in some cases, will be contestable. Despite this failing, the distinction between policy and principle is useful in distinguishing between the legislature and courts. The practical distinction is that judges do not arise in the morning and decide, for instance, that it would be a good thing for people to have comprehensive, government-funded health care, and so rule. The constraints of the constitutional community will prevail against such usurpation. For one thing the judge must have a suitable case before her. Controversial constitutional adjudication involves conflicts over deep, often incommensurate, perspectives concerning human values and political organization. On pragmatist grounds concepts and principles must be revised or reinterpreted with each new constitutional era. Otherwise we may forgo a better version of that concept or principle, or lose it entirely. Additionally, legislatures are concerned with addressing general problems that typically involve balancing competing interests. Courts are concerned with the individual's permanent rights and liberties, as well as with the constitutional authority of federal and state governments. Consequently, courts might alter constitutional principles without trespassing on legitimate legislative authority to make changes in policy.

Admittedly, questions of principle are not always easily distinguished from questions of policy. The former, however, refer to the Constitution's meaning, whereas the latter are debates over which constitutionally permitted policy is best in the given circumstances. For example, the New Deal judicial revolution held that legislatures should be responsible for economic decisions. This principle permits both free-market laws as well as progressive laws; it requires neither. Hence, when the New Deal Court overturned the *Lochner* paradigm, it had an important effect on politics. It permitted, but did not require, Congress and the state legislatures to regulate the economy. The Court said, in effect, that any rational decision Congress makes concerning the economy is constitutionally permissible. The role of the Court ended here, and so too the judicial function. It is up to the legislature to enter the arena and establish the best policy within the parameters of the permitted judicial principle. This creates a useful dialogue between the legislature and the courts in which deliberation among branches contributes to the overall deliberative dimension of American constitutionalism.

However, the critic might insist that no governmental branch should alter constitutional principles, or replace one constitutional principle with another not found in the Constitution. In one sense this objection is absolutely right. If the Court were to interpret a provision of the Constitution to require or even permit theocracy, monarchy, fascism, or communism, the Court would be overstepping its bounds. No American Court has even come close to such interpretations. Yet every branch of government has altered, sometimes radically, some constitutional principles. The original constitutional principle of limited government was altered through both the Marshall Court and the New Deal Court decisions. The principle of the original role of the presidency has been altered drastically in the twentieth century. The advent of the administrative state as a fourth branch of governmental authority is not in the original Constitution. So the objection is right that courts should be unable to add concepts to the Constitution, concepts having no purchase in constitutional and cultural practice, but it does not follow that courts should be unable to alter constitutional principles that are constitutive of this practice.[22]

A corollary of this objection is that the theory of constitutional revolutions fails to preserve the distinction between law and politics. When one understands law to involve principles and policies, the theory of constitutional revolutions preserves the distinction between law and politics.[23] However, if law means neutral principles, and politics means substantive principles, then the theory rejects this distinction. The theory recognizes no neutral principles. Even if it did, neutral principles would not be useful in constitutional law. The best of law translates the best of politics into legal form. Indeed, the best of law and the best of politics amount to the same thing: reflective responses about how to structure the good society.

Is the Theory of Constitutional Revolutions Consistent with the Rule of Law?

A compelling criticism of the theory of constitutional revolutions is that it fails to explain the rule of law. A constitutional system in which judges are permitted, if not required, to engage in revolutionary adjudication fails to achieve the impartial and neutral administration of the law. The importance of the rule of law in Anglo-American constitutionalism can be expressed in the following way.[24] Any acceptable constitutional scheme must maintain the rule of law, and any acceptable constitutional theory must preserve the importance of this doctrine. Consequently, preserving the rule of law is a constraint or condition of adequacy for any theory of constitutional adjudication. Because the theory of constitutional revolutions permits important decisions to derive from factors extrinsic to the Constitution or to constitutional practice, it must fail as an adequate constitutional theory. More specifically, because the theory of constitutional revolutions insists on the existence of two different approaches to constitutional adjudication, it cannot preserve the virtues of notice, predictability, and reliability, virtues that express the rule of law. Hence, according to this objection, the theory of constitutional revolutions must concede that a constitutional scheme need not preserve the rule of law. If true, this argument admittedly defeats the theory.

To assess the validity of the criticism, we need to define the meaning of "the rule of law." First, the rule of law must mean that decisions concerning a citizen's rights and obligations must be predictable and not arbitrary. In this way there is no rule of law if a person's right to free speech is determined solely by whatever a particular individual, a king or a bureaucrat, decides it to be. Second, there is no rule of law if law arbitrarily protects particular classes of people — the wealthy, whites, men — but not others, as arguably the original Constitution did. Third, there is no rule of law if there are substantive laws but no procedural protections for implementing them. Fourth, there is no rule of law if there are good substantive and procedural laws but no one to enforce them, or when those entrusted with their enforcement are corrupt. The theory of constitutional revolutions maintains the rule of law in each of these instances. Further, it promotes notice, predictability, and reliance, but it goes beyond these virtues by also revealing the existence of three additional judicial virtues, namely, flexibility, coordination, fundamental justice.[25] Moreover, it permits the Court to respond to the urgent demand to recognize undeclared individual rights that have developed as an integral part of our constitutional scheme, or rights that exist in large part independently of any system of positive law in the political and cultural environment that gives law meaning.[26]

The critic might reply that when revolutionary adjudication is permitted, the government ceases to be a government of laws, but becomes a government of men.[27] Conventionalist virtues such as notice, predictability, and stability are sacrificed on the altar of revolution. According to this objection, courts cannot decide like cases alike, because judges can always engage in revolutionary adjudication and, therefore, overturn precedents.[28] Deciding like cases alike appears to be a requirement of elementary consistency that any adequate constitutional theory must satisfy. Hence, because the theory of constitutional revolutions cannot satisfy this requirement, it must be rejected as an adequate constitutional theory. This objection to the the-

ory results from an impoverished conception of the rule of law. In particular, this conception of the rule of law as consistency is ambiguous. It might
refer to some elementary conception of consistency, or it might, instead,
refer to a deeper sense of consistency with underlying cultural values, which
insists that we treat people with equal concern and respect, even if that
means violating elementary consistency in a revolutionary case. In normal
adjudication the rule of law is satisfied by elementary consistency. In revolutionary adjudication the rule of law is better satisfied by this deeper sense of
consistency than with conventionalist theories adhering to elementary consistency. Sometimes revolutionary adjudication is required to extend digni-
fied treatment throughout the population.[29] For example, *Brown* fails to
satisfy the rule of law as elementary consistency but succeeds in satisfying
the rule of law in the deeper sense of consistency of what in 1954 was a
minority view that was about to sweep the nation. The Court treated Ms.
Linda Brown with equal concern and respect, the way she should have been
treated by the law.[30] In short, in the Court's view moral, political, or cultural values sanctioned overturning elementary consistency in this case.
Consequently, unlike monist conceptions, the theory of constitutional revolutions provides a more comprehensive approach to the rule of law, one
that permits both elementary consistency in normal conditions and deep
consistency in revolutionary circumstances.

   When a society is governed by the rule of law, there must be reliable ways
to resolve conflicts. Reliability in this sense has two elements: First, it provides a basis for reasonable expectation. Second, it guarantees that the conflict will be settled in the right manner according to the society's basic
principles, or such principles that a reflective majority of Americans are beginning to see as fundamental ones. Because these principles are almost always subject to debate, different conclusions will be generated by different
background assumptions. This is one of the bases of constitutional revolution. It is not at all obvious why the rule of law is trampled upon by courts
engaging in revolutionary adjudication. Instead we might describe a court
that searches for a new paradigm better adapted to each new generation's
culture as protecting the spirit of law better than alternative conceptions.[31]

   A corollary of this objection accuses the theory of constitutional revolutions of abandoning reliance as an important legal value. According to this
objection, law is designed to satisfy people's legitimate expectations, which
enables them to rely on the law to structure their lives. Revolutionary
adjudication is antithetical to reliance, and, therefore, the theory must be

inadequate. However, no one believes that reliance is absolutely dispositive in all cases. Especially in constitutional law, the value of reliance, though important, is not primary. In constitutional law we do not want people to rely on unconstitutional statutes or pragmatically impoverished interpretations of the Constitution. Instead, conservative and progressive alike want the Court to overturn unconstitutional laws. This is the reason stare decisis does not have the same significance in constitutional law as it does in the common law. Overcoming constitutional crises is more critical than elementary consistency with the past.[32] Paraphrasing the late Senator Barry Goldwater: Restraint in the face of constitutional crisis is no virtue, and activism in pursuit of democratic justice is no vice.

Should Judges Be Restrained or Activist?

The short answer is that, if the theory of constitutional revolutions is justified, judges should be both. In normal adjudication judges should be restrained; in revolutionary adjudication they should be activist. The question of when a judge should adopt one or another form of adjudication has no general answer. Instead, it can be resolved only by determining the judge's methodological and political values, which are central to a judge's decisions, despite the popular view that these values should be virtually irrelevant in confirming a judge. The theory of constitutional revolutions permits judicial activism, though there is still room for controversy over when it is appropriate, and how far it should go. The theory describes American constitutional practice as one requiring judicial activism in order to explain the evolution of American constitutional practice. One traditional criticism of judicial activism is that activist judges fail in the primary judicial duty to find or discover law, not to make it. This is a general legal imperative, but it assumes greater importance in constitutional adjudication. Because federal judges are not elected, and therefore are not accountable as are officials of the legislative and executive branches, judicial lawmaking is, according to this objection, unremittingly illegitimate.

According to the theory of constitutional revolutions, the distinction between restraint and activism, as a choice between mutually exclusive alternatives, flies in the face of actual constitutional practice. In fact, the development of constitutional law is cyclical and periodic. A given period of revolutionary constitutional adjudication often begins with judge-made law, which then becomes a normal paradigm. If the normal decisions fail to resolve a future crisis, the cycle continues with either the ultimate resolution through normal adjudication or the advent of revolutionary adjudication. This stage of constitutional adjudication is one wherein microrevolutions and subparadigms predominate. During this period judges continue to make law, but now in terms of the accepted constitutional paradigm and *some* pragmatic factors. During this period the reliance on revolutionary methods decreases. Finally, when reliance on pragmatic factors sufficiently cease, normal adjudication predominates in which judges merely apply the law. In these circumstances the judge functions conventionally, seeking well-accepted constitutional authorities upon which to base his decisions. When he cannot find such conventions, it may be due to an impending constitutional crisis. In that event a judge must consider instituting a revolutionary constitutional decision. Notice that the two leading theories, conventionalism and pragmatism, have a role to play in the dualistic dimension of constitutional adjudication. During constitutional revolutions pragmatism is the fundamental judicial philosophy. During normal adjudication conventionalist legal philosophy prevails.

Doesn't the Theory of Constitutional Revolutions Abandon the Idea of Constitutionalism?

Some readers by now have asked themselves whether the theory abandons the idea of constitutionalism. According to this objection, the theory of constitutional revolutions consists of external principles for explaining and justifying constitutional adjudication, thus failing to account for the internal perspective so conspicuous in Anglo-American law. According to this objection, the relevant explanatory principles must provide standards for constitutional actors to use in deciding cases, not merely a social scientific methodology for describing constitutional practice. Internal principles of constitutional adjudication show how constitutional law depends upon coherent moral principles explaining and justifying the practice. Any theory not preserving the importance of coherence in constitutional adjudication is unacceptable. This objection goes further than merely requiring coherence. In fact, it says that constitutionalism must be guided by permanent rules that do not change except through a stated constitutional process if there is one. Consequently, the theory of constitutional revolutions in effect is abandoning constitutionalism for something less defined. The reply is that normal adjudication is constitutional adjudication through and through.

Hence, rather than abandon the idea of constitutionalism, the theory embraces it. Second, revolutionary adjudication, though not an example of normal constitutionalism, is certainly an example of constitutionalism. It says that constitutionalism means appreciating the appropriateness of different kinds of adjudication. If that is a modified constitutionalism, so be it.

Is the Theory of Constitutional Revolutions Superfluous?

Some critics argue that because we already have the conceptual resources to describe constitutional change, the theory of constitutional revolutions is superfluous. This objection points to our existing constitutional conceptual scheme, in which we describe the phenomena that the theory of constitutional revolutions refers to in perfectly commonsensical terms. For example, one could say that "normal adjudication" refers to "well-settled law," where judges "apply, but do not make law." Our present constitutional conceptual scheme describes revolutionary cases as "landmark" or "seminal," insisting that law has a "creative," or "evolutionary," dimension. The latest term used by mainstream theorists, sensitive to revolutionary adjudication but unwilling to embrace revolution, is "transformative." Further, in the civil rights revolution, the precursors to *Brown* "eroded" the viability of *Plessy*. This objection, though common, is not compelling. It overlooks that the ordinary ways of describing these phenomena deliberatively fudge the issue of revolution and do not consider whether the new law is derivable through normal conventions from prior law. Law cannot be both novel and constant. This is the myth of the standard account. Characterizing the precursors of *Brown* as "eroding" *Plessy* partakes in this charade. Somehow these precursor cases followed and eroded *Plessy,* but did not overturn it. Then *Brown* followed from the discontent in the precursor cases, if not in *Plessy*. So the precursor cases are connected to *Plessy,* and the precursors are connected to *Brown,* and *Brown* is connected to *Plessy* through the precursors. Hence, *Brown* is anything but revolutionary, because it follows from the precursors that follow from *Plessy*. This reasoning distorts the change involved in *Brown* and the precursors. If the precursors eroded *Plessy*, they were the beginning of a series of revolutionary decisions temporarily concluding in *Brown* and the per curiam cases, which resulted in the rejection of *Plessy*. It is impossible to have it both ways.

The mainstream view sees seminal or landmark cases as novel, but somehow this novelty is tied to prior law. Something is conceptually wrong with this picture as an exhaustive account of constitutional change. The mainstream view has no room for the genuine revolutionary nature of constitutional law. Although we can quarrel over which cases are revolutionary, the theory of constitutional revolutions maintains that one has not properly identified constitutional practice if one believes that normal adjudication can explain all the relevant cases. The commonsense conceptualization of this practice radically (purposefully?) distorts this practice. Hence, we need another way of conceptualizing constitutional change.

The theory of constitutional revolutions is offered as a candidate for a different way of understanding constitutional change. It represents a new language for appreciating the subtlety and complexity of change in any living conceptual system. No talk of "seminal" or "landmark" cases can capture this postmodern feature of both constitutional and conceptual systems. A corollary objection challenges the theory of constitutional revolutions to distinguish between normal seminal adjudication and revolutionary seminal adjudication. Without the distinction, seminal and revolutionary appear to be the same. If so, why replace one lexicon for another? The reason is twofold: First, seminal cases do not follow from the Constitution or constitutional practice. The term "revolutionary" reflects this better than alternative terms. Second, the theory of constitutional revolutions better depicts the role revolutionary adjudication has in generating normal adjudication.

A related criticism maintains that the theory of constitutional revolutions is banal because it merely describes what we must do anyway.[33] According to the banality objection, the theory of constitutional revolutions requires that judges sometimes make narrow decisions, sometimes broad, including decisions based on coherency. The theory adds nothing of value to the practice; instead, it is merely an inevitable feature of human inquiry, and therefore it is pointless to offer the theory as a competing theory that practitioners may or may not adopt.

The banality objection must be evaluated carefully. If the objection suggests that constitutional practice cannot function according to one paradigm alone, it merely reiterates the position of the theory of constitutional revolutions. That does not mean practitioners cannot believe that they can adhere to one paradigm alone, and this belief may cause them to distort constitutional practice. In fact, they may use normal adjudication to decide some cases that should be decided by revolutionary adjudication. This is one of the mistakes the theory attempts to prevent. Consequently, though the theory of constitutional revolutions describes how American constitutionalism functions, its value lies in encouraging self-conscious adherence to the practice described. When a judge views American constitutionalism through the lens of the theory of constitutional revolutions, she may perfect the revolutionary dimension of our practice more effectively than if she were to adopt an alternative theory. Hence, it is not pointless to endorse the theory of constitutional revolutions. Although arguably we cannot avoid revolutionary adjudication, we can do it much better when we do it self-consciously.

This implicates the issue of legitimacy. If, instead of justifying revolutionary adjudication in conventionalist terms, the constitutional community emphasized how revolutionary change was responsive to crisis and therefore better able to deal with change than conventionalism, the dialogue about revolutionary adjudication might change in ways beneficial to the political system. This functionalist conception of legitimacy warns us to rely on what now makes constitutional adjudication better, not what some remote statesmen found plausible. It seeks a different vocabulary for conceptualizing constitutional problems, one that better reflects American constitutionalism and American democracy.

How Can the Theory Be the Theory of American Constitutionalism If It Is Inconsistent with Most Judges' Self-Conceptions?

The theory of constitutional revolutions depicts what judges do, not what they say they do, but this hardly negates the appropriateness of the theory. Just as Kuhn's point did not imply that scientists from Copernicus on embrace the theory of scientific revolutions, I do not mean that judges and lawyers have self-consciously embraced the theory of constitutional revolutions in its own terms. Nor do I mean that judges and lawyers would necessarily characterize what they do in terms of the theory. What I do mean is that almost all judges and lawyers would, upon giving the theory a fair hearing, understand the plausibility of the claim that the theory accurately describes pathbreaking opinions and innovative Supreme Court justices. If one agrees with this point, then the remaining historical question is to discover whether every Court engaged in these two strands of adjudication. In candor I believe that both so-called activist and so-called restrained judges will accept this view. Ironically, conservative justices often preach judicial restraint, yet practice, at least selectively, activism. For example, Justice Scalia, especially in *Employment Division v. Smith*, does not hesitate to radically revise the constitutional paradigm governing free exercise cases.[34] Clearly, *Smith* is a constitutional revolution that radically altered the meaning of the free exercise clause. Congress entered this crisis by passing the Religious Freedom and Restoration Act, reestablishing strict scrutiny for laws of general applicability that burden religious freedom. The Court protected its revolutionary decision by striking down this federal statute giving itself the ultimate authority in this case.

There are three approaches to testing theories of constitutional jurisprudence: intentionalist, functionalist, and de facto approaches. A judge uses the theory in an intentionalist sense, when she self-consciously intends to apply this theory to her adjudication. By contrast a judge uses the theory in a functionalist manner when her internal point of view, and her conception of what she's doing, translate into the theory. A judge uses the theory in a de facto sense when the internal perspective of a judge is replaced by an external account of judicial history that conforms to the theory.

The theory of constitutional revolutions is a functionalist theory. I do not contend that any court or justice ever used the theory in an intentionalist sense. Although history reveals some close calls, the theory's accuracy does not depend on finding judges who would self-consciously describe their decisions as congruent with the theory of constitutional revolutions. However, judges have used the theory in a functionalist sense; they have decided cases pragmatically utilizing both revolutionary adjudication and normal adjudication. Moreover, many judges' self-conscious conceptions of what they do translate into the theory. Because the theory enables nonpragmatist conceptions of adjudication to be redescribed in pragmatist terms, it is easy to conclude that every justice has used the theory in a de facto sense deciding cases according to the theory though characterizing it in standard terms. The test of the theory is whether it provides a functionalist explanation of constitutional adjudication.[35] For example, William Brennan certainly embraced the theory in its functionalist sense, as did John Marshall, though neither embraced the theory in its intentionalist sense. Although using the language of convention, Chief Justice Marshall's style of adjudication clearly embraces the distinction between the legitimacy of revolutionary and normal adjudication. A change in judicial practice embracing the theory would have pragmatist benefits for the political system generally. Doing so means, first of all, reconceiving our talk about when to hear a case, when to sustain the current law, when to make minor and major modifications, and when to abandon the law and replace it with a new constitutional paradigm. For example, now we argue about whether judges should merely apply the law and not make law. Under the theory of constitutional revolutions, justices would all concede that judges make law in revolutionary adjudication. The arguments should then be not whether the court should change the law but whether it should engage in normal adjudication or revolutionary adjudication in a given case.

I have argued that a descriptive interpretation of constitutional practice has normative implications in two ways. First, if the theory accurately characterizes the practice, then, barring reasons against the practice, it is valuable because it depicts our practice. What happens when a challenge to the practice is raised? One way of meeting this challenge is to determine whether the practice is a vital or important part of a larger, more fundamental practice. If so, the normative reasons associated with the larger practice apply also to the practice now challenged. To achieve a full normative defense of the theory, a more precisely normative justification of revolutionary adjudication is appropriate. For this we need to sketch a description of the relationship between the theory of constitutional revolutions and political theory, especially a progressive theory of democracy.[36]

The Political Defense

What Is the Relationship between Revolutionary Judicial Review and Politics?

Revolutionary judicial review is self-consciously concerned about politics in the sense of political theory, not partisan politics. Revolutionary judges scrutinize calls for action by determining which lawsuits should be disposed of through normal adjudication, and which should be creatively resolved through revolutionary adjudication. Pragmatism drives the processes of constitutional change, thus judges sometimes have positive reasons to stick closely to a constitutional paradigm, and at other times they have little or no reason to do so. On the other hand, pragmatism recognizes the importance and — in the American context — the inevitability of constitutional revolutions. The processes of change, of refining, perfecting, and stabilizing the change to reach normalization, efficiently translate cultural and ethical and political meaning into constitutional law and contribute to the vigor and health of our constitutional democracy.[37] To achieve good health, the theory of constitutional revolutions exploits the strengths of conventionalism, coherentism, pragmatism, and naturalism. In normal adjudication conventionalism reigns, whereas in revolutionary adjudication pragmatism and naturalism dominate, and, of course, in postrevolutionary adjudication coherentism plays an important, though not exclusive, role.

The theory of constitutional revolutions has an advantage over competing monist theories in its capacity to accommodate and integrate them into one pragmatist conception of constitutional practice. It is a syncretic conception of American constitutional practice that incorporates the strengths of each of the competing theories into a unified jurisprudential account of that practice. Even if our constitutional practice were different, we would have an affirmative reason to reform it according to the theory of constitutional revolutions because the theory has the widest jurisprudential reach. In this view constitutional law is a product of the Constitution and revolutionary interpretations of the text, which then become refined, perfected, and stabilized with the ultimate goal of quelling crisis and reaching normalization. This is a deliberative process within the judiciary, as well as among the judiciary, the other federal branches, state governments, and the people. It is designed to provide a procedure for conversing about common problems, finding solutions to these problems, and recognizing that sometimes permanent barriers preclude resolution.

Like pragmatist theories generally, the theory of constitutional revolutions favors concrete results over theory. A pragmatic judicial philosophy is designed to overcome crisis. It eschews overtly ideological factors. Pragmatist judicial philosophy tolerates experimental solutions to difficult questions. It avoids the quest for foundational constitutional principles, which lay down univocal constitutional methodologies once and for all. The theory generates comparative judgments concerning the constitutionality of governmental acts. It requires and creates further need for accommodation between and among different groups and individuals. Ideally, democratic citizens relinquish the conviction that their fundamental values must prevail over others.

Arguably, the theory of constitutional revolutions is closely allied to such constitutional values as equality, community, and liberty. Understood in a progressive sense, these values are concerned with producing a community in which equally free citizens deliberate to establish constitutional and public policy. This conception is a progressive conception because, as Robin West states so eloquently, the progressive concerns herself with the plight of lesser lives.[38] Progressive constitutionalism seeks to eradicate various types of domination that make a life painful and incomplete. The progressive keeps a careful vigil against inequality, old and new, that prevents an individual's life from flourishing. She seeks a community, a sense of belonging, which ideally is concerned with elevating lesser lives. This community should be the forum and vehicle for people who are equally free to deliberate with one another in order to solve social conflicts and to deliberatively construct their future together. People are tied to communities through deliberative conversation, and a sense that all citizens are equally subjects of the political world. Given human history, securing these values typically involves revolutionary change, whereas authority, hierarchy, and domination usually represent the status quo.

Although the labels "conservative" and "progressive" are undeniably vague, progressives seek to expand the values of equality, community, and liberty throughout the citizenry, whereas conservatives typically are more restricted in their zeal to exhaust the moral resources of these concepts. Conservatives tend to seek narrow interpretations of these salient political philosophical concepts and, therefore, require the use of revolutionary adjudication in fewer situations than do progressives. Progressives must be vigilant in protecting their values from erosion and ensuring that they be realized in the right way. The possibility of revolutionary constitutional change is essential to this vigilance.

This is not to say that conservatives never engage in revolutionary adjudication.[39] To the contrary, every constitutionalist has endorsed such adjudication at one time or another.[40] The point here is only that the theory of constitutional revolutions is antithetical to a Burkean conception of change. A constitutional Burkean sees constitutional change as incremental and occurring not so much from individual choice and utopian reform as from the multiplicity of choices people make every day in social interaction. The Burkean, however, cannot explain how these factors are incorporated into the law. Consequently, the Burkean regards the theory of constitutional revolutions as anathema. However, other varieties of conservative jurists have embraced the theory of constitutional revolutions. Indeed, my contention that the theory of constitutional revolutions is *the* theory of our constitutional change precludes denying its role in conservative adjudication. According to the theory of constitutional revolutions, the difference between judicial conservatives and judicial progressives is that the former sees normal adjudication occupying a wider piece of the judicial landscape than progressives do.

Indeed, the differences between conservatives and progressives are made more intelligible when seen through the lens of the theory of constitutional revolutions. Although conservatives do engage in revolutionary adjudication, there is a greater conceptual connection between the theory of constitutional revolutions and progressive political theory. Progressive political theory, as a thoroughly pragmatist theory, though committed to evaluation, denies that any particular value is necessarily sacrosanct or that any argument is immune from criticism. Any value may be abandoned in the appropriate circumstances, although not all at once.[41] Pragmatism, therefore, needs a form of adjudication that encourages revising, replacing, abandoning, and creating values. The theory of constitutional revolutions is the only theory that integrates these jurisprudential paradigms in a unified manner. Consequently, any pragmatic progressive political theory will naturally ally itself with the theory. Progressives will seek a theory of constitutional adjudication that permits systemic change in order to protect these developing values vigilantly.

A judge must answer two questions concerning the relationship of political theory to the case before the court. First, she must determine how the history of the nation's political values bears on the decision. This is always her conception of these values. Nevertheless, the object of the judge's inquiry must be "the nation's fundamental political values," not her own. Generally, when the answer to this question is clear, the judge's pursuit of fundamental values is complete. When it is unclear, the judge must then consult her own fundamental values, not because there's something sacrosanct about "her values," but rather because her values are the nation's best values from her perspective. We ask the impossible of a judge when we forbid her from appealing to the nation's best values (from her perspective), and, more important, we set the stage for judicial self-deception in the name of what "the law" commands. The theory of constitutional revolutions is a theory of judicial review's role in the American democracy. As mentioned above it is *the* theory of American constitutional change. However much it captures both restrained and activist strategies of adjudication, it has progressivist or activist proclivities when seen against a background of pragmatist constitutionalism and democracy.

Two Theories of Democracy

The relationship between communitarian democracy and revolutionary judicial review reveals, in broad outline, the progressive character of the theory of constitutional revolutions. This theory of democracy stands in contradistinction to majoritarian democracy. The countermajoritarian argument against revolutionary judicial review is straightforward. If nine unelected justices, using the theory of constitutional revolutions, can overturn the product of the majoritarian branches of government, then they defeat or curb the democratic will. A majoritarian democracy cannot tolerate unelected and unaccountable officials making major changes in the law, and sometimes overturning the law and replacing it with what they think the law should be. This usurps the purpose of the majoritarian branches of government and leads to judicial tyranny.

The theory of constitutional revolutions is countermajoritarian, though it is not necessarily antidemocratic. For the theory to succeed it must cohere with a favorable conception of democracy. Two very different conceptions of democracy are involved in an appropriate defense of this theory: majoritarian and communitarian democracy.[42] Majoritarian democracy conceives of the role of democratic government primarily as consisting of a procedure for making decisions. In this respect majoritarian democracy may be skeptical concerning morality and politics; it might contend that because no one moral procedure for settling political and constitutional controversies is generally accepted, such as God's will or a Kantian imperative, we should prefer to make political decisions by asking a majority of the people to decide. Two problems immediately arise. One might plausibly contend that a majority is required for political decision, but it is not obvious why a simple majority of 51 percent is always the preferred choice. Second, and more importantly, if majoritarianism is a skeptical doctrine, it is not at all apparent how the question of determining the best course of action is answered by a majority, simple or compound. If skepticism is plausible concerning politics, the majority's wishes need not be superior to any one else's. The skeptical majoritarian agrees but continues by pointing out that when there is no truth of the matter, or when we cannot know the truth of the matter, we are likely to achieve greater stability by seeking a wide consensus. Of course, the skeptical majoritarian must answer why stability is desirable if skepticism appropriately applies to politics. The skeptic cannot regard moral equality as the touchstone of democracy without abandoning her skepticism. Consequently, no completely skeptical majoritarianism is likely. And any nonskeptical majoritarian theory of democracy must then appeal to the moral reasons for embracing majoritarianism, reasons that also explain when the majority should be restricted.

The majoritarian position might also be explicitly nonskeptical. In this version of the doctrine, procedure is the hallmark of collective decision making, not substantive conclusions. Substance, however, is the justification of this procedural democracy. Because each person has intrinsic value, each is entitled to be equally a part of the process of setting policy. Moreover, because no person is more intrinsically valuable than any other, no one can have a greater part in the decision-making process as a matter of that person's inherent status. This nonskeptical majoritarianism finds expression in certain forms of classical liberalism. In this view equal freedom is the value sought by the democratic polity. Equal freedom is valued primarily for its impact in one's private life. To be sure, no one can live an entirely private life in a democratic society, but the real value in life is to promote the private lives of independent individuals. The democratic state is necessary, on prudential grounds, but government is far from the apex of human value. According to nonskeptical majoritarianism the focus of value and meaning resides in the individual life, essentially conceived of independently of social interactions. This does not mean that this form of majoritarianism is committed to social or political isolation and solipsism. Human relationships can be confirmed as valuable, forming part of the meaning of life. Moreover, in this version of majoritarianism social structures may be empirically necessary for growth and development. Thus majoritarians of this kind can love and be loved, raise families, be members of guilds and churches, have loyalties, and so forth. What they cannot have, however, is an obligation to value their lives in conjunction with others. This does not mean that such individuals must be egoistic in the Hobbesian sense of that term. Instead, one is a liberal majoritarian when one believes that one's set of values, egoistic or altruistic, should prevail over the values of others. A liberal majoritarian sees majoritarian rule as an ultimate vehicle for persuading others to her values, not to work out principled solutions based on collective value. As such, majoritarians do not embrace as the paramount value of human existence the realization of the self as that self interacts with and teaches and learns from other equals in a web of essential human relationships.

In contrast to majoritarianism, communitarian democracy seeks to invoke procedures for determining the community's will, not a statistical account of what people believe. These procedures will consist of constraints and filters on majoritarian processes. Just as minorities can block the community's will, so too can the majority. Communitarian democracy seeks a form of government that encourages citizens to rise above their personal interests, if possible, to seek the common good. One salient goal of communitarian democracy is self-government, or more generally, living a self-governing life in a community of equals. This form of democracy is communitarian because it prizes an intentionalist community, not a natural one, a community that, in principle, each person voluntarily joins.[43] In such a community one's racial, ethnic, or ancestral allegiances are secondary to the idea of a new society based on deliberative reason and willingness to resolve social conflicts within the community according to what a reasonable citizen would consider fair. Moreover, each member of this community has a special connection to other members. Knowledge that citizens are committed to fair resolutions of common problems is what gives a person a sense of belonging in a communitarian republic.

Unlike classical liberalism, communitarian democracy eschews a sharp dichotomy between the private and the public. Defenders of this dichotomy contend that we can systematically distinguish between two different arenas, one concerning self-regarding actions, or actions that primarily affect the agent alone or those entering voluntary associations with the agent; and a second arena emphasizing actions that necessarily implicate others, including others not voluntarily associated with the agent, at least concerning the action in question. Communitarian democracy accepts a distinction between these two arenas but denies its systematic application as a justification of constitutional and political principles. Instead, communitarian democracy evaluates all decisions in terms of how they affect individuals attempting to live self-governing lives in the context of communitarian relations with other self-governing individuals.

Communitarian democracy eschews majoritarian democracy because simple majoritarian considerations do not guarantee that a particular policy will have a positive effect on self-governing lives. Communitarian democracy insists that we ask the following kinds of questions: Of what does a self-governing life consist? What is the role of individualism in the communitarian democracy? How do we guarantee equal consideration under the law? When should minority concerns take precedence over the concerns of majorities? Communitarian democracy seeks to provide answers to these questions for the sake of truly understanding whether (and how) self-governing individuals can best live self-governing lives, lives integrated with other self-governing individuals.

Moving the focus away from the libertarian ideal of political society, constructed for the self-growth of independent beings living private lives, toward communitarian democracy will not automatically resolve constitutional and political controversies, but in changing the focus it will provide a common framework for evaluating these issues. No longer will the clarion call be concerned merely with individual freedom, but rather with self-governing individuals interacting with other self-governing individuals in a community of equals. Communitarian democracy is conceived as the public philosophy or public faith of the American communitarian Republic that develops through a civic discourse and that any reasonable citizen should use as a sign of her commitment to the perpetuation of the community.

Two features of communitarian democracy deserve special attention: its deliberative function and its participatory function. The hallmark of communitarian democracy resides in the notion of having a stake in one's own development and in the development of the community. Further, it involves a mechanism, or series of mechanisms, for preserving that stake or in instantiating that stake in concrete institutional and noninstitutional structures in one's daily life. Individuals in such a society must develop elaborate forms of deliberation for conversing with other members of the community, and policies should be embraced only when they display the best reasons. This conversation must have political instantiation as well as social and economic instantiation. Therefore, true democracy involves much more than either of the two forms of majoritarian democracy previously described. Deliberative reasoning and conversation must be part of the good of the individual as well as the good of the society. Constitutional and political structures of government will then be evaluated in terms of their impact on self-government. This is the context for evaluating judicial review, understood in terms of the theory of constitutional revolutions. Thus, if revolutionary judicial review is conducive to a communitarian democracy fulfilling the essential role of deliberative "second thought," it is justified on democratic grounds, not because it doesn't offend majoritarian inclinations, but precisely because it does. Majoritarianism then is seen not to be equivalent to democracy, and critical reflection by a government entity contributes overall to the creation of the community's considered judgment.

Judicial review, understood in terms of the theory of constitutional revolutions, is justified in the following manner. In a democracy people generate at least two kinds of judgments: unreflective judgments about individual preferences, and considered judgments about social obligation or utility. The society should seek methods for transforming, if possible, judgments

236 Constitutional Revolutions

about preferences into considered, reflective social judgments through conversation and deliberation, with the aim of ascertaining the collective considered judgments of the community. Such reflection involves considering one's own interests, other people's interests, how these interests interact, and the effect of these interactions upon the good and civility of society. If democracy requires this capacity for considered judgment, and if the Court can do the job, the Court acts democratically, though not in a majoritarian fashion, by serving as the institution and repository of our most central reflective, considered judgments.[44]

The pragmatist foundation of communitarian democracy, in contrast to majoritarian democracy, requires the political community to create standards for institutionalized deliberation to determine what counts as a mere preference and what counts as a considered judgment of the community. Just as an individual learns to distinguish between her first reaction or decision, and her considered judgment derived after reflection, and after attending to important factors not explicit in her situation of choice, so too a polity must have a mechanism for making this distinction. In essence, this context, however we ultimately describe it, reflects the most persuasive paradigm of epistemically favorable situations of choice. In principle judicial review in the American context functions as one instantiation of these epistemically favorable circumstances; it is a mechanism for critical reflection — for a "second look" at a problem, and the first-order decision made to solve it.

There are at least two kinds of mechanism for this reflection. Call the first the "quantitative mechanism," and the second the "qualitative mechanism." In the quantitative mechanism, both the first- and second-order decisions are of the same type. In this case the mechanism for determining our considered judgments would involve layers of majoritarian scrutiny. The Founders might have devised a majoritarian institution, such as the president in conjunction with the Senate, or any other combination of institutions, or even an entirely new institution to perform this corrective function.

The qualitative mechanism creates a different form of reasoning in the second order to scrutinize conclusions from the first order. In American constitutionalism the Founders chose this second path. American judicial review is performed by unelected judges, and their concerns are less with policy than with determining whether a particular law passed by the majoritarian forces can withstand the scrutiny of a second look. The dissatisfaction with the qualitative mechanism because it is countermajoritarian does not obviate the need for some mechanism of critical reflection. Communitarian democracy maintains that such critical reflection must be part of the deliberative process, because communitarian democracy looks inward to the political culture to determine the standards for generating judgments and resolving conflicts. No external standard is possible. Similarly, communitarian democracy looks to the actual citizens in the polity and not to eternal truths or external standards to generate political truth. This inward direction is designed in part to preclude the alienation and moral torpor that arises from a purely procedural, majoritarian conception of political life. Communitarian democracy is deliberative and as such has a vested interest in the procedures of deliberation, but it must build into these procedures constraints that best express the idea of democracy as a communitarian construct, concerned with individual flourishing, because that contributes to the realization of an especially attractive conception of community.

The role judicial review plays in the American communitarian Republic is pragmatic in that it permits the distinction between first-order and second-order practical judgments. As such, it institutionally permits a polity to reflect on its first-order judgments and alter them when appropriate. We can, if we wish, change the nature of such reflection from a qualitative to a quantitative mechanism, but it would be foolish to abolish or severely restrict judicial review without first replacing it with a mechanism designed to formulate the considered judgments of the people independently.

The original arguments against the creation of judicial review have been recast in contemporary discussions of influential jurists. The strategy is to restrict it by calling it countermajoritarian, or judicial tyranny, or some equally misleading epithet. The next best step for the antijudicial review position, short of abolition, is to advocate restricting judicial review severely by insisting that reliance on the text, intent, or structure of the Constitution, or a majoritarian conception of democracy, entails a narrow understanding of the Court's role in our democracy. This flies in the face of actual judicial practice. More important for present purposes, it rejects the idea that either a qualitative or a quantitative mechanism exists for self-correction, and tends to degenerate into a skeptical form of majoritarianism. Communitarian democracy, on the other hand, insists on the need for some kind of corrective mechanism because a pragmatist democracy recognizes the need for fallibility, correction, and redirection. Only then can developing values be hewn and extended across the community to those who find themselves excluded from full membership.

Conclusion

Revolutionary change drives judicial review by translating cultural factors external to the judicial system itself into judicially and politically workable constitutional principles and rules. The theory of constitutional revolutions integrates a theory of constitutional moments with a theory of judicial reasoning by combining Kuhn's theory of conceptual change with the concept of wide reflective equilibrium, that is, a pragmatist interpretation of the relationship between constitutional fit and justification. The Court revolutionizes constitutional practice when a majority of judges perceive a constitutional crisis that demands resolution in contemporary terms not contained in that form in the Constitution. Ackerman's dualism is a theory of this sort. However, Ackerman's dualism gives the Court merely a preservationist role and binds it to three different constitutions, or constitutional regimes, exclusively. By contrast, the theory of constitutional revolutions supports a prophetic role for the Court that is both restricted to and liberated by constitutional practice. For a majority of judges to institute a revolution, each justice must believe that a particular decision, though short on history, is nevertheless the morally best, or pragmatically necessary, decision in the relevant circumstances. This reconstruction of constitutional moments and judicial reasoning creates a syncretic conception of American constitutional practice, a conception necessary in explaining American constitutional change accurately. This explanatory claim itself has normative force because, in the absence of neutral perspectives, a presumption exists in favor of the way we do things, unless there are formidable reasons to the contrary. Once a theory adequately satisfies this explanatory dimension of constitutional practice, it has initial normative force. A full justification of the practice of revolutionary review can occur only by showing how it supports and is supported by a preferred theory of American democratic constitutionalism — in my view, communitarian democracy. The legitimacy of judicial review rests in its explanatory accuracy and its support of communitarian democracy. For a viable sense of legitimacy, the central normative question is functionalist: Does revolutionary review contribute positively to efficiency and justice in a communitarian democratic society?

The goal of communitarian democracy is to determine, if possible, the good of the community, or at least its considered judgments concerning the good. This process is a two-step process at least. First, the majoritarian branches speak; then if their voice is unclear or in some other way problematic, causing a constitutional crisis, the nonmajoritarian branch reconsiders, or takes a "second look" at, their decision. The communitarian democratic point here is that to ascertain the community's good, or the community's considered judgment, some mechanism for reconsideration is required. This does not render revolutionary judicial review inevitable, but rather reflects how American judicial practice has in fact developed independently, whether or not its original structure was designed in this manner. One could argue that a particular nonjudicial mechanism of reconsideration may be more compatible with one's preferred conception of democracy, but some mechanism is necessary, and in the context of American constitutional practice, and according to communitarian democracy, revolutionary judicial review has assumed that role. If there exists a better nonjudicial mechanism for second-order judgments that is more compatible with democratic self-rule, its proponents must articulate it.

Although revolutionary judicial review is not limited to progressive political theory, it is more compatible with such theory than with competing ones. Given the need in progressive political theories to keep a vigil against domination, progressive values need a mechanism for extension, beyond simple majoritarianism. Thus, it is not surprising that the New Deal and Warren courts issued many progressive decisions. However, revolution breeds counterrevolution. The Rehnquist Court is now engaged in major revolutionary adjudication, prompting Linda Greenhouse to remark "the Court [is] a single vote shy of reinstalling the Articles of Confederation."[1] In my view the basis of this counterrevolution is precisely the nullification of the progressive effects of contemporary constitutional law. Progressive or not, the Court engages in revolution and counterrevolution as part of a deliberative process designed to determine the community's good. Thus, the theory explains how judges of all political ideologies use the same constitutional methodology and arrive at very different substantive conclusions. When judges have different substantive values, the theory of constitutional revolutions explains why the same judicial methodology yields different constitutional conclusions.

In our constitutional culture the theory of constitutional revolutions exhorts us to end the interminable, internecine bickering over proper constitutional methodology, which no one can win. Instead, substantive battles should be waged without permitting the choice of methodology itself to restrict or expand the possible answers. Judges should, instead, reconsider and reconstruct our public discourse reflecting the substantive values expressed in American constitutionalism, and should also appreciate the fact that when legislators fail to resolve a constitutional issue, as they will in some cases, it is judges who must exercise creative judicial insight and decide the case according to their best conception of the moral and political ideals in American constitutional law. The theory of constitutional revolutions maintains that such revolutionary decisions are a fundamental feature of American constitutionalism and that judges and academic lawyers do more harm than good when they insist otherwise.

This book's central purpose has been to dispel a myth that constitutional interpretation is or should be restricted to a narrow range of constitutional conventions. Traditional constitutional theory, Ackerman's interpretive history of constitutional moments, and Dworkin's coherentism perpetuate this myth in different ways. Instead, postmodern pragmatist constitutionalism must seek new vistas, new ways of providing insight into the creation of constitutional meaning. The theory of constitutional revolutions provides a constitutional aesthetic, a way of feeling critically comfortable with constitutional theory. Postmodern pragmatist constitutionalism need not be a chaotic free-for-all. Instead, it can be an opportunity for integrating disparate values in order to confront pragmatically the problems American constitutionalism and democracy will face in the next millennium.

NOTES

Preface

1   In this book the question of the legitimacy of state authority over the individual is determined by whether the state is democratic. Hence, this sense of legitimacy applies to democratic governments alone, and not to other forms of government.

2   Robert Bork is one of the chief critics calling for a mechanism permitting Congress to overrule a Supreme Court decision simply by majoritarian legislation. Robert Bork, *The Tempting of America* (1990). If the fruits of judicial review are necessary for having second-thoughts concerning the results of the majoritarian process, this suggestion is implausible. If a legislative solution is desirable here, only a *supermajoritarian* will seriously constrain the majoritarian processes. If not, the charge that the fox is left to guard the henhouse appears irrefutable.

3   Robert Bork also argues that justices are unable to appeal to moral theories without simply imposing their own "preferences" on the law. But if this is systemic, and no one can accurately appeal to moral and political theory in explicating the meaning of a constitutional provision, then majoritarianism cannot be the (morally?) best (preferred) strategy.

Introduction

1   In the American context the Constitution functions as a general rule of recognition through which structural features of government and the rights of individuals are identified and justified. American constitutionalism creates a government based on what Madison called "the Empire of Reason," the formation of a community wherein deliberative reasoning concerning the common good is one of the central conditions of membership.

2   Alternatively, the crisis of American constitutionalism is a crisis over the role of reason in politics and practical affairs. That the Framers intended American government to be based on reason is uncontrovertible. However, the problem arises concerning which conception of reason they employed and how it relates

to contemporary conceptions of reason. For an illuminating account of this issue, see Steven Smith, *The Constitution and the Pride of Reason* (1998). In my view Smith asks the right questions, but I disagree with his contention that the Framers could (and did) constitutionalize conclusions about reason in politics, not the process of reasoning itself. See J. G. A. Pocock, "States, Republics, and Empires: The American Founding in Early Modern Perspective," in *Conceptual Change and the Constitution,* 55, 56 (T. Ball and J. G. A. Pocock eds. 1988). Instead, the Revolution and the Constitution created a tradition of problem solving together with a self-correcting process of public practical reasoning.

3   For corroboration that this crisis is real or at least perceived to be real by important constitutional scholars, see Morton J. Horwitz, "Foreword: The Constitution of Change: Legal Fundamentality without Fundamentalism," 107 *Harv. L. Rev.* 30, 40 (1993); Sanford Levinson, *Constitutional Faith* 172 (1988); Paul W. Kahn, *Legitimacy and History* 210 (1992); and S. Smith, *The Constitution and the Pride of Reason,* at 125–26. For an informative discussion of this crisis in law generally, see Michel Rosenfeld, *Just Interpretations: Law between Ethics and Politics* (1998).

4   By "culture" I refer to a "human community . . . that is associated with ongoing ways of seeing, doing, and thinking about things." Amy Gutmann, "The Challenge of Multiculturalism in Political Ethics," 22 *Phil. & Pub. Aff.* 171 (1993). By "American" culture I mean those distinctive strategies and values for ordering social life, especially the resolution of various kinds of conflicts that have developed in American society. For example, the general American commitment to liberty and equality is more than just constitutional or legal values. Instead, they inform a certain culture, or way of life. More commonly, many American communities, but not all, have a commitment to taking one's place in line at bus stops. These norms and strategies contribute to forming American character. To talk about a national culture does not obviate the importance of recognizing the existence of minority cultures; nor does it suggest that cultural conflict is not an essential feature of American culture.

5   It might not be obvious that the United States Constitution is or should be considered a progressive document. By "progressive" I mean a form of politics or constitutionalism that seeks to enlarge the scope of individual and collective freedom by rooting out the structures that dominate and exclude individuals. I do not insist that American constitutionalism *entails* progressive politics or constitutionalism. My point here is that such a connection must remain an open question. For a recent discussion distinguishing progressive constitutionalism politics from liberal and conservative constitutionalism, see Robert Justin Lipkin, "Foreword: Is American Progressive Constitutionalism Dead?" 4 *Widener L. Sym. J.* 1 (1999).

6   The Constitution includes in article 5 a process for amending the Constitution.

This does not explain how the Constitution can be relevant to unforeseen circumstances for the following reason. If there were no non-article-5 method for effecting constitutional change, or if the process were very difficult to use, the Constitution remains stagnant without emendation. If it is relevant only through article 5, and article 5 were easier to use, then it would render the Constitution as prolix as a legal code. In this event either the Constitution remains stagnant and irrelevant to contemporary matters, or it is relevant but indistinguishable from ordinary law. Chief Justice Marshall warned us against the latter course early on in *McCulloch v. Maryland*. See infra note 87, chap. 4. The reply that the Constitution proscribes informal change is inadequate because nowhere in the Constitution is informal change discussed. This means the Founders believe article 5 exhausted constitutional change, or that they thought constitutional change inevitable and good, or that they forgot to address the issue.

7   The culture wars are systemic conflicts over the proper interpretation of American culture: what it is, what it should be, and how it changes. Typically, the parties to these conflicts, sometimes broadly characterized as conservatives and liberals, have very different ideas concerning the roles religion, education, and the family play in American society. See J. D. Hunter, *Culture Wars* (1990); see also Gerald Graff, *Beyond the Culture Wars: How Teaching the Conflicts Can Revitalize American Education* (1992). American constitutionalism is a form of cultural criticism and as such constitutes a process of constitutional and cultural change. For a discussion of progressive cultural change, see Robert Justin Lipkin, "Pragmatism, Cultural Criticism, and the Idea of the Postmodern University," in *Ethics and the University: Community, Diversity and Morality in the American Academy* 49 (M. N. S. Sellers ed. 1994); see also Sanford Levinson, "Law as Literature," in *Interpreting Law as Literature* 155 (S. Levinson and S. Mailloux eds. 1988).

8   The American constitutional culture rejects majoritarianism because majorities can tyrannize just as effectively as minorities. See James Madison, *Federalist Papers*.

9   I distinguish between a deliberative culture and a dedicated one in Robert Justin Lipkin, "The Possibility of Liberal Constitutionalism: The Distinction between Deliberative and Dedicated Cultures," 29 *U. Rich. L. Rev.* 765 (1995); and Robert Justin Lipkin, "Can Liberalism Justify Multiculturalism?" 45 *Buffalo L. Rev.* 1 (1997), among other places. A deliberative culture or community is one committed to the ideal of openness through pragmatic reasoning, whereas dedicated cultures seek to authoritatively explicate canonical values without subjecting them to fallibilist reasoning.

10   In general, republicanism can be contrasted with liberalism. Republicanism is committed to the liberty of self-government, which in part encourages and requires civic virtue. Freedom, for republicanism, is twofold: First, it repre-

244 Notes to Introduction

sents the collective capacity of citizens to govern themselves in a community. Second, it represents the civic component of the good life. The civic component is related to personal aspects of freedom and the good life; it reflectively guides personal preferences and encourages the individual to think in terms of the common good. Most contemporary forms of American republicanism are committed to deliberativism in collective choice. By contrast, liberalism appears more concerned with individual freedom, viewing government as a necessary evil at best. In republicanism the idea of the common good refers to something beyond the total preferences of citizens. In some forms of liberalism, at least, democratic rule means the unconstrained rule of the majority.

11   Cass R. Sunstein, *The Partial Constitution* (1993). But see Robert Justin Lipkin, "The Quest for the Common Good: Neutrality and Deliberative Democracy in Sunstein's Conception of American Constitutionalism," 26 *U. Conn. L. Rev.* 1039 (1995).

12   R. Bork, *The Tempting of America* at 2, preface; M. Perry, *The Constitution in the Courts: Law or Politics?* (1994).

13   That we have minimal agreement on such moral and political issues as murder, fraud, theft, torture, and so forth should not be taken as the beginning of complete moral agreement. The aspiration toward consensus hopes that minimal agreement will yield general principles that will settle the remaining differences. Few theorists consider the possibility that only minimal agreement is possible. See M. Walzer, "Minimal Moralism," in *The Twilight of Probability* 3 (William R. Shea and Antonio Spadafora eds. 1992).

14   Cf. S. Levinson, "Law as Literature."

15   I am aware of the problems associated with the notion of an "American national character." However, American liberal constitutionalism has always proceeded as if there exists a distinct, unique model of American values embodied in a particular kind of moral and political personality. Some features of this model are fairness, impartiality, meritocracy, and justice. Of course, denying the feasibility of one such model does not preclude the existence of a small set of mutually incompatible models that accurately depict the several different moral personalities associated with American constitutionalism. For a discussion of this last possibility, see Robert Justin Lipkin, "Beyond Skepticism, Foundationalism, and the New Fuzziness: The Role of Wide Reflective Equilibrium in Legal Theory," 75 *Cornell L. Rev.* 811 (1990).

16   Ibid.

17   Postmodernity rejects the quest for principles validating all we know and value. See Jean-François Lyotard, *The Postmodern Condition: A Report on Knowledge* xxiv (1984) (defining postmodernity "as incredulity toward metanarratives"). Metanarratives "subordinate, organize and account for other narratives; so that every other local narrative . . . is given meaning by the way it echoes and

confirms the grand narrative." Steven Connors, *Postmodernist Culture: An Introduction to Theories of the Contemporary* 30 (1989). Losing faith in metanarratives implies that philosophy, the metanarrative of metanarratives, can never be the queen of the sciences. J-F. Lyotard, *The Postmodern Condition,* at 41 ("Speculative or humanistic philosophy has been forced to relinquish its legitimation duties, which explains why philosophy is facing a crisis wherever it persists in arrogating such functions and is reduced to the study of systems of logic or the history of ideas where it has been realistic enough to surrender them"). This should not tempt us to describe the failure of the great narratives as "the great narrative of the decline of great narratives." Jean-François Lyotard, "Universal History and Cultural Differences," in *The Lyotard Reader* 314, 318. (A. Benjamin ed. 1989); Seyla Benhabib, *Situating the Self: Gender, Community, and Postmodernism in Contemporary Ethics* 224 (1992) (discussing what philosophy becomes when it ceases aspiring to a metadiscourse of legitimation).

18   Challenging these dichotomies is not equivalent to denying distinctions between the paired terms. Instead, it denies that the distinction exhaustively defines the domain under investigation.

19   Integration refers to the process of salvaging what is attractive in past paradigms and discarding the rest. Do not think this process represents a grand narrative in itself, since it merely exhorts us to deliberate about cultural and constitutional values.

20   This book regards "pragmatism" and its cognates as signifying a willingness to resolve constitutional and cultural conflicts normatively by balancing competing factors in an attempt to create consensus, or, if consensus is impossible, by explaining why these conflicts are intractable.

21   S. Levinson, *Constitutional Faith* 10 (1988).

22   The crisis of American constitutionalism is the downside of this process. In remaking others into one's self-conception, one must have a sufficiently capacious conception of the self if tolerance and diversity are to reign.

23   Robert Cover, "The Supreme Court 1982 Term: Foreword: Nomos and Narrative," 97 *Harv. L. Rev.* 4 (1983).

24   Additionally, constitutional theory must be concerned with the question of the constitutional scheme's competence. How does constitutional reasoning generate answers to constitutional questions? The question of competence is conceptually prior to the question of legitimacy. We must know how to generate constitutional conclusions before addressing the question of whether these conclusions are legitimate. See Lipkin, "Beyond Skepticism," at 834–36. It is this question of competence that survives the demise of modernity's foundationalist hold on constitutionalism.

25   Coercion might be presumptively invalid, yet ultimately valid if it involves the defense of liberty.

26   But see Robert A. Burt, *The Constitution in Conflict* 9 (1992) (arguing that the question of legitimacy in constitutional contexts is spurious).

27   R. Bork, *The Tempting of America,* at 187–240 (discussing liberal and conservative attempts to justify judicial activism).

28   Furthermore, there is little evidence, if any, that the Framers intended a purely majoritarian government. Indeed, most commentators agree that the republican design of American government was to thwart, not encourage, pure majoritarian rule.

29   The countermajoritarian problem assumes that the legislative branches are not countermajoritarian. It is difficult to see how such a claim can be sustained. Not only are such institutions as the Senate countermajoritarian, but so are the rules of Congress, which set up entrenched committee chairpersons and parliamentary rules that often stifle majority decisions. The reply is that at least these branches and policies are subject to the people's ultimate endorsement whereas the Court is not. I do not see a significant difference between entrenched rules of the legislature and entrenched "reasoned" decisions by courts. Both render constitutional and political change enormously difficult.

30   Steven Shiffrin, *First Amendment, Romance, and Dissent* 84 (1990).

31   It is important to distinguish between majoritarian processes in selecting judges and majoritarian processes in holding judges accountable. One could argue that justices survive the majoritarian process of appointment and confirmation. The real problem is that once a justice is confirmed, no effective procedure exists (beyond impeachment) for holding the justice accountable to the people. Consequently, informal constraints are necessary to avoid judicial tyranny. Still, prudential and institutional concerns discipline most judges precluding their riding roughshod over every piece of legislation.

32   One such factor would be a referendum or referenda designed to confirm or reverse an errant Supreme Court decision. Another would be a two-thirds congressional override of such decisions. Some argue that section 5 of the Fourteenth Amendment permits Congress to override errant Supreme Court decisions concerning those rights incorporated by its due process clause. Recently, however, the Court rejected this argument in *City of Boerne v. Flores,* 117 S.Ct. 2157 (1997).

33   Both the political right and the political left have used this criticism against the Court in different historical eras.

34   See Alexander M. Bickel, *The Least Dangerous Branch* (1962).

35   Presumably, this argument's plausibility rests on the fact that if we are committed (nonskeptically) at least to one principle that self-government is good, then if no other principles prove dispositive about individual rights and powers, we should simply appeal to the first principle of government to settle all

future controversies. Few skeptics, however, would plausibly break with skepticism in order to admit that this first principle of government is knowable. Without further constraints, precluded by skepticism, this first principle is indistinguishable from mob rule. To deal with the unprecedented size of the American Republic, Madison broke with traditional republicanism by placing a great trust, tinged with fear, in the people. For Madison it was "[u]ltimately, the civic virtue of the people that would have to prevent republican government from degenerating into mobocracy." Jack N. Rakove, *Original Meanings: Politics and Ideas in the Making of the Constitution* 49 (1996).

36   Article 5 is the normal constitutional procedure for constitutional change. However, once a constitutional amendment is ratified, the Court, in the appropriate circumstances, will interpret the amendment and sometimes subject it to revolutionary adjudication. According to the theory of constitutional revolutions, the procedure in article 5 applies to adding text formally to the Constitution; it says nothing about the informal process of judicial amendments.

37   H. Berman, *Law and Revolution* 21 (1983).

38   One writer seriously considers the possibility of returning to the past: C. Wolfe, *The Rise of Modern Judicial Review* (1986) (arguing that modern judicial review is much more radical than traditional judicial review). One of this book's salient aims has been to demonstrate that this contention rests on a misconception of the nature of the Marshall Court. Marshall was as activist as any modern judge; his concerns were different, now appearing obvious to the contemporary perspective.

39   For an interesting discussion pointing out that the Framers of the Fourteenth Amendment themselves passed laws containing racial classifications for the purpose of helping black women and children, see Jeb Rubenfeld, "Affirmative Action," 107 *Yale L. J.* 427, 430 (1997).

40   Originalism is back in vogue primarily through the efforts of Robert Bork, Raoul Berger, Michael McConnell, and, surprisingly, Michael Perry and Ronald Dworkin. But these originalisms are very different from one another. Interestingly, Michael Perry's originalism is not committed to judicial restraint. It could be argued that Ronald Dworkin's "moral reading of the Constitution" is a form of originalism or textualism. Perry's and Dworkin's "originalism" appeals to the Framers for the initial abstract political theoretical terms for constitutional adjudication, such as freedom, equality, and procedural justice. However, it leaves these terms to be specified by latter-day judges and political actors. As such it distorts the common conception of originalism, which attempts to tie the details of future application to the Framers' actual beliefs, intentions, and expectations. With friends like Perry and Dworkin, the standard conception of originalism needs no enemies.

41   Robert Justin Lipkin, "The Anatomy of Constitutional Revolutions," 66 *Neb. L. Rev.* 701 (1989).

42   Some believe that there is wide agreement on this point. See S. Smith, *The Constitution and the Pride of Reason.* However, without the recognition that these changes are revolutionary, that they depict and drive American constitutional law, and that they are constitutive of American democracy, this agreement fails to draw the startling conclusion that this functionalist account of revolutionary adjudication deploys history and normative political theory to legitimize judicial review.

43   This should not be read as an endorsement of ethical or political relativism. However, it does caution against assuming that some neutral Archimedean constitutional perspective exists that can be used to determine constitutional meaning once and for all.

44   See *Fordham Symposium,* for a useful discussion of different conceptions of fidelity.

45   Chief Marshall's conception of American constitutionalism explicitly acknowledges the relationship between constitutionalism and resolving "crises of human affairs." *McCulloch v. Maryland,* see infra chap. 4, note 87.

46   Robert J. Lipkin, "Conventionalism, Pragmatism, and Constitutional Revolutions," 21 *U.C. Davis L. Rev.* 645 (1988); Lipkin, "Indeterminacy, Justification, and Truth in Constitutional Theory," 60 *Fordham L. Rev.* 595 (1993).

47   See infra chap. 1.

48   Although this book stresses constitutional revolutions, similar revolutions occur in all areas of the law, especially in the common law.

49   This may not always be so. Conventionalism can be defended because a conventionalist legal system provides processes of adjudication as an uncontrovertible social fact. However, this raises the question of legitimacy from the start.

50   See Lipkin, "Beyond Skepticism."

51   The terms "revolutionary," "transformative," "evolutionary," and so forth are part of a practice of change that renders them mutually interdependent. A change is "revolutionary" in a domain when reference to the domain cannot explain its genesis. A decision is "transformative" when the domain can partially explain its genesis. Finally, a decision is "evolutionary" when the domain completely explains its genesis. Most theorists regard the terms "transformative" and "evolutionary" to be incompatible with revolutionary decisions, yet they simultaneously acknowledge the new directions that such decisions generate. Understood in this manner, they share the same fate as "seminal" or "landmark" decisions.

52   Contemporary republicanism is not restricted to stability as perhaps its classical counterpart is. Instead, contemporary republicanism emphasizes deliberating over the common good and chooses formal and informal methods for doing so.

53 This attempt was born in conflict and duplicity, which included brutal treat-
    ment of Africans and indigenous peoples, the lack of enfranchisement for
    women, and discrimination against Catholics, Jews, and other minority reli-
    gions and cultures. I do not intend to defend early American republicanism.
    Instead, I want to show the role judicial review plays in American constitu-
    tionalism and to connect that role to the founding political ideals.
54 Gerald Rosenberg, *The Hollow Hope: Can Courts Bring about Social Change?*
    (1991).
55 J. Madison, *Federalist Papers* No. 10 (1961).

1   Constitutionalism and Dualist Politics

1 Bruce Ackerman, 1 *We the People* (1991).
2 Even if the countermajoritarian problem cannot be overcome, all is not lost.
   One could argue that political and constitutional wisdom derive from the clash
   of these competing values. Renouncing either one sacrifices its importance as
   well as the importance of the clash. See David Dow, "When Words Mean What
   We Believe They Say: The Case of Article V," 76 *Iowa L. Rev.* 1, 10 (1990).
3 Ackerman's pragmatism insists that even if formalist — rule-based — constitutional development is possible, it is undesirable. Any vital constitutional
   democracy will develop informal — sometimes even unconscious — ways of engaging in constitutional change. The pragmatic imperative drives these informal processes. That's the whole point of the pragmatist injunction "Let's try it
   out!" It also conducts a constant, unremitting vigil for mistakes that arise out of
   this process.
4 Postmodernity need not be a nihilist doctrine. Indeed, some conceptions of
   pragmatism are compatible with postmodern sensibilities. Robert Justin Lipkin, "Can American Constitutional Law Be Postmodern?" 42 *Buff. L. Rev.* 317
   (1994). For my conception of "reflective pragmatism," see Robert Justin Lipkin, "Pragmatism — The Unfinished Revolution: Doctrinaire and Reflective
   Pragmatism in Rorty's Social Thought," 67 *Tul. L. Rev.* 1561 (1992).
5 Ackerman doesn't distinguish between judicial dualism and political dualism.
   American constitutionalism is politically dualist on its face because ordinary
   legislative processes create most laws, whereas superordinary laws through
   article 5 amend the Constitution. Claiming judicial dualism, as the theory of
   constitutional revolutions does, is more surprising.
6 Both dualism and the standard view accept the New Deal's *political* revolution.
   However, dualism regards the judicial "switch in time" to be preservative; the
   standard view considers it transformative. However, the term "transformative"
   is obscurantist; it describes constitutional change as both novel, yet based in

prior law. According to the theory of constitutional revolutions "transformative" changes are, for the most part, revolutionary; they represent the process
courts use to translate cultural and political values (sometimes inchoate values)
into constitutional law.

7   Bruce Ackerman, "Why Dialogue?" 86 *J. Phil.* 5, 10 (1989).

8   Following the Framers, Ackerman contends that American democracy is
    unique and cannot be understood as the mere instantiation of European politi-
    cal theories.

9   Robert Justin Lipkin, "Pragmatism — The Unfinished Revolution."

10 Richard Rorty, "Inquiry as Recontextualism: An Anti-Dualist Account of Inter-
    pretation," in 1 *Philosophical Papers: Objectivity, Relativism, and Truth* 93 (1991).

11 We must await the third volume of this multivolume work for Ackerman to
    unveil his theory of constitutional interpretation, as nothing in his chapter
    "The Possibility of Interpretation" reveals such a theory. B. Ackerman, 1 *We the
    People,* at 131.

12 See Laurence Tribe, "Taking Text and Structure Seriously: Reflections on Free-
    form Method in Constitutional Interpretation," 108 *Harv. L. Rev.* 1221 (1995).

13 This chapter was written before the publication of 2 *We the People: Transforma-
    tions* (1997). In 1 *We the People: Foundations* Ackerman gives a promissory note
    to show that article 5 does not exhaust the legitimate procedures for amending
    the Constitution. In *Transformations* Ackerman attempts to make good on
    these promises. One weakness in Ackerman's theory is revealed in the evidence
    he marshals in favor of abnormal changes in the Founding, Reconstruction,
    and New Deal. Even if, arguably, his evidence is real, why should we regard
    these vents as alternative ways of legitimately amending the Constitution rather
    than lawlessness or pragmatic necessity?

14 Some resist the notion of "pragmatic principle" on the ground that pragmatism
    eschews principles. No doubt pragmatism eschews certain kinds of principles,
    just like formalism and other conceptions of law. However, it does not follow
    from this that pragmatism is incapable of incorporating any type of principle.
    In my view pragmatism clearly can embrace prima facie principles. A prima
    facie principle includes a statement of principle's content and purpose, together
    with some such caveat as *all things being equal.*

15 B. Ackerman, *Social Justice and the Liberal State* (1980).

16 Constitutional and political theorists rarely, if ever, consider the possibility that
    irreducibly different paradigms concerning freedom and equality underlie our
    commitment to constitutionalism. A postmodern conception of American
    constitutionalism might explain this possibility.

17 I ignore the question of whether modernity is a distinct period in human
    history. Whether distinct or merely part of modernity, postmodernity chal-
    lenges us to reevaluate our epistemic values.

18 Arguably, the very nature of law, especially democratic law, entails the possibility of prior majorities controlling subsequent ones. Indeed, the very idea of
democratic constitutionalism requires it. See R. Bork, 170–71. A corollary of
this conclusion is that it is misleading to think that the Constitution reflects the
will of the people *tout court*. Instead, it reflects, at best, the will of certain people
in the past. Indeed, the notion of "the people" or "the will of the people" is a
metaphor. In fact, such locutions refer to different, sometimes fractionated,
groups of people. See Edward S. Morgan, "The Fiction of the People," *N.Y.
Rev. Bks.,* Apr. 23, 1992, at 46–48 (stating that the instances of constitutional
politics Ackerman stresses may not have come by the will of the people).
Indeed, in 1787 "the people" were a much larger group than "We the People,"
including Africans, women, indigenous people as well as others. How, then,
can the Founding serve as one of the key paradigms of American constitutional
democracy? Even if the Founding referred to the right "people," how can a
people have a will? All the important theoretical questions concerning the
legitimacy of democracy arise in answering this last question. Consequently,
"We the People" derives from a preferred conception of democracy; it does not
ground such a conception.

Along different lines Akhil Reed Amar makes the interesting observation
that the notion of popular sovereignty precludes a prior majority from abrogat-
ing the present majority's right to amend the Constitution. See Akhil R. Amar,
"Philadelphia Revisited: Amending the Constitution outside Article V," 55 *U.
Chi. L. Rev.* 1043 (1988). Amar, like Ackerman, endorses the possibility of
amending the Constitution outside the constraints of article 5. Ibid.

19 Michael McConnell, "The Forgotten Constitutional Moment," 11 *Const. Commentary* 115 (1994).

20 B. Ackerman, 1 *We the People,* at 3.

21 R. Bork, at 139. But see Dow, "When Words Mean," at 15–16 ("[D]espite our
general commitment to majority rule, we also believe, we believe passionately,
that mere majorities may not do whatever they want simply because they are
majorities"). Even Bork concedes that this majoritarian prerogative is constrained by rights set out in the text of the Constitution. No one can accept the
United States Constitution as it is written and be a monist in Ackerman's sense
of the term. Indeed, the father of the Constitution, James Madison, certainly
wasn't a monist. Instead Madison was convinced of the dangers of a mobilized
majority; majority factions could become equally as oppressive as monarchy.
Therefore, monism flies in the face of constitutional history.

I am convinced that Robert Bork is the perennial modernist judge. Bork still
believes that "a judicial philosophy is either correct or incorrect," as if some
formal feature of reason or "correspondence with reality" makes it so, with
nothing more to say, as if that alone settles some important issue, or has

relevance to our practical deliberations over constitutional matters. Robert Bork, *Crossfire*, CNN, March 26, 1993. It is difficult to understand why Bork persists in advancing this position, when he is the first to insist that we cannot know or prove which *substantive* values are correct. Even if Bork's distinction between correct and incorrect judicial philosophies is conceptually sound, how can he believe that we can reliably know or prove when a judicial philosophy is correct or when a constitutional methodology is incorrect? Modernity aside, what can it mean in postmodern pragmatist constitutionalism for a judicial philosophy to be correct or incorrect? Postmodern pragmatist constitutionalism advocates that we drop such notions and, instead, try to delineate a picture of American constitutionalism that is rich and suggestive, and, at least for some Americans, renders constitutional reasoning meaningful.

22   B. Ackerman, 1 *We the People*.

23   Ibid. at 11.

24   Ibid. at 10–11.

25   Ibid. at 11.

26   Ibid. at 12.

27   Ibid.

28   See Suzanna Sherry, "The Ghost of Liberalism Past," 105 *Harv. L. Rev.* 918, 924 n. 19 (1992) (reviewing B. Ackerman, *We the People* [1991]) ("Does anyone really believe . . . that [d]emocracy requires the grant of plenary law-making authority to the winners of the last general election . . .?").

29   Ibid. at 923.

30   Ackerman made these remarks specifically in reply to my criticism at the Association of American Law School Conference on Constitutional Law in Ann Arbor, June 13, 1993, where I presented an earlier version of this chapter in a workshop. As I understand it, the "symbolic Constitution" is expressed by the formal rhetoric of American constitutionalism, whereas the "effective Constitution" is expressed by how constitutional change actually occurs. For example, a monist might say that she embraces rights as constraints on majoritarianism but rarely, if at all, finds a law that violates a right. Thus, her formal stance maintains a commitment to rights, but her actual judicial practice suggests that majorities may rule simply because they are majorities.

31   Ackerman also mentions Woodrow Wilson, James Thayer, Charles Beard, Oliver Wendell Holmes, and Robert Jackson as "monistic democrats." B. Ackerman, 1 *We the People*, at 7. The evidence against this contention is plentiful but can only be selectively scrutinized here. For example, it is unclear in Woodrow Wilson's case that the label "monist" applies. In contrasting our constitutional system with the British, Wilson maintained that the English courts do not restrict Parliament, but in the United States "[t]he powers of our law-making bodies are, on the contrary, very definitely defined and circumscribed in docu-

ments which are themselves part of the body of our law, and the decisions of the courts interpreting those documents set those law-making bodies their limits." Woodrow Wilson, *Constitutional Government in the United States* 145 (1907). Wilson described the court as "the balance-wheel of the whole system taking the strain from every direction and seeking to maintain what any unchecked exercise of power might destroy." Ibid. at 149. Consequently, it is difficult to see how Wilson advocates plenary power for the majoritarian branches of government in normal politics.

Ackerman's case is best supported by John Hart Ely. John Hart Ely, *Democracy and Distrust* 105 (1980). One way to demonstrate that a theorist is committed to monism is to show that he avoids interpreting the Constitution as containing substantive, as opposed to procedural, values. Ely argues that "[t]he general strategy [of the constitutional design] has . . . not been to root in the document a set of substantive rights entitled to permanent protection." Ibid. at 100. Ely, however, does recognize "a few provisions that do not comfortably conform to this pattern." "But they're an odd assortment," he goes on, "the understandable products of particular historical circumstances — guns, religion, contract, and so on — and in any event they are few and far between. To represent them as a dominant theme of our constitutional document one would have to concentrate quite single-mindedly on hopping from stone to stone and averting one's eyes from the mainstream." Ibid. at 101.

The obvious rejoinder is that Ely's emphasis on process and representation-reinforcement itself "averts its eye" from the mainstream. American constitutionalism has other elements besides these factors, and surely they do not adequately characterize the mainstream. If Ely is a monist, he ought not to be one. More important, even in representation-reinforcing terms, Ely rejects the idea that even a qualified absolutism permits a present majority from overturning certain constraints on this process.

Another way to prove the charge of monism is to show that a theorist embraces the present majority as the final authority over constitutional interpretation. However, few theorists, if any, embrace such a thing, certainly not Ely. Even Ely argues that present majoritarian decisions should be thwarted when restricting democratic values such as free speech and the right to vote.

Similarly, Ackerman's inclusion of Jesse Choper as a paradigmatic monist is unwarranted. Although Choper concerns himself with antimajoritarian elements of the Supreme Court, he is concerned equally with antimajoritarian elements of Congress and even the presidency. Jesse Choper, *Judicial Review and the National Political Process: A Functional Reconsideration of the Role of the Supreme Court* (1980). Choper, though a parliamentarian, is no monist. Rather, Choper insists that "the essential role of judicial review in our society is to guard against certain constitutional transgressions which popular majorities specifically seek to impose." Choper insists that "[t]he great task . . . for the Court . . . is how best to reject majority will when it must." Ibid. at 59. Finally, Choper suggests that "if judicial review were nonexistent for popularly frustrated minorities, the fight, already lost in the legislative halls, would have only one remaining battleground, the streets." He concluded that without judicial review, "violence and decadence" are the only viable alternatives. Ibid. at 128.

The case of Robert H. Jackson is ambiguous at best. Although Jackson wants courts to defer unless the law is clearly wrong, he also believes that "[t]he Supreme Court is . . . the voice of the Constitution in vindicating the rights of the individual under the federal Constitution against both the national and state governments." Robert H. Jackson, *The Struggle for Judicial Supremacy* 22, 323 (1979). Consequently, Ackerman needs to provide additional evidence that Jackson was a monist. Even Robert Bork's *The Tempting of America* is replete with references to the legitimacy of judicial review understood as review committed to the original understanding of the Constitution. For example, in his introduction Bork writes: "The judiciary's greatest office is to preserve the constitutional design. It does this not only by confining Congress and the President to the powers granted them by the Constitution and seeing that the powers granted are not used to invade the freedoms guaranteed by the Bill of Rights, but also, and equally important, by ensuring that the democratic authority of the people is maintained the full scope given by the Constitution." Bork, at 4. According to Bork, "we retain the institution of judicial review because we have found that it does much good." Ibid. at 11. It is true that Bork contends that the first principle of a Madisonian system is the principle of self-government, "which means that in wide areas of life majorities are entitled to rule, if they wish, simply because they are majorities." But the second principle of the Madisonian system "is that there are nonetheless some things majorities must not do to minorities, some areas of life in which the individual must be free of majority rule." Further, the Bill of Rights "directly addresses the specific liberties minorities are to have." Ibid. at 139. Moreover, even Bork, the majoritarian, believes that "there should be a presumption that individuals are free, and to justify coercion by [the majority] a case must be made that overcomes that presumption." Ibid. at 79–80.

32 Indeed, one might accuse Ackerman of circular reasoning here. The distinction between constitutional monists and rights foundationalists is a dichotomy purporting to describe the constitutional landscape exhaustively. Because everyone embraces *some* rights, Ackerman's framework is suspect. By distinguishing between embracing rights effectively or only symbolically, Ackerman supports the original distinction. But this begs the question because it assumes that Ackerman characterizes monists correctly; and this is precisely the conclusion that must be argued for, not assumed.

33   J. Noel Ryan, "The Central Fallacy of Canadian Constitutional Law," 22 *McGill L. J.* 40, 42 (1976).

34   Sherry, at 923, 927.

35   Ackerman fails to consider the rights foundationalist who believes that the right to self-government is the principal right the Constitution protects. In that event no conflict exists between monism and rights foundationalism. Concerning rights of this kind, the countermajoritarian problem cannot even arise. If judicial review is predicated on protecting rights of self-government, the Court acts democratically when it exercises judicial review. Similarly, Cass Sunstein writes:

> [T]he much-vaunted opposition between constitutionalism and democracy, or between rights and democracy, tends . . . to dissolve entirely. Many rights are indispensable to democracy and to democratic deliberation. If we protect such rights through the Constitution, we do not compromise self-governments at all. On the contrary, self-government depends for its existence on firmly protected democratic rights. Constitutionalism can thus guarantee the preconditions for democracy by limiting the power of majorities to eliminate those preconditions.
>
> Moreover, rights-based constraints on the political process are necessary for a well-functioning democracy; they are not antithetical to it. Unchecked majoritarianism should not be identified with democracy. A system in which majorities are allowed to repress the views of those who disagree could hardly be described as democratic. (Cass R. Sunstein, *The Partial Constitution*, at 142)

36   Miriam Galston and William A. Galston, "Reason, Consent, and the U.S. Constitution: Bruce Ackerman's *We the People*," 104 *Ethics* 446 (1994). This essay appeared in an edition of *Ethics* devoted to Ackerman's 1 *We the People*, which hereinafter will be cited as *Ackerman Symposium*.

37   Don Herzog, "Democratic Credentials," in *Ackerman Symposium*, at 467, 471.

38   Ibid.

39   Ibid.

40   Bruce Ackerman, "Rooted Cosmopolitanism," in *Ackerman Symposium*, at 516, 520.

41   Ibid.

42   Ibid.

43   Ibid.

44   This is part of the attraction of Ackerman's dualism. If normal politics gives us 90 percent of the promise of monism, and if constitutional politics gives us 90 percent of the promise of rights foundationalism, then dualism gives us what most American constitutionalists desire.

45   It could be argued that any normatively desirable conception of democracy

requires a more engaged involvement in normal politics on the part of the private citizen. If so, then Ackerman's conception of a private citizen points to an undesirable feature of American constitutionalism.

46   B. Ackerman, 1 *We the People,* at 31.

47   Ibid. at 30 (footnote omitted). But see Harold J. Berman, "The Impact of the Enlightenment on American Constitutional Law," 4 *Yale J. L. and Human.* 311, 332 (1992) (arguing against conflating liberalism and republicanism).

48   It also has some obvious defects. For instance, higher lawmaking is not always lawmaking concerning rights, it is also lawmaking concerning powers or structural features of government (which in turn imply the absence of particular rights). Thus rights foundationalism must be more broadly conceived, for Ackerman's purposes; it must include individual rights and sometimes the rejection of individual rights through the right of self-government.

49   B. Ackerman, 1 *We the People,* at 12.

50   Ibid.

51   Ibid.

52   This suggests that we must look at the Constitution, in some sense, as continuous with the Articles of Confederation. The better view, however, would be that the Constitution was a fresh start. One can argue that the Articles of Confederation was a compact between the states creating a weak central government, which was the reason for the compact's failure. If this failure abrogated the Articles of Confederation, then the Constitution is not illegal for failing to follow the process of amendment in the Articles of Confederation. In this view Ackerman's dualism, which rests on the conventional illegality of the Founding, is a nonstarter.

53   One might argue that this explains only the political or constitutional transition, which was revolutionary because of its changed criteria of constitutional validity; it does not explain the conceptual transition, which was relatively minimal.

54   The situation after the Revolutionary War quickly deteriorated. Debtors and creditors were at odds, and debtor rebellions were not uncommon. States were dangerously bickering over tariffs, among other issues. King George was pleased by this discord and predicted that the new political entity would not last more than a few years. In fact, history tells us that the odds were in favor of the king.

55   See David A. J. Richards, *Conscience and the Constitution: History, Theory, and Law of the Reconstruction Amendments* 136 (1993).

56   B. Ackerman, 1 *We the People,* at 120.

57   Ibid. at 86.

58   The question of whether the Constitution is ever amended without creating new constitutional text is examined in Sanford Levinson ed., *Responding to Imperfection* (1995).

59 Ackerman needs to provide a methodology for determining who counts as the people as well as for determining the people's will.

60 Keep in mind that the Founding occurred in terms of article 7, but in embracing article 7 as the standard of legitimacy, the Framers repudiated (unjustifiably?) the Articles of Confederation. The Civil War amendments occurred through article 5 but only, according to Ackerman, in an improper way.

61 S. Levinson, *Responding to Imperfection*, at 9.

62 Ibid. at 9–10.

63 Suzanna Sherry argues that Ackerman fails to show that judges have any incentive to preserve the higher lawmaking processes. But surely Ackerman's theory provides incentives for judges to resist "acquiescing to popular passions." The judiciary should be the primary preservationist branch because it is the only fully nonmajoritarian branch of government. If all governmental officials accept Ackerman's story, then they all might have reason to support the dualist democracy in the appropriate circumstances, but judges are the only officials who have an obligation to engage in systemic defense of higher lawmaking. For it is judges alone whose very raison d'être is to protect constitutional politics. Nevertheless, it is true that Ackerman's "identification of the judiciary as the primary preservationist branch still does not take us beyond simple judicial review to a dualist Constitution." Sherry, at 927.

64 Ibid. at 10.

65 Ibid.

66 Ibid. at 22.

67 B. Ackerman, 1 *We the People,* at 139.

68 Ibid.

69 Ibid.

70 Ibid. at 139–40.

71 Ackerman cannot seriously contend that this collective majority intended that *Brown* and *Griswold* follow from the New Deal. If conceded, Ackerman's dualism is left in the unenviable position of insisting that despite the ratifiers' intentions, justices must devise synthetic interpretations that add content to the last constitutional moment. Ackerman fails to describe how his theory overcomes these conceptual and epistemic problems. For example, do transformative appointments give us evidence of the intended break, or did the break occur when the appointments took place? If the former, how does Ackerman know this? If the latter, the argument is circular. The president is warranted, according to dualistic politics, in making such appointments only when he knows the people intend such a break. But the people intend such a break only when the appointments occur. Therefore, making the appointments cannot be the truth conditions of the intent. And, consequently, when making the transformative appointment, the president never has the evidence to do so. Even if

one concedes that political circumstances in 1937 could have been interpreted as breaking with the past, did the majority intend the break to be permanent? Did they intend the break to be canonical as authorizing an alternative method for amending the Constitution? I submit that Ackerman has no way to answer these questions. He merely assumes that the identification, content, significance, and legitimacy of a new constitutional moment is somehow self-evident.

72　It is not obvious that 1937 illustrates Ackerman's point here, although, arguably, the "switch in time" may be the result of pure individual prudence on the part of some justices, or an institutional concern for the viability of the Court. It need not be that the justices adhered to substantive (economic) due process until they recognized that "We the People" had constitutionally spoken in the revolution of 1937. Of course, Ackerman would say his account fits the facts, but it fits the facts only in broad strokes; it tells us nothing as to what motivational factors prompted the key actors. Moreover, if motivational factors are irrelevant, then in what sense can we say that the *people* gave new marching orders to their leaders?

73　B. Ackerman, 1 *We the People*, at 266–68. For a detailed elaboration of these processes, see id. at 266–94. Additionally, the support for a movement must have "depth, breadth and decisiveness." Id. at 272.

74　U.S. Constitution, art. 27.

75　One can accept this point and still agree that article 5 is at times laborious, ineffective, and slow. If so, we might decide to make the formal method for constitutional amendment more susceptible to reflective change. This is a far cry from embracing Ackerman's structural amendment.

76　B. Ackerman, 1 *We the People*, at 72.

77　Ibid.

78　Ibid. at 74.

79　B. Ackerman, 1 *We the People*, at 289.

80　Kent Greenawalt, "Dualism and Its Status," *Ackerman Symposium*, at 480, 491.

81　See Jennifer Nedelsky, "The Puzzle of Modern Constitutionalism," in *Ackerman Symposium*, at 500, 504.

82　See B. Ackerman, 1 *We the People*, at 291.

83　Ibid.

84　Ibid.

85　Bruce Ackerman, "Rooted Cosmopolitanism," in *Ackerman Symposium*, at 529. Ultimately, the people control the circulation of governing elites by frequent elections. Id. Ackerman still must articulate in great detail who constitutes "the people."

86　This does not suggest that the problem of legitimization was the same (or even existed) in medieval Europe.

87　Ackerman's is-ought deduction rests constitutional legitimacy on a few important, but atypical, periods in American constitutional history. Thus, even if his description of what actually occurs is accurate, it does not follow that constitutional actors *should* act this way. Indeed, normative conceptions of democracy might count against dualism.

88 *United States v. Carolene Products Co.,* 304 U.S. 144, 152, n. 4 (1938). B. Ackerman, 1 *We the People,* at 120.

89 This is due to the failure or incompleteness of the New Deal. Had the New Deal Court explicitly established the fundamental right to education, food, shelter, and health, or had the Court viewed wealth as a suspect class, normal politics would have been unable to reverse this constitutional revolution.

90 History certainly supports the claim that judicial appointments are designed to affect the philosophy of the Supreme Court. Ackerman is not, however, similarly enamored with the idea of transformative appointments serving as the principal means of constitutional politics. Given the role the New Deal plays in Ackerman's dualism, it is difficult to understand why. Ackerman would reply that transformative appointments represent a bad way to engage in constitutional change because they do not focus the issues in the appropriate way so as to generate the right degree of deliberation. Bruce Ackerman, "Transformative Appointments," 101 *Harv. L. Rev.* 1164 (1988). This is a contingent matter, and nothing in the nature of the appointment process precludes mobilized deliberation.

91 *Lochner v. New York,* 198 U.S. 45 (1905). Such a conception advocates a laissez-faire system of government.

92 See Bruce Ackerman, "Transformative Appointments," at 1172–74.

93 Ibid. at 1182. Ackerman himself proposes an amendment to article 5 that requires a total of three presidential elections, including a referendum on the second and third ballots requiring a supermajority for ratification.

94 The Bork confirmation period was a mixed bag concerning the depth of deliberation. Two consequences seem clear: First, the ordinary person believes, pace Bork, that a general right of privacy is constitutionally protected. And second, the Constitution's meaning is contestable.

95 B. Ackerman, 1 *We the People,* at 139.

96 Mark Tushnet indicates that "Ackerman has now suggested that transformations can be consensual, in which case the Court can straightforwardly endorse ongoing transformations." Mark Tushnet, "Living in a Constitutional Moment," 46 *Case West. Res. L. Rev.* 845, 851 (1996). If so, Ackerman's dualism becomes virtually indistinguishable from the theory of constitutional revolutions.

97 An even stronger counterexample can be framed. What if everyone agreed on the propriety of a particular constitutional change? Suppose tomorrow everyone awakes agreeing that the Fourteenth Amendment requires affirmative action, or prohibits abortion. Why should an Ackermanian Court prevent the

people from making the constitutional change through judicial interpretation? How do we know that this is an example of normal politics or one of
constitutional politics? The problem here is that the distinction between normal and constitutional politics does not explain the myriad ways the constitution is altered.

98   More generally, the Middle Republic stands for a reconception of the notion
of federalism.

99   *Plessy v. Ferguson*, 163 U.S. 537 (1896). *Brown v. Board of Education*, 347 U.S.
483 (1954).

100   *Plessy*'s conception of segregated equality is abstract and formal. The argument
runs something like this: How can segregation between X and Y stigmatize X
only, as both X and Y are treated exactly the same? Only one's self-image can be
responsible for the stigma, not the formal relation between X and Y. In effect,
this argument decontextualizes racism. Uttered today, this argument is implausible due to the systemic historical mistreatment of X (Africans), not because the New Deal changed government's role in creating social reality. Moreover, why couldn't a *Plessy*-sensitive Court in *Brown* grant that law may never
eradicate racism, yet it might still embrace social equality? The problem is that
Ackerman takes the Court's distinction in *Plessy* too seriously. A more cynical
explanation is warranted. For example, how could anyone insist that two
groups should associate with one another only if they voluntarily do so, while
at the same time upholding a law requiring them to remain segregated? Barring racial animus in *Plessy,* the distinction between political and social *racial*
equality is not affected by an activist government regarding economic equality.

101   In Justice Brown's words: "We consider the underlying fallacy of the plaintiff's
argument to consist in the assumption that the enforced separation of the two
races stamps the colored race with a badge of inferiority. If this be so, it is not by
reason of anything found in the act, but solely because the colored race chooses
to put that construction upon it." *Plessy v. Ferguson,* 163 U.S. 537 (1896).

102   *Plessy*'s argument rests not on a conception of the government's role, but
rather on a logical point. Segregation between the races burdens and benefits
both races equally; therefore, if one race claims that segregation stigmatizes, it
cannot logically be anyone's fault but their own. The Court is decontextualiz-
ing the actual historical circumstances of *Plessy* to create an argument that is no
more plausible in the Middle Republic than after the New Deal. Ackerman
fails to consider the obvious, that Brown's *logical* point flies in the face of
history and common knowledge concerning America's racial past.

103   B. Ackerman, 1 *We the People,* at 146.

104   If Ackerman's point is that judges need lawyerly skills of integrating the old
with the new, he is surely right. Intergenerational synthesis is possible in
nondualist conceptions of constitutional interpretation. Judges often refer

back to early constitutional periods to integrate a new constitutional under-standing with the old. However, this occurs fluidly without the conviction that an identifiable, canonical process exists through which we can pull it off, and which is the sine qua non of judicial interpretation.

105   B. Ackerman, 1 *We the People,* at 1175.

106   Ibid.

107   *Griswold v. Connecticut.* 381 U.S. 479 (1965).

108   For an important theory of constitutional translation, see L. Lessig, "Fidelity and Constraint," 65 *Fordham L. Rev.* 1365 (1997) (journal hereafter cited as *Fordham Symposium,* devoted to a symposium on fidelity in constitutional theory).

109   Suzanna Sherry indicates that "[Ackerman's] argument that we are absolutely bound by the popular intent underlying constitutional moments of the past suffers from all the problems that beset originalists generally." Sherry, at 923.

110   Ibid.

111   The internal perspective is required to identify what the new paradigm says and whether the people consented to it as a constitutional moment. But see Bruce Ackerman, "A Generation of Betrayal?" *Fordham Symposium* at 1519.

112   R. Dworkin, *Law's Empire.*

113   Ackerman should answer the problems of intent and purpose. Did the Fram-ers intend to amend the Constitution, and in doing so, was their purpose in part to create a legitimizing process outside of article 5?

114   See Terrance Sandalow, "Abstract Democracy: A Review of Ackerman's *We the People,*" 9 *Const. Comm.* 309, 324 (1992) (book review) ("[I]n attempting to codify [the meaning of constitutional moments], Ackerman falls into the same error as those who seek to fix the meaning of the written Constitution by the way it was understood at the time of its adoption"); Sherry, at 923 (char-acterizing Ackerman's theory as a type of originalist theory). But see San-dalow, at 315 ("Ackerman's thesis is certain to be rejected out of hand of originalists of every stripe").

115   R. Dworkin, "The Forum of Principle," 56 *N.Y.U. L. Rev.* 461 (1981); see also R. Dworkin, *Law's Empire,* at 47; see also Michael Perry, *The Constitution in the Courts: Law or Politics?* (1993).

116   Kent Greenawalt, "Dualism and Its Status," at 486.

117   B. Ackerman, 1 *We the People,* at 88.

118   Ackerman's view fails to acknowledge that most judicial decisions occur dur-ing normal politics, and these decisions must be, in part, forward looking. Often these decisions produce interpretations of the Constitution that are functionally equivalent to formal amendments. Moreover, the majoritarian branches of government, though primarily concerned with normal politics, also must be prepared to preserve higher lawmaking. Although the distinction

between normal and higher lawmaking might survive, there is no evidence that the judiciary is the only preservationist institution. The Congress and presidency should be equally concerned about preserving the fruits of the most recent constitutional moment. However, these branches, in Ackerman's world, must have multiple personalities. They must simultaneously be concerned about normal politics, preserving the last constitutional moment, as well as being prepared for the inchoate beginnings of higher lawmaking. This is equally true of the Court, perhaps more so. Moreover, regarding the Court, no criteria exists to enable them to identify the precise moment normal politics transform into constitutional politics. In Ackerman's universe questions concerning the Court's role abound: What is the Court's responsibility when a relevant constitutional issue arises in normal politics that was never addressed by the most recent constitutional moment? Should the Court abstain? Should it defer? What if the constitutional issue involved is neither constitutionally prescribed nor prohibited by the most recent regime, but was prescribed or prohibited by a prior regime? How does the synthesis work in these circumstances? Ackerman seeks to combine a democratically sensitive conception of originalism and majoritarianism, on the one hand, with progressive change, on the other. Thus Ackerman attempts to show the legitimacy of *Brown* and *Griswold* by appealing to the Founding, the Reconstruction, and the New Deal. Although Ackerman grounds these decisions in instances of higher lawmaking, he permits wide latitude in judicial interpretations reflecting changing social and cultural circumstances.

119 Sandalow, at 331.
120 Ibid.
121 Ibid.
122 Ackerman's theory needs to address other areas of constitutional law more comprehensively, such as the religion clause of the First Amendment. For example, how do we evaluate Justice Scalia's opinion in *Smith* according to Ackerman's theory of constitutional change? See *Employment Div. v. Smith*, 494 U.S. 872 (1990). Let me point out that most constitutional cases are due to normal adjudication, but we seldom teach many of these cases. Most important constitutional cases are revolutionary, prerevolutionary, or postrevolutionary. See chap. 3 for an explication of these terms.
123 William Fischer III, "The Defects of Dualism," 59 *U. Chi. L. Rev.* 955, 971 (1992) (reviewing Bruce Ackerman, *We the People* [1991]).
124 See Michael J. Klarman, "Constitutional Fact/Constitutional Fiction: A Critique of Bruce Ackerman's Theory of Constitutional Moments," 44 *Stan. L. Rev.* 759, 770 (1992) (reviewing Bruce Ackerman, *We the People* [1991]).
125 Ibid. at 771.
126 B. Ackerman, 1 *We the People*, at 159.

127   Ackerman and other liberals overlook the differences between *Griswold* and its progeny. Arguably, *Griswold* concerned the communitarian value of marriage and the family, whereas latter privacy cases were more concerned with individualist choice. Michael J. Sandel, *Democracy's Discontent* 96–97 (1996).

128   The formal component of a right is the kind of right it is—for example, whether it is an individual or collective right. Its substantive component describes the interests the right protects, for example, free speech or religious freedom. One might say that the substantive component can change preserving the importance of some (newly defined) individual right. If the Framers valorized individual rights in terms of property, the individual right component is the formal component, whereas the substantive component involves property. In principle we can jettison the property component and still seek individual rights that are no longer property rights but now become, for example, privacy rights. However, this process is suspect. The Framers were not concerned with protecting the formal concept of individual rights. Instead, they sought to protect the substance of certain kinds of individual rights. The substantive dimension of individual rights is not fungible in the way that Ackerman suggests. As a pragmatist, Ackerman would have a much easier time showing how new substantive rights serve the same purpose as their earlier relatives.

129   Bruce Ackerman, "Liberating Abstraction," 59 *U. Chi. L. Rev.* 317, 347 (1993). I would rephrase this point to emphasize the underlying core value of independence, which is a guarantor of civic equality and applies to both property and privacy.

130   See *United States v. Carolene Products Co.,* 304 U.S. 144, 152 n. 4 (1938).

131   See Jeremy Waldron, "Book Review," 90 *J. Phil.* 149, 153 (1993) (reviewing Bruce Ackerman, 1 *We the People* [1991]).

132   To say that somehow this script was intended or became an official, nonformal (canonical) method of amending the Constitution begs the important question of how we know this. Further, we must determine what legitimizes this informal change and whether the only legitimate nonformal process of amendment is structural amendment. Instead, one could argue that judicial as well as political changes in American constitutional culture occur throughout our history, given that our constitutional culture is essentially pragmatist and communitarian.

2   Dworkin's Constitutional Coherentism

1   As I understand it, pragmatism identifies the correct judicial decision with what is right on balance, including the virtue of stability or consistency with

the past. Consequently, constitutional pragmatism can appeal to politics, economics, or natural law as the basis for what is right, all things considered.

2   Contrary to traditional understanding, this interpretation of natural law, or naturalism, for short, is a pragmatist theory; it counsels judges to serve justice and bring about a better community by incorporating naturalist imperatives into the law. Other kinds of pragmatist theory, such as law and economics, reject naturalism as not having pragmatist benefits.

3   Ronald Dworkin, *Law's Empire* (1986).

4   Positivism, typically, permits judicial discretion. However, discretion should fill in only minor lapses in the law. The more a positivist theory permits a wide form of judicial discretion, the more it begins to look like the theory of constitutional revolutions.

5   Of course, this does not preclude a purely causal explanation of such legal phenomena. Dworkin, however, needs an interpretive account. Consider Dworkin's earlier remarks: "No theory can count as an adequate justification of institutional history unless it provides a good fit with that history; it must not expose more than a low threshold number of decisions, particularly recent decisions, as mistakes." Ronald Dworkin, *Taking Rights Seriously* 340 (1977).

6   Raz's positivism may allow overruling precedent whenever the judge believes with certainty that the new rule is superior to the old rule. J. Raz, "Dworkin: A New Link in the Chain," 74 *California L. Rev.* 1103, 1110, 1115–16 (1986). Raz's theory thus appears to be capable of explaining constitutional revolutions and legal change; the question remains *how* it does so. By making morality relevant to judicial discretion only, Raz's theory distorts the unifying rationale of pragmatism and revolutionary adjudication.

7   347 U.S. 483 (1954).

8   Previously, Dworkin distinguished between fidelity and principle and argued that principle was the superior virtue. Ronald Dworkin, *Life's Dominion* (1992). More recently it appears that Dworkin interprets fidelity to refer to principles that can change depending upon the best conception of the principle in a given constitutional period. In reality, fidelity isn't needed here; nor is it illuminating. Instead, interpretation should discover the appropriate principles, the principles that fit and justify constitutional practice best. Then attribute those principles to the Framers, if one wishes, but recognize that many Framers might repudiate these new principles as unfaithful to their actual intent.

9   Ronald Dworkin, *Freedom's Law* 7 (1996); R. Dworkin, "The Arduous Virtue of Fidelity: Originalism, Scalia, Tribe, and Nerve," *Fordham Symposium* at 1249.

10 Dworkin, *Freedom's Law,* at 7.

11 Constitutional concepts refer to those terms that determine constitutional meaning. For instance, "liberty," "due process," "equal protection," and so

forth. Consequently, a concept is constitutional if it is required to explain constitutional meaning, irrespective of whether it is contained in the text.

12   Dworkin begs the question in favor of abstraction by insisting that "[n]othing counts as someone's conviction unless he recognizes that what actually follows from it depends on what is in fact true, not on what he thinks is true." R. Dworkin, *Law's Empire,* at 331. This vastly oversimplifies the possibilities. Dworkin fails to realize that when a conviction has undesirable implications — because these implications depend on what is true, not what I think is true — a person is always entitled to give up the original conviction.

13   The process of redefining a concept is only one possible way to avoid its undesirable implications. There are at least two others. First, a person might always reject the untoward implications in cases when concepts and implications conflict. Or a person might always give up the concept in such circumstances. Second, the person might decide which to prefer on a case-by-case method, depending upon the comparative importance of the concept and its implications in a given case.

14   One could argue that someone must determine the basic structure of political society, and in our tradition that power resides in the Framers. However, this doesn't reveal the procedure for discovering their intentions, nor does it explain what counts as the Framers' intentions.

15   R. Dworkin, *Freedom's Law* at 293.

16   Ibid.

17   Ibid.

18   Despite the fact that a given individual may not hold the two intentions as potentially conflicting, they are in fact potentially conflicting. If the two judgments can be individuated, it is irrelevant that the agent holds them as one judgment. In the context of argument and justification, one would want to bring him to see that there are two judgments, or at least two conceptually distinct parts of a single judgment, involved. If two judgments exist for the interpreter, they exist for the agent.

19   I have in mind Rawls's conception of wide reflective equilibrium.

20   Dworkin searches for some distinction between a linguistic designation and a political one. Somehow the linguistic designation is tied more closely to what the concept actually is, whereas the political merely reflects a particular conception of the subject of the concept.

21   For a discussion of the concept of dedicatedness and the distinction between dedicated and deliberative reasoning, see Robert Justin Lipkin, "Can Liberalism Justify Multiculturalism?" and "The Possibility of Multicultural Constitutionalism: The Distinction between Deliberative and Dedicated Cultures."

22   There are of course (weaker) deliberative defenses of these methodologies.

23   As far as I can tell, no one has an adequate theory of who counts as a constitu-
     tional Founder and why. Some theorists distinguish between Madison and
     Jefferson by embracing the former as a Founder, but not the latter. Narrowly
     speaking, this is correct. Yet, more broadly, understanding Jefferson's thought
     is essential to understanding the tenor of the times, and, consequently, to the
     thought of the citizens ratifying the Constitution.

24   R. Dworkin, *Law's Empire*.

25   Ibid.

26   Ibid. at 117.

27   Ibid. at 159.

28   Ibid. at 225.

29   Ibid. Thus Dworkin rejects the dichotomy between finding or inventing law.
     Integrity holds that legal reasoning does "both and neither."

30   Legal pragmatism is used here as a general term for a variety of legal theories
     including both legal realism and natural law theory (naturalism). Legal prag-
     matism provides a theory of adjudication counseling judges to adopt the deci-
     sion best suited to the community's future. What is best can be construed
     ethically, economically, or sociologically. Ibid. at 160. Regarding ethics, legal
     pragmatism is not committed to any traditional conception of ethics. It is not,
     for example, conceptually committed to either consequentialist or deontologi-
     cal ethics.

31   A legal right is a right to win a lawsuit, and so, in Dworkin's view, pragmatism
     cannot countenance legal rights. Ibid. at 152. I think Dworkin is wrong in
     characterizing pragmatism as a skeptical doctrine concerning legal rights. Prag-
     matism can countenance *derivative* legal rights, and that should be sufficient to
     show that pragmatism fits constitutional practice without either embracing the
     "noble-lie" theory or requiring "epicycles to survive as an eligible interpretation
     of our own practice." Ibid. at 160. A pragmatist judge might endorse act-
     pragmatism or rule-pragmatism. Only an act-pragmatist judge must appeal to
     pragmatic factors in each and every case. The rule-pragmatist judge adopts
     rules that might have no direct or immediate pragmatic benefit in each case just
     so long as the *adoption* of the rule has pragmatic benefits. Consequently, a rule-
     pragmatist need not appeal directly to any pragmatic factors at all.

32   H. L. A. Hart, *The Concept of Law* 273 (1994). Hart, of course, acknowledges
     that judges apply law and make law. As such, his positivism seems to be an
     unexplained blend of what Dworkin calls "strict conventionalism" and what I
     call pragmatism.

33   The notion of the law running out refers to those situations in which explicit
     rules or conventions do not resolve the controversy at hand. (Or is it that
     it resolves the controversy unsatisfactorily according to one's perspective?)

H. L. A. Hart and others have rejected Dworkin's conception of conventionalism or positivism. In Hart's view there can be implicit conventions in the law. Hart, *The Concept of Law,* at 272.

34 According to Dworkin's conception of strict conventionalism, a conventionalist judge can use his (strong) discretion to make new law when old law runs out. The problem, of course, is that in *Brown* the (old) law did not run out. *Plessy* is the precedent a strict conventionalist judge should follow. Thus strict conventionalist judges could not use their discretion to embrace the principle in *Brown.* Theories of conventionalism permitting only weak discretion would also be unable to explain *Brown.* By contrast, pragmatism can explain the decision in *Brown* because pragmatism permits revolutionary adjudication.

35 Constitutional revolutions occur in the executive and legislative branches also. This chapter is concerned with revolutionary *adjudication.* The term "revolutionary adjudication" is more germane than "transformative adjudication" because the type of adjudication I have in mind has altered American constitutional practice in unpredictable, even startling, ways. Revolutionary adjudication concerning both form and content has *created* constitutional law and practice; it has not merely expressed what is latent in the law.

36 I owe this and the following sense of containment to Ken Kress.

37 An interpretation of a legal practice, according to Dworkin, involves three stages. The first, or preinterpretive, stage involves a tacit agreement on the paradigms of legal practice, for example, statutes and judicial decisions. The second stage provides an interpretation of the practice that characterizes its point or meaning. Finally, the postinterpretive stage includes a theory of mistakes that helps us refine and reform our view about law according to the interpretation presented in the second stage. This process is similar to Rawls's method of "wide reflective equilibrium," a process by which we explain and justify our scheme of pretheoretical moral intuitions by devising a theory of the scheme's rationale that helps us sort out which intuitions we wish to retain. John Rawls, *A Theory of Justice* (1971). But see Brian Bix, *Law, Language, and Legal Determinacy* 61 (1993) (contending that Rawls's approach "is not suited for interpretation of practices"). For an application of wide reflective equilibrium to legal theory, see Robert Justin Lipkin, "Beyond Skepticism"; Robert Justin Lipkin, "Kibitzers, Fuzzies, and Apes without Tails: The Art of Conversation in Legal Theory," 66 *Tulane L. Rev.* 69 (1991); and Robert Justin Lipkin, "Indeterminacy," at 638–42. Wide reflective equilibrium is an interpretive theory in Dworkin's sense of "interpretive," and the methodology in law as integrity, in my estimation, is a version of wide reflective equilibrium. See R. Dworkin, *Law's Empire,* at 255–75. See Lipkin, "Kibitzers, Fuzzies, and Apes without Tails."

38 Constitutional law is a practice that has a point, perhaps—more accurately,

several points. A judge, as a socialized participant in this practice, will develop
opinions of what the point is. She will develop a sense of what counts as
continuing a practice and what counts as revising or abandoning it.

39   Although it is ultimately necessary, I have not supplied a theory of the individuation of principles demonstrating how to differentiate one principle from
another. Instead, I have relied on reasonable consensus. One might accuse this
criterion, in one sense, of begging the question against Dworkin's conception
of interpretation, which attempts to show how meaning may be far from
obvious yet still be contained in the Constitution. I do not believe that there
exists a knock-down argument against this controversial view generally. However, I know of no successful argument purporting to establish such a method,
and certainly Dworkin's argument fails to do so without being recast as a
pragmatist theory. For the sake of argument, even if some cases can be explained by such a method, constitutional revolutions such as *Brown* cannot.
Finally, in no way does this view entail textualism.

40   See also *Railroad Company v. Brown*, 84 U.S. (17 Wall.) 445 (1873) (a statutory
case not involving the Fourteenth Amendment holding that railway cars must
be desegregated).

41   The rule in *Plessy v. Ferguson* was the final understanding of the equal protection
clause. *Corbin et al. v. County School Board*, 84 F.Supp. 253 (1949) (affirming the
separate but equal doctrine in public schools, transportation, and the enforcement of attendance laws); *Briggs v. Elliott*, 98 F.Supp. 529 (1951) (affirming
separate but equal in education); *Carr v. Corning, Browne Junior H.S. Parent-
Teacher Ass'n v. Magdeburger*, 182 F. 2d 14 (1950) (upholding separate but equal
in education); *Boor v. Garrett*, 183 F. 2d (1950) (affirming separate but equal
despite the fact that *Plessy* had been weakened); *Boyer v. Carret*, 88 F.Supp. 353
(1949) (holding that the board of recreation could segregate athletic activities); *Gong Lum v. Rice*, 275 U.S. 78 (1927) (upholding segregation of Chinese
students); *Berea College v. Kentucky*, 211 U.S. 45 (1908) (upholding a fine
levied on a private college for integrating classes); *McCabe v. Atchison, T. & S.F.
Railway Co.*, 235 U.S. 151 (1914) (upholding segregation on trains).

In *Commonwealth ex rel v. Carolina Coach Co.*, 192 Va. 745 (1951), a black
man argues an exception to a Virginia statute mandating segregation on buses.
Essentially, his argument is that when there is one seat left contiguous to a seat
occupied by a member of one race, someone from an opposite race should be
allowed seating there. So well settled was the *Plessy* doctrine that both the court
and petitioner would not consider challenging it.

42   Perhaps justice, understood abstractly, abhors the rule in *Plessy*. Understood
constitutionally, *Plessy* determines in part what equality means. To overrule
Plessy, one must appeal to abstract justice or some other conception of justice

found neither in constitutional law nor in the constitutional theory reflecting that law. So, in overruling a case, a justice can ignore fit and appeal directly, as a pragmatist would, to an extrinsic conception of the relevant concept.

43 Determining the appropriate role and force of the sources of constitutional law—for example, precedent—is itself an interpretive question and does not precede and constrain interpretation. Frederick Schauer, "The Occasions of Constitutional Interpretation," 72 *B. U. L. Rev.* 729, 746 (1992). It is unclear, however, what the notion of taking constitutional practice seriously means without supposing that foundational constitutional decisions play a role of central importance in constitutional interpretation.

44 Dworkin may say at this point that fifty-eight years of *Plessy* showed the "separate but equal" doctrine to be an abomination. But then he is permitting nonlegal influences, social and moral concerns, to enter into a judge's "interpretation." There is no reason why Dworkin should not do this. But it should be clear that if he does, law as integrity is a pragmatist theory incorporating cultural changes into the law. These cultural changes are contestable, and therefore, when the Court incorporates them, it does so through revolutionary adjudication. Is Dworkin's point that constitutional provisions may be overruled when they conflict with abstract moral or political theory? Isn't this pragmatism plain and simple?

45 Robert Westmoreland, "Dworkin and Legal Pragmatism," 11 *Oxford J. Leg. Stud.* 174, 183, 188 (1991) ("Law as integrity edges toward pragmatism when it dismisses the particular restraints on judicial power. . . . [T]he citizens of the community of integrity have reason to lose interest in the arcane intentional distinctions between [integrity and pragmatism], and to conclude that where fundamental rights are concerned they are ruled by pragmatist judges").

46 Dworkin insists that the Constitution mandates an individual right not to be the victim of state-imposed invidious racial discrimination. If *Plessy* controls, however, "separate but equal," racial discrimination is not invidious. Dworkin walks right over the question, How does law as integrity permit a justice to overrule a prior foundational decision?

47 One problem with Dworkin's approach is in identifying the object of interpretation. Just what is an interpretation an interpretation *of*? The precise nature of law as integrity, as a distinct theory of law, depends on his answer to this question. If the data include only the Constitution and case law, Dworkin's theory will be one kind of theory. If they include additionally other political decisions, it might be a different theory. If they include also significant cultural meaning, it will be a very different theory.

48 Frederick Schauer describes Dworkin's theory of interpretation as an interpretation of "the text of the Constitution, reported cases of the Supreme Court,

and other political acts not necessarily emanating from the courts, as raw data from which the interpreter constructs interpretations of the Constitution." Frederick Schauer, "The Occasions of Constitutional Interpretation," at 736.

49   R. Dworkin, *Law's Empire,* at 230.

50   Ibid. at 230–31.

51   Ibid. at 231.

52   Dworkin takes it as uncontroversial that a correct interpretation of a legal practice will show that practice in its best light. Moreover, judges should consciously seek such interpretations. However, a conventionalist, having coherentist sympathies, might argue that a judge should not *try to show* the legal practice in its best light. Rather, she should merely provide the best explanation of the practice and how it applies to the present case, ignoring justification entirely. If she follows this proposal, so the argument goes, the legal practice will appear in its best light without her self-consciously trying to portray it in that way.

53   R. Dworkin, *Law's Empire,* at 231.

54   Consider:

> So the distinction between the two dimensions is less crucial or profound than it might seem. It is a useful analytical device that helps us give structure to any interpreter's working theory or style. He will form a sense of when an interpretation fits so poorly that it is unnecessary to consider its substantive appeal, because he knows that this cannot outweigh its embarrassments of fit in deciding whether it makes [the law] better, everything taken into account, than its rivals. But he need not reduce his intuitive sense to any precise formula; *he would rarely need to decide whether some interpretation barely survives or barely fails, because a bare survivor, no matter how ambitious or interesting it claimed the text to be, would almost certainly fail in the overall comparison with other interpretations whose fit was evident.* (Ibid.; emphasis added)

This passage suggests that the distinction between fit and justification is always a *comparative* one. If so, it simply does not follow that "a bare survivor . . . would almost certainly fail in the overall comparison with other interpretations whose fit was evident." Ibid. This conclusion follows only if we deny that sometimes a justification is so normatively compelling that it overcomes a poor fit. Not only is there no reason to deny this in a comparative approach to fit and justification, but Dworkin, in fact, appeals to such a comparative approach in his treatment of *Brown.*

55   Some commentators point out that the stronger one's conception of a theory of mistakes, the greater the role of justification in interpreting a legal practice. Consider: "[T]he greater the power of the theory of mistakes the more morality becomes the primary consideration in the best justifying theory, relating

institutional fit to the status of a marginal constraint. But, the more frugal one's theory of mistakes the less easy it is to write off great chunks of institutional history and the less easy it is to give compelling moral considerations . . . their head." D. Beyleveld and R. Brownsword, *Law as Moral Judgment* 412 (1986).

56   Ultimately, however, the right answer thesis might be inadequate. See Robert Justin Lipkin, "Beyond Skepticism," at 843; see also, John Fellas, "Reconstructing Law's Empire," 73 *Boston U. L. Rev.* 715, 739 (1993).

57   It is important to recognize that integrity is not alone in emphasizing the importance of constitutional background theories. Conventionalism and pragmatism also refer to such theories. Conventionalism includes a weak theory of mistakes requiring a normative principle to explain most cases, or at least certain critical cases in a particular area. Pragmatism's background theory contains a theory of mistakes requiring conformity with past cases in normal adjudication. However, pragmatism's strong theory of mistakes permits a minimal fit with practice when the normative interpretation is sufficiently compelling.

58   In some circumstances strong judicial discretion permits judges to make law. Weak judicial discretion permits judges only to use their discretion to formulate principles implicit in the law. Thus, weak judicial discretion involves determining the best way to continue past legal practice. See R. Dworkin, *Taking Rights Seriously.*

59   The lexical conception of fit and justification should involve a severe constraint on interpretation, not just because fit has a descriptive dimension, but more important, because a judge has every reason to believe that she has made a mistake when her interpretation differs wildly from her brethren's. Thus, under the lexical conception, agreement with other practical reasoners or judges is required for justification to get off the ground. Dworkin denies the role of other members of the constitutional interpretive community. Instead, "Dworkin's conception of interpretive protestantism implies that judges characteristically are not and should not be concerned with the rival interpretations that others will predictably develop." Richard H. Fallon Jr., "Dworkin and the Two Faces of Law," 67 *Notre Dame L. Rev.* 553, 560 (1992). See R. Dworkin, *Law's Empire,* at 64 ("Each of the participants in a social practice must distinguish between trying to decide what other members of his community think the practice requires and trying to decide, for himself, what it really requires"). If other judicial decisions are part of constitutional practice, then deciding what other judges think constitutional practice is amounts to interpreting the practice itself, and certainly must count as evidence of what the practice is.

60   Dworkin, *Law's Empire,* at 221. In another place Dworkin refers to "the scheme of principles necessary to justify [rights and duties]." Ibid. at 227. In discussing the kind of community associated with integrity, Dworkin writes: "The integrity of a community's conception of justice demands that the moral principles

necessary to justify the substance of its legislature's decision be recognized in the rest of the law." Ibid. at 166. Finally, in referring to the structure of the post–Civil War amendments, Dworkin admonishes us to "ask what principles of equality are necessary to justify that structure." Ibid. at 363. This pragmatic process of positing principles necessary to justify a practice is the beginning of a holistic conception of constitutional change. In positing a scheme of justificatory principles, this process permits a pragmatist resolution. If the justificatory principles are attractive enough, the absence of fit does not preclude embracing them.

61 Dworkin can reply that integrity is just one virtue among many legal virtues such as justice, fairness, and procedural due process. Integrity applies when justice doesn't trump it. Constitutional revolutions are, then, cases wherein justice is the superior virtue. Moreover, Dworkin might say that a constitutional revolution is the straw that breaks the camel's back in a series of incremental changes recalling Neurath's image of sailors forced to rebuild a ship at sea plank by plank. For the first reply to work, justice must arbitrate between two or more principles that satisfy integrity. In the case of overruling a foundational decision, the new principle does not satisfy integrity. The second reply fails because if the constitutional revolution consists of a series of incremental decisions, then either the first member of the series is the revolution, or the series itself is revolutionary.

62 See B. Ackerman, 1 *We the People*.

63 If constitutional revolutions cannot be explained in this manner, Dworkin would reject them as an illegitimate exercise of judicial power.

64 It should be noted that constitutional "interpretation is never *just* exposition of an 'existing' principle; it is also a positing of the very principle it reads into the case through the enunciation of the 'should be' inherent in the justification of principles." Drucilla Cornell, "Institutionalization of Meaning, Recollective Imagination, and the Potential for Transformative Legal Interpretation," 136 *U. Pa. L. Rev.* 1135, 1144 (1988).

   As such Dworkin reads what he considers to be the best principle of racial equality "back into" the law. This process is perfectly legitimate; but I do not believe that it is available to law as integrity. A coherentist judge must follow the principles in actual practice, and such principles must be closely tied to the explicit case law if fit is to be a serious constraint on adjudication.

65 R. Dworkin, *Law's Empire*, at 29.

66 From the ratification of the Fourteenth Amendment (at least) the American Constitution contained an equal protection element. Thus, African Americans had a right to be free from state-imposed inequality at least in certain circumstances. In my view this equal protection element did not entail a right against

segregation until *Brown* and the civil rights revolution. Robert Justin Lipkin, "The Anatomy of Constitutional Revolutions," at 755–77.

67   R. Dworkin, *Law's Empire,* at 30.

68   Ibid. This sentiment reveals a commitment to the *rhetoric* of American constitutional law, not its substance. The genius of American constitutionalism is its ability to translate needed moral and political values from the wider culture to constitutional practice in order to resolve constitutional and political crises. See Robert Justin Lipkin, "Can American Constitutional Law Be Postmodern?"

69   As mentioned earlier, an intuitively plausible conception of what is "in the law" can be explicated in terms of a community of reasonable judges. In such a community significant consensus will exist over a host of routine, and even moderately difficult, questions. This conception permits using the location "in the law," despite not possessing a theory that systematically explicates the force of this locution.

70   Dworkin's characterization also begs the question against a form of constitutional pragmatism that is as old as the Marshall Court. See supra chapter 4.

71   Ludwig Wittgenstein, *Philosophical Investigations* (1950).

72   By contrast, "conscientious judges do acknowledge that they are making new law, breaking new ground . . . by choice, a new commitment, not mere discovery and application." John Finnis, "On Reason and Authority in Law's Empire," 6 *Law & Phil.* 357, 376 (1987). For an interesting discussion of the relevance of judicial testimony on the nature of judicial reasoning, especially on judicial discretion, see W. J. Waluchow, *Inclusive Legal Positivism* 213–19 (1994).

73   Although I believe there is a complex explanation of this phenomenon, I reject the "noble lie" theory exhorting judges to use conventionalist rhetoric while acting as pragmatists. Candor is far better; therefore, judges, lawyers, academics, and others should clearly identify the revolutionary changes in American constitutional law, not conceal them with rhetorical flourishes. More important, constitutional discourse should acknowledge self-consciously the importance of revolutionary adjudication in explaining and justifying constitutional law.

74   It is hornbook law that *Brown* does not technically overrule *Plessy.* J. Nowak, R. Rotunda, and A. Young, *Constitutional Law* 574 (1986).

75   Dworkin overlooks the legally abrupt or discontinuous changes in American constitutional law that enable it to reflect changes in moral and political reality.

76   In fact, constitutional pragmatism can take practice seriously except when a compelling justification disallows doing so.

77   Although the term "preinterpretive" is misleading, I would argue that the

equal protection clause and the *Plessy* Court's interpretation of that clause are partly preinterpretive paradigms of equality in American constitutional practice. Thus, any theory explaining and justifying American law must explain and justify that paradigm if it is to take actual legal practice seriously.

78   Alexander Bickel, "The Original Understanding and the Segregation Decisions" 69 *Harv. L. Rev.* 1 (1955). But see Michael W. McConnell, "Originalism and the Desegregation Decisions," 81 *Virginia L. Rev.* 947 (1995). Conceptually and historically, the equal protection clause was designed and best suited for expressing the kind of formal equality denied by the Black Codes. In this context the privileges or immunities clause was designed and best suited for expressing substantive equality. However, in the *Slaughterhouse Cases*, 83 U.S. 36 (1872), the Court nullified the privileges or immunities clause as a vehicle for expressing substantive equality. In my estimation this presents a major obstacle to originalists who want to argue that the equal protection clause precluded segregation. As originally understood, it was the privileges or immunities clause that was principally designed to defeat what later became known as Jim Crow segregation. The equal protection clause, if not an afterthought, was clearly secondary. For an important discussion of the privileges or immunities clause, see Michael Perry, *The Constitution in the Courts,* at 116–60, and David A. J. Richards, *Conscience and the Constitution,* at 199–232.

79   In an earlier article Dworkin seems to share this view when he writes that "[b]ecause of the practice of precedent, the court's view, even if wrong, becomes part of the sources which I must take into account in making fresh judgments of law in the future." R. Dworkin, "Philosophy and the Critique of Law," in *The Rule of Law* 147, 161 (R. Wolff ed. 1971).

To say, as Justice Kennedy said during his confirmation hearing, that "*Plessy* was wrong on the day it was decided" can be understood in two ways. First, it might mean that the equal protection clause contains some determinate, relatively obvious, paradigm precluding racial segregation in schools. If such a paradigm exists, it must be revealed. Second, it could mean that an antisegregation paradigm provides the best normative account of the equal protection clause. If so, either historical factors—such as the text or original intent—constrain this account, or not. If they constrain, what historical factors show that the equal protection clause contains an antisegregation paradigm? If historical factors do not constrain this account, then only normative factors are required. In this case justification, not fit, is all we need.

80   Equally mysterious are the complexities associated with the dimension of fit. Suppose, for example, the only foundational Court decision concerning a constitutional provision interprets it incorrectly, rejecting the provision's obvious purpose. But suppose this erroneous interpretation (erroneous textually or historically) provides the best normative interpretation of the provision. Thus,

practice and normative desirability favor the accepted interpretation despite its inadequate fit with the constitutional document itself. What does fit require in this context? Should we follow history and moral desirability or the Constitution as originally written and understood? How do we decide between these different paradigms?

81   R. Dworkin, *Law's Empire*, at 382. But the Constitution mandates an individual right not to be the victim of state-imposed *invidious* racial discrimination. If *Plessy* controls, "separate but equal" racial discrimination is not invidious.

82   It is not sufficient for Dworkin to say that social facts have changed from 1896 to 1954, other cases undermined the principles in *Plessy*, justices no longer believe that the principle behind *Plessy* is part of the best interpretation of law as a whole, or that justice trumps integrity. If other cases eroded *Plessy*, they are the revolutionary decisions. As for the other factors, none establish how a foundational decision can be overruled if fit is a necessary constraint on interpretation.

83   Even *Brown* is reluctant to declare itself, self-consciously, a revolution.

84   See section "Deciding *Brown*" in R. Dworkin, *Law's Empire*, at 387–89.

85   It should be noted that the *Plessy* Court was not the first Court to deploy the "separate but equal" doctrine. Forty-six years earlier a Massachusetts court validated a statute authorizing separate school systems for blacks and whites. *Roberts v. City of Boston, 59 Mass.* (5 Cush.) 198 (1850). Thus, racial apartheid permitted segregated schools prior to the ratification of the Fourteenth Amendment. It could be argued that unless the Fourteenth Amendment specifically rejected this feature of constitutional practice, it continued to be constitutionally permissible even after the amendment's ratification. In my estimation, denying this amounts to a complete rejection of constitutional history and practice.

86   Dworkin might argue that the Constitution contains a robust conception of equality derived from such provisions as the First Amendment or the structure of the document itself. *Brown* then fits *this* conception of equality. Two remarks are in order: First, what judicial decisions characterize the First Amendment or the structure of the Constitution in this manner? This equality claim as a partially descriptive claim about the constitutional document is tendentious. These other sources of constitutional law do not obviously contain a principle of racial equality. Second, how can this "implicit" conception of equality override the equality of the Fourteenth Amendment (and its history and interpretation by the courts) and satisfy the dimension of fit? Surely, the equal protection clause must be given primacy over other conceptions of equality in the Constitution, even if we grant for argument's sake that such other conceptions exist.

It should be emphasized again that Dworkin never states clearly what an interpretation is an interpretation *of*. What data must a proposed principle fit?

What justifies Dworkin's contention that "the Constitution mandates some individual right not to be the victim of official, state-imposed racial discrimination"? R. Dworkin, *Law's Empire,* at 382. What actual constitutional cases, statutes, or principles does this alleged right fit? If fit is understood independently of justification, and fit is a requirement of constitutional law, the principle in *Brown* should be summarily dismissed because it fails so thoroughly to fit existing judicial practice regarding equal protection. If, on the other hand, *Brown* must be embraced by any adequate theory of adjudication, then fit can in such cases be ignored. In these cases the normative attractiveness of the principle of equality in *Brown* overcomes the absence of fit entirely. This move rendering fit inconsequential shows how the analytic device of fit and justification can be reconceived as a pragmatic conception.

87   In 1954 shepardizing *Plessy* would show that the *Plessy* principle of equality explains the actual cases, and the principle in *Brown* fails to explain these .cases. What, then, can the principle in *Brown* explain better than *Plessy*? The normative conception of constitutional equality? If so, this result is entirely circular. The admittedly better normative principle of equality in *Brown* explains constitutional practice when that practice is understood normatively as the principle in *Brown*. What this admittedly better normative principle does not explain is the actual case law, and explaining the case law should be part of what it means to take constitutional practice seriously. In order to desegregate American society, "a vast number of statutes and regulations, incorporating centrally or marginally the rule of segregation, would require change." Alexander Bickel, *The Least Dangerous Branch,* at 248. How can a judge change current foundational law — or, in Dworkin's terms, "what has been thought to be law" — without ignoring fit and endorsing the justificatory dimension as sufficient methodology to do the job?

88   Dworkin does discuss three theories of racial equality: suspect classifications, banned categories, and banned sources. Only suspect classifications can be used to generate the principle in *Plessy.* In other words, only suspect classifications fit American practice concerning racial equality. Dworkin fails to explain how given the fit requirement Hercules can even begin to consider rejecting this theory of suspect classifications.

89   R. Dworkin, *Law's Empire,* at 387.

90   But see Gerald Rosenberg, *The Hollow Hope.* (1991).

91   381 U.S. 479 (1965).

92   405 U.S. 238 (1972). I purposely avoid inquiring whether principle 2 can explain this line of cases, given that some judicial opinions (Harlan's opinion in *Poe v. Ullman*) specifically exclude homosexual intimacy from the right to privacy.

93   I do not wish to suggest that Dworkin's treatment of *Hardwick* is flawless. In

chap. 4 I discuss the problem with Tribe and Dworkin's condemnation of *Hardwick.*

94 Precursors to revolutionary adjudication, however, do exist. For example, *Korematsu v. United States,* 323 U.S. 214 (1944) was such a precursor to the revolutionary adjudication in *Brown.* Interestingly, Thurgood Marshall's brief in *Brown* raised the *Korematsu* strict scrutiny analysis, but the opinion in *Brown* contains no such analysis. Marshall tried to raise the *Korematsu* analysis in oral argument but, curiously, Chief Justice Warren redirected him to discuss the issue of judicial power. Bernard Schwartz, *Super Chief Earl Warren and His Supreme Court* 83 (1983). *Korematsu* cannot help Dworkin, however, because Dworkin rejects the theory of racial equality (suspect classifications) in *Korematsu* for the normatively more compelling theory of banned sources, the theory Dworkin contends justifies *Brown.*

95 The argument that the Constitution's structure entails an antisegregation principle, or that such a principle follows "from the totality of the constitutional scheme under which we live" (*Poe v. Ullman,* 367 U.S. 497 [1961]) promises a unique and powerful constitutional methodology, but its promise has never been fulfilled. Given the Constitution's toleration of slavery, the Black Codes, Jim Crow, and so forth, how can an antisegregation principle be derived from history? One might reply that this same history contains certain pearls of constitutional rectitude, unfortunately lying with the dregs of racism, causing the failure of government, and these pearls are awaiting the right person to pluck them from the ocean floor and reveal the pristine normative structure of American constitutional practice. If this methodology is supposed to constrain judges, it must be spelled out in much greater detail. If not, it is indistinguishable from pragmatism.

96 At a conference on "Dworkin and his critics," at Millersville University, Dworkin mentioned that *Brown* fit constitutional practice because it fit the civil rights cases that were immediate precursors to *Brown. McLaurin v. Oklahoma State Regents,* 339 U.S. 637 (1950); *Sweatt v. Painter,* 339 U.S. 629 (1950); *Sipuel v. Board of Regents,* 332 U.S. 631 (1948); *Missouri ex rel. Gaines v. Canada,* 305 U.S. 337 (1938); *Gong Lum v. Rice,* 275 U.S. 78 (1927); *Cumming v. Board of Education,* 175 U.S. 528 (1899). The problem with this reply is twofold: First, the Court in *Brown* describes none of these cases as calling for a reconsideration of *Plessy.* Instead, these precursors, like most precursors to revolution, are restricted cases — Kuhnian anomalies — and stop short of revolutionizing and redefining the paradigm in that area of the law. Consequently, *Brown* cannot follow as a matter of normal adjudication from such cases without introducing different paradigmatic elements. Second, the simple answer is that if *Brown* follows from one or more of these precursors, then the precursor is the constitutional revolution, and Dworkin's jurisprudential point fails.

97   Perhaps Dworkin could argue that *Strauder v. West Virginia,* 100 U.S. (10 Otto) 303 (1879) reveals the true purpose of the equal protection clause, and that purpose is incompatible with *Plessy.* However, *Strauder* is inapposite for two reasons. First, if it is read narrowly, its interpretation of the Fourteenth Amendment's equal protection clause at most refers to the amendment's purpose in invalidating the Black Codes. Thus interpreted, the amendment's purpose was designed to preclude racial discrimination concerning the formal processes associated with courts, contracts, and owning property. Understood more broadly, as including a more general racial antisegregation principle, *Strauder* was simply not followed by the courts. It was superseded in practice by *Plessy.* Thus, understood broadly, *Strauder* played only an insignificant role in American constitutional practice concerning racial equality. Interpreted broadly, *Shelly v. Kramer,* 334 U.S. 1 (1949) was a precursor to the *Brown* revolution. Nevertheless, because *Shelly* involved just the sort of activities that the Fourteenth Amendment was intended to prevent, *Brown* and the per curiam cases represent a revolution of much greater magnitude than anything in *Shelly.*

98   See R. Dworkin, "Philosophy and the Critique of Law." Integrity, according to Dworkin, is thus "more demanding and more radical in circumstances like those of *Brown,* when the plaintiff succeeds in showing that an important part of what has been thought to be law is inconsistent with more fundamental principles necessary to justify law as a whole." However, even if more fundamental principles can be formulated to justify law as a whole, it simply does not follow that these same principles *explain* law as a whole also.

99   Should Dworkin alter his position by saying that the decision in *Brown* follows from principles posited to *justify* constitutional practice? Then integrity can account for *Brown,* but only by embracing pragmatism.

100   This is not to say that the principle in *Plessy* is a legal principle, not a moral one. On the contrary, the principle in *Plessy* is both a legal *and* a moral principle and is contained in a background theory of the law. Of course, this analysis does not preclude insisting that the *Plessy* principle is morally wrong.

101   This does not mean that controlling law cannot be overruled. Rather, it means that theories of adjudication taking constitutional practice seriously must be more circumspect in explaining the possibility of overruling such decisions. Such theories must identify other foundational paradigms, such as an alternative constitutional provision or constitutional decision that warrants overruling the controlling decision. Absent these alternative paradigms, a controlling decision can be overruled only by constructively satisfying the fit requirement, which is to say, by embracing pragmatism.

102   For this distinction between surface and deep structure to be convincing, we must first explain how we individuate these different levels, and what is the relationship between them.

103 One dramatic way to do this is to show that equality — even "separate but equal" equality — requires a more fundamental principle in the law's deep structure, that is, a principle of racial equality precluding segregation. If the more fundamental principle is required to warrant "separate but equal," it is not obvious how it can then preclude it.

104 Why not say that *Brown* fits *Sweatt v. Painter,* 339 U.S. 629 (1950)? Indeed, *Sweatt* is, in my estimation, a precursor to the revolutionary adjudication in *Brown.* However, the decision in *Brown* is in no way a logical (as opposed to a pragmatic) extension of *Sweatt. Brown* in conjunction with the per curiam cases constitutes a much broader antisegregation principle than conceivably contained in *Sweatt.*

105 J. Wilkinson III, *From Brown to Bakke* 25 (1979).

106 The practical implications would be either desegregation due to unequal facilities, or continued segregated facilities that were equal in all important ways.

107 My intention is not to disparage revolutions in practical results or remedies. Changes in legal remedies often save a person's life, or free her from jail, or enable her to be treated as an equal citizen.

108 This does not mean that no social or political revolution would occur, or that these revolutions would have no benefits for blacks.

109 Thus, a Dworkinian argument for *Sweatt* based on *Plessy* might be successful.

110 R. J. Lipkin, "The Anatomy of Constitutional Revolutions," at 746. There are two issues here. First, what is the role of foundational constitutional decisions in determining actual practice? Second, how does actual practice constrain the choice of justificatory principles? If foundational constitutional decisions determine constitutional practice, then *Plessy,* during its reign, determined the meaning of the equal protection clause. Second, if justificatory principles must be consistent with actual practice, no justificatory principle can deny *Plessy* and still claim to fit constitutional practice.

111 Perhaps the Constitution cannot be coherently read as a single document, but rather must be understood in Ackerman-like terms as referring to more than one constitutional paradigm. In this way different parts, or different constitutional texts, support claims of fidelity, and Dworkin's nonpragmatist conception works in *Brown.* But no matter — if law as integrity can pick and choose among different constitutional texts, any decision is bound to fit some part of constitutional practice. Moreover, these different texts presumably contain foundational decisions; thus the question of how to overrule a foundational provision is replicated in the notion of different constitutional texts containing different paradigms. Last, and most importantly, if different constitutional texts contain conflicting paradigms, it is difficult to see how consensus is possible.

112 E. Corwin, *Court over Constitution* 86 (1938).

113   Ibid. at 87.

114   Dworkin, "Is Law a System of Rules?" 35 *U. Chi. L. Rev.* 14, 26 (1967).

115   But see R. Tur, "Positivism, Principles, and Rules" (arguing against Dworkin's distinction between principles and rules), in *Perspectives in Jurisprudence* 42 (Elspeth Attwool ed. 1977).

116   See generally, W. Ross, *The Right and the Good* (1930).

117   Professor Laurence Tribe writes: "It was not the concept embodied in the equal protection clause that changed between 1896 and 1954, but only our relevant perceptions and understandings." Laurence H. Tribe, *American Constitutional Law* 1478 (1986). In Tribe's view *Brown* was always the correct interpretation of the equal protection clause. Cf. Charles Black, *Law as an Art* 6 (1978) ("If the *Brown* decision was right, then it was right all along"). If we accept such a view, constitutional meanings are independent of judicial practice.

118   In this view there are unstated *principles* in our system of law that may have force in a given situation. Ronald Dworkin, "Is Law a System of Rules?" at 26.

119   Remember that "authoritative interpretations of the text . . . create a new meaning for it, and the original meaning . . . ceases to be the current meaning." Stephen R. Munzer and James Nickles, "Does the Constitution Mean What It Always Meant?" 77 *Colum. L. Rev.* 1029 (1977). Arguably, a foundational constitution decision should govern all explicit constitutional norms as well as implicit and extraconstitutional norms. See Thomas Grey, "Origins of the Unwritten Constitution: Fundamental Law in American Revolutionary Thought," 30 *Stan. L. Rev.* 843 (1978) (arguing "that an enacted constitutional norm takes hierarchical precedence over an unenacted norm where the two conflict").

120   Here Dworkin appears to be committed to a natural law conception. At one time Dworkin doesn't appear to view this as an objection to his theory. Ronald Dworkin, "'Natural' Law Revisited," 34 *U. Fla. L. Rev.* 165 (1982). In this article Dworkin embraces a looser conception of "fit." A strong justificatory principle can compensate for a weak fit. Such a relaxation of the fit requirement does help Dworkin explain *Brown*. But, in that case, the fit requirement has a value of zero, something Dworkin's theory in *Law's Empire* does not seem to allow.

121   R. Dworkin, *Law's Empire*, at 221.

122   Ibid. at 166.

123   Whether this is really the position of our constitutional culture is open to serious challenge.

124   R. Dworkin, *Law's Empire*, at 378.

125   Ibid. It is not clear what actual legal tradition, other than Benthamite act-utilitarianism and the law and economics school, Dworkin has in mind. In-

deed, it is not obvious that Dworkin recognizes the possibility of a nonconsequentialist pragmatism.

126 Alternatively, one could say that in revolutionary adjudication the object of fit changes from constitutional decisions interpreting the Constitution to the evolving, reflective convictions of the society. However, it is not clear that *Brown* fits even these.

127 Keep in mind that in my view this newly declared principle is now law. It was not law when we started our inquiry. Even if a new rule is in some sense implicit in the constitutional practice, there has still been a change in the law. Neil MacCormick, *Legal Reasoning and Legal Theory* 188 (1978) (arguing that "the law is changed the moment after a great 'leading case' is decided from what it was the moment before").

128 In effect, taking the future seriously requires more than extending a principle implicit in past legal practice. It requires the recognition that present legal practice is fast becoming future legal practice. Just what fits the present state of a dynamic legal system is unclear.

129 One argument against justification as the sole methodological concern is that it really means the end of law. If we need not take fit seriously, then there is no real distinction between law and politics. This entails nihilism. I do not believe this is true. More accurately, discovering that law is illusory might help us discover values behind and deeply related to the rule of law that are more important than law itself. Professor Brest eloquently states a similar point: "[T]he lesson I carry away from contemporary literary and social theory is that its very location is a question of politics. I do not think this is nihilism. *Rather, I believe that examining 'rule of law'—even at the risk of discovering that it is entirely illusory—is a necessary step toward a society that can satisfy the aspirations that make us hold to the concept so tenaciously*" (emphasis added). Paul Brest, "Interpretation and Interest," 34 *Stan. L. Rev.* 765, 773 (1982).

130 R. Dworkin, *Law's Empire,* at 356.

131 It could be argued that a theory is worthwhile if it explains ordinary cases, despite being able to explain constitutional revolutions. Even if true, we still need a theory that can explain both ordinary and revolutionary cases equally, especially if the revolutionary cases drive the ordinary.

132 Jack Balkin, "Taking Ideology Seriously: Ronald Dworkin and the CLS Critique," 55 *UMKC L. Rev.* 392 (1987).

133 R. Dworkin, *Law's Empire,* at 392.

134 The notion of a minimal fit indicates only that a proposed principle be related to American political culture. This means that all the various conceptions of society that have been part of our heritage are a basis for a proposed principle.

135 Suppose someone interprets the entitlement cases as implying a principle of general economic democracy. *Goldberg v. Kelly,* 397 U.S. 254 (1970) ("It may

be realistic today to regard welfare entitlements as more like property than a 'gratuity'"); *Funnies v. Shevin*, 407 U.S. 67 (1972); *Sniadach v. Family Finance Corp.*, 395 U.S. 67 (1969). Such a principle might be an embarrassment of fit yet provide such a good justification of evolving American ideals that it's preferable to a principle providing a better fit but not as good a justification. Surely, it is wrong to close off this possibility in advance.

136   The pragmatist need only show that a principle has a good fit with the American "civic culture," not that it fits all the formal decisions or statutes. In Dworkin's terminology pragmatist constitutionalism contains a large theory of mistakes.

137   It needn't be a progressive political principle. The same conclusion follows if we choose a libertarian principle.

138   Dworkin's reply would insist that this is the price we pay to keep the Court a court and not a superlegislature. But in the domain of human rights, the Court *is* a superlegislature. It decides that people have rights or do not have rights. Either decision affects an individual's rights.

139   Similarly, if libertarianism or laissez faire capitalism is the correct political theory, its correctness compensates for its insufficient fit. This is what we learn from the structure of constitutional revolutions. It would be fruitful to describe the possible objects of fit and their role in different types of constitutional adjudication.

140   R. Dworkin, *Law's Empire,* at 225.

141   Ibid. at 190, 413.

142   A. Peczenik, "Moral and Ontological Justification in Legal Reasoning," 4 *Law & Phil.* 289, 305–06 (1985).

143   Much of Dworkin's argument against external skepticism derives from his frustration over making claims about what is "out there," or whether there exists an "independent reality" and so forth. Dworkin does not conceive of his true interpretations as saying anything about what there is — that is, they do not have any ontological commitment. But why not say that if one interpretation is better than any alternative, the rights it entails actually exist. See W. V. O. Quine, "Ontological Relativity," in *Ontological Relativity and Other Essays* 26 (1969); see also W. Quinn, "Truth and Explanation in Ethics," 96 *Ethics* 524, 530 (1986) (arguing that Quinean and Harmanian epistemology allows for moral facts).

144   Philosophers perennially have been seeking external procedures for validating particular enterprises. For example, in evaluating the question of the objectivity of morals, Hampshire distinguishes four kinds of questions, the last of which is relevant here: "there is . . . a question of whether there is a respectable procedure, recognized in other contexts, for establishing the acceptability of moral judgments of various kinds, or whether moral judgment is in this re-

spect *sui generis* and for this reason problematic." S. Hampshire, *Morality and Conflict* 126 (1983). Here Hampshire seeks a procedure external to ethics that could validate ethics. Further, one could argue that every theory consists of formal and substantive principles. The formal principles include a conception of critical adequacy. It is perfectly possible to generalize from each theory's formal principles and come up with a more comprehensive theory of criticism. Such a theory of criticism may then be used to evaluate the legitimacy of different areas of human inquiry.

145 But see J. Mackie, *Ethics: Inventing Right and Wrong* 24 (1978) ("The difficulty of seeing how values could be objective is a fairly strong reason for thinking that they are not so . . . but it is not a good reason for saying that this is not a real issue"). Dworkin's disclaimers notwithstanding, the question of whether there are objective values is of vital intellectual and moral importance. J. Mackie, at 24–25.

146 Both a critical morality and a conception of law must have as a goal that they "eventuate in agreement." Michael Walzer, "Minimal Moralism," in *From the Twilight of Probability: Ethics and Politics* (William R. Shea and Antonio Spadafora eds. 1992).

147 Putnam makes a moral principle's "width of appeal" a condition of its objectivity. H. Putnam, *Meaning and the Moral Sciences,* 93 (1978).

148 Dworkin wants to disprove the positivists' contention that in hard cases a judge is disputing what the law *ought* to be, not what it *is*. But unless there are principles that guarantee agreement in hard cases, there is no way to distinguish between what the law is and what it ought to be. Dworkin's contention that there are nonconventionalist moral principles that one can infer from legal conventions might be true. But how do we know that such principles exist? Further, even granting their existence, how do we know the content of such principles?

149 The most obvious practical result is to settle the conflict. Having an orderly way to settle conflicts provides stability and predictability in a social system.

150 The most obvious example of this is for an appellate court to agree with how the trial judge disposed of the case. If the trial judge employed principles in the ordinary case that he did not believe could generate such agreement, it would be difficult to understand his conduct. Of course, in extraordinary cases he might dispose of the case in an idiosyncratic manner in order to make a point or to educate the public concerning an erroneous law.

151 In other words, law is a practical art—one that seeks principles of reasoning whose conclusions generate action. See J. Hall, *Foundations of Jurisprudence* 150 (1973).

152 The distinction between external and internal skepticism can be criticized for another reason. Suppose people played a game called "fess." Fess is the same

game as chess with the qualification that players believe that each correct move establishes the truth of statements that morally evaluate the players. So that if you check my king, you are courageous and I am cowardly. Now, suppose someone comes along and offers the following skeptical argument: I know that making this move means that I am courageous and you are cowardly within the game of fess. But the game of fess doesn't really decide these things. (The skeptic's argument here might be that it doesn't really decide these things because there are alternative ways of making such decisions, or that there are no ways of doing so.) Hence, you can continue playing fess if you choose, but don't think it is really a reliable guide regarding courage. It really says nothing at all about the way the world is.

The skeptical attack here is external, yet perfectly legitimate. Dworkin's argument that the existence of problem-solving rules within an enterprise precludes an external attack is fallacious. As in the example of fess, such external attacks are often warranted. Dworkin's arguments against external skepticism are not really arguments but an attempt to bypass external skepticism. Like other attempts at defeating external skepticism, "[t]he old epistemological problems are not so much by-passed, as ignored." S. Sayers, *Reality and Reason* 110 (1985).

153   Dworkin's point also overlooks the social nature of knowledge. In such a view answers to difficult questions are determined not by some idiosyncratic standard but rather by shared rules and paradigms. Hence, in such a view, for there to be a right answer, it is necessary to have principles of proof.

154   Further, Dworkin's conception of truth and justification makes him vulnerable to attack by constitutional skeptics generally, and in particular by scholars associated with the critical legal studies movement. According to critical legal studies, our legal system embodies contradictory principles; hence solution to legal conflict is illusory. The ruling class exploits this illusion to generate conclusions most conducive to its interests. See Duncan Kennedy, "The Structure of Blackstone's Commentaries," 28 *Buff. L. Rev.* 205 (1979); William Singer, "The Legal Rights Debate in Analytical Jurisprudence from Bentham to Hohfeld," 1982 *Wis. L. Rev.* 975.

155   Dworkin's view is interesting only by revealing uniquely right answers across the judicial community and not merely for an individual judge. Yet it seems that Dworkin refuses to speculate on what such collective principles of proof might be like. On the other hand, his view is plausible only on the level of an individual practical reasoning. Consequently, Dworkin's view is interesting but incomplete or false, or it is true but uninteresting.

156   For a discussion of the determinacy issue in law, see Ken Kress, "Legal Indeterminacy," 77 *Calif. L. Rev.* 283 (1988); Robert Justin Lipkin, "Beyond Skepticism"; and Lipkin, "Indeterminacy," at 638–42.

157 Without such rules or principles, it is permissible for each judge to generate his own independent decision. By "independent" I mean that each judge's decision is equally valuable, not that the correct methodology eschews other judicial opinions. In law, as in any domain, independence in the latter sense is impossible.

158 Consider the following characterization of the rationality associated with interpretive statements: "Interpretative statements express a social and rational attitude of an individual towards a real or imagined situation. They result from a deliberation in which an individual tries to adapt his reworking of an [attitude] not only to the demands of consistency, coherence and generality but also to the demands of acceptability, that is, to his expectations of consensus from other rational individuals. One can meaningfully criticize interpretative statements not only when they contain inconsistencies or when their coherence or generality is insufficient but also when *they are not sufficiently acceptable from the point of view of other deliberators*" (emphasis added). A. Peczenik, at 294.

3   The Theory of Constitutional Revolutions

1   Richard Rorty extends Kuhn's distinction to normal and revolutionary discourse. Consider his words: "[N]ormal discourse [adjudication] is that which is conducted within an agreed-upon set of conventions about what counts as a relevant [factor], what counts as answering a question, what counts as having a good argument for that answer or a good criticism of it. Abnormal discourse [adjudication] is what happens when someone . . . sets [these conventions] aside." Richard Rorty, *Philosophy and the Mirror of Nature* 320–321 (1979).

2   A theory of constitutional moments explains how courts follow and redirect constitutional law. Theories of this type emphasize the *Court's* role in redirecting constitutional law, whereas a theory of judicial reasoning emphasizes how individual *justices* reason in integrating historical and moral factors to yield a decision in the present case.

3   As mentioned earlier, Dworkin implies that this objection conflates metaphysical and epistemic concerns. For Dworkin two questions exist: First, what does it mean to say that there is a uniquely correct balance? Second, how can we prove (know) that one such balance *is* correct? For Dworkin the first question is answered in terms of integrity. The second question does not have a general answer. In my view this violates the pragmatist imperative to abandon pursuing truths that are unprovable.

4   My argument establishes only that this strong conception of judicial review is permissible, not necessarily required by deliberative democracy. However, we

ought not to jettison this institution and the role it plays in a deliberative democracy until we have designed an alternative practice with a highly probable chance of success. Any durable democracy must designate some institution to serve this purpose. The Court is not the only possibility here. Other institutional arrangements might serve this goal better than the Court. If so, we must describe these arrangements and overcome what has become a presumption in favor of the Court.

5   Other constitutional actors also change constitutional law outside of article 5. For example, the modern role and power of the executive, the executive-legislative "treaty" agreements, and congressional veto are examples of the informal redistribution of governmental power occurring outside of article 5.

6   These revolutions clearly occur without the benefit of article 5.

7   Ernest Gellner characterizes this evolutionary conception of history as a "world-growth story." Ernest Gellner, *Thought and Change* 12–13 (1964). Instead, human history is marked by abrupt transformations.

8   The story of American constitutionalism is "one of continuous and . . . upward growth," a growth that is "only occasionally interrupted by plateaus or even retrogressions." Ibid. (characterizing Western history).

9   See John Stick, "Can Nihilism Be Pragmatic?" 100 *Harv. L. Rev.* 332 (1986). This book embraces a skeptical view concerning the existence of a distinctive form of legal reasoning. See Richard Posner, "The Jurisprudence of Skepticism," 86 *Mich. L. Rev.* 827 (1988) (arguing that "[t]here is no distinctive methodology of legal reasoning"). Progress in constitutional theory will be impeded until we recognize that there is no distinctive form of constitutional reasoning. Instead, in my view, constitutional reasoning is a species of practical reasoning. This is more than a banal semantic distinction. If constitutional reasoning is a unique form of reasoning thoroughly distinguishable from other kinds of reasoning, or reasoning in other domains, then its autonomy might be established (though not necessarily) in a way that supports formalism.

10   Herbert Wechsler, "Toward Neutral Principles of Constitutional Law," 73 *Harv. L. Rev.* 1, 34 (1959). But see Mark Tushnet, "Following the Rules Laid Down: A Critique of Interpretivism and Neutral Principles," 96 *Harv. L. Rev.* 781 (1983). In fact, this familiar conception of law is really a spectrum of related conceptions. At one end of the spectrum there is "mechanical jurisprudence," holding that formal legal rules will generate particular answers to legal questions. See Lawrence Friedman, *Law and Society: An Introduction* 94 (1977). Some hold the view that legal decisions must be principled. Alexander Bickel, *The Supreme Court and the Idea of Progress* 87 (1978) (insisting that constitutional argument must be principled and based on reason); R. Dworkin, "The Forum of Principle," 56 *N.Y.U. L. Rev.* 461, 469 (1981). It is not obvious that a principled decision is always in harmony with reason. That question must be

determined by a more comprehensive conception of "principle" and "reason." When a constitutional scheme is either formally or substantively defective, a principled decision in a given case often includes flawed principles.

To oppose the view that legal decisions must be principled is not to endorse arbitrariness in legal reasoning. Rather, it is a call to recognize the futility in seeking a consensus concerning what counts as a "principle." Moreover, most theories concerning how principles generate legal results are marginally true at best. See R. J. Lipkin, "Conventionalism, Pragmatism, and Constitutional Revolutions," at 685, n. 124. Most importantly, one need not be totally disenchanted with principle and consistency to acknowledge that an excessive concern with either distorts legal and moral reality. See John Coons, "Consistency," 75 *Calif. L. Rev.* 59 (1987) (criticizing consistency as an ideal and recommending instead the prudent use of inconsistent outcomes); Cornelius Murphy, "Dworkin on Judicial Discretion: A Critical Analysis," 21 *U.C. Davis L. Rev.* 767, 784 (1988) (arguing that judicial discretion cannot be explained by an appeal to principle); Steven Shiffrin, "Radicalism, Liberalism, and Legal Scholarship," 30 *UCLA L. Rev.* 1103 (1982) (arguing against Dworkin's devotion to fundamental general principles in political philosophy). The defect in mechanical conceptions of judicial reasoning is that the judge is viewed as a technician, a mechanic, capable of starting the engine but not influencing its operation. See Catherine Haines, "General Observations on the Effects of Personal, Political, and Economic Influences in the Decisions of Judges," 17 *U. Ill. L. Rev.* 96–98 (1922). Even theories like Dworkin's, recognizing the role of moral and political theory in adjudication, depict judges as discoverers, not inventors. Or perhaps Dworkin would insist that they are a little bit of both. Cf. M. R. Cohen, *Law and Social Order* 112 (1933) (arguing that had judges never made law, the common law could never have developed and changed).

My conception of "mechanical jurisprudence" refers to any conception of adjudication that does not take into account the judge as an independent moral evaluator, or moral philosopher. If that is true, we should be more concerned with the purely philosophical and theoretical credentials of judges than whether they are in the mainstream. No justice to my knowledge has ever been a bona fide legal, moral, or political philosopher. See Paul Freund, "Umpiring the Federal System," 54 *Colum. L. Rev.* 561, 574 (1954) (stating that a Supreme Court justice should be a philosopher, but not too much of a philosopher). The fear of philosophy (and moral theory) in constitutional adjudication is only partially justified. Certainly, philosophy in constitutional law will not necessarily resolve the great controversies. However, it might very well help each party to understand the depth of her own views as well as her opponent's views. This fear of philosophy is illustrated in Judge Learned Hand's remark that he would not want to be governed by Platonic guardians even if he knew how to choose them.

Given the role of reasoning and reflection in the American communitarian Republic, it is a priori irrational to ignore the judgments of these super-reflectors. Careful reflection on policy and law is necessary to the vibrancy of any democracy. On the other hand, these super-reflectors must learn the people's language.

11   That the quest for a neutral perspective, if taken seriously, would be a quest for a perspective that is value laden and value free. As such, this quest inevitably fails. However, other conceptions of neutrality may be more likely in law and in politics. One can imagine a neutral perspective that supports a constitutional democracy whose principles are not *intrusively* value laden, despite being committed to the values of constitutionalism and democracy. This means that it supports both the procedural and substantive conditions of a constitutional democracy, not the intrusive values of partisan perspectives.

12   However, we must distinguish between the judge's personal values and public, defensible values that the judge holds personally. Robert Bennett, "Objectivity in Constitutional Law," 132 *U. Penn. L. Rev.* 445 (1984).

13   In rejecting this view, I do not say that judges should feel free to appeal to any "preference" they have at the moment of decision. For example, a judge ought not to decide consciously or unconsciously the case before her because of what she had for breakfast. Nor should she appeal to political principles having no currency in American constitutional experience. But within these confines a judge ultimately must appeal not to her preferences, but rather to what she conscientiously believes is the right answer based on her background values and beliefs concerning the nation's best interest. This is certainly a difficult task; but without some distinction between mere preferences and reflective convictions judicial reasoning seems doomed from the start.

14   The entire constitutional landscape — including Supreme Court decisions, constitutional scholarship, and constitutional education in law school — adopts some versions of the classical view. Central to this notion is the idea that judges do not govern, but regulate. As Justice Brewer remarked, "The court . . . makes no laws, they establish no policy, they never enter the domain of public action. They do not govern." David J. Brewer, "The Nation's Safeguard," in *Proceedings of the N.Y. State Bar Association* 46 (1893).

15   Any attempt to restrict constitutional change to normal adjudication is destined to fail; it simply cannot accommodate the facts and, instead, distorts the modalities of constitutional change. Should one suppose that one of these normal modalities permits or encourages revolutionary change, then the importance of the distinction between normal and revolutionary adjudication diminishes. In this event normal adjudication contains as one of its components revolutionary adjudication. In my view, besides muddying the conceptual waters, this approach does not give revolutionary adjudication its due in American constitutional practice.

16 This familiar picture refers to "explicit constitutional conventions" as one model of constitutional meaning. By "explicit constitutional conventions" I mean those constitutional provisions associated with what Bickel refers to as the "manifest constitution." Alexander Bickel, *The Morality of Consent* 30 (1975). Here Bickel argues that there is a moral obligation to obey the manifest constitution. Bickel tells us, for instance, that the president cannot decide to stay in office for six rather than four years. "To deny this idea is in the most fundamental sense to deny the idea of law itself." Ibid.

However, this proposition does not explain many important developments in our constitutional design, for example, how the imperial presidency informally acquired its place in our constitutional structure. Surely, the office of president today has much greater power than that anticipated by the Framers. See Arthur Schlesinger Jr., "After the Imperial Presidency," 47 *Md. L. Rev.* 54, 70 (1987) (arguing that the Framers explicitly rejected the notion that the executive has sole responsibility for foreign policy). Nor are these powers derived from the manifest constitution. Does the imperial presidency deny the idea of law itself? What Bickel fails to recognize is that many fundamental changes in constitutional law have occurred without either "judicial" or formal amendment.

17 Langdellian formalism contends that an indefinite number of legal problems can be resolved by applying a distinct number of legal concepts and rules. According to this view the essence of law is its logical form and principles of reasoning. Law is a formal science the principles of which can be extrapolated from case decisions. C. C. Langdell, *Cases on Contracts* vi (1871); C. C. Langdell, *Brief Survey of Equity Jurisprudence* 220 (1905).

More contemporary conceptions of formalism insist minimally on a separation of law and policy. See Herbert Hovenkamp, "The Political Economy of Substantive Due Process," 40 *Stan. L. Rev.* 379 (1988). Formalism holds that "the law must be internally consistent and self-contained." Ibid. at 382. See also Frederick Schauer, "Formalism," 97 *Yale L. J.* 509 (describing some of the virtues of formal rules restricting judicial choice); Mark Tushnet, "Anti-Formalism in Recent Constitutional Theory," 83 *Mich. L. Rev.* 1502 (1985) (criticizing certain "formalistic" solutions to the countermajoritarian challenge in constitutional theory); James J. Wilson, "The Morality of Formalism," 33 *UCLA L. Rev.* 431, 434 (1985) (arguing that "doctrinal formalism" is a desirable and essential feature of constitutional jurisprudence).

Legal realism maintains that we must study legal phenomena from a scientific point of view. The legal realist seeks to discover the causes and effects of legal phenomena. Joseph Bingham, "What is Law?" 11 *Mich. L. Rev.* 1, 9 (1912). Legal realists deny the existence of an irreducibly internal point of view consisting of rules, principles, arguments, and reasons. The internal point of view maintains that legal rules function as critical standards of conduct for participants in a social practice. H. L. A. Hart, *The Concept of Law* (1994). The external perspective emphasizes the view of a nonparticipatory observer concerned with describing regularities in behavior.

One must bear in mind that legal realists are a diverse group and no simple definition captures the richness of their views. See generally Wilfrid E. Rumble Jr., *American Legal Realism* (1968). Legal realism is usually characterized as abandoning a conceptual or theoretical view of the law and instead seeking principles or strategies for predicting judicial decisions, thereby gaining some control over social and political life. See Theodore Benditt, *Law as Rule and Principle* 11–16 (1978).

Although there were many significant differences between the Langdellian formalists and legal realists, their views share a structural similarity. Both of these perspectives were committed to the mistaken position that there was a science of law. Consider Gilmore's view: "The Legal Realists of the 1930s embraced the fallacy quite as enthusiastically as the Langdellian formalists. As a group, the Realists unquestioningly accepted the idea of the one true rule of law which was waiting to be discovered if only the search was conducted in the right way. Realist jurisprudence proposed a change of course, not a change of goal." Grant Gilmore, *The Ages of American Law* 100 (1977). The theory of constitutional revolutions differs from legal realism in that the former adopts both an internal and an external perspective toward constitutional questions, whereas legal realism adopts only an external perspective. One feature that the theory of constitutional revolutions shares with legal realism is that both theories are committed to "accurate recording of things as they are, as contrasted with things as they are imagined to be, or wished to be, or as one feels they ought to be." Roscoe Pound, "The Call for a Realist Jurisprudence," 44 *Harv. L. Rev.* 697 (1931).

18   One argument against the possibility of explaining case law is that legal principles are indeterminate. See Mark Tushnet, "A Note on the Revival of Textualism in Constitutional Theory," 58 *S. Cal. L. Rev.* 683, 685 (1985) (evaluating recent attempts to formulate a textualist mode). For differing views on determinacy, see Ken Kress, "Legal Indeterminacy," at 283; R. J. Lipkin, "Beyond Skepticism"; R. J. Lipkin, *Indeterminacy*. In reply some scholars maintain that "theorists who matter least are those who find language so indeterminate that any text can mean almost anything. These theorists seem to assume that a statute is not essentially different from a poem. They deny one of the fundamental premises of the polity [that we try to govern ourselves with legal texts, not town meetings or Platonic guardians], and consequently make themselves irrelevant." Douglas Laycock, "Constitutional Theory Matters," 65 *Tex. L. Rev.* 767, 773–74 (1987). Laycock's premise is implausible. No serious observer can argue that *poems* can mean anything at all. For example, imagine someone

suggesting that the most obvious interpretation of Hamlet's famous soliloquy is that it is an attempt to determine whether two plus two equals four, or whether it is possible to square the circle. Moreover, it is far from obvious that a society operating with a Platonic guardian or a town meeting could dispense with interpretation. The problem of interpretation affects these methods of government just as much as it affects a society operating with texts. Finally, of course, it is foolish to contend that constitutional or statutory language is so indeterminate as to mean anything at all. However, within certain parameters, key provisions of our Constitution can be interpreted in conflicting ways. For example, the equal protection clause can be interpreted in Nozickian or Rawlsian terms, or even in terms of radical egalitarianism. The great constitutional controversies are indeterminate in the sense that no set of background values yields a uniquely right answer to a question of interpretation. Moreover, even if such answers followed from background values, few background values are required for rationality in interpretation. Consequently, conflicting interpretations would be possible with no way to decide between them. The problem with the indeterminacy argument is that it needs to be spelled out in greater detail. Does it rule out the possibility of constraints on interpretation? If not, is this a sufficient response to the indeterminacy argument? If textual meaning is fundamentally cultural, constraints may exist that defeat or dissipate the force of the indeterminacy argument. Cf. J. Boyd White, "Thinking About Language," 96 *Yale L. J.* 1960, 1973 (1987) (describing meaning as cultural and communal and residing in a background of unstated assumptions).

19   Drucilla Cornell, "Institutionalization of Meaning, Recollective Imagination, and the Potential for Transformative Legal Interpretation," at 1144.

20   The fundamental problem of constitutional methodology (indeed, of legal methodology generally) is to specify in what sense a decision follows from prior law. Because only systematically controversial answers to this specific question exist, it is dubious that anyone will succeed in delineating an intersubjective conception of what it is for a decision to "follow" from the authorities. What counts as following, in Gallie's terms, is "an essentially contested concept."

21   In one sense not all interpretations of constitutional language are foundational. A decision interpreting the constitutional requirement that presidents be thirty-five years of age is not foundational—in the sense that such an age requirement is not designed to affect age requirements throughout the entire legal system—though it is authoritative regarding the president's age.

22   Cf. J. David Greenstone, "Against Simplicity: The Cultural Dimensions of the Constitution," 55 *U. Chi. L. Rev.* 428, 431–32 (1988) (constitutional interpretation must reflect social realities). This forward-looking attitude is a central element in American constitutional practice, though many judges and theorists deny it.

23   The pragmatist turn appeals to such extrinsic factors for interpreting foundational constitutional provisions as morality, culture, or common sense or common knowledge. For many "[i]t will be apparent how much of our constitutional law is merely getting at the common sense of the matter when we
consider how few of the questions of constitutional law are answered by any
specific language in the Constitution. When the language is really specific
questions seldom arise." Thomas Reed Powell, "The Logic and Rhetoric of
Constitutional Law," in *Essays in Constitutional Law* 85, 89 (R. McCloskey ed.
1957) [hereafter cited as *Essays in Constitutional Law*].

24   I have in mind Robert Bork's "Madisonian conception of democracy," which
Bork maintains asserts that the Constitution and the Bill of Rights ultimately
imply that majorities are empowered to prevail simply because they are majorities. Robert Bork, *The Tempting of America*. In the first instance Bork radically
distorts Madison's conception of the Constitution. Madison was concerned
with the tyranny of the majority, not the tyranny of the courts. Second, Bork's
position overlooks Madison's commitment to the common good; Madison
fervently believed that governmental structure should vitiate the effects of
majoritarian decisions conflicting with the common good. Majoritarianism,
therefore, was not *Madison's* idea of American constitutionalism.

25   Pragmatism, as a legal theory, has other meanings. A pragmatist approach to
law can be concerned with making legal decisions on a case-by-case basis rather
than enunciating sweeping legal principles. Pragmatism can be understood as
commonsense decisions not guided by logic or theory. Another kind of pragmatism holds that reason, as opposed to sentiment, is inappropriate to explain
legal practice. Pragmatism might also refer to a consequentialist or utilitarian
approach to ethics and political theory. See generally P. S. Atiyah, *Pragmatism
and Theory in English Law* (1987). See also Robert S. Summers, *Instrumentalism and American Legal Theory* 20–22 (1982) (describing pragmatic instrumentalism). One brand of pragmatism concerns itself with reason as opposed to
tradition, seeking change based on reason and experience rather than depending upon formal structures in legal theory. Gary Jacobsohn, *Pragmatism, Statesmanship, and the Supreme Court* 40–41 (1977). Pragmatism may also be described as "the view that the ultimate test is always experience." Daniel Farber,
"Pragmatism," 72 *Minn L. Rev.* 1331 (1988). Some forms of pragmatism suggest that there are usually diverse perspectives on any issue. Catherine Hantzis,
"Legal Innovation within the Wider Intellectual Tradition: The Pragmatism of
Oliver Wendell Holmes, Jr.," 82 *Nw. U.L. Rev.* 541, 587 (1988).
    My use of "pragmatism" maintains that judicial decisions should be evalu-
ated in terms of whether the decision would make a positive contribution to
the community's constitutional and political future. In my view a pragmatist
theory might embrace principles or theories; it can be monistic or pluralistic. A

pragmatist theory of law can include consequentialistic or nonconsequentialistic conceptions of what is right and what is good. Therefore, the type of pragmatist theory I am concerned with should not be confused with "pragmatic instrumentalism," which is an essentially consequentialist legal theory. See Robert S. Summers, "Professor Fuller's Jurisprudence and America's Dominant Theory of Law," 92 *Harv. L. Rev.* 444, 437–38 (1978). For clarity I have suggested that we call "superpragmatist" any theory of adjudication primarily concerning itself with how judicial decisions contribute to the future of the republic. R. J. Lipkin, "The Anatomy of Constitutional Revolutions," at 729. There are more radical forms of philosophical pragmatism that have important implications for legal theory. See generally Richard Rorty, *Contingency, Irony, and Solidarity* (1989). I critically examine Rorty's social thought in R. J. Lipkin, "Pragmatism — The Unfinished Revolution," and his liberal ironism in "Beyond Skepticism."

26 Like conventionalists, pragmatists value continuity with the past for its stabilizing effects. Contemporary society confronts problems of coordination, which cannot be solved without protecting reasonable expectation. Pragmatists also value the past for making the present and future possible in a nontrivial way. To understand the present and speculate about the future, some framework characterizing the past is necessary. To value the past in this manner does not entail sanctifying the past with normative authority to determine present and future decisions.

27 That a particular judge is a pragmatist does not entail that she draw the balance between fit and justification in a particular way, just that she consider both factors in making her decision. Because no deductively satisfactory manner of balancing these factors exists, one might contend that the pragmatist dictum that history and morality must be balanced is rather trivial. If everyone, or almost everyone, can be a pragmatist, the term loses all meaning. If every theory is pragmatist, it doesn't help to depict a theory as pragmatist as opposed to something else. What is interesting about the convergence from different quarters to the pragmatism summit is that the agreement is not trivial — not, at least, unredeemably trivial. The interesting feature of pragmatist discourse is that it permits the replication of different, allegedly nonpragmatist, positions in a pragmatist form. This will not automatically resolve constitutional controversies. However, it will provide a framework that will make agreement more likely, or at least explain systematically why agreement is improbable in a given case.

28 The notion of a better future as the test of truth and justice is an essential tenet of pragmatism. See G. Jacobsohn, *Pragmatism, Statesmanship, and the Court,* at 51. Consider the contrary view: "People are always shouting they want to create a better future. It's not true. The future is an apathetic void of no interest to anyone. The past is full of life, eager to irritate us, provoke and insult us,

tempt us to destroy or repaint it. The only reason people want to be masters of the future is to change the past." Milan Kundera, *The Book of Laughter and Forgetting* 22 (1981).

29 A source or factor is "extrinsic" when a reasonable community of judges would reject it as a preinterpretive paradigm of constitutional practice.

30 For an account of how "natural law" theory may be tied to different historical epochs, see Olefumi Taiwo, *Legal Naturalism* (1996).

31 See Bernard Bailyn, *The Origins of American Politics* 161 (1944).

32 The Framers endorsed a conception of public reason, the view that civic discourse could be formulated for settling conflicts between different individuals' conceptions of the good. Most historians of the period emphasized how different early colonialists felt from one another; thus, a Virginian did not appreciate or understand a Massachusettsan, nor did he care.

33 Cooley gives one conventional statement of this "living constitution" perspective: "No instrument can be the same in meaning today and forever and in all men's minds. As the people change so does their written constitution change also. They see it in new lights and with different eyes: events may have given unexpected illumination to some of its provisions, and what they read one way before they read in a very different way now." Lawrence Lessig, *Translating Federalism: United States v. Lopez,* 1995 Sup. Ct. Rev. 125, 126, n. 3 (quoting Cooley). I understand Cooley's remarks to embrace the idea of a "living constitution," which sanctions revolutionary adjudication, even to make it inevitable. Both Ackerman and Dworkin are attempts to explain the "living constitution"; however, neither can explain revolutionary adjudication.

34 See Ronald Dworkin, " 'Natural Law' Revisited." Dworkin argues that instrumentalism, a form of pragmatism, denies the existence of such rights. But instrumentalism is only one, and not the most refined, form of pragmatism. Constitutional pragmatism, as Dworkin admits on another occasion, can appeal to any kind of substantive conception of the right and the good, just as long as it counsels judges to decide constitutional cases according to this conception in the appropriate circumstances.

35 R. Dworkin, *Freedom's Law.*

36 Until at least he became thirty-five.

37 At the time Ford became president, no one occupied the vacated vice presidency.

38 See Stanley Fish, "Still Wrong after All These Years," 6 *Law & Phi.* 401, 404 (1987).

39 This does not settle, though it should temper, the debate over originalism. The present community's historical gaze can and should be directed; and one possible direction can be the meaning of the past community. However, it is always *our* conception of the past that controls.

40 We need to understand the appeal of originalism. Not only does it connect us

with the past, and a particular hallowed past, at that, it also allegedly provides for the rule of law and democratic values.

41 See J. Boyd White, *When Words Lose Meaning* 265–66 (1984).

42 Without mentioning the concept of a constitutional revolution, one writer describes eloquently the constitutionally revolutionary process: "Constitutional law is a dynamic process of creativity. Through the continual interpretation and reinterpretation of the text of the document, the Supreme Court perpetually creates new meaning for the Constitution. . . . Notwithstanding the orthodox protestation that it is illegitimate for the Court to 'revise' or to 'amend' the Constitution, this is in fact what the Court has always done by continually creating new constitutional meaning." Jeffrey Shaman, "The Constitution, the Supreme Court, and Creativity," 9 *Hastings Const. L.Q.* 257, 258–66 (1982). See also Jeffrey Shaman, "Constitutional Fact: The Perception of Reality by the Supreme Court," 35 *U. Fla. L. Rev.* 236, 253 (1983).

43 Interpretation can be stable, transformative, or revolutionary. The theory of constitutional revolutions does not entirely preclude incremental evolution in normal adjudication. However, the theory of constitutional revolutions rejects the notion that incremental evolutionary change can ever yield new constitutional concepts and principles. If a change is truly evolutionary, normal conventions alone can explain its development. Nor does the theory reject transformations in postrevolutionary adjudication. The theory does insist, however, that the foundational cases in American constitutional history are driven by interpretations that cannot be characterized as incremental evolution or as merely transformative. Instead, the concept of revolution, in its Kuhnian and Rortyan sense, is required. Only such a concept can explain Marshall's creating the practice of judicial review or the practice reversing *Plessy*'s conception of equal protection; these decisions determine a qualitatively different paradigm creating or reversing formal or substantive answers to constitutional questions. Hence, we discover a special sense of "revolution" applying to American constitutionalism and law generally.

44 A formal constitutional principle is concerned with the method for getting results, not the result itself. For example, the principle of judicial review is a formal principle of constitutionalism. It does not resolve the substantive issue of whether a statute is unconstitutional or whether an individual's right to free speech has been violated. A substantive constitutional principle implicates a particular substantive value, for example, that segregated schools are constitutionally invalid.

45 See, e.g., *Cohens v. Virginia*, 19 U.S. (6 Wheat.) 264 (1821); *Martin's v. Hunter's Lessee*, 14 U.S. (1 Wheat.) 304 (1816); *Fletcher v. Peck*, 10 U.S. (6 Cranch) 187 (1810); *Marbury v. Madison*, 5 U.S. (1 Cranch) 137 (1803).

46 Thomas Kuhn, *The Structure of Scientific Revolutions* (1969). Even if Kuhn is

arguably wrong about science, a Kuhnian-inspired theory might still be right about constitutional revolutions.

47   Science, law, and even morality operate according to the distinction between normal and revolutionary reasoning. See Kathryn Parsons, "Nietzsche and Moral Change," in *Nietzsche* 169 (Robert C. Solomon ed. 1973) (describing moral revolutions). But see D. Palmer and M. Scarring, "Moral Revolutions," *Phil. & Phenom. Res.* 262 (1974).

48   Constitutional paradigms can be procedural or substantive, and a particular constitutional paradigm can exhibit both substantive and procedural dimensions at the same time. For example, the different levels of review include both substantive and procedural elements. They are procedural because they provide an analytic device for conceptualizing a case. But they are also substantive in recognizing that certain kinds of governmental burdens constitutionally and morally require greater scrutiny.

49   The term "undetermined" might be preferable to "indeterminacy." Yet significant differences between these terms might remain.

50   J. Craven, "Paean to Pragmatism," 50 *N.C. L. Rev.* 977 (1972). *Korematsu v. United States,* 323 U.S. 214 (1944), had already established strict scrutiny in cases involving racial classifications, and so ultimately must be regarded as a key precursor to *Brown.*

51   This theory is concerned primarily with revolutionary constitutional *adjudication* and not with constitutional revolutions in the legislative or executive branches of government. Moreover, the theory of constitutional revolutions is primarily concerned with *constitutional* revolutions, though revolutionary adjudication occurs in both the common law and statutory law.

52   The American concern with fidelity to the Constitution is nonexistent in England. Instead, "debate in England centers on the right or wrong of a particular bill, not on its fidelity to a presumptively authoritative text that stands above parliamentary activity." Sanford Levinson, "Law as Literature," at 156.

53   The substantive theory that formalists mistake for neutrality is a distinctive American conception of democracy through which equal citizens, devoted to working out solutions to common problems together, deliberate over the community's future.

54   By "judicial actors" I mean everyone having a stake in the outcome of a constitutional controversy, including citizens, attorneys and judges, and so forth.

55   I do not say that the distinction between a minor question of law and a major question of law can be answered mechanically. Whether a change is minor or major depends upon the context, scope, and depth of the change.

56   Or if it does, it does so only trivially.

57   For example, deciding not to run for political office because one is too young, or claiming the right to a jury trial in a criminal case, both qualify as interpreta-

tions of the Constitution. Frederick Schauer, "The Occasions of Constitutional Interpretation."

58 Adjudication, or litigation, starts at the time of the injury and continues through selecting a lawyer and going to court, trying the case, and satisfying the judgment. Thus, when a lawyer convinces her client that the client has no case, the lawyer and the client are engaged in normal adjudication.

59 Dworkin argues for a distinction between the semantic intention or "what the Framers meant to say" and the "political or expectation intention," or "what would be the consequences of their saying it." Ronald Dworkin, "The Arduous Virtue of Fidelity," *Fordham Symposium* at 1256 (1997). Unfortunately, this begs the question in favor of two kinds of originalism; more strongly, without sufficient argument it begs the question against the possibility of interpreting what the Framers meant to say in terms of their expectations or hopes that they will be understood in a certain way.

60 The different phases of constitutional adjudication are interrelated and are driven by a single principle: constitutional pragmatism. The ultimate goal of a democratic system of adjudication is that justices have the power and prerogative to correct mistakes in constitutional practice. Sometimes correcting the mistake requires formal amendment; most times it requires the informal amending power that is an integral part of constitutional interpretation.

61 Arthur Bestor, "The American Civil War as a Constitutional Crisis," 69 *Am. Hist. Rev.* 327, 328 (1964).

62 Consider: "A constitution, after all, is nothing other than the aggregate of laws, traditions, and understandings — in other words, the complex of institutions and procedures — by which a nation brings to political and legal decision the substantive conflicts engendered by changes in all the varied aspects of its societal life." A. Bestor, at 328. In this sense revolutionary adjudication is a central part of the United States Constitution.

63 Revolutionary constitutional decisions are judicial decisions composed of extra-constitutional, sometimes contraconstitutional, factors. Contraconstitutional interpretation contrasts with extraconstitutional interpretation, which permits the Court to breathe new (but not conflicting) life into a constitutional provision. See Robert N. Clinton, "Original Understanding, Legal Realism, and the Interpretation of 'This Constitution,'" 72 *Iowa L. Rev.* 1177, 1265 (1987); see also Michael J. Perry, *The Constitution, the Court, and Human Rights* 20 (1982).

64 The problem of "fidelity to" or "following the Constitution" partakes of all the difficulties Wittgenstein diagnosed in the conventional conception of identity and in the idea of following a rule. Ludwig Wittgenstein, *Philosophical Investigations*. Much of Wittgenstein's later philosophy is an attempt to understand the concept of rule-governed activities, a concept that itself depends on the notion of sameness. For Wittgenstein no univocal criterion of identity is possible in

ordinary language. Instead, Wittgenstein proposes to replace identity with the idea of "family resemblance." L. Wittgenstein, ibid.; L. Wittgenstein, *Remarks on the Foundations of Mathematics* (1956); L. Wittgenstein, *On Certainty* (1967); L. Wittgenstein, *Zettel* (1970). There is always some rule that one could formulate to account for the "rule-likeness" of certain behavior no matter how complex or unilluminating the rule is. In revolutionary adjudication almost any result can plausibly be based on the Constitution in this rather trivial sense.

65   For example, several precursors to *Brown* attempted to repair the paradigm in *Plessy.* See R. J. Lipkin, "The Anatomy of Constitutional Revolutions," at 635, n. 172.

66   This process is not always forward looking. Sometimes precursors can be identified only after the revolution. *Korematsu v. United States* was a precursor to *Brown,* but it was also revolutionary in its own right. If we include in the "*Brown Revolution*" the post-*Brown* per curiam cases desegregating at least the public dimension of American society, the *Korematsu* is revolutionary in the sense that it makes *Brown* possible. Today both *Brown* and *Korematsu* are cited as authorities for the contemporary conception of racial equality.

67   *Korematsu v. United States.*

68   Revolutionary decisions have been a critical feature of every stage of American constitutional change. Besides the formative cases, some notable revolutionary decisions are: *Dred Scott v. Sanford,* 60 U.S. (19 How.) 393 (1857); *Slaughterhouse Cases,* 83 U.S. (16 Wall.) 36 (19873); *Plessy v. Ferguson,* 163 U.S. 537 (1896); *Lochner v. New York,* 198 U.S. 45 (1905); *Nebbia v. New York,* 291 U.S. 502 (1934); *United States v. Carolene Products Co.,* 304 U.S. 144 (1938); *Brown v. Board of Education of Topeka (Brown I),* 347 U.S. 483 (1954); *Reynolds v. Sims,* 377 U.S. 533 (1964); *Griswold v. Connecticut,* 381 U.S. 479 (1965); *Roe v. Wade,* 410 U.S. 113 (1973); *Home Building and Loan Association v. Blaisdell,* 290 U.S. 398 (1934); and *New York Times Co. v. Sullivan,* 376 U.S. 254 (1964). *Bolling v. Sharpe,* 347 U.S. 497 (1954), is an especially interesting case. In Bolling the Court read an "equal protection component" into the Fifth Amendment's due process clause on the ground that due process already includes an equal protection component. One wonders if that makes the Fourteenth Amendment's equal protection clause redundant. Such a revolutionary decision might embarrass even some ardent supporters of revolutionary adjudication.

69   3 U.S. (1 Cranch) 137 (1803).

70   14 U.S. (1 Wheat.) 304 (1816).

71   17 U.S. (4 Wheat.) 316 (1819).

72   22 U.S. (9 Wheat.) 1 (1824).

73   A potentially potent individual rights revolution was quelled in *Barron v. Mayor Baltimore,* 32 U.S. (7 Pet.) 243 (1933).

74   But see B. Ackerman, 1 *We the People.* The *Slaughterhouse Cases* give evidentiary
      support to the theory of constitutional revolutions. In this case, the Court's
      interpretation of the Fourteenth Amendment effectively repealed the amend-
      ment's privileges or immunities clause.

75   163 U.S. 537 (1896).

76   *Griswold v. Connecticut,* 381 U.S. 479 (1965).

77   *Eisenstat v. Baird,* 405 U.S. 438 (1972); *Roe v. Wade,* 410 U.S. 113 (1973); *Moore
      v. City of East Cleveland,* 431 U.S. (1977); *Zablocki v. Redhail,* 434 U.S. 374
      (1978). The precursors to *Griswold* are an interesting line of cases. *Skinner v.
      Oklahoma,* 316 U.S. 535 (1942); *Peirce v. Society of Sisters,* 268 U.S. 510; *Meyer v.
      Nebraska,* 262 U.S. 390 (1923). One could argue that this area of law was never
      stabilized. The conservative position is that the notion of privacy doesn't lend
      itself to stabilization. On pragmatist grounds one wonders how we can know
      this in advance.

78   Crises do not always announce themselves in terms everyone identifies. When-
      ever normal constitutional practice cannot resolve some thorny issue of gov-
      ernmental structure or individual rights, identifying crises will be fairly ob-
      vious. It is not so obvious how to resolve these crises. Without a concept akin
      to revolutionary adjudication most of these crises cannot be resolved short of
      invoking the process in article 5.

79   *McCulloch v. Maryland,* 17 U.S. (4 Wheat.) 316 (1819).

80   Ibid.

81   Ibid.

82   Other constitutional actors, such as the executive and the legislative branches of
      government, have just as much responsibility as the courts in appreciating con-
      stitutional meaning. Historically, though, a structural feature of American con-
      stitutionalism requires the courts to make the final decision on constitutionality.

83   A critical cultural theory seeks a coherent cultural perspective, a perspective
      about American culture held by a (culturally) reasonable person. When no
      single perspective achieves this, a critical cultural theory seeks to identify the
      conflicting perspectives involved in our cultural wars.

84   A theory of mistakes is a method for determining when constitutional decisions
      are erroneous, which should follow from constitutional theory.

85   See Note, "Dualistic Legal Phenomena and the Limitations of Positivism," 86
      Colum. L. Rev. 823, 826 (1986).

86   5 U.S. (1 *Cranch*) 137 (1803).

87   See Deryck Beyleveld and Roger Brownsword, *Law as a Moral Judgment,* at
      423. Critical cultural theories include abstract components, but, in addition,
      they take particularized cultural conditions more seriously than do abstract
      moral and political theories. In fact, a critical cultural theory is related to com-

mon sense and reasonableness. See T. R. Powell, "The Logic and Rhetoric of Constitutional Law," at 85, 87. A principle is included in a critical cultural theory if a reasonable citizen, upon reflection, would endorse it. Such a procedure may not always yield one unequivocal answer. Indeed, there may exist more than one reasonable answer to many important constitutional matters. It may be a general feature of practical reasoning that, though being able to rule out many proposals, one is always left with two or more competing views, neither of which is decidable in terms of reason or law. In fact, two or perhaps three irreducible, general, moral, and political perspectives may exist that yield incompatible answers. R. J. Lipkin, "Beyond Skepticism." Justices often appeal, albeit tacitly, to principles of critical cultural theory in deciding cases. See Charles P. Curtis Jr., *Lions under the Throne* 332 (1947). If there are more than one equally reasonable competing principles in a critical cultural theory, a judge's appeal to this theory will produce a different constitutional result depending upon the judge. Ibid.

88   Cf. A. Bickel, *The Supreme Court and the Idea of Progress,* at 86 (arguing that justification of a constitutional judgment "turns on issues of moral philosophy and political theory, which we abstract from the common political process").

89   R. Dworkin, *Freedom's Law,* at 382. But see Charles Black, *Law as an Art,* at 6 (stating that in 1950 *Plessy* appeared to be "quite a serious piece of work"). Furthermore, the attitude toward blacks expressed in *Plessy* "predated the founding of the Republic and may even have preceded slavery in England's North American colonies." Charles A. Lofgren, *The Plessy Case: A Legal-Historical Interpretation* 7 (1987).

I do not know what evidence Dworkin has to support his sanguine view, because it seems clearly false. In fact, as late as 1956 more than half the population disapproved of integration. Jonathan D. Casper, *The Politics of Civil Liberties* 169 (1972). By 1963, probably as a result of *Brown,* almost two-thirds of the population approved of school integration. Ibid. at 16–70. See also Mark Tushnet, "Book Review," 57 *Tex. L. Rev.* 1295, 1303 (1979) (arguing that the significant Warren Court decisions were not endorsed by local, and probably not endorsed by national, majorities).

Besides, subsequent history during the civil rights movement seems to suggest that many Americans have no great commitment to real integration. D. Cornell, at 1169, n. 109. Look what happened in Yonkers in 1988 and 1989, when a federal judge found the city council guilty of contempt for failing over the course of forty years to provide low-income housing. Such recalcitrance can be explained only in terms of negative stereotypes concerning blacks and poor people. Indeed, stereotypes about blacks "serve a hegemonic function by perpetuating a mythology about both blacks *and* whites even today, reinforcing an illusion of a white community that cuts across ethnic, gender and class lines."

Kimberle Crenshaw, "Race, Reform, and Retrenchment: Transformation and Legitimation in Antidiscrimination Law," 101 *Harv. L. Rev.* 1331, 1371 (1988).

In 1954, Chief Justice Vinson himself was not ready to overrule *Plessy*. Bernard Schwartz, *Super Chief Earl Warren and His Supreme Court,* at 74–75. Similarly, Justices Clark and Jackson were originally disinclined to outlaw segregation. Ibid. at 88–89. Justice Black believed that the South would reject integration. Ibid. at 118. It is also arguable whether President Eisenhower ever believed that *Brown* had been decided correctly. Indeed, referring to the South, he told Warren: "These are not bad people. All they are concerned about is to see that their sweet little girls are not required to sit in school alongside some big black bucks." Ibid. at 112–13. See A. Bickel, *The Supreme Court and the Idea of Progress,* at 265–66 (describing Eisenhower's lack of commitment to the principle in *Brown*). In light of this judicial culture, the unanimity in *Brown* is astounding. See Richard Kluger, *Simple Justice: The History of Brown v. Board of Education and Black America's Struggle for Equality* 693–99 (1975).

What further evidence could we adduce as evidence against Dworkin's contention? One possible reply here is illuminating. Dworkin might respond that the law is not determined by polls; deeper moral and political convictions are involved, or, in my terms, judges often extract meaning from the wider political culture, transforming constitutional law. This is a complex process; it is unhelpful to describe this extraconstitutional meaning as already part of the law before the Court acts. One does not need to embrace conventionalism to recognize that law is restricted to what reasonable citizens say it is. When reasonable people disagree it is misleading to characterize as already law a judicial decision justifying one competing view. Rather, the judicial decision concerns revision, repair, and re-creation.

90   In order to distinguish his theory from conventionalism, from Dworkin's perspective, he must describe the judicial decision in *Brown* as law as it is, not law as it should be. If not, the law changed and equal protection contained a new constitutional paradigm. Dworkin cannot admit this. But see John Finnis, "On Reason and Authority in Law's Empire," 6 *Law & Phil.* 357, 376 (1987) (arguing that "Hercules' claim obscured the reality that conscientious judges do acknowledge that they are making new law, breaking new ground . . . by choice, a new commitment, not mere discovery and application").

91   Dworkin believes that "[t]he American people would almost unanimously have rejected [the rule in *Plessy*], even in 1954, as not faithful to their convictions about racial justice." R. Dworkin, *Law's Empire,* at 387. There are two important problems with Dworkin's argument. First, even if most people rejected the rule in *Plessy* in 1954, it does not follow that the principle in *Brown* was contained in the relativized constitutional theory of our Constitution. If

foundational constitutional decisions define what the Constitution means, then prior to *Brown* the Constitution permitted state-imposed racial segregation. Because these decisions are the basic building blocks or data of relativized constitutional theories, only by appealing to extrinsic theories can this decision be overturned. Second, as an empirical matter, it just seems wrong to contend that the right Dworkin advocates was part of the political culture of the time. Perhaps some reasonable citizens endorsed such a right, but other reasonable citizens did not. In the final analysis Dworkin conflates the relativized theory with the critical cultural theory. In essence, his view assumes that the critical cultural theory is as authoritative as the relativized theory in determining the law. This conceals the revolutionary dimension of appealing to the critical cultural theory. However, it does give added significance to the idea of a "living Constitution," and if Dworkin's account recognizes that revolutionary adjudication is what makes the Constitution live, then it is closer to the theory of constitutional revolutions than Dworkin would lead us to believe in arguing against constitutional pragmatism.

92   Simple abhorrence, or any other preference, is not sufficient for inclusion in the critical cultural theory. Instead, individuals must reflect in an unbiased, informed manner, considering arguments in favor of their position as well as those in favor of their opponents. A culture's commitments are not determined statistically. Nevertheless, antiabortion proponents could argue that protecting abortion rights is not sufficiently grounded in critical cultural theory to warrant characterizing that culture as proabortion.

93   Two qualifications are in order. First, abstract theory is not a uniform conception we can identify and utilize throughout different stages of American history. Second, slave owners, following Locke, believed that the right to own slaves was an abstract moral right. Thus, whenever applying this framework for classifying theories, we need to ask, "Abstract according to whom?" Distinguish also between what a thinker abstractly holds and what his abstract theories imply. That Aristotle approved of slavery, therefore, does not mean slavery is an ineluctable element in his theory of practical reasoning and virtue.

94   347 U.S. 483 (1954).

95   163 U.S. 537 (1896).

96   Just prior to *Brown* several cases progressively revealed discomfort with *Plessy: McLaurin v. Oklahoma State Regents,* 339 U.S. 637 (1950); *Sweatt v. Painter,* 339 U.S. 629 (1950); *Sipuel v. Board of Regents,* 332 U.S. 631 (1948); *Missouri ex rel. Gaines v. Canada,* 305 U.S. 337 (1938); *Gong Lum v. Rice,* 275 U.S. 78 (1927); *Cumming v. Board of Education,* 175 U.S. 528 (1899). The seeds of the revolution can be observed in a discrete number of prior cases; this is one way a constitutional revolution occurs.

97   Kai Nielsen, *Equality and Liberty: A Defense of Radical Egalitarianism* 27 (1985).

98   The theory of constitutional revolutions is Kuhnian as a theory of constitutional moments; it also includes a Rawlsian theory of judicial reasoning.

99   This methodology, a pragmatic methodology, was popularized by J. Rawls, *A Theory of Justice*, 48–51 (describing how reflective equilibrium works). See also Alvin I. Goldman, *Epistemology and Cognition* 66 (1986) (endorsing reflective equilibrium as a method in epistemology); Norman Daniels, "Reflective Equilibrium and Archimedean Points," 10 *Can. J. Phil.* 83 (1980). The origins of wide reflective equilibrium go back to the work of Willard van Orman Quine and Nelson Goodman, if not as far back as Socrates.

Considered constitutional values in constructing a constitutional theory are akin to moral intuitions in ethical theory construction. R. M. Hare, *Moral Thinking: Its Levels, Method, and Point* 11 (1981) (contrasting the allegedly different epistemic roles of linguistic and moral intuitions). See also R. M. Hare, "Liberty and Equality: How Politics Masquerades as Philosophy," in *Liberty and Equality* 1, 3, 6 (Ellen Frankel Paul et al. eds. 1985) (all illustrating Hare's ethical formalism); R. M. Hare, "Rawls' Theory of Justice," in *Reading Rawls* 81 (Norman Daniels ed. 1975); Peter Singer, "Sidgwick and Reflective Equilibrium," 58 *The Monist* 490, 516 (1974) (denigrating the role of intuitions in ethical theory). Cf. W. V. O. Quine, "Truth and Explanation in Ethics," 96 *Ethics* 524, 530 (distinguishing three kinds of moral intuitions).

100   In evaluating a constitutional theory, we test it against our considered beliefs and certain formal or metatheoretical factors. A theory should conform to our critical constitutional values, but it should also be elegant. A theory is elegant when it is simple, general, fecund, and reenforced or supported by theories in other domains. W. Quinn and J. Ullian, *The Web of Belief* (1970); W. V. O. Quine, "Posits and Reality," in *The Ways of Paradox* (1966) (describing various metatheoretical virtues such as fecundity and simplicity).

101   One must be certain here not to beg a number of questions. I do not claim that the description of this perspective is uncontestable; nor do I claim that this perspective guarantees consensus. Rather, I'm suggesting that it is a pragmatically verifiable fact that certain perspectives ("states of mind") are better than others for generating our favored judgments.

102   For a more extensive discussion of wide reflective equilibrium, see R. J. Lipkin, "Indeterminacy, Justification, and Truth," at 638–42; Lipkin, "Kibitzers, Fuzzies, and Apes without Tails," at 69; Lipkin, "Beyond Skepticism," at 865–77; Lipkin, "The Anatomy of Constitutional Revolutions," at 723–26, n. 94–96.

103   How would a judge write a judicial opinion according to the theory of constitutional revolutions? Would she write a homily? A story? In my estimation a revolutionary judicial opinion has three salient parts. Part 1 should be a comprehensive statement of the relevant principles of law. The second part

should show why the answer that follows from these legal principles is morally, politically, or practically wrong. And the third part should be a coherent revised statement of political philosophy supporting a novel answer to the question.

4   The Historical Defense of the Theory

1   Van Alstyne's examination of *Marbury* is an exemplar in this regard. William Van Alstyne, "A Critical Guide to *Marbury v. Madison,*" 1969 *Duke L. J.* 1.

2   See Jeffrey Shaman, "Constitutional Fact"; and J. Shaman, "The Constitution, the Supreme Court, and Creativity."

3   For some purposes American constitutional history can be divided into three periods. During the first period, from the Founding through the Civil War, the central constitutional theme "was directed toward forging as strong a national union as law could produce." A. S. Miller and R. F. Howell, "The Myth of Neutrality," in *Judicial Review and the Supreme Court* 1, 198, 213 (L. Levy ed. 1967). But see L. Tribe, *American Constitutional Law,* at 3 (arguing that the Marshall period was based on the model of checks and balances and a federalism giving the states their proper autonomy). The second period, from 1870 to 1937, found the Court struggling with the appropriate role of government in economic and social affairs. Finally, the last period, from 1937 to the present, saw the greatest movement toward big government, and toward protecting individual civil rights and liberties.

4   347 U.S. 483 (1954). Dworkin contends that it is possible to argue that slavery was unconstitutional prior to the Thirteenth Amendment. Ronald Dworkin, "The Law of the Slave-catchers," *Times Literary Supplement* 1437 (December 5, 1975). See Christopher Eisgruber, "Justice Story, Slavery, and the Natural Law Foundations of American Constitutionalism," 55 *U. Chi. L. Rev.* 273, 325 (1988) (arguing that Dworkin fails to "distinguish philosophy grounded in experience from philosophy that is speculative, theoretical and visionary").

5   T. Kuhn, *The Structure of Scientific Revolutions,* at 181. The type of change must significantly change the way the relevant constitutional provision is conceptualized. Many constitutional revolutions, though not all, have a revolutionary impact on everyday lives. For example, consider the words of Judge Anthony Kennedy during his confirmation hearings before the Senate Judiciary Committee: "Well, the *Miranda* rule, as I say, is in place; it was a sweeping, sweeping rule. It wrought . . . it was almost a revolution. And it [is] not clear to me that it necessarily followed from the words of the Constitution. Yet it is in place now, and I think it's entitled to great respect." In response to questions by Senator Leahy, December 15, 1987. Kennedy, a conservative Reagan

appointee, clearly raises doubts that the particular rule follows from the Constitution. Yet he concedes that the results of revolutionary adjudication are sometimes, at least, legitimate. Given public awareness of the *Miranda* rule, reversing it would have catastrophic effects.

6   Of course, some cases in casebooks are examples of normal adjudication. However, this leaves an enormous number of normal cases in the reporters, and even more cases never litigated because of their obvious solutions.

7   Constitutional revolutions also occur when the Court renders a constitutional provision a dead letter, as in the *Slaughterhouse Cases.*

8   The relevant phrase, "New States may be admitted by the Congress into this Union," fails to include the phrase "on an equal basis." For a description of the history of this provision, see C. Curtis, at 4–7.

9   Ibid.

10 This is a clear example of contraconstitutional interpretation as distinguished from extraconstitutional interpretation. The former permits a reading of a constitutional provision that conflicts with the original interpretation of its language, whereas extraconstitutional interpretation permits "whatever interpretive means are appropriate to breathe precisely the same evolutionary interpretive life into the Constitution that Madison envisioned in *The Federalist* No. 49." R. Clinton, "Original Understanding, Legal Realism, and the Interpretation of 'This Constitution.'" In this view extraconstitutional interpretation is evolutionary and legitimate, whereas contraconstitutional interpretation is revolutionary and illegitimate. Id. See M. Perry, *The Constitution, the Court, and Human Rights,* at 20. The reason for skepticism concerning this distinction is that we lack any reliable procedure for determining when an addition reverses constitutional meaning or adds to it. In either case, factors beyond the Constitution determine the result.

11 C. Curtis, at 3.

12 A. Cox, *The Role of the Supreme Court in American Government* 12 (1976).

13 Ibid.

14 There are many different senses of the term "judicial review." Two broad senses roughly correspond to a procedural/substantive distinction. W. Van Alstyne, "A Critical Guide to *Marbury v. Madison,*" at 23–24. Furthermore, the character of judicial review varies in different political and judicial systems. See generally David Deener, "Judicial Review in Modern Constitutional Systems," 46 *Am. Pol. Sci.* 1079 (1952). See also E. McWhinney, *Judicial Review in the English-Speaking World* (1965).

15 Textualists and originalists are especially bothered by the question of legitimacy. They argue that the countermajoritarian problem is resolved or diminished by following the text of the Constitution, or, where interpretation is required, by interpreting the Constitution in terms of the Framers' original

understanding. However, neither textualism nor originalism resolves the countermajoritarian challenge. Both methods permit judicial review and the cancellation of majoritarian policies. See E. Chemerinsky, *Interpreting the Constitution* 11 (1987). Furthermore, a careful inspection of the early revolutionary years makes it clear that a written constitution was *not* designed to replace appeals to extrinsic constitutional sources. See Suzanna Sherry, "The Founders' Unwritten Constitution," 54 *U. Chi. L. Rev.* 1127 (1987) (arguing that the Founders intended both the written Constitution and natural law to serve as sources of law). See also Bernard Bailyn, *The Ideological Origins of the American Revolution* 184–98 (1967) (describing the reliance on natural law during the period prior to the Revolution).

One writer contends that the relevant "original understanding" or "intentions" are not the Founders', but that of the parties to the compact, the states. H. J. Powell, "The Original Understanding of Original Intent," 98 *Harv. L. Rev.* 885 (1985). See also Thomas Grey, "Constitutionalism: An Analytic Framework," in *Constitutionalism* 189, 202–3 (J. Pennock and J. Chapman, eds. 1979) (arguing that normative principles of ethics and politics have always been an accepted source of constitutional norms); H. J. Powell, "Rules for Originalists," 73 *Va. L. Rev.* 659 (1987) (describing the limited role of history in constitutional interpretation).

16   Christopher Wolfe, "A Theory of U.S. Constitutional History," 43 *J. Pol.* 292, 313–14 (1981) (arguing that there are three kinds of judicial review: narrow, broad and loose).

17   Joseph Grano, "Judicial Review and a Written Constitution in a Democratic Society," 28 *Wayne L. Rev.* 1, 12 (1981).

18   Ibid. But see Robert Sedler, "The Legitimacy Debate in Constitutional Adjudication: An Assessment and a Different Perspective," 44 *Ohio St. L. J.* 93, 113 (1983) (arguing that "the Court's institutional behavior does not indicate that the Court recognizes any distinction between interpretive and noninterpretive review").

19   J. Grano, "Judicial Review," at 11.

20   Furthermore, interpretivist review requires a political justification, a justification not found in the Constitution's text, history, structure, or logic. Thus, interpretivism, if true, can only be justified by an appeal to noninterpretivist principles.

21   U.S. Constitution, art. 2, cl. 1; art. 2, sec. 3.

22   See Jesse Choper, *Judicial Review and the National Political Process* 61 (1980) (stating that "the Constitution consists of a mass of anti-majoritarian imperatives"). See also Carl Wellington, "The Nature of Judicial Review," 91 *Yale L. J.* 486 (1982).

23   For a comparative point about our northern neighbors, see B. Strayer, *The*

Canadian Constitution and the Courts 53 (1983) (describing the counterma-joritarian problem concerning the Canadian constitution).

24 The countermajoritarian problem becomes troublesome depending upon whose ox is gored. Conservatives raise the problem when the Court is liberal. Liberals raise the problem when the Court is conservative. Cf. Wallace Mendelson, "Jefferson on Judicial Review: Consistency through Change," 29 *U. Chi. L. Rev.* 327 (1962) (describing Jefferson's attitude toward the Court as depending upon how tyrannical in any given period he thought the Court was).

25 One could argue that when the majoritarian branches of government act in a countermajoritarian fashion, they present less danger than when the Court does the same. Remedying Congress's defective interpretation of a constitutional provision can be overturned by majoritarian means, whereas court decisions generally can be reversed only by the Court or through constitutional amendment. However, when there is a right answer to a constitutional problem overlooked by the legislature, the present majority is countermajoritarian with regard to our continuing *constitutional* majority.

26 See B. Strayer, *Canadian Constitution*. See also M. Cappelletti and John Adams, "Judicial Review of Legislation: European Antecedents and Adaptations," 79 *Harv. L. Rev.* 1207, 1224 (1966) (characterizing the value of judicial review as a "sobering and ennobling experience that befalls those who check their acts against their principles and strive in performing the former never to lose sight of the latter").

27 Majoritarian democracy defines the "community's will" simply as the majority decision (with or without side constraints); however it is calculated, it derives from the aggregated decisions of individuals. A different form of democracy insists on two levels of the people's will. First, what do the people want? Then, what do they reflectively judge concerning public policy after their wants are filtered through a series of deliberative processes? Judicial review is one such process. Judicial review enables the polity to function in the way a pragmatic individual functions, that is, it gives her important critical distance or a second-look at her first-order judgments.

28 Besides the formative revolutions, Marshall's pragmatic creativity can be seen in his response to federal judge Richard Peters's query concerning when a judge should set aside the verdict in a jury trial due to irregularities during the trial. Marshall writes that "if [he] approved the verdict [he] would let it stand; if [he] did not, although [his] disapprobation might not be sufficient to set it aside had all been perfectly *en regle*, [he] would avail himself of the irregularity to award a new trial." Jean Edward Smith, *John Marshall: Definer of a Nation* 426 (1996).

29 Consider the following example of the present perspective fallacy:

When our government was created as a federal system, it was evident that the Supreme court would be the umpire. As the head of the hierarchy of the federal courts, and, on some questions, of the state courts also, it had the final power to review all questions of the federal division of powers and of jurisdiction; this was recognized in the debates on the convention and in *The Federalist* papers. It was a power decried by foes and defended by supporters. But there was little doubt it existed under the Constitution. It only remained for the statesmanship of John Marshall to show its uses in strengthening the new federal government. There was talk of resistance in some of the states. There was annoyance on the part of Jefferson. But the great Federalist (nationalist) jurist won out. The logic of our national development fought on his side. (William Yawed Elliott, *The Need for Constitutional Reform* 147 [1935])

30   5 U.S. (1 Cranch) 137 (1803). The first instance of judicial review by the Supreme Court occurred in *Hylton v. United States,* 3 U.S. (3 Dall.) 171 (1796) (upholding a congressional tax on carriages). In this case the three separate opinions "paid little heed to the Constitution's words." David Currie, "The Constitution in the Supreme Court," 48 *U. Chi. L. Rev.* 819, 855 (1981). Instead, "[p]olicy considerations dominated all three opinions." Id. at 856. The concept of judicial review goes back at least as far as Dr. Bonam's Case, 77 *Eng. Rep.* 638 (C. P. 1610). There Lord Coke adopted a naturalist conception of law, insisting that acts of Parliament were void when inconsistent with "common right and reason." Ibid. at 652.

31   The results of the Philadelphia Convention were themselves revolutionary in that scrapping the Articles of Confederation and designing a new Constitution exceeded the authority of the convention. Michael Kammen, ed., *The Origins of the American Constitution: A Documentary History* xix (1986) [hereafter *Origins*]. Ackerman's dualism rests on this arguably illegal act by the Framers. Bruce Ackerman, 1 *We the People.* The fundamental defect in the Articles of Confederation was that the document did not create "a government at all, but rather the central agency of an alliance." Edward Corwin, "The Progress of Constitutional Theory between the Declaration of Independence and the Meaning of the Philadelphia Convention," 30 *Amer. Hist. Rev.* 511, 527 (1925). See also *The Federalist* No. 15. In other words, its defect was that it was a compact among the states and not among the people. This is not to deny that even the Articles of Confederation had a rudimentary federal system, but its defects were too numerous for salvaging it. For a list of the defects in the Articles of Confederation, see Max Farrand, "The Federal Constitution and the Defects of the Confederation," 2 *Amer. Pol. Sci. Rev.* 132, 149 (1908). Leonard Levy, "The Making of the Constitution," in *A Grand Experiment: The Constitution at 200: Essays from the Douglass Adair Symposia* 1, 5 (J. Moore Jr. and J. Murphy eds. 1987).

32   J. Thayer, "The Origin and Scope of the American Doctrine of Constitutional Law," in *Essays in Constitutional Law*, at 71. See also Learned Hand, *The Bill of Rights* 15–18 (1958). See *Northwestern Symposium*.

33   In this regime the Court is presupposed to uphold the constitutionality of a statute, except when it must decide that the statute is clearly erroneous.

34   J. Thayer, "The Origin and Scope of the American Doctrine of Constitutional Law," at 410.

35   Cf. R. McCloskey, "Introduction," in *Essays in Constitutional Law*, at 12 ("If judicial review as we know it in America can be justified at all, it must be justified as an attempt by men to think coherently about the ordering of human affairs").

36   Because Marshall never invalidated another congressional statute, this might not appear obvious. However, Marshall's broad interpretations of constitutional text — interpretations that expressed the political philosophy of nationalism — clearly transcend the Thayerian imperative. For an interesting extension of this imperative, see Mark Tushnet, *Taking the Constitution Away from the Courts* (1999).

37   For perhaps the most comprehensive critique on this subject, see W. Van Alstyne, at 37 ("There is . . . no doctrine of national, substantive judicial supremacy which inexorably flows from *Marbury v. Madison itself*"). Others include: Edward Corwin, "*Marbury v. Madison* and the Doctrine of Judicial Review," 12 *Mich. L. Rev.* 538 (1914); B. Thayer, "The Origin and Scope of the American Doctrine of Constitutional Law," at 143–44 (arguing that judicial review might have been construed to apply only when the legislature's mistake "is not open to rational question"); C. Warren, *The Supreme Court in United States History* 232, 242–43 (1926) ("It seems plain . . . that it would have been possible for Marshall, if he had been so inclined, to have construed the language of the section of the Judiciary Act which authorized writs of mandamus, in such a manner as to have enabled him to escape the necessity of declaring the section unconstitutional"); L. Hand, *The Bill of Rights*, at 1–11; J. Ely, *Democracy and Distrust* 186, n. 11 (1980); L. Levy, *Judicial Review and the Supreme Court* (1967).

38   Felix Frankfurter, "John Marshall and the Judicial Function," 69 *Harv. L. Rev.* 217, 219 (1955) ("The courage of *Marbury v. Madison* is not minimized by suggesting that its reasoning is not impeccable and its conclusion, however wise, not inevitable"). This recognizes but does not candidly state that wisdom dictates propriety in American constitutional practice.

39   L. Tribe, *American Constitutional Law*, at 25.

40   W. Crosskey, *Politics and the Constitution*, at 944–75. Furthermore, Hamilton believed judicial review to be an essential part of judicial prerogative. Nevertheless, the practice of judicial review was an assumed power. *Origins*, at xii. No

consensus on this issue existed. Moreover, it is not obvious that even Hamilton's view supports the practice of judicial review as it developed over the years.

41   F. Aumman, *The Changing American Legal System* 193 (1969).

42   See generally S. Bloch and M. Marcus, "John Marshall's Selective Use of History in *Marbury v. Madison*," 1986 *Wis. L. Rev.* 301. Without a relatively obvious procedure for determining when a concept is implicit in the Constitution, the term "implicit" distorts constitutional reasoning, usually in favor of its proponent's position.

43   Some state courts engaged in judicial review. However, even if all state courts did so, why should that be a reason for assuming that the federal judicial function necessarily includes review?

44   There is some evidence that Marshall achieved this goal. A. Cox at 16, 29–30.

45   These principles need to fit with judicial practice, yet in most cases they do not.

46   I do not mean to suggest that most scholars contend that the decision in *Marbury* is wrong. Marshall's "judicial reasoning" comes under attack, not his result. Some scholars, however, are candid in crediting Marshall with creating modern judicial review. Sylvia Snowiss, *Judicial Review and the Law of the Constitution* (1990).

47   R. Dworkin, *Law's Empire* at 356.

48   Ibid.

49   One standard argument is that there were preconstitutional precedents for judicial review in the state governments. But why should these precedents normatively entail federal judicial review?

50   See R. Dworkin, *Law's Empire*.

51   Dworkin uses the model of a chain novel to explain constitutional adjudication. R. Dworkin, *Law's Empire*, at 228. But see R. J. Lipkin, "Conventionalism, Pragmatism, and Constitutional Revolutions," at 669–77. However, it is not at all clear that at the early stages of a novel there must be, or that there can be, a discernible structure indicating *the* right way to continue the story.

52   See generally M. White, *Philosophy, The Federalist, and the Constitution* (1987).

53   Here I am taking liberties with Alasdair MacIntyre's interesting argument concerning the superiority of scientific paradigms. MacIntyre argues that epistemological crises are remedied by reconstructing the tradition in which two apparently incompatible paradigms operate in order to compare and evaluate them. MacIntyre, "Crises, Narrative, and Science," in *Paradigms and Revolutions* 54, 70 (1970). MacIntyre's theory echoes Dworkin's argument. Each writer believes respectively that the best scientific methodology or the best jurisprudential methodology is the one making the history of the field — science or law — the best it can be. Ibid. at 120. See Dworkin, *Law's Empire*, at 52.

54   *Marbury* was the first case in which the Court struck down a federal statute. However, in *Hayburn's Case*, 2 U.S. (2 *Dall.*) 409 (1792), the justices, sitting

on the circuit courts, decided that the Court could not be compelled to give advisory opinions to the president. Additionally, in *Hylton v. United States,* 3 U.S. (3 Dall.) 171 (1796), the Supreme Court held that a federal tax on carriages was constitutional. Finally, in *Calder v. Bull,* 3 U.S. (3 Dall.) 386 (1798), the Court held a state law to be an ex post facto law, and therefore unconstitutional.

55   *The Federalist Papers* No. 78.

56   See Jean Edward Smith, *John Marshall,* at 315.

57   Paul W. Kahn argued that Marshall's form of constitutional adjudication fused political science (reason) with popular consent (will). The object of consent was the Constitution, and the content of the Constitution was explicated in terms of political science. In short, Marshall appealed to factors extrinsic to the Constitution — reason and science — to be the source of constitutional meaning. Paul W. Kahn, "Reason and Will in the Origins of American Constitutionalism," 98 *Yale L. J.* 449, 479–87 (1989). This view supports the contention that Marshall's form of constitutional interpretation was pragmatic and revolutionary.

58   See Robert Gordon, "Critical Legal Histories," 36 *Stan. L. Rev.* 57, 71 (1984).

59   See T. R. Powell, "The Logic and Rhetoric of Constitutional Law," at 85.

60   It is important to point out that merely *saying* that the structure, or intent, or history of the Constitution requires or permits a particular statute does not make it so. Because these terms were originally introduced to provide a method for settling constitutional controversies, their utility is limited because they simply replicate the substantive controversy on a methodological level. If we cannot agree substantively about first-order constitutional values, how can we find a second-order value that provides an exceptionless methodology for settling first-order disputes?

61   Relativistic constitutional theory cannot explain Marshall's creation of judicial review. Rather than explaining or justifying judicial review, the relativistic constitutional theory itself depends on judicial review for its existence.

62   However, many provisions of the Constitution do not lend themselves to revolutionary adjudication. Instead, these provisions are constitutional paradigms that control normal adjudication. In such circumstances ordinary constitutional conventions such as the Constitution's text, intent, history, structure, or logic can be used to decide constitutional issues.

63   14 U.S. (1 *Wheat.*) 304 (1816).

64   In *Martin* the state's argument was that the U.S. Supreme Court could not exercise jurisdiction over a state supreme court.

65   See C. Warren, "Legislative and Judicial Attacks on the Supreme Court of the United States — A History of the Twenty-Fifth Section of the Judiciary Act," 47 *Am. L. Rev.* 1, 161 (1913).

66   Imagine in 1803 arguments, from skeptics like Bork, that the Constitution

contains neither the language "judicial review," nor the intent to create such an institution.

67 There may be good reasons for uniformity in federal law, but the Court fails to state what these reasons might be. The Court needs to state why the reasons for uniformity should prevail over diversity, especially when diversity enables the states to exercise their sovereignty. Certainly, diversity and pluralism might result from different states interpreting the federal constitution in different ways. In that event one could vote with one's feet against the state judiciary's interpretation of the Constitution in one's state. Certainly, a conception of federalism is served in this scenario.

68 W. Crosskey, *Origins,* at xvi.

69 There is an interesting parallel between the argument over federalism that existed between Federalists and Anti-Federalists, and the contemporary debate between those favoring a strong federal government to guarantee individual rights against state majorities and those who want state majorities to be relatively supreme. Anti-Federalists would come down on the side of individual rights against the federal government. Federalists would endorse a strong national government and a limited conception of individual rights, except for property rights. Since the adoption of the Fourteenth Amendment, the controversy must be realigned. Conservatives come down on the side of state majorities against individual rights guaranteed by the federal courts. Liberals choose a strong federal court system guaranteeing individual rights against state majorities. Marshall and Jefferson initiated this controversy, although it began in different terms. C. Warren, *The Supreme Court in United States History,* 169–230 (1922).

70 14 U.S. (1 Wheat.) 304, 350 (1816).

71 "Note, Judge Spencer Roane of Virginia: Champion of States' Rights Foe of John Marshall," 66 *Harv. L. Rev.* 1242, 1256 (1953).

72 He continues:

> [It] seems to me Congress could have provided for this even without an article III, simply by creating a court and endowing it with the power to perform this necessary and proper function. Insofar, then, as legitimacy in origin is relevant to judicial or public attitude toward the judicial work, the Court ought to feel no slightest embarrassment about its work of reviewing state acts for their federal constitutionality. It seems very clear, moreover, that all present-day political considerations strongly impel toward the same conclusion. In policing the actions of the states for their conformity to federal constitutional guarantees, the Court represents the whole nation, and therefore the whole nation's interest in seeing those guarantees prevail, in their spirit and in their entirety.
> (C. Black, *Structure and Relationship in Constitutional Law* 74–75 [1969])

See L. Tribe, *American Constitutional Law,* at 13, n. 7 (arguing that the result in *Martin* "was quite plainly compelled by the structure of the federal system"). See also O. Holmes, *Collected Legal Papers* 295–96 (1920) ("I do not think the United States would come to an end if [the Court] lost [its] power to declare an Act of Congress void. I do think that the Union would be imperiled if we could not make that declaration as to the laws of the several States. For one in my place sees how often a local policy prevails with those who are not trained to national views and how often action is taken that embodies what the commerce clause was meant to end"). Both Tribe and Holmes are better understood as asserting that the necessity of federal judicial supremacy refers to a particular *conception* of the Union, rather than the Union under any description. True, a "union" in which federal courts could not reverse state court decisions might be, from our point of view at least, less unified than our present system; it is nevertheless possible for such a system to work, respecting the continuing commitment to the equal sovereignty of the states. Consequently, nothing compels federal judicial supremacy except the conclusory view that structure entails it. There are many kinds of republics and many reasons for or against federal judicial supremacy. See D. Currie, "The Constitution in the Supreme Court: The Powers of the Federal Courts 1801–35," 49 *U. Chi. L. Rev.* 646, 685–86 (1982).

73 C. Black, *Structure and Relationship in Constitutional Law,* at 74–75.

74 A useful definition of federalism is "that system of political order in which powers of government are separated and distinguished and in which these powers are distributed among governments, each government having its quota of authority and each its distinct sphere of activity." A. McLauglin, "The Background of American Federalism," 12 *Am. Pol. Sci. Rev.* 15 (1918).

75 See G. Stone, L. Seidman, C. Sunstein, and M. Tushnet, *Constitutional Law* 43 (1986).

76 Federalism as a structural principle of American Constitutionalism suffers from two major defects. First, nowhere in the Constitution does it *say* that the United States Republic is a federalist one. Moreover, if it implies a federal structure, it does not imply a particular conception of federalism. Therefore, like penumbras and emanations, judicial opinions resting on some ill-defined notion of federalism encourage judicial tyranny.

77 C. Warren, *The Supreme Court and Sovereign States* 3–13 (1972).

78 Consider: "Where a federal judicial construct is found not to extend to certain official behavior because of institutional concerns rather than analytical perceptions, it [is] strange to regard the resulting decision as a statement about the meaning of the constitutional norm in question. . . . [C]onstitutional norms which are underenforced by the federal judiciary should be understood to be legally valid to their full conceptual limits, and federal judicial decisions which

stop short of these limits should be understood as delineating only the boundaries of the federal courts' role in enforcing the norm: By 'legally valid,' I mean that the unenforced margins of underenforced norms should have the full status of positive law which we generally accord to the norms of our Constitution." L. Sager, "Fair Measures: The Legal Status of Underenforced Constitutional Norms," 91 *Harv. L. Rev.* 1212, 1221 (1978).

79   Essentially, American federalism attempts to "enable the American people to secure the benefits of national union without imperilling their republican institutions. E. Corwin, "The Passing of Dual Federalism," in *Essays in Constitutional Law,* at 185, 207. Not everyone believed that states' sovereignty would survive ratification of the Constitution. Federalists insisted that it would, though Anti-Federalists believed that ratification would create a perpetual union. K. Stampp, "The Concept of a Perpetual Union," 65 *J. Amer. Hist.* 5, 18 (1978).

80   D. Currie, "The Constitution in the Supreme Court."

81   19 U.S. (6 Wheat.) 264 (1821).

82   *Cohens v. Virginia,* 19 U.S. (6 Wheat.) 264 (1821).

83   A. Kelly and W. Harbison, *The American Constitution: Its Origins and Development* 287–88 (1970).

84   This controversy over states' powers was ultimately resolved by the Civil War.

85   See generally C. Beard, *An Economic Interpretation of the Constitution of the United States* (1913).

86   A. Miller, *The Secret Constitution and the Need for Constitutional Change* 17 (1987). But see R. Bork, *The Tempting of America,* at 21 (arguing that Marshall's decisions were faithful to the Constitution).

87   17 U.S. (4 Wheat.) 316 (1819). In an earlier case, *United States v. Fischer,* 6 U.S. (2 Cranch) 358 (1805), the Court interpreted the necessary and proper clause to uphold federal legislation.

88   See Nowak et al., *Constitutional Law,* at 124–30.

89   Thomas Jefferson, "Opinion on the Constitutionality of the Bill for Establishing a National Bank," in 19 *Papers of Thomas Jefferson* 275, 278 (J. Boyd ed. 1974). But see Alexander Hamilton, "Final Version of an Opinion on the Constitutionality of an Act to Establish a Bank," in 8 *Papers of Alexander Hamilton* 97, 102–3 (H. Syrett ed. 1965).

90   But see B. Siegen, *The Supreme Court's Constitution* 11–14 (1987) (arguing that the decision in *McCulloch* reflects a very different political philosophy than the one endorsed by Hamilton and Madison). Indeed, Marshall fails to mention that the Philadelphia Convention rejected Madison's proposal to include a provision authorizing a national bank in the text of the Constitution. This is just the sort of evidence the classical view regards as dispositive, or at least presumptively valid.

91 Marshall clearly sided with the Federalists against the Anti-Federalists in a struggle that persists today over the proper role of government. It is not obvious that the contemporary mind has the capacity to appreciate the fact that the inevitable Federalist victory was not, at the time, considered inevitable. See F. Broderick, *The Origins of the Constitution* 59 (1964) (describing the battle over ratification in Virginia).

92 Ibid.

93 J. Taylor, *Construction Construed and Constitutions Vindicated* 177 (1820) ("But this interpolation of the words, 'convenient, useful and essential,' into the constitution is in my view not even a plausible argument. It is merely a tautology of the phrase 'necessary and proper,' but excluding the restriction attached to the latter").

94 One argument Marshall advances equates "necessary means" with "best means." In this view if M is the best means to E, then M is necessary. To deny that Congress may take action in this sense of "necessary," is "[t]o have declared that the best means shall not be used, but those alone, without which the power given would be nugatory, would have been to deprive the legislature of the capacity to avail itself of experience, to exercise its reason, and to accommodate its legislation to circumstances. If we apply this principle of construction to any of the powers of the government, we shall find it so pernicious in its operation that we shall be compelled to discard it." *McCulloch v. Maryland,* 17 U.S. (4 Wheat.) 316 (1819).

   One can argue that when Congress declares that X is the best means, the Court should defer and declare it necessary. But it is unclear why this should be so. If the necessary and proper clause is designed to restrict legislative choice, then in taking this route the Court amends the Constitution, that is, the meaning of "necessary" changes to "most conducive." And that is revolutionary adjudication. One could argue that reason compels us to accept the principle of legislative discretion. Consequently, if you want a legislature, you must accept legislative discretion. Yet this proposition is clearly false. Having a legislature such as ours may require legislative discretion. However, a more limited government does not need this discretion, and, indeed, it was the hope of some that the American legislature would be limited.

95 J. Boyd White, *When Words Lose Meaning*, at 24–63.

96 See R. Brown, *Society as Text: Essays on Rhetoric, Reason, and Reality* 148 (1987).

97 *McCulloch v. Maryland,* 17 U.S. (4 Wheat.) 316 (1819). This led Justice Frankfurter to reply that "[p]recisely *because* 'it is a *constitution* we are expounding,' we ought not to take liberties with it." *National Mutual Insurance Co. v. Tidewater Transfer Co.,* 337 U.S. 582, 647 (1949) (Frankfurter, J., dissenting). See also Philip Kurland, "Curia Regis: Some Comments on the Divine Right of Kings and Courts 'To Say What the Law Is,'" 23 *Ariz. L. Rev.* 581, 591 (1981).

However, it is not obvious that *interpreting* a constitution in terms of our contemporary understanding is "taking liberties with it." Indeed, there are powerful arguments that we avoid taking liberties with the language of the Constitution only by interpreting a Constitution in the context of our contemporary interpretive community.

98   Such middle-theoretical factors as structure, intent, history, or logic are useful considerations in normal adjudication, but function as a talismanic display in revolutionary adjudication.

99   I take libertarians to be making such an argument. No doubt our society would be very different had Marshall adopted such a position; it probably would render our society less vibrant. However, that does not change the point that Marshall's argument does not involve normal adjudication. In normal constitutional adjudication, the text, intent, history, structure, and logic of the Constitution determine the outcome.

It is important to note that the current controversy over judicial review has its roots in the Marshall Court. Those advocating a narrow role for judicial review are still concerned about its legitimacy. In one very important sense judicial review, as Marshall conceived it, is not legitimate; it never was authorized by the Constitution. Indeed, Marshall was the first truly revolutionary justice: "Chief among the founders of American constitutional law was John Marshall. A maker rather than a follower of precedents, he never hesitated to argue from principles of right and justice. . . . Certainly, he did not hesitate to go beyond the express statements of a written constitution to find bases for his decisions." B. Wright Jr., *American Interpretations of Natural Law* 294–95 (1931). Marshall wrote that "[i]n exploring an unbeaten path, with few, if any aids, from precedents or written law, the court has found it necessary to rely much on general principles." The *Schooner Exchange v. M'Faddon*, 11 U.S. (7 Cranch) 116, 136 (1812). On the other hand, Marshall's conception of judicial review is now a fundamental tenet of American constitutionalism. Narrowing judicial review flies in the face of the nature of constitutional practice.

100   *McCulloch v. Maryland* 17 U.S. (4 Wheat.) 316 (1819).

101   Ibid.

102   Black also argues against linguistic or textual analysis in favor of structuralism. Consider:

I am inclined to think well of the method of reasoning from structure and relation. [B]ecause to succeed it has to make sense — current, practical sense. The textual-explication method, operating on general language, may often — perhaps more often than not — be made to make sense, by legitimate enough devices of interpretation. But it contains within itself no guarantee that it will make sense, for a court may always present itself or even see itself as being bound by the stated intent, however nonsensical, of somebody else. [Using a structural approach,] we can and must begin to argue at once about the practicalities and proprieties of the thing, without getting out dictionaries whose entries will not really respond to the question we are putting, or scanning utterances, contemporary with the text, of persons who did not really face the question we are asking. We will have to deal with policy and not with grammar. (C. Black, *Structure and Relationship in Constitutional Law*, at 23)

Thus stated, Black's account of structural analysis sounds very much like pragmatism.

103   *McCulloch v. Maryland*, at 415 (emphasis in original).

104   W. Berns, *Taking the Constitution Seriously* 207–8 (1987).

105   C. Black, *Structure and Relationship in Constitutional Law*, at 15.

106   This is not limited to the Supreme Court or judicial decision making generally. In any complex, fecund practice involving a text, actors determine the text through deliberative debates over appropriate applications. The text is still relevant in determining the general character of the practice. However, the text and the practice are interdependent factors.

107   *Panhandle Oil Co., v. Mississippi ex. rel. Knox.*, 277 U.S. 218, 223 (1928) (Holmes, J., dissenting).

108   R. McCloskey, *The American Supreme Court* 67 (1960).

109   Van Alstyne demurs when he writes that "[d]iversity and pluralism are . . . [the essence] 'of federalism,' " suggesting that the kind of federalism we have today is less than ideal. William Van Alstyne, "Federalism, Congress, the States, and the Tenth Amendment: Adrift in the Cellophane Sea," 1987 *Duke L. J.* 769, 775. At the time, states' rights advocates denounced Marshall's decision in *McCulloch*. However, "it was clear to Marshall, as it has been to posterity, that a national government restricted in its powers by Maryland's narrow interpretation would be incapable of the great tasks that might lie before it." R. McCloskey, *The American Supreme Court*, at 66. This observation might be true, but it is irrelevant to whether the decision in *McCulloch* was inherent in the Constitution. Of course, it is apparent that had the narrow interpretation prevailed, we would not now have a national government as we know it.

110   Revolutionary adjudication is now necessary if constitutional practice is to be redirected as in *Lopez v. United States*, 514 U.S. 549 (1995), or *New York v. United States*, 505 U.S. 144 (1992).

111   Though Madison argued that the federalism in the new Constitution was not pure federalism, but rather a blend of federalism and nationalism, Marshall was clearly a nationalist. For Marshall: "Local government was associated in his mind with the petty bickerings of narrow ambition and a dangerous indifference to rights and property. The need for a strong central government, as the indispensable bulwark of the solid elements of the nation, was for him the

deepest article of his political faith." F. Frankfurter, *The Commerce Power under Marshall, Taney and Waite* 14 (1937). See also Albert J. Beveridge, *The Life of John Marshall* (1916). Marshall clearly desired "to restrain local legislatures from hampering the free play of commerce among the states," but not by "tying the Court to rigid formulas for accomplishing such restrictions." F. Frankfurter *Commerce Power,* at 14.

112　Jean Yarbrough, "Federalism in the Foundation and Preservation of the American Republic," in 6 *Publius: The Journal of Federalism* 43, 45 (1976).

113　Alexander Hamilton believed "that the state governments constituted so much unnecessary furniture for a strong national government." R. Rutland, *The Birth of the Bill of Rights* 111 (1983).

114　J. Ranney, "The Bases of American Federalism," 3 *Wm. & Mary Q.* 1, 25 (1946).

115　Indeed, "Marshall's version of commerce was an importation; it did not correspond to the accepted usage at the time the Constitution was adopted." R. Berger, *Federalism: The Founders' Design* 124 (1987). Nor did Marshall's version of "commerce" conform with other obvious authorities. Ibid. Such "terms of art" generally indicate a revolutionary decision.

116　Intercourse among the states is one of the broadest possible interpretations of "commerce." Such a broad interpretation is not required by the constitutional text or the Framers' intentions; neither is it required by the structure or logic of the Constitution. Similarly, the particular question in this case, whether commerce entails navigation, was not decided by referring to the constitutional text or the Framers' original understanding of the commerce clause, although Marshall purports to rely on them. C. Black, *The People and the Court* 166 (1960). The fundamental question concerning the scope of the commerce clause is whether we are to form a strong national government. See ibid.

117　22 U.S. (9 Wheat.) 1, 197 (1824).

118　F. Frankfurter, *Commerce Power,* at 40.

119　Ibid.

120　Ibid. at 12. In the case of the commerce clause "the Supreme Court had to create doctrines without substantial guidance or restriction by previous discussion and analysis." Marshall used the occasion to restrict the authority of local legislatures. Ibid. at 13–14. In effect, it contributes to the construction of a government of unenumerated powers, arguably an idea the Constitution specifically rejects.

121　P. Hay and R. Rotunda, *The United States Federal System: Legal Integration in the American Experience* 71 (1982).

122　E. Prentice & J. Egan, *The Commerce Clause of the Federal Constitution* 11 (1981).

123　Albert S. Abel, "The Commerce Clause in the Constitutional Convention and in Contemporary Comment," 25 *Minn. L. Rev.*, 432, 468–81 (1941); Richard Epstein, "The Proper Scope of the Commerce Power," 73 *Va. L. Rev.* 1387 (1987) (arguing against the inaccuracy of a broad interpretation of the commerce clause).

124   Marshall's interpretation of the commerce clause has ramifications for the dormant commerce clause. What is the legitimacy of the dormant commerce clause? The dormant commerce clause maintains that even without federal legislation, the commerce clause prohibits states from regulating their own commercial activities in a prejudicial fashion. No normal convention implies this interpretation; in fact, it can be brought about only through revolutionary adjudication. The alternative would be to say that where Congress does not speak, the commerce clause is silent. See Julian Eule, "Laying the Dormant Commerce Clause to Rest," 91 *Yale L. J.* 425 (1982).

125   Moreover, it can be argued that the decisions in *McCulloch* and *Ogden* were necessary features of the counterrevolution ultimately culminating in the reversal of the *Lochner* era in *United States v. Darby*, 312 U.S. 100 (1941). E. Corwin, "John Marshall, Revolutionist, Malgré Lui," 104 *U. Pa. L. Rev.* 9, 21–22 (1955). It is possible, though far from plausible, to suggest that *McCulloch, Gibbons,* and *Darby* were all erroneous. If they are wrong, important currents in American constitutional practice are false. However, saying this requires retreating into ideology as opposed to candidly looking at American constitutional practice.

126   Any pragmatic successful decision that becomes an integral part of our national political culture may now appear to be written in stone. It does not follow, however, that, at the time, anyone could have predicted that Marshall's pragmatic choice would succeed. Pragmatic decisions, consistent with fundamental values and social aspirations, often appear to be historically inevitable. We must resist this appearance. History and familiarity breed only the appearance of inevitability. The commerce power could have been defined differently, and, if so, this different interpretation would now appear inevitable. If we are ever to fully understand the legal dimension of human behavior, we must begin to take cognizance of these historical and psychological processes that encourage us to accept constitutional doctrine as necessary or inevitable when, in fact, it is contingently based.

127   U.S. Constitution, art. 1, sec. 10 [1].

128   17 U.S. (4 Wheat.) 122 (1819).

129   25 U.S. (2 Wheat.) 213 (1827) (holding that state insolvency laws regarding preexisting contracts are constitutional valid).

130   *Fletcher v. Peck*, 10 U.S. 87 (1810); *Dartmouth College v. Woodward*, 17 U.S. 518 (1819).

131   The issue here is that if the allegedly offending state law existed at the time of

the contract, the contract clause is not implicated because a contract is understood against the backdrop of other statutes. Only contracts existing before the allegedly offending law could survive scrutiny under the clause.

132   *Ogden v. Saunders,* 25 U.S. (12 Wheat.) 213 (1827).

133   H. Maine, *Popular Government* 247–248 (1885).

134   *Caulder v. Bull,* 3 U.S. (3 Dall.) (1798).

135   The Court in *Proprietors of Charles River Bridge v. Proprietors of Warren Bridge,* 36 U.S. (11 Pet.) 420 (1837) upheld Massachusetts's prerogative to alter a public contract.

136   *Home Building and Loan Association v. Blaisdell,* 290 U.S. 398 (1934).

137   Ibid.

138   Ibid.

139   Ibid.

140   Ibid.

141   Ibid.

142   E. Corwin, "The Passing of Dual Federalism," in *Essays in Constitutional Law,* at 186.

143   For example, Jean Edward Smith, *John Marshall.* It is similarly doubtful that Marshall would accept any interpretation of separation of powers, federalism, and the supremacy of the federal courts if it failed to generate a strong conception of national power over state power.

144   32 U.S. 243 (1833).

145   The Court again examined this issue, finding that the Constitution does not protect a citizen's religious liberties from state interference. *Permoli v. First Municipal,* 44 U.S. 589 (1845).

146   W. Crosskey, *Politics and the Constitution,* at 1066–76. But see C. Fairman, "The Supreme Court and the Constitutional Limitations on State Governmental Authority," 21 *U. Chi. L. Rev.* 40 (1953). Crosskey's rejoinder appears in W. Crosskey, "'Legislative History' and the Constitutional Limitations on State Authority," 22 *U. Chi. L. Rev.* 1 (1954). Crosskey's point is that textualism supports Marshall's decision in *Barron,* but only regarding the First Amendment and part of the Seventh Amendment. The principles in the Second through the Eighth Amendments apply to the states.

147   W. Crosskey, *Politics and the Constitution,* at 1059.

148   *People v. Goodwin,* 18 Johns. (N.Y.) 187, 201 (1920).

149   W. Rawle, *A View of the Constitution of the United States of America* 124–25 (1829). See also J. Angell, "Restrictions on State Power in Relation to Private Property," 1 *U.S.L. & Intelligence Rev.* 4, 64 (1829); W. Rawle, at 119–43; *Houston v. Moore,* 18 U.S. (5 Wheat.), 1 (1820); *Bank of Columbia v. Okely,* 17 U.S. (4 Wheat.), 235 (1819). For a discussion of these cases and of state court opinions supporting the view that the provisions of the Second through the

Eighth Amendments apply to state governments, see R. Smith, *Public Prayer and the Constitution* 137–44 (1987).

150   Most constitutional cases are decided by appeal to normal constitutional conventions. But most constitutional cases are not reprinted in casebooks; they are argued, decided, and recorded affecting few beyond the parties involved. Sometimes, in seemingly normal cases, a controversy erupts over the priority of the conventions and turns into a crisis requiring revolutionary adjudication. The legal community often achieves consensus over the relative importance of normal conventions. For example, most constitutional decisions seek to identify the constitutional text that implicates a problem as well as the text of the offending statute. Further, most judges, Justice Scalia notwithstanding, view the intent of a constitutional provision and the offending text to be relevant to the statute's constitutionality. Similarly, historical, structural, and logical arguments always seem to be appropriate. When none of these conventions alone or in combination explain a decision, the decision is revolutionary.

151   W. B. Gallie, "Essentially Contested Concepts" 56 *Proc. Aristotlean Soc'y* 167, 169 (1956).

152   Ibid.

153   Marshall was a dedicated Federalist, not a neutral, impartial judge. See Charles A. Beard, *The Supreme Court and the Constitution* 109 (1962) (quoting Justice Story's view of Marshall). *Ogden v. Saunders,* 25 U.S. (12 Wheat.) 213, 353 (1827) (appealing to political philosophical treaties to understand how the Framers used certain political concepts).

154   Marshall's version of federalism was much closer to a form of nationalism, the latter being a monist form of government, deriving its authority from the people rather than from a federation of states. A. Kelly and W. Harbison, *The American Constitution* (1970). The Marshall revolutions can be characterized as comprising decisions that created a stronger and more pervasive national government. This must be considered revolutionary, for both the Federalists and Anti-Federalists claimed that they disapproved of a national form of government. The Federalists denied that the Constitution created a national government, whereas the Anti-Federalists feared that it did. To pacify some of these fears, Madison wrote: "The proposed constitution, therefore, even when tested by the rules laid down by its antagonists, is, in strictness, neither a national nor a federal constitution; but a composition of both. In its foundation it is federal, not national; in the sources from which the ordinary powers of the government are drawn, it is partly federal, and partly national: in the operation of these powers, it is national, not federal; in the extent of them again, it is federal, not national; and finally in the authoritative mode of introducing amendments, it is neither wholly federal, nor wholly national." J. Madison, *The Federalist Papers* No. 39, at 195–96.

Madison seemed unaware of the conceptual problems introduced by his hybrid conception of government. Unless one is able to integrate federalism and nationalism coherently, the situation is rife for conflict and revolution. Unless we are able to identify the hybrid under some coherent rubric, simply making a compilation of the ways in which the government was federal, and the ways in which it was national, leads inevitably to usurpation by other political actors to achieve one or the other. This "other political actor" could be the judicial branch. This is precisely what John Marshall achieved in revolutionary fashion. But see Martin Diamond, "Commentaries on the Federalist: The Federalist on Federalism: Neither a National nor a Federal Constitution, but a Composition of Both," 86 *Yale L. J.* 1273, 1281 (1977) (arguing that "[t]he Federalist's theory of federalism is not only analytically superior to our contemporary approach in explaining the American political system as originally devised, but that it also better illuminates the federal-national balance of the system as it has developed historically"). See P. Kahn, "Reason and Will."

155   In fact, appealing to original intent is a ritualized style of constitutional rhetoric that accompanies an independently derivable constitutional argument. It is a device for announcing a constitutional conclusion, not deriving it. Whether they approved or not, the Founders surely knew that the original meaning of constitutional discourse would be altered. Madison writes: "What a metamorphosis would be produced in the code of law if all its ancient phraseology were to be taken in its modern sense! And that the language of our Constitution is already undergoing interpretations unknown to its founders will, I believe, appear to all unbiased inquirers into the history of its origin and adoption." Letter from James Madison to Henry Lee (June 25, 1824), quoted in M. Farrand ed., *The Record of the Federal Convention of 1787* 464 (1966). See H. J. Powell, "The Modern Misunderstanding of Original Intent," 54 *U. Chi. L. Rev.* 1513 (1987).

156   William E. Nelson, "The Eighteenth Century Background of John Marshall's Jurisprudence," 76 *Mich. L. Rev.* 893, 894 (1978).

157   S. Bloch and M. Marcus, at 336.

158   For example, given the appropriate interpretation of "high crimes and misdemeanors," what would have prevented "Congress from using its power of impeachment to override the President and the Supreme Court at will, on ordinary policy questions, whenever a sufficiently numerous faction is so moved"? C. Kesler ed., *Saving the Revolution* (1987). Unfortunately, the precise meaning of "high crimes and misdemeanors" became relevant to the survival of William Jefferson Clinton's presidency.

159   347 U.S. 483 (1954). But see William E. Nelson, "The Changing Meaning of Equality in Twentieth-Century Constitutional Law," 52 *Wash. & Lee L. Rev.* 3

(1995) (arguing that New York caselaw contains the seeds of the new conception of equality affirmed in *Brown*).

160   *Brown* did not formally overrule *Plessy* because the Court in *Brown* was concerned with the special stigmatizing effects of segregation in education only. Despite such a literalist interpretation of *Brown,* one can safely say that *Brown* and the several subsequent per curiam decisions successfully began to dismantle segregation.

161   Like other constitutional provisions, the equal protection clause arguably can be read in a narrow or expansive way. If so, any decision—either prohibiting or permitting separation—would be revolutionary. The problem is there is nothing neutral in most controversial cases to generate an uncontroversial result. When two reasonable constitutional actors differ on how to interpret a constitutional provision, the situation is ripe for revolution. Consequently, *Plessy* itself can be viewed as a constitutional revolution—a bad one at that.

162   We must guard against the view that the Constitution's meaning is constant, while only our conception of its meaning changes. L. Tribe, *American Constitutional Law,* at 1478 (arguing that it was not the concept embodied in the equal protection clause that changed between 1896 and 1954, but only our relevant perceptions and understandings"). This type of view can be supported only by embracing naturalism in constitutional adjudication. On the contrary, Frankfurter wrote that "[i]t is not fair to say that the South has always denied Negroes 'this constitutional right.' It was NOT a constitutional right 'till May 17/54.'" Bernard Schwartz, *Super Chief Earl Warren and His Supreme Court,* at 108–9.

    In Tribe's view *Brown* was always the correct interpretation of the equal protection clause, despite the fact that constitutional practice declared the contrary. Cf. C. Black, *Law as an Art,* at 6 (stating that "[i]f the *Brown* decision was right, then it was right all along"). If we accept such a view, constitutional meanings have a life of their own, independent of judicial practice. The problem with such a view is that we have no clue as to how constitutional provisions acquire their meaning. Are constitutional meanings eternal truths? If so, then whatever the "true meaning" of the Constitution is, it need not have anything to do with actual constitutional practice. Consequently, actual constitutional practice might be totally wrong. Of course, it might be that whatever the true meaning of the Constitution, it is read back into the Constitution despite Supreme Court decisions. However, if that is so, then why even bother with the Constitution and actual constitutional practice? Why not decide important "constitutional" questions in terms of abstract moral and political theory?

163   The source of the new principle is not contained in the Constitution or judi-

cial decisions. Instead, it is derived from critical cultural theory or abstract moral and political theory. It is important to note that the new principle is normative, even if empirical factors are relevant to its justification. In *Brown* social scientific evidence was adduced to support the normative judgment that separate school facilities were inherently unequal. For a discussion of the desirability of using social scientific data upon which to base constitutional decisions, see M. Cohen, *Law and the Social Order* 380–81 (1933) ("If, however, we recognize that courts are constantly remaking the law, then it becomes of the utmost social importance that the law should be made in accordance with the best available information, which it is the object of science to supply"); Edmond Cahn, "Jurisprudence," 30 *N. Y. U. L. Rev.* 150, 157–58, 167 (1955). Cf. Ronald Dworkin, "Social Sciences and Constitutional Right: The Consequences of Uncertainty," 6 *J. L. & Ed.* 3 (1977) (arguing that legal judgments are interpretive, not merely factual).

164 For example, the *Plessy* Court was not the first court to deploy the "separate but equal" doctrine. Forty-six years earlier a Massachusetts court validated a statute authorizing separate school systems for blacks and whites. *Roberts v. City of Boston*, 59 Mass. (5 Cush.) 198 (1850). Further, the doctrine was adopted in various forms by many judicial decisions. How, then, can Dworkin say that it is obvious that the Constitution gives us the right not to be victimized by state-approved discrimination? How does he know that the Constitution gives us such a right without first seeing whether the doctrine fits legal practice? If Dworkin followed his own methodology, he would soon learn that the separate but equal doctrine fits more of legal practice than the *Brown* doctrine, and informally more of cultural practice generally. And of course that's not surprising, as *Brown* embodied a constitutional revolution.

165 The term "discretion" is ambiguous. A weak form of discretion simply means that a judge must use judgment; she must eschew mechanical methods for deciding a case. A stronger conception of discretion authorizes a judge to make a decision within the parameters of certain standards, but the judge is the final authority in so deciding. An even stronger conception of discretion permits the judge to decide what standards he is to use to make such decisions. See R. Dworkin, *Taking Rights Seriously*, at 32–33. It is this sort of discretion that some conventionalist theories permit.

166 According to both theories, there is a clear distinction between what the law *is* and what it *ought* to be. Minutes before the decision the principle enunciated in *Brown* was what the law *ought* to be, not what it *was*.

Just as the original decision in *Brown* (*Brown I*) was a progressive step into the future, the decision in *Brown v. Board of Education*, 349 U.S. 294 (1955) (*Brown II*) — ordering desegregation "with all the deliberate speed" — was a retrogressive step into the past. Charles Black correctly observed that "[t]here was just exactly no reason, in 1955, for thinking it would work better than an order to desegregate at once." C. Black, "The Unfinished Business of the Warren Court," 46 *Wash. L. Rev.* 3, 22 (1970).

167 *Griswold v. Connecticut,* 381 U.S. 479 (1965).

168 R. Posner, "Privacy in the Supreme Court," 1979 *Sup. Ct. Rev.* 173, 197.

169 The revolution's present hold on the American people was probably one of the key factors in derailing Robert Bork's appointment to the Supreme Court.

170 See *Griswold v. Connecticut,* at 484.

171 Ibid.

172 Ibid.

173 367 U.S. 497 (1961) (Harlan, J., dissenting). Other precursors were: *Skinner v. Oklahoma,* 316 U.S. 535 (1942) (invalidating, on equal protection grounds, a law permitting sterilization for certain types of repeat offenders); *Pierce v. Society of Sisters,* 268 U.S. 510 (1925) (invalidating a law requiring students to attend public schools); *Meyer v. Nebraska,* 262 U.S. 390 (1923) (invalidating a law requiring teaching only English in grade schools).

174 Ibid. at 521.

175 Ibid. at 522.

176 *Griswold v. Connecticut.* Paul G. Kauper, "Penumbras, Peripheries, Emanations, Things Fundamental and Things Forgotten: The Griswold Case," 64 *Mich. L. Rev.* 235, 244 (1965).

177 See Burt Henly, " 'Penumbra': The Roots of Legal Metaphor," 15 *Hast. Const. L. Q.* 81, 96–99 (1987) (discussing some of the problems with "penumbra" as a spatial metaphor).

178 Sometimes this general right is referred to as "the right to be let alone," a right that is "implicit in many of the provisions of the Constitution and in the philosophical background out of which the Constitution was formulated." Erwin Griswold, "The Right to Be Let Alone," 55 *Nw. U. L. Rev.* 216 (1960). Consider this eloquent statement of the right involved: "The makers of our Constitution undertook to secure conditions favorable to the pursuit of happiness. They recognized the significance of man's spiritual nature, of his feelings and of his intellect. They knew that only a part of the pain, pleasure and satisfactions of life are to be found in material things. They sought to protect Americans in their beliefs, their thoughts, their emotions and their sensations. They conferred, as against the Government, the right to be let alone — the most comprehensive of rights and the right most valued by civilized men." *Olmstead v. United States,* 277 U.S. 438, 478 (1928) (Brandeis, J., dissenting).

179 A defender of *Griswold* would contend that this objection is circular, insisting upon a decisive distinction between law and morality, which is just the point at issue. Additionally, it could be argued that this objection suffers from a faulty, nondeliberative conception of judicial reasoning, as if judicial reason

functions in merely a mechanical manner. Of course, this reply is always met with cries of countermajoritarianism, judicial tyranny, superlegislatures, or abdicating the rule of law.

I think a deeper rationale explains the reluctance to embrace a revolutionary role for the Court, a rationale having nothing to do with countermajoritarianism or the rule of law. This Burkean rationale says that reason and deliberation cause more bad than good. Judges should strike down a statute only when it is clearly erroneous, because evaluating change theoretically is bound to have serious untoward effects. This view distrusts innovation because consensus concerning what ought to be is so much more elusive than consensus over what is.

180   Defenders of *Griswold* find the decisions in *Roe v. Wade,* 410 U.S. 113 (1973) and *Planned Parenthood of Southeastern Pennsylvania v. Casey,* 112 S.Ct. 2791 (1992) to be refinements of the *Griswold* paradigm, whereas opponents generally find *Roe* and *Casey* to be revolutionary within the privacy paradigm. One method of characterizing the controversy over abortion is to indicate that those who believe the fetus to be a constitutionally protected person perceive *Roe* and *Casey* as radical departures from the paradigm in *Griswold*.

181   Other cases refining this paradigm are: *Eisenstadt v. Baird,* 405 U.S. 438 (1972); *Roe v. Wade,* 410 U.S. 113 (1973); *Planned Parenthood of Southeastern Pennsylvania v. Casey,* 505 U.S. 833 (1992); *Moore v. City of East Cleveland,* 431 U.S. 494 (1977); *Quilloin v. Walcott,* 434 U.S. 246 (1978); *Zablocki v. Redhail,* 434 U.S. 374 (1978); *Kelly v. Johnson,* 425 U.S. 238 (1976); *Kart v. Schmidt,* 460 F. 2d 609 (5th Cir. 1972); *In Re* Quinine, 70 N.J. 10, 355 A. 2d 647 (1976); *Washington v. Glucksberg,* 521 U.S. 702 (1997).

182   The paradigm in *Griswold* is a principle of personal inviolability or individual sovereignty, which conservatives contend precludes the possibility of refinement to the extent necessary for normal adjudication. In their view such paradigms are inherently unstable, and therefore courts should avoid them unless the legislature gives them no choice.

183   478 U.S. 186 (1986) (holding that private consensual homosexual sodomy is not constitutionally protected). The abortion cases also involved a challenge to refine and perfect the *Griswold* paradigm.

184   The problem here is that if the Court arbitrarily ends a revolution, it does so through revolutionary adjudication. In other words, if normal adjudication is used when postrevolutionary adjudication is warranted, the decision is arbitrary. A judge knows that postrevolutionary, not normal, adjudication is warranted when there exists controversy over a range of the paradigm's applications.

185   Ronald Dworkin, "Bork to Kennedy," 34 *N.Y. Rev. Bks.* 36, 41 (1987); L. Tribe, *American Constitutional Law,* at 1422. One commentator contends

that what divides the Court in *Hardwick* is a commitment "to two incommensurable and incompatible systems of fundamental values: classical liberalism and classical conservatism." Anne Goldstein, "History, Homosexuality, and Political Values: Search for the Hidden Determinants of *Bowers v. Hardwick*," 97 *Yale L. J.* 1973, 1099 (1988). If so, the coherentist argument that the majority opinion commits a *judicial* mistake is erroneous. Further, the coherentist argument begs the question against the majority opinion.

186 Justice Harlan's dissent in *Poe v. Ullman,* 367 U.S. 497, 546 (Harlan, J., dissenting) (1961) is taken by many to express the paradigm ultimately made law in *Griswold.* Harlan writes: "The laws regarding marriage which provide both when the sexual powers may be used and the legal and societal context in which children are born and brought up, as well as laws forbidding adultery, fornication, and homosexual practices . . . [confine] sexuality to lawful marriage, [and] form a pattern so deeply pressed into the substance of our social life that any Constitutional doctrine in this area must build upon that basis." Further, Justice Goldberg's concurrence in Griswold clearly states that the holding in this case "in no way interferes with the State's proper regulation of sexual promiscuity or misconduct." 381 U.S. 498–99 (Goldberg, J., concurring). These remarks suggest clearly that the essential feature paradigm in *Griswold* is to defend the traditional conception of marriage and family.

187 L. Tribe, *American Constitutional Law,* at 423; Kenneth Karst, "The Freedom of Intimate Associations," 88 *Yale L. J.* 33 (1980). See also Charles Fried, "Privacy," 77 *Yale L. J.* 475 (1968) (characterizing privacy as necessary for love, friendship, and trust). Let me say at the outset that I agree with the coherentist argument for *extending* protection for consensual homosexual sodomy. My criticism of the coherentist argument is not with its conclusion. What I object to is the coherentist position that this conclusion captures what the law *is* in contradistinction to what it *should* be. Skepticism is appropriate, in my estimation, when we move from what should be a right to what allegedly already is a right. See, e.g., David Richards, "Sexual Autonomy and Right to Privacy," 30 *Hast. L. J.* 957, 1006 (1979) (arguing that laws instructing us how to have sex and with whom are constitutionally invalid absent a compelling moral justification). Alternatively, we can avoid the issue of whether a principle protecting consensual homosexual sodomy inheres in constitutional practice. Instead, we could argue that even if homosexual privacy does not trigger strict scrutiny, it is irrational in the extreme to criminalize such conduct. It is irrational because the state can have no nonarbitrary goal in criminalizing this conduct. Of course, to achieve victory here, rational basis scrutiny must have *some* teeth.

188 L. Tribe, *American Constitutional Law,* at 1421–35.

189 Ibid. at 1422–23. See David Richards, *Toleration and the Constitution* 280 (1986) (presenting a functionalist argument for extending constitutional

protection to consensual sodomy). But see Thomas Grey, "Eros and Civilization and the Burger Court," 43 *Law & Contemp. Prob.* 83, 85 (1980) (arguing
that Griswold "contains no hint of any endorsement of the sexual freedom of
consenting adults. Three of the concurring opinions expressly disavowed any
notion that the right of privacy cast doubt on sex laws. The opinion for the
Court . . . stressed the ancient and sacred character of marriage as the basis of
the decision"). Additionally, Grey argues that the Court's decisions in the
privacy cases are "dedicated to the cause of social stability through the rein-
forcement of traditional institutions and have nothing to do with sexual liber-
ation of the individual. . . . Where the less traditional values have been directly
protected, the decisions reflect . . . the stability-centered concerns of moderate
conservative family and population policy." T. Grey, "Eros and Civilization
and the Burger Court," at 88, 90.

190   For example, it can be argued that "[i]mpermanent relationships that perform some intimate or associational 'functions' cannot claim the same position as marriage and kinship in ensuring a political structure that limits governments, stabilizes social patterns, and protects pluralistic liberty through the
power of its own relational permanency." B. Hafen, "Marriage, Kinship, and
Sexual Privacy," 81 *Mich. L. Rev.* 463, 482 (1983). But see D. Richards, *Toleration and the Constitution,* at 277 ("There is no good reason to believe that the
legitimacy of [sodomy] devitalizes social cooperation"). I do not find persuasive the argument purporting to show that homosexuality devitalizes. For one
thing, even if marriage is important, why should we not tolerate other kinds of
sexual unions? Nevertheless, those endorsing the view that we should not,
have a principled position. They just have the wrong principle. That in itself
cannot show that they are wrong about the paradigm in the sexual privacy
cases. Similarly, the Supreme Court has described marriage as "the most important relation in life" and "the foundation of the family and of society,
without which there would be neither civilization nor progress." *Maynard v.
Hill,* 125 U.S. 190, 205, 211 (1988). But see "Note, *Hardwick v. Hardwick:* The
Right of Privacy — Only within the Traditional Family?" 26 *J. Fam. L.* 373
(1987) (arguing that the principle in the sexual privacy case has application
broader than the family).

191   Some argue that the "privacy" involved in sexual privacy cases is not privacy at
all, but much more like an important kind of autonomy or freedom. R. Posner, "Privacy in the Supreme Court," at 195.

192   Tribe argued this case before the Court with the dissent essentially adopting
his position.

193   This distinction does not necessarily presuppose a positivistic conception of
law. Indeed, this book has attempted to show that neither conventionalism,

nor pragmatism, nor any other single jurisprudential theory can explain the different moments of constitutional adjudication.

194   I take as a truism that for a rule of conduct to be a law, it must be promulgated. See A. Ross, *On Law and Justice* 101–2 (1974) (describing the degree of probability as the factor determining whether a source of law is law itself); William Blackstone, *Commentaries on the Laws of England* 44 (1809) (arguing that municipal law derives from the supreme power of the state); J. Gray, *The Nature and Sources of the Law* 84 (1948) (arguing that courts create law).

195   Hafen, "Marriage, Kinship, and Sexual Privacy," at 527 ("If the activity, regardless of what it is, is presumed to be within the 'right of privacy' simply because it was carried out in seclusion or in 'intimate' circumstances, a strong presumption against any social or state interest is created before any real analysis takes place").

196   See J. Austin, *Lectures on Jurisprudence* 60 (1885).

197   William McBride, "Towards a Phenomenology of International Justice," in *Law, Reason, and Justice* 137, 149 (G. Hughes ed. 1969).

198   Neil MacCormick, "Jurisprudence and the Constitution," 36 *Current Legal Problems* 13, 28 (1983).

199   So too are notions like "the best theory" or "the soundest conception of law."

200   R. Dworkin, *Law's Empire*, at 377.

201   The more general right to privacy might also include questions about nonsexual family life.

202   It is unclear how a principle extending privacy to homosexuals fits the privacy cases when some of those cases explicitly deny that constitutionally protected privacy extends that far. To characterize these explicit remarks as dicta is circular.

203   For an interesting examination of the moral and constitutional reasons against the *Hardwick* decision, see David Richards, "Constitutional Legitimacy and Constitutional Privacy," 61 *N.Y.U. L. Rev.* 800 (1986).

204   Ronald Dworkin, "'The Bork Nomination': An Exchange," 34 *N.Y. Rev. Books* 59, 60 (1987).

205   See R. Dworkin, *Bork to Kennedy*, at 41.

206   Ibid.

207   There are at least two possible arguments for this position. The first argument maintains that homosexuality is itself morally justifiable. (I believe this argument to be *morally* superior to alternative positions.) The second argument denies that it is morally justifiable but insists that homosexuality should be tolerated. This second argument gains appeal when we realize that intolerance of homosexuals is a conspicuously modern phenomenon. See John Boswell, *Christianity, Social Tolerance, and Homosexuality* 269–302 (1980). But

Dworkin's insistence that homosexuality is constitutionally protected does not entail that it is morally justifiable. And that is what is so wrong about Dworkin's position. Toleration in the hands of some usually degenerates into persecution.

208   Legions of moral philosophers from Kant to Hare, Gewirth, and Singer have embraced principles of generalization or universalization to prove particular moral judgments. To my knowledge no one believes that any of these important thinkers succeeded in this task.

209   The Burkean principle is part of a more sweeping condemnation of deliberative constitutional change. Consider Bickel's description of Burke's view in the latter's *Reflections on the French Revolution:*

> You cannot start from scratch . . . and expect to produce anything but a continued round of chaos and tyranny, until you return to the remnants of what you sought to destroy. Perfection is unlikely in human contrivances, and so the professed purpose of any scheme that attempts to start fresh will be defeated. The old vices tend to reappear in new institutions if their causes have not been attacked, but only their outward manifestations, which were the old institutions. Meanwhile the price has been paid of teaching men to yield as little respect to new institutions as was shown for the old, and, in continual round of change, men unmoored from their past "become little better than the flies of summer." Even in pursuit of the most radical reforming ends, it is, moreover, simple practical common sense "to make the most of the existing materials." (A. Bickel, *The Morality of Consent,* at 22)

210   Such a principle would counsel against the decision in *Griswold* on the grounds that it is revolutionary. In my view the fact that thoughtful Americans would probably choose to retain the privacy principle shows that it was revolutionary and legitimate at the same time.

211   Two members of the Court explicitly limit sexual privacy to heterosexual relations. *Poe v. Ullman,* 367 U.S. 497 (1961) (J. Harlan, dissenting); *Griswold v. Connecticut* 381 U.S. 479 (1965), at 498–99 (Goldberg, J., concurring).

212   See generally, B. Hafen, "The Constitutional Status of Marriage, Kinship, and Sexual Privacy — Balancing the Individual and Social Interest"; *Skinner v. Oklahoma,* 316 U.S. 535 (1942) (invalidating a statute authorizing the sterilization of certain types of criminals); *Poe v. Ullman,* 367 U.S. 497 (1961) (J. Harlan, dissenting); *Griswold v. Connecticut,* 381 U.S. 479 (1965); *Roe v. Wade,* 410 U.S. 113 (1973); *Eisenstadt v. Baird,* 405 U.S. 438 (1972).

213   See K. Karst, "The Freedom of Intimate Association"; Robert Gerstein, "California's Constitutional Right to Privacy: The Development of the Protection of Private Life," 9 *Hastings Const. L. Q.* 387 (1982) (arguing that the value of

privacy is what affords us an opportunity to live a private life). It has been argued that homosexual relations are natural and permissible. See David Richards, *The Moral Criticism of the Law* 77–134 (1977). In fact, there is an interesting, if somewhat strained, sociobiological argument that homosexuality in humans is grounded in evolutionary theory. E. Wilson, *On Human Nature* (1977).

214   For such an argument, see D. Richard, *Sex, Drugs, Death, and the Law* 84–127 (1982).

215   Dworkin never explains why polygamy or private drug use in intimate settings aren't constitutionally protected instances of privacy. If consenting adults choose to enter into a polygamous relationship, why should we object?

5   The Conceptual and Political Defenses of the Theory

1   This view supports a conceptual conservatism concerning the development of social practices and traditions. Logically, a distinction exists between having no reason to change and having a reason not to change, but in constitutional adjudication, for some not having a reason to change provides a reason not to change. Moreover, conceptual conservatism has little to do with political or judicial conservatism or progressivism.

2   In my view a constitutional paradigm is always *conceptually* indeterminate; in the appropriate circumstances it can take on a meaning significantly different from its normal or default meaning. However, some paradigms are also *practically* indeterminate. For instance, many provisions of the Constitution, such as the necessary and proper clause, the commerce clause, the due process and equal protection clause are conceptually indeterminate, but in addition they are practically indeterminate. On the other hand, the requirement that a president be thirty-five years of age is conceptually indeterminate, but practically determinate. We can imagine circumstances in which the age requirement for the presidency could be interpreted as "sufficient maturity," but because these circumstances will never obtain, we can treat the age requirement as if it were conceptually determinate. For a discussion of constitutional indeterminacy, see Robert Justin Lipkin, "Indeterminacy, Justification, and Truth in Constitutional Theory," at 599–619.

3   Although the distinction between normal adjudication and revolutionary adjudication cannot be drawn mechanically, it is a useful analytic device for understanding and teaching American constitutional practice. A constitutional law professor should try thinking of most lead cases in a casebook as revolutionary, depending upon the case, of course. The remaining major cases

in that section should be seen as prevolutionary or postrevolutionary, the minor and note cases as normal. This taxonomic framework alone illuminates the development of constitutional law for many law students.

4 This modernist objection, if correct, applies to all other modern and postmodern theories of constitutionalism, and not merely to the theory of constitutional revolutions.

5 See Frederick Schauer, "The Occasions of Constitutional Interpretation."

6 See G. E. Moore, *Principia Ethica* (1911); see also David Hume, *A Treatise Concerning Human Nature* (1965).

7 See generally William Frankena, *Ethics* (1973).

8 What would we do in the following circumstances? Suppose we found incontrovertible evidence that the Founders intended actual American constitutional practice to be very different from what it is. Would that render two hundred years of actual constitutional practice unconstitutional or illegitimate? In a constitutional republic such as ours, legitimacy must be defined in part in terms of actual practice. And concerning actual practice, "constitutional adjudication is concerned with defining constitutional provisions, many of which are broadly phrased and open ended and so do not convey much meaning in their text alone. The Court has done this ever since Marbury asserted and recognized the power of judicial review. In establishing the meaning of the Constitution the court has not recognized any distinction between interpretive and noninterpretive review." R. Sedler, at 115.

9 Actual practice must have at least a modicum of normative force, because it defines the context for deliberating over constitutional change. Consequently, the fact that some procedure is a part of actual constitutional practice means that procedure is good, all things being equal. This doesn't take us very far when we consider how few problems actual practice resolves.

10 The notion of a prima facie good is simply something that is good, all things being equal. See David Ross, *The Foundations of Ethics* (1930).

11 198 U.S. 45 (1905).

12 See Robert Justin Lipkin, "Pragmatism—the Unfinished Revolution," 67 *Tul. L. Rev.* 1561 (1992).

13 Ludwig Wittgenstein, *Remarks on the Foundation of Mathematics,* pt. 3, sec. 74, at 74 (1964).

14 A pragmatic judicial philosophy rejects descriptive-normative dichotomies, though it doesn't reject a contextual distinction between descriptive and normative claims. The problem with such dichotomies in justificatory contexts is that choosing one branch over the other risks begging the question against one's opponent.

15 Western philosophy has periodically attempted to explicate the meaning of this essentialism.

16   See Cass Sunstein, *The Partial Constitution*; Frank Michelman, "Law's Republic," 97 *Yale L. J.* 1493 (1988); and Frank Michelman, "The Supreme Court, 1985 Term — Forward: Traces of Self-government," 100 *Harv. L. Rev.* 4 (1986).

17   Some structuralists consider their arguments to be a function of normal adjudication. Whatever else it does, normal adjudication tells us which political concepts set the stage for constitutional interpretation. Normal adjudication functions as a default mode in constitutional law. Unless there is a reason to change modes, the Constitution should be understood in terms of its default mode. Conceptually, there is always the possibility of switching, but practically, the default mode of normal adjudication determines many constitutional issues. Yet American constitutionalism has embraced revolutionary adjudication to resolve the great controversial cases. Indeed, our constitutional scheme would be recognizably different if it embraced only normal adjudication.

18   This objection is similar to one lodged at Kuhn's distinction between revolutionary and normal science. Consider:

By 1965, he [Kuhn] was conceding that his first distinction between "normal" and "revolutionary" change in science might have been too sharply drawn; but he was arguing, in reply, that scientific revolutions were in fact, not less frequent, but more frequent than he had previously recognized. His critics' objections had convinced him that the sciences are exposed to profound conceptual changes . . . continually. So he went on to redescribe theoretical change in science as comprising an unending sequence of smaller revolutions or . . . "micro-revolutions." Every serious theoretical change in science, even if less than a complete "paradigm-switch," now committed us to refashioning our concepts in a "revolutionary" way. (Stephen Toulmin, "Does the Distinction between Normal and Revolutionary Science Hold Water?" in *Criticism and the Growth of Knowledge* 39 [I. Lakatos and A. Musgrave, eds. 1970])

The objection continues:

[A]ny scientific change whatever will normally have both something "normal" and something "revolutionary" about it. And if this were indeed all that Kuhn had ever meant by his use of the phrase "scientific revolutions," that choice of phrase was grossly misleading; for it simply disguised a familiar (but atemporal) logical distinction in an irrelevantly historical fancy dress. Rather than distinguishing two historical kinds of scientific change, it merely indicated two logically distinct aspects of any theoretical change in science. (Ibid. at 115)

19   A case may involve normal adjudication concerning one aspect of the issue and revolutionary adjudication concerning others. For example, all cases involving judicial review are instances of normal adjudication regarding their reviewability. The judicial paradigm in this instance is clear. Consequently, *Brown,* a

paradigm of revolutionary adjudication regarding equal protection, is simultaneously an example of normal adjudication regarding judicial review. Of course, arguably *Brown* is a case of revolutionary adjudication regarding both judicial review (in the circumstances of *Brown*) and equal protection. In fact, those uneasy with *Brown* usually ascribe to the equal protection revolution while rejecting the revolution in judicial review. I see no reason why this complexity vitiates the force of the distinction between normal and revolutionary adjudication.

20   Some circuits have procedural rules for deciding cases without oral argument or opinion. Presumably, in cases of this sort there is a clear application of a substantive rule to the facts of the particular case. Of course, in one sense every application of a settled rule to a new fact situation gives us a greater understanding of the rule. But this is entirely trivial; the new application does not affect the constitutional paradigm upon which the rule is based.

21   Robert Bork is the most prominent advocate of this approach. See *The Tempting of America*. Others have made similar appeals, for example, Robin West, Cass Sunstein, and Bruce Ackerman. But judicial review plays a much less prominent role in Bork's constitutionalism than in the others.

22   Some alterations can result in increasing the store of constitutional concepts, but not all do. For the most part, we know the relevant constitutional concepts concerning liberty, equality, community, fairness, wealth, and so forth. Adding to constitutional structure means invoking a concept — for example, monarchy or theocracy — that changes the deep structure of the Constitution. Altering constitutional principles means replacing one paradigm of liberty, say, for an alternative one. One sees this in the distinction between law and revolutionary politics. Revolutionary constitutional change *in* a legal system is different from revolutionary political change *of* that legal system, or in one of its parts. Of course, it is a conceptual truth that at some point revolutionary change *in* a legal system is tantamount to a revolutionary change *of* that legal system.

23   This distinction is a rather recent phenomenon; prior to modernity, courts typically engaged in both legislative and adjudicative functions.

24   A rough but useful conception of the rule of law informs us that laws cannot be arbitrary; legal decisions must be public and rationally defensible. See I. Harden and N. Lewis, *The Noble Lie* 302 (1986). The argument in the text is that flexibility, coordination, and justice are also conditions of adequacy that any acceptable legal system must exhibit. J. Finnis, *Natural Law and Natural Rights* 270 (1980) (describing the rule of law as "the specific virtue of legal systems" consisting of certain formal conditions any acceptable legal system must meet).

25   Paul W. Kahn insists that "[w]hat the rule of law attempts to conceal is political action — a politics constituted by novelty, self-defining subjects, and presence."

Paul W. Kahn, *The Reign of Law: Marbury v. Madison and the Construction of America* 34 (1998).

26   In other words there may exist undeclared rights that develop in certain cultural circumstances and not in others. For example, the right or entitlement to governmental financial assistance may be regarded as a fundamental right that has not yet been declared to be a constitutional right. Such rights might not have developed in a more libertarian society, but they have developed in ours, although not entirely through the legal system. Hence they are nonpositive rights that should be judicially recognized. Textually, the Ninth Amendment assists in this analysis, because a conceptual link exists between the theory of constitutional revolutions and the Ninth Amendment, an amendment that insists on there being rights independently of the constitutional scheme, and which makes possible revolutions in the area of individual rights. It has been argued in effect that the Ninth Amendment's purpose is to encourage revolutionary adjudication in the contexts of rights. B. Patterson, *The Forgotten Ninth Amendment* 19 (1955). According to Patterson, "these inherent rights, whether enumerated in the Constitution of the United States or not, are entitled to protection, not only against the Federal Government, but also as against the government of the several states." Ibid. at 38. See also *Griswold v. Connecticut,* 381 U.S. 479 (1965) (Goldberg, J., concurring) (indicating the existence of unenumerated rights); Sotorious Barber, "The Ninth Amendment: Inkblot or Another Hard Nut to Crack," 64 *Chic.-Kent L. Rev.* 67 (1988) (arguing that the Ninth Amendment indicates that some natural rights are justiciable); but see Michael W. McConnell, "A Moral Realist Defense of Constitutional Democracy," 64 *Chic.-Kent L. Rev.* 89 (1988) (arguing against the justiciability of Ninth Amendment natural rights); see also Sotorious Barber, "Whither Moral Realism in Constitutional Theory? A Reply to Professor McConnell," 64 *Chic.-Kent L. Rev.* 111 (1988); Norman Redlich, "Are There Certain Rights . . . Retained by the People?" 37 *N.Y.U. L. Rev.* 787, 804–5 (1962) (arguing that the purpose of the Ninth Amendment was to show that the enumerated rights did not exhaust the rights retained by the people); Calvin Massey, "Federalism and Fundamental Rights: The Ninth Amendment," 38 *Hast. L. J.* 305 (1987) (arguing that there are Ninth Amendment natural rights that can be a check on the federal government and even in a limited fashion against state government). But see Russell Caplan, "The History and Meaning of the Ninth Amendment," 69 *Va. L. Rev.* 223, 261 (1983) (arguing that the Ninth Amendment can check neither federal nor state legislation); "Note, The Uncertain Renaissance of the Ninth Amendment," 33 *U. Chi. L. Rev.* 814 (1966) (arguing that the Ninth Amendment is not the source of independent rights, nor is it a means for protecting them); R. Barnett ed., *The Rights Retained by the People* (1993).

27 Thus, judicial changes in the law satisfy the rule of law when such decisions are public and rationally defensible, not when judges maintain the status quo. Further, the distinction between a government of laws or a government of men is unilluminating. All government is government by men constrained in part by a distribution of power in different institutional settings.

28 This objection should also apply to any theory that permits reversing precedent.

29 This "deeper" consistency is usually a consistency with critical cultural or abstract principles of politics and morality. As such, this "deeper" consistency refers to factors extrinsic to the constitutional scheme and is almost always contestable.

30 Of course, the primacy of this notion of "respect and concern" is contestable and will, therefore, necessitate revolutionary adjudication.

31 Indeed, this view might have been part of what Jefferson said when he called for getting rid of the Constitution and the laws of land every generation. The theory of constitutional revolutions, in principle, makes good on this Jeffersonian proposal.

32 Moreover, the theory of constitutional revolutions takes elemental consistency seriously in normal adjudication.

33 This is a version of an argument that Stanley Fish has made prominent. See generally Stanley Fish, *Doing What Comes Naturally* (1989).

34 494 U.S. 872 (1990).

35 Counterfactual confirmation is available if those judges who functionally embrace it would intentionally embrace it if given the chance.

36 I attempt a more complete conception of American constitutionalism in a manuscript tentatively titled *Democracy at Reason's Door: The Idea of the American Communitarian Republic in American Constitutionalism, Politics, and Culture.*

37 I elaborate these notions in Robert Justin Lipkin, "Progressivism as Communitarian Democracy," 4 *Widener Symp. L. J.* 229 (1999) and "Religious Freedom in the American Communitarian Republic," 25 *Cap. L. Rev.* 765 (1997).

38 Robin West, "Is Progressive Constitutionalism Possible?" 4 *Widener Symposium L. J.* 1 (1999).

39 It is uncertain whether any tight conceptual connection exists between the theory of constitutional revolutions and progressive political theory. It is conceivable that an aggressive conservative judicial ideology can find the theory of constitutional revolutions useful, for example, in the hands of Robert Bork or Justice Scalia. For an interesting discussion of Justice Scalia's revolutionary proclivities, see David A. Schultz and Christopher E. Smith, *The Jurisprudential Vision of Justice Antonin Scalia* (1996).

40 Anyone supporting *Brown,* for example, supports revolutionary constitutional change, although sometimes the alleged reasoning in support of such change is disingenuous and borders on the ridiculous. Robert Bork, for example, rejects

revolutionary adjudication, yet he endorses *Brown*. Bork, *The Tempting of America*, at 139. Indeed, in Bork's view *Brown* is decided correctly because the *Brown* Court picked one of the two intentions the Framers possessed when ratifying the Fourteenth Amendment. The Framers believed in equality but did not believe that school desegregation was violative of equality. And because it would be an administrative nightmare for the Court to be tied up supervising a "separate but equal" school regime, the *Brown* Court was right to reject the constitutional permissibility of equal, segregated schools. Bork presents this argument without irony, surely aware of the Supreme Court's administrative nightmare in integrating the schools. Do the school desegregation cases represent any less of an administrative nightmare than judicially enforcing equal, but segregated, schools? I cannot see that they do. Administrative nightmare aside, Bork never tells us whether there exists a general answer to the question of which intention prevails when the Framers have two incompatible intentions relevant to a constitutional question. Dworkin has a general answer to this question that I have argued in chapter 2 is unsatisfactory.

Bork adds a second argument that crudely echoes Dworkin's, namely, that the Framers of the Fourteenth Amendment valued equality and segregation but "[s]ince equality and segregation were mutually inconsistent, though the ratifiers did not understand that, both could not be honored. When that is seen, it is obvious the Court must choose equality and prohibit state-imposed segregation. The purpose that brought the Fourteenth Amendment into being was equality before the law, and equality, not separation, was written into the text." R. Bork, *The Tempting of America*, at 139. But the notion that equality and segregation are "mutually inconsistent" is question begging, surprisingly, against "originalism." For an originalist understanding of "equality" as it appears in the Fourteenth Amendment, we must consult the Framers' understanding of "equality." And their understanding renders equality and segregation compatible. The fact that the amendment contains the word "equality," not "segregation," might be persuasive for a textualist, but it cannot do the work Bork wants it to do if he is really an originalist. For an originalist, textual evidence is one form of evidence of original intent, but it is in no way necessarily dispositive.

41 Of course, it may be inconceivable to reject a value under certain descriptions, for example, murder. Murder is defined as unjustifiable, unexcused homicide. No one can seriously (linguistically) reject that proscription. But that is a trivial result. The real test is whether certain forms of behavior must always be described as murder. Pragmatism denies that linguistic descriptions are necessarily related to certain forms of behavior and not to others.

42 I could have said "nonmajoritarian democracy" in place of "communitarian democracy," because other forms of nonmajoritarian democracy can justify

judicial review also. I use "communitarian democracy," because it is my choice for the best conception of nonmajoritarian democracy, and because every conception of democracy must include a principle of majority rule.

43 This choice is in principle voluntary because the ideal is for each individual to ratify, after careful reflection, the normative attraction of the community.

44 Arguably, the original Senate could also serve this purpose.

Conclusion

1   Linda Greenhouse, "Focus on Federal Power," *N.Y. Times,* May 24, 1995, at A1.

BIBLIOGRAPHY

Abel, Albert S. "The Commerce Clause in the Constitutional Convention and in Contemporary Comment." 25 *Minn. L. Rev.* 432 (1941).

Ackerman, Bruce. "A Generation of Betrayal?" 65 *Fordham L. Rev.* 1519 (1997). (Journal cited as *Fordham Symposium*).

———. "Liberating Abstraction." 59 *U. Chi. L. Rev.* 317 (1993).

———. "Rooted Cosmopolitanism." 104 *Ethics* 446 (1994). (Journal cited as *Ackerman Symposium*).

———. *Social Justice and the Liberal State*. New Haven: Yale University Press, 1980.

———. "Transformative Appointments." 101 *Harv. L. Rev.* 1164 (1988).

———. *We the People*. Vol. 1: *Foundations*. Vol. 2: *Transformations*. Cambridge: Harvard University Press, Belknap Press, 1991 and 1997.

———. "Why Dialogue?" 86 *J. Phil.* 5 (1989).

Ackerman Symposium. "Bruce Ackerman's *We the People*." 104 *Ethics* 446–535 (1994).

Amar, Akhil R. "Philadelphia Revisited: Amending the Constitution Outside Article V." 55 *U. Chi. L. Rev.* 1043 (1988).

Angell, J. "Restrictions on State Power in Relation to Private Property." 1 *U.S.L. & Intelligence Rev.* 4 (1829).

Atiyah, P. S. *Pragmatism and Theory in English Law*. London: Stevens, 1987.

Aumman, F. *The Changing American Legal System*. New York: Da Capo Press, 1969.

Austin, J. *Lectures on Jurisprudence: The Philosophy of Positive Law*. London: J. Murray, 1885.

Bailyn, Bernard. *The Ideological Origins of the American Revolution*. Cambridge: Harvard University Press, Belknap Press, 1982.

———. *The Origins of American Politics*. 1944. New York: Knopf, 1968.

Balkin, Jack. "Taking Ideology Seriously: Ronald Dworkin and the CLS Critique." 55 *UMKC L. Rev.* 392 (1987).

Ball, Terence, and J. G. A. Pocock, eds. *Conceptual Change and the Constitution*. Lawrence: University Press of Kansas, 1988.

Barber, Sotorious A. "The Ninth Amendment: Inkblot or Another Hard Nut to Crack." 64 *Chic.-Kent L. Rev.* 111 (1988).

——. "Whither Moral Realism in Constitutional Theory? A Reply to Professor McConnell." 64 *Chic.-Kent L. Rev.* 111 (1988).

Barnett, Randy E., ed. *The Rights Retained by the People: The History and Meaning of the Ninth Amendment.* Fairfax, Va.: George Mason University Press, 1989.

Beard, Charles A. *An Economic Interpretation of the Constitution of the United States.* 1935. New York: Free Press, London: 1986.

——. *The Supreme Court and the Constitution.* New York: Paisley Press for the Facsimile Library, 1938.

Benditt, Theodore. *Law as Rule and Principle.* Stanford: Stanford University Press, 1978.

Benhabib, Seyla. *Situating the Self: Gender, Community and Postmodernism in Contemporary Ethics.* New York: Routledge, 1992.

Bennett, Robert W. "Objectivity in Constitutional Law." 132 *U. Penn L. Rev.* 445 (1984).

Berger, R. *Federalism: The Founder's Design.* Norman: University of Oklahoma Press, 1987.

Berman, Harold J. "The Impact of the Enlightenment on American Constitutional Law." 4 *Yale J. L. & Human* 311 (1992).

——. *Law and Revolution: The Formation of the Western Legal Tradition.* Cambridge: Harvard University Press, 1983.

Berns, Walter. *Taking the Constitution Seriously.* New York: Simon and Schuster, 1987.

Bestor, Arthur. "The American Civil War as a Constitutional Crisis." 69 *Am. Hist. Rev.* 327 (1964).

Beveridge, Albert J. *The Life of John Marshall.* New York: Houghton Mifflin, 1919.

Beyleveld, D., and R. Brownsword. *Law as Moral Judgment.* London: Sweet and Maxwell, 1986.

Bickel, Alexander. *The Least Dangerous Branch.* New Haven: Yale University Press, 1962.

——. *The Morality of Consent.* New Haven: Yale University Press, 1975.

——. "The Original Understanding and the Segregation Decisions." 69 *Harv. L. Rev.* 1 (1955).

——. *The Supreme Court and the Idea of Progress.* New Haven: Yale University Press, 1978.

Bingham, Joseph. "What is Law?" 11 *Mich. L. Rev.* 1 (1912).

Bix, Brian. *Law, Language, and Legal Determinacy.* New York: Oxford University Press, 1993.

Black, Charles. "The Unfinished Business of the Warren Court." 46 *Wash. L. Rev.* 3 (1970).

——. *Law as an Art.* Knoxville: University of Tennessee Press, 1978.

———. *Structure and Relationship in Constitutional Law*. Baton Rouge: Louisiana State University Press, 1969.

———. *The People and the Court*. Englewood Cliffs, N.J.: Prentice-Hall, 1970.

Blackstone, William. *Commentaries on the Laws of England*. London: A. Strahan, T. Cadell, and W. Daviews, 1809.

Bloch, Susan Low, and Maeva Marcus. "John Marshall's Selective Use of History in *Marbury v. Madison*." 1986 *Wis. L. Rev.* 301.

Bork, R. *The Tempting of America: The Political Seduction of the Law*. New York: Free Press, 1990.

Boswell, John. *Christianity, Social Tolerance, and Homosexuality: Gay People in Western Europe from the Beginning of the Christian Era to the Fourteenth Century*. Chicago: University of Chicago Press, 1980.

Brest, Paul. "Interpretation and Interest." 34 *Stan. L. Rev.* 765 (1982).

Brewer, David J. "The Nation's Safeguard." in *Proceedings of the N.Y. State Bar Association* 46 (1893).

Broderick, F. *The Origins of the Constitution*. New York: Macmillan, 1964.

Brown, Richard. *Society as Text: Essays on Rhetoric, Reason, and Reality*. Chicago: University of Chicago Press, 1987.

Burt, Robert A. *The Constitution in Conflict*. Cambridge: Harvard University Press, Belknap Press, 1992.

Cahn, Edmond. "Jurisprudence." 30 *N.Y.U. L. Rev.* 150 (1955).

Caplan, Russell. "The History and Meaning of the Ninth Amendment." 69 *Va. L. Rev.* 223 (1983).

Cappelletti, M., and John Adams. "Judicial Review of Legislation: European Antecedents and Adaptations." 79 *Harv. L. Rev.* 1207 (1966).

Casper, Jonathan D. *The Politics of Civil Liberties*. New York: Harper and Row, 1972.

Chemerinsky, Erwin. *Interpreting the Constitution*. New York: Praeger, 1987.

Choper, Jesse. *Judicial Review and the National Political Process: A Functional Reconsideration of the Role of the Supreme Court*. Chicago: University of Chicago Press, 1980.

Clinton, Robert N. "Original Understanding, Legal Realism, and the Interpretation of 'This Constitution.'" 72 *Iowa L. Rev.* 1177 (1987).

Cohen, M. R. *Law and the Social Order: Essays in Legal Philosophy*. New York: Harcourt, Brace, 1933.

Connors, Steven. *Postmodernist Culture: An Introduction to Theories of the Contemporary*. New York: Basil Blackwell, 1989.

Coons, John E. "Consistency." 75 *Calif. L. Rev.* 59 (1987).

Cornell, Drucilla. "Institutionalization of Meaning, Recollective Imagination, and the Potential for Transformative Legal Interpretation." 136 *U. Pa. L. Rev.* 1135 (1988).

Corwin, Edward. *Court over Constitution*. 1938. Gloucester: P. Smith, 1957.

———. "John Marshall, Revolutionist, Malgré Lui." 104 *U. Pa. L. Rev.* 9 (1955).

———. "*Marbury v. Madison* and the Doctrine of Judicial Review." 12 *Mich. L. Rev.* 538 (1914).

———. "The Passing of Dual Federalism." In *Essays in Constitutional Law,* Robert McCloskey ed. New York: Knopf, 1957.

———. "The Progress of Constitutional Theory between the Declaration of Independence and the Meaning of the Philadelphia Convention." 30 *Amer. Hist. Rev.* 511 (1925).

Cover, Robert. "The Supreme Court 1982 Term: Foreword: Nomos and Narrative." 97 *Harv. L. Rev.* 4 (1983).

Cox, Archibald. *The Role of the Supreme Court in American Government.* New York: Oxford University Press, 1976.

Craven, J. "A Paean to Pragmatism." 50 *N.C. L. Rev.* 977 (1972).

Crenshaw, Kimberle. "Race, Reform, and Retrenchment: Transformation and Legitimation in Antidiscrimination Law." 101 *Harv. L. Rev.* 1331 (1988).

Crosskey, W. *Politics and the Constitution.* Chicago: University of Chicago Press, 1953.

———. " 'Legislative History' and the Constitutional Limitations on State Governmental Authority." 22 *U. Chi. L. Rev.* 1 (1954).

Currie, David. "The Constitution in the Supreme Court: 1789–1801." 48 *U. Chi. L. Rev.* 819 (1981).

———. "The Constitution in the Supreme Court: The Powers of the Federal Courts, 1801–35." 49 *U. Chi. L. Rev.* 646 (1982).

Curtis, Charles P. Jr. *Lions under the Throne.* Boston: Houghton-Mifflin, 1947.

Daniels, Norman. "Reflective Equilibrium and Archimedean Points." 10 *Can. J. Phil.* 83 (1980).

Deener, David. "Judicial Review in Modern Constitutional Systems." 46 *Am. Pol. Sci.* 1079 (1952).

Diamond, Martin. "Commentaries on the Federalist: The Federalist on Federalism: Neither a National nor a Federal Constitution, but a Composition of Both." 86 *Yale L. J.* 1273 (1977).

Dow, David. "When Words Mean What We Believe They Say: The Case of Article V." 76 *Iowa L. Rev.* 1 (1990).

Dworkin, Ronald. " 'The Bork Nomination: An Exchange.' " 34 *N.Y. Rev. Bks.* 59 (1987).

———. "Bork to Kennedy." 34 *N.Y. Rev. Bks.* 36 (1987).

———. "The Arduous Virtue of Fidelity: Originalism, Scalia, Tribe, and Nerve." In *Fordham Symposium* at 1249.

———. "The Forum of Principle." 56 *N.Y.U. L. Rev.* 469 (1981).

———. *Freedom's Law.* Cambridge: Harvard University Press, 1996.

——. "Is Law a System of Rules?" 35 *U. Chi. L. Rev.* 14 (1967).

——. "The Law of the Slave-catchers." *Times Literary Supplement* 1437 (December 5, 1975).

——. *Law's Empire.* Cambridge: Harvard University Press, 1986.

——. *Life's Dominion.* New York: Knopf, 1993.

——. " 'Natural Law Revisited.' " 34 *U. Fla. L. Rev.* 165 (1982).

——. "Philosophy and the Critique of Law." In *The Rule of Law.* R. Wolff ed. New York: Simon and Schuster, 1971.

——. "Social Sciences and the Constitutional Right: The Consequences of Uncertainty." 6 *J.L. & Ed.* 3 (1977).

——. *Taking Rights Seriously.* Cambridge: Harvard University Press, 1977.

Eisgruber, Christopher. "Justice Story, Slavery, and the Natural Law Foundations of American Constitutionalism." 55 *U. Chi. L. Rev.* 273 (1988).

Elliott, W. Y. *The Need for Constitutional Reform.* New York: McGraw-Hill, 1935.

Ely, John Hart. *Democracy and Distrust: A Theory of Judicial Review.* Cambridge: Harvard University Press, 1980.

Epstein, Richard. "The Proper Scope of the Commerce Power." 73 *Va. L. Rev.* 1387 (1987).

Eule, Julian. "Laying the Dormant Commerce Clause to Rest." 91 *Yale L. J.* 425 (1982).

Fairman, Charles. "The Supreme Court and the Constitutional Limitations on State Governmental Authority." 21 *U. Chi. L. Rev.* 40 (1953).

Fallon, Richard H., Jr. "Dworkin and the Two Faces of Law." 67 *Notre Dame L. Rev.* 553 (1992).

Farber, Daniel. "Pragmatism." 72 *Minn. L. Rev.* 1331 (1988).

Farrand, Max. "The Federal Constitution and the Defects of the Confederation." 2 *Amer. Pol. Sci. Rev.* 132 (1908).

——, ed. *The Record of the Federal Convention of 1787.* New Haven: Yale University Press, 1966.

Fellas, John. "Reconstructing Law's Empire." 73 *Boston U.L. Rev.* 715 (1993).

Finnis, John. *Natural Law and Natural Rights.* Oxford: Clarendon Press, 1980.

——. "On Reason and Authority in Law's Empire." 6 *Law & Phil.* 357 (1987).

Fischer, William, III. "The Defects of Dualism." 59 *U. Chi. L. Rev.* 955 (1992).

Fish, Stanley. *Doing What Comes Naturally: Change, Rhetoric, and the Practice of Theory in Literary and Legal Studies.* Durham: Duke University Press, 1989.

——. "Still Wrong after All These Years." 6 *Law & Phi.* 401 (1987).

Fordham Symposium. "Fidelity in Constitutional Theory." 65 *Fordham L. Rev.* 1247–1818 (1997).

Frankena, William. *Ethics.* Englewood Cliffs, N.J.: Prentice-Hall, 1973.

Frankfurter, Felix. "John Marshall and the Judicial Function." 69 *Harv. L. Rev.* 217 (1955).

——. *The Commerce Power under Marshall, Taney, and Waite*. Chapel Hill: University of North Carolina Press, 1937.

Freund, Paul. "Umpiring the Federal System." 54 *Colum. L. Rev.* 561 (1954).

Fried, Charles. "Privacy." 77 *Yale L. J.* 475 (1968).

Friedman, Lawrence. *Law and Society: An Introduction*. Englewood Cliffs, N.J.: Prentice-Hall, 1977.

Gallie, W. B. "Essentially Contested Concepts." 56 *Proc. Aristotlean Soc'y.* 167 (1956).

Galston, Miriam, and William A. Galston. "Reason, Consent, and the U.S. Constitution: Bruce Ackerman's *We the People.*" *Ackerman Symposium* at 446.

Gellner, Ernest. *Thought and Change*. London: Weidenfeld and Nicolson, 1964.

Gerstein, Robert. "California's Constitutional Right to Privacy: The Development of the Protection of Private Life." 9 *Hastings Const. L. Q.* 387 (1982).

Gilmore, Grant. *The Ages of American Law*. New Haven: Yale University Press, 1977.

Goldman, Alvin I. *Epistemology and Cognition*. Cambridge: Harvard University Press, 1986.

Goldstein, Anne. "History, Homosexuality and Political Values: Search for the Hidden Determinants of *Bowers v. Hardwick.*" 97 *Yale L. J.* 1073 (1988).

Gordon, Robert. "Critical Legal Histories." 36 *Stan. L. Rev.* 57 (1984).

Graff, Gerald. *Beyond the Culture Wars: How Teaching the Conflicts Can Revitalize American Education*. New York: Norton, 1992.

Grano, Joseph. "Judicial Review and a Written Constitution in a Democratic Society." 28 *Wayne L. Rev.* 1 (1981).

Gray, J. *The Nature and Sources of the Law*. 2d ed. Gloucester: Peter Smith, 1972.

Greenawalt, Kent. "Dualism and Its Status." In *Ackerman Symposium* at 480.

Greenhouse, Linda. "Focus on Federal Power." *New York Times*, May 24, 1995, A1.

Greenstone, J. Davis. "Against Simplicity: The Cultural Dimensions of the Constitution." 55 *U. Chi. L. Rev.* 428 (1988).

Grey, Thomas. "Eros and Civilization and the Burger Court." 43 *Law & Contemp. Prob.* 83 (1980).

——. "Origins of the Unwritten Constitution: Fundamental Law in American Revolutionary Thought." 30 *Stan. L. Rev.* 843 (1978).

Griswold, Erwin. "The Right to Be Let Alone." 55 *Nw. U. L. Rev.* 216 (1960).

Gutmann, Amy. "The Challenge of Multiculturalism in Political Ethics." 22 *Phil. & Pub. Aff.* 171 (1993).

Hafen, B. "The Constitutional Status of Marriage, Kinship, and Sexual Privacy — Balancing the Individual and Social Interest." 81 *Mich. L. Rev.* 463 (1983).

Haines, Catherine. "General Observations on the Effects of Personal, Political, and Economic Influences in the Decisions of Judges." 17 *U. Ill. L. Rev.* 96–98 (1922).

Hall, J. *Foundations of Jurisprudence*. Indianapolis: Bobbs-Merrill, 1973.

Hamilton, A. "Final Version of an Opinion on the Constitutionality of an Act to

Establish a Bank." In 8 *Papers of Alexander Hamilton* 97. H. Syrett ed. New York: Columbia University Press, 1974.

Hampshire, Stuart. *Morality and Conflict.* Cambridge: Harvard University Press, 1983.

Hand, Learned. *The Bill of Rights.* Cambridge: Harvard University Press, 1958.

Hantzis, Catherine. "Legal Innovation within the Wider Intellectual Tradition: The Pragmatism of Oliver Wendell Holmes, Jr." 82 *Nw. U. L. Rev.* 541 (1988).

Harden, I., and N. Lewis. *The Noble Lie: The British Constitution and the Rule of Law.* London: Hutchinson, 1986.

Hare, R. M. "Liberty and Equality: How Politics Masquerades as Philosophy." In *Liberty and Equality,* 1 Ellen Frankel Paul, F. D. Miller Jr., and J. Paul eds. New York: Basil Blackwell, 1985.

——. *Moral Thinking: Its Levels, Method, and Point.* Oxford: Clarendon Press, 1981.

——. "Rawls' Theory of Justice." In *Reading Rawls* 81. Norman Daniels ed. New York: Basic Books, 1975.

Hart, H. L. A. *The Concept of Law.* 2d ed. Oxford: Clarendon Press, 1994.

Hay, P., and R. Rotunda. *The United States Federal System: Legal Integration in the American Experience.* New York: Oceana Publications, 1982.

Henly, Burt. "'Penumbra': The Roots of Legal Metaphor." 15 *Hast. Const. L. Q.* 81 (1987).

Herzog, Don. "Democratic Credentials." In *Ackerman Symposium* at 467.

Holmes, O. *Collected Legal Papers.* New York: Harcourt, Brace, 1920.

Horwitz, Morton J. "Foreword: The Constitution of Change: Legal Fundamentality without Fundamentalism." 107 *Harv. L. Rev.* 30 (1993).

Hume, David. *A Treatise Concerning Human Nature.* London: J. M. Dent, 1965.

Hunter, J. D. *Culture Wars: The Struggle to Define America.* New York: Basic Books, 1991.

Jackson, Robert H. *The Struggle for Judicial Supremacy.* 1941. New York: Octagon Books, 1979.

Jacobsohn, Gary. *Pragmatism, Statesmanship, and the Supreme Court.* Ithaca: Cornell University Press, 1977.

Jefferson, Thomas. "Opinion or the Constitutionality of the Bill to Establish a National Bank." In 19 *Papers of Thomas Jefferson* 25, Julian Boyd ed. Princeton: Princeton University Press, 1994.

Kahn, Paul W. "Reason and Will in the Origins of American Constitutionalism." 98 *Yale L. J.* 449 (1989).

——. *Legitimacy and History.* New Haven: Yale University Press, 1992.

——. *The Reign of Law: Marbury v. Madison and the Construction of American.* New Haven: Yale University Press, 1998.

Kammen, Michael. *The Origins of the American Constitution: A Documentary History.* New York: Penguin, 1986.

Karst, Kenneth. "The Freedom of Intimate Associations." 88 *Yale L. J.* 33 (1980).

Kauper, Paul G. "Penumbras, Peripheries, Emanations, Things Fundamental and Things Forgotten: The Griswold Case." 64 *Mich. L. Rev.* 235 (1965).

Kelly, A., and W. Harbison. *The American Constitution: Its Origins and Development.* New York: Norton, 1970.

Kennedy, Duncan. "The Structure of Blackstone's Commentaries." 28 *Buff. L. Rev.* 205 (1979).

Kesler, C. *Saving the Revolution: The Federalist Papers and the American Founding.* New York: Free Press, 1987.

Klarman, Michael J. "Constitutional Fact/Constitutional Fiction: A Critique of Bruce Ackerman's Theory of Constitutional Moments." 44 *Stan. L. Rev.* 759 (1992).

Kluger, Richard. *Simple Justice: The History of Brown v. Board of Education and Black America's Struggle for Equality.* New York: Knopf, 1975.

Kress, Ken. "Legal Indeterminacy." 77 *Calif. L. Rev.* 283 (1988).

Kuhn, Thomas. *The Structure of Scientific Revolutions.* Chicago: University of Chicago Press, 1969.

Kundera, Milan. *The Book of Laughter and Forgetting.* New York: Knopf, 1981.

Kurland, Philip. "Curia Regis: Some Comments on the Divine Right of Kings and Courts 'To Say What the Law Is.'" 23 *Ariz. L. Rev.* 581 (1981).

Langdell, C. C. *Brief Survey of Equity Jurisprudence.* Cambridge: Harvard Law Review Association, 1905.

——. *Cases on Contracts.* Boston: Little, Brown, 1871.

Laycock, Douglas. "Constitutional Theory Matters." 65 *Tex. L. Rev.* 767 (1987).

Lessig, Lawrence. "Fidelity and Constraint." In *Fordham Symposium* at 1365.

——. *Translating Federalism: United States v. Lopez.* 1995 Sup. Ct. Rev. 126.

Levinson, Sanford. "Law as Literature." In *Interpreting Law as Literature: A Hermeneutic Reader* 155, Sanford Levinson and Steven Mailloux eds. Evanston: Northwestern University Press, 1988.

——. *Constitutional Faith.* Princeton: Princeton University Press, 1988.

——, ed. *Responding to Imperfection.* Princeton: Princeton University Press, 1995.

Levy, Leonard. "The Making of the Constitution." In *A Grand Experiment: The Constitution at 200: Essays From The Douglass Adair Symposia* 1, J. A. Moore Jr. and J. E. Murphy eds. Wilmington, Del.: Scholarly Resources, 1987.

Lipkin, Robert Justin. "The Anatomy of Constitutional Revolutions." 66 *Neb. L. Rev.* 701 (1989).

——. "Beyond Skepticism, Foundationalism, and the New Fuzziness: The Role of Wide Reflective Equilibrium in Legal Theory." 75 *Cornell L. Rev.* 811 (1990).

——. "Can American Constitutional Law Be Postmodern?" 42 *Buff. L. Rev.* 317 (1994).

——. "Can Liberalism Justify Multiculturalism?" 45 *Buffalo L. Rev.* 1 (1997).

———. "Conventionalism, Pragmatism and Constitutional Revolutions." 21 *U.C. Davis L. Rev.* 645 (1988).

———. "Foreword: Is American Progressive Constitutionalism Dead?" 4 *Widener Symposium L. J.* i (1999).

———. "Indeterminacy, Justification, and Truth in Constitutional Theory." 60 *Fordham L. Rev.* 595 (1993).

———. "Kibitzers, Fuzzies, and Apes without Tails: The Art of Conversation in Legal Theory." 66 *Tulane L. Rev.* 69 (1991).

———. "Pragmatism, Cultural Criticism, and the Idea of the Postmodern University." In *An Ethical Education: Community and Morality in the Multicultural University* 49, M. N. S. Sellers ed. Oxford: Berg, 1994.

———. "Pragmatism—The Unfinished Revolution: Doctrinaire and Reflective Pragmatism in Rorty's Social Thought." 67 *Tul. L. Rev.* 1561 (1992).

———. "The Possibility of Liberal Constitutionalism: The Distinction Between Deliberative and Dedicated Cultures." 29 *U. Rich. L. Rev.* 765 (1995).

———. "Progressivism as Communitarian Democracy." 4 *Widener Symposium L. J.* 229 (1999).

———. "The Quest for the Common Good: Neutrality in Sunstein's Conception of American Constitutionalism." 26 *U. Conn. L. Rev.* 1039 (1995).

Lofgren, C. *The Plessy Case: A Legal-Historical Interpretation.* New York: Oxford University Press, 1987.

Lyotard, Jean-François. *The Postmodern Condition: A Report on Knowledge.* Minneapolis: University of Minnesota Press, 1984.

———. "Universal History and Cultural Differences." In *The Lyotard Reader* 314, A. Benjamin ed. Oxford: Basil Blackwell, 1989.

MacCormick, Neil. "Jurisprudence and the Constitution." 36 *Current Legal Problems* 13, L. Lloyd, R. Rideout, and J. Dysob eds. 1983.

———. *Legal Reasoning and Legal Theory.* Oxford: Clarendon Press, 1978.

MacIntyre, Alasdair. "Crises, Narrative and Science." In *Paradigms and Revolutions: Appraisal and Applications of Thomas Kuhn's Philosophy of Science* 54, Gary Gutting ed. Notre Dame: University of Notre Dame Press, 1980.

Mackie, J. *Ethics: Inventing Right and Wrong.* Harmondsworth, England: Penquin Books, 1978.

Madison, James. *Federalist Papers.* New York: New American Library, 1961.

Massey, Calvin. "Federalism and Fundamental Rights: The Ninth Amendment," 38 *Hast. L. J.* 305 (1987).

McBride, William. "Towards a Phenomenology of International Justice." In *Law, Reason, and Justice* 137, G. Hughes ed. New York: New York University Press, 1969.

McCloskey, Robert. *The American Supreme Court.* Chicago: University of Chicago Press, 1960.

——. "Introduction." In *Essays in Constitutional Law*. New York: Knopf, 1957.

McConnell, Michael W. "The Forgotten Constitutional Moment." 11 *Const. Commentary* 115 (1994).

——. "A Moral Realist Defense of Constitutional Democracy." 64 *Chic. Kent L. Rev.* 89 (1988).

——. "Originalism and the Desegregation Decisions." 81 *Virginia L. Rev.* 947 (1995).

McLaughlin, Andrew C. "The Background of American Federalism." 12 *Am. Pol. Sci. Rev.* 15 (1918).

McWhinney, E. *Judicial Review in the English-speaking World*. Toronto: University of Toronto Press, 1965.

Mendelson, Wallace. "Jefferson on Judicial Review: Consistency through Change." 29 *U. Chi. L. Rev.* 327 (1962).

Michelman, Frank. "Law's Republic." 97 *Yale L. J.* 1493 (1988).

——. "The Supreme Court, 1985 Term-Forward: Traces of Self-Government." 100 *Harv. L. Rev.* 4 (1986).

Miller, A. *The Secret Constitution and the Need for Constitutional Change*. New York: Greenwood Press, 1987.

Miller, A., and R. Howell. "The Myth of Neutrality." In *Judicial Review and the Supreme Court*. Leonard Levy ed. New York: Harper and Row, 1967.

Moore, G. E. *Principia Ethicai*. Cambridge: Cambridge University Press, 1911.

Morgan, Edward S. "The Fiction of the People." *N.Y. Rev. Bks.* Apr. 23, 1992: 46.

Munzer, Stephen R. and James Nickles. "Does the Constitution Mean What It Always Meant?" 77 *Colum. L. Rev.* 1029 (1977).

Murphy, Cornelius. "Dworkin on Judicial Discretion: A Critical Analysis," 21 *U.C. Davis L. Rev.* 767 (1988).

Nedelsky, Jennifer. "The Puzzle of Modern Constitutionalism." In *Ackerman Symposium* at 500.

Nelson, William E. "The Changing Meaning of Equality in Twentieth-Century Constitutional Law." 52 *Wash. & Lee L. Rev.* 3 (1995).

——. "The Eighteenth Century Background of John Marshall's Jurisprudence," 76 *Mich. L. Rev.* 893 (1978).

Nielsen, Kai. *Equality and Liberty: A Defense of Radical Egalitarianism*. Totowa, N.J.: Rowman and Allanheld, 1985.

Northwestern Symposium. "One Hundred Years of Judicial Review." 88 *Nw. L. Rev.* 1–468 (1993).

Note: "Dualistic Legal Phenomena and the Limitations of Positivism." 86 *Colum. L. Rev.* 823 (1986).

Note: "Judge Spencer Roane of Virginia: Champion of States Rights, Foe of John Marshall." 66 *Harv. L. Rev.* 1242 (1953).

Nowak, J., R. Rotunda, and A. Young. *Constitutional Law.* 3d ed. St. Paul, Minn.: West Publishing, 1986.

Palmer, D., and M. Scarring. "Moral Revolutions." *Phil. & Phenom. Res.* 262 (1974).

Parsons, Kathryn. "Nietzsche and Moral Change." In *Nietzsche: A Collection of Critical Essays* 169, Robert C. Solomon ed. Garden City, N.Y.: Anchor Press, 1973.

Patterson, B. *The Forgotten Ninth Amendment.* Indianapolis: Bobbs-Merrill, 1955.

Peczenik, Alexander. "Moral and Ontological Justification in Legal Reasoning." 4 *Law & Phil.* 289 (1985).

Perry, Michael J. *The Constitution, the Court, and Human Rights.* New Haven: Yale University Press, 1982.

———. *The Constitution in the Courts: Law or Politics?* New York: Oxford University Press, 1994.

Pocock, J. G. A. "States, Republics, and Empires: The American Founding in Early Modern Perspective." In *Conceptual Change and the Constitution* 55, T. Ball and J. G. A. Pocock eds. Lawrence: University Press of Kansas, 1988.

Posner, Richard. "The Jurisprudence of Skepticism." 86 *Mich. L. Rev.* 827 (1988).

———. "Privacy in the Supreme Court." 1979 *Sup. Ct. Rev.* 173, 197.

Powell, H. J. "The Modern Misunderstanding of Original Intent." Book review. 54 *U. Chi. L. Rev.* 1513 (1987).

———. "The Original Understanding of Original Intent." 98 *Harv. L. Rev.* 885 (1985).

———. "Rules for Originalists." 73 *Va. L. Rev.* 659 (1987).

Powell, Thomas Reed. "The Logic and Rhetoric of Constitutional Law." In *Essays in Constitutional Law* 85, Robert McCloskey ed. New York: Knopf, 1957.

Prentice, E. P., and J. G. Egan. *The Commerce Clause of the Federal Constitution.* 1898. Littleton, Colo.: F. B. Rothman, 1981.

Putnam, Hilary. *Meaning and the Moral Sciences.* London: Routledge and Kegan Paul, 1978.

Quine, W. V. O. *Ontological Relativity and Other Essays.* New York: Columbia University Press, 1969.

———. "Posits and Reality." In *The Ways of Paradox.* New York: Random House, 1966.

Quine, W. V. O., and J. S. Ullian. *The Web of Belief.* New York: Random House, 1970.

Quinn, W. "Truth and Explanation in Ethics." 96 *Ethics* 524 (1986).

Rakove, Jack N. *Original Meanings: Politics and Ideas in the Making of the Constitution.* New York: Knopf, 1996.

Ranney, J. "The Bases of American Federalism." 3 *Wm. & Mary Q.* 1, 25 (1946).

Rawle, W. *A View of the Constitution of the United States of America.* 2d ed. New York: DaCapo Press, 1970.

Rawls, John. *A Theory of Justice*. Cambridge: Harvard University Press, 1971.

Raz, J. "Dworkin: A New Link in the Chain." 74 *Calif. L. Rev.* 1103 (1986).

Redlich, Norman. "Are There Certain Rights . . . Retained by the People?" 37 *N.Y.U. L. Rev.* 787 (1962).

Richards, David A.J. *Conscience and the Constitution: History, Theory, and Law of the Reconstruction Amendments*. Princeton: Princeton University Press, 1993.

———. "Constitutional Legitimacy and Constitutional Privacy." 61 *N.Y.U. L. Rev.* 800 (1986).

———. *The Moral Criticism of the Law*. Encino, Calif.: Dickenson Publ. Co., 1977.

———. *Sex, Drugs, Death, and the Law*. Totowa: Rowman and Littlefield, 1982.

———. "Sexual Autonomy and Right to Privacy." 30 *Hast. L. J.* 957 (1979).

———. *Toleration and the Constitution*. New York: Oxford University Press, 1986.

Rorty, Richard. *Contingency, Irony and Solidarity*. Cambridge: Cambridge University Press, 1989.

———. "Inquiry as Recontextualism: An Anti-Dualist Account of Interpretation." 1 *Philosophical Papers: Objectivity, Relativism and Truth* 93. Cambridge: Cambridge University Press, 1991.

———. *Philosophy and the Mirror of Nature*. Princeton: Princeton University Press, 1979.

Rosenberg, Gerald. *The Hollow Hope: Can Courts Bring about Social Change?* Chicago: University of Chicago Press, 1991.

Rosenfeld, Michel. *Just Interpretations: Law between Ethics and Politics*. Berkeley and Los Angeles: University of California Press, 1998.

Ross, A. *On Law and Justice*. Berkeley and Los Angeles: University of California Press, 1974.

Ross, David. *The Foundations of Ethics*. Oxford: Oxford University Press, 1930.

Rubenfeld, Jeb. "Affirmative Action." 107 *Yale L. J.* 427 (1997).

Rumble, Wilfrid E. *American Legal Realism: Skepticism, Reform, and the Judicial Process*. Ithaca: Cornell University Press, 1968.

Rutland, R. *The Birth of the Bill of Rights*. Boston: Northeastern University Press, 1983.

Ryan, Noel. "The Central Fallacy of Canadian Constitutional Law." 22 *McGill L.J.* 40 (1976).

Sager, L. "Fair Measures: The Legal Status of Underenforced Constitutional Norms." 91 *Harv. L. Rev.* 1212 (1978).

Sandalow, Terrance. "Abstract Democracy: A Review of Ackerman's *We The People.*" 9 *Const. Comm.* 309 (1992).

Sandel, Michael J. *Democracy's Discontent*. Cambridge: Harvard University Press, 1996.

Sayers, S. *Reality and Reason*. Oxford: Basil Blackwell, 1985.

Schauer, Frederick. "Formalism." 97 *Yale L. J.* 509.

——. "The Occasions of Constitutional Interpretation." 73 *B. U. L. Rev.* 729 (1992).

Schlesinger, Arthur, Jr. "After the Imperial Presidency." 47 *Md. L. Rev.* 54 (1987).

Schultz, David A. and Christopher E. Smith. *The Jurisprudential Vision of Justice Antonin Scalia.* Lanham, Md.: Rowman and Littlefield, 1996.

Schwartz, Bernard. *Super Chief Earl Warren and His Supreme Court.* New York: New York University Press, 1983.

Sedler, Robert. "The Legitimacy Debate in Constitutional Adjudication: An Assessment and a Different Perspective." 44 *Ohio St. L. J.* 93 (1983).

Shaman, Jeffrey. "The Constitution, the Supreme Court, and Creativity." 9 *Hastings Const. L.Q.* 257 (1982).

——. "Constitutional Fact: The Perception of Reality by the Supreme Court." 35 *U. Fla. L. Rev.* 236 (1983).

Sherry, Suzanna. "The Founders' Unwritten Constitution." 54 *U. Chi. L. Rev.* 1127 (1987).

——. "The Ghost of Liberalism Past." 105 *Harv. L. Rev.* 918 (1992).

Shiffrin, Steven. *First Amendment, Romance, and Dissent.* Cambridge: Harvard University Press, 1990.

——. "Radicalism, Liberalism and Legal Scholarship." 30 *UCLA L. Rev.* 1103 (1982).

Siegen, B. *The Supreme Court's Constitution.* New Brunswick, N.J.: Transaction, 1986.

Singer, Peter. "Sidgwick and Reflective Equilibrium." 58 *The Monist* 490 (1974).

Singer, William. "The Legal Rights Debate in Analytical Jurisprudence From Bentham to Hohfeld." 1982 *Wis. L. Rev.* 975.

Smith, Jean Edward. *John Marshall: Definer of a Nation.* New York: H. Holt, 1996.

Smith, R. *Public Prayer and the Constitution: A Case Study in Constitutional Interpretation.* Wilmington: Scholarly Resources, 1987.

Smith, Steven. *The Constitution and the Pride of Reason.* New York: Oxford University Press, 1998.

Snowiss, Sylvia. *Judicial Review and the Law of the Constitution.* Yale University Press: New Haven, 1990.

Stampp, Kenneth M. "The Concept of a Perpetual Union." 65 *J. Amer. Hist.* 5 (1978).

Stick, John. "Can Nihilism Be Pragmatic?" 100 *Harv. L. Rev.* 332 (1986).

Stone, G., L. Seidman, C. Sunstein, and M. Tushnet. *Constitutional Law.* Boston: Little, Brown, and Company, 1986.

Strayer, B. *The Canadian Constitution and the Courts.* Toronto: Butterworth's, 1983.

Summers, Robert S. *Instrumentalism and American Legal Theory.* Ithaca: Cornell University Press, 1982.

——. "Professor Fuller's Jurisprudence and America's Dominant Theory of Law." 92 *Harv. L. Rev.* 444 (1978).

Sunstein, Cass R. *The Partial Constitution*. Cambridge: Harvard University Press, 1993.

Taiwo, Olefumi. *Legal Naturalism*. Ithaca: Cornell University Press, 1996.

Taylor, J. *Construction Construed and Constitutions Vindicated*. 1820. New York: Da Capo Press, 1970.

Thayer, James B. "The Origin and Scope of the American Doctrine of Constitutional Law." 7 *Harv. L. Rev.* 129 (1893).

Toulmin, Stephen. "Does the Distinction between Normal and Revolutionary Science Hold Water?" In *Criticism and the Growth of Knowledge* 39, I. Lakatos and A. Musgrave eds. New York: Cambridge University Press, 1970.

Tribe, Laurence H. *American Constitutional Law*. Mineola: Foundation Press, 1986.

———. "Taking Text and Structure Seriously: Reflections on Free-form Method in Constitutional Interpretation." 108 *Harv. L. Rev.* 1221 (1995).

Tur, Richard. "Positivism, Principles, and Rules." In *Perspectives in Jurisprudence* 42, Elspeth Atwood ed. Glasgow: University of Glasgow Press, 1977.

Tushnet, Mark. "Anti-Formalism in Recent Constitutional Theory." 83 *Mich. L. Rev.* 1502 (1985).

———. Book Review. 57 *Tex. L. Rev.* 1295 (1979).

———. "Following the Rules Laid Down: A Critique of Interpretivism and Neutral Principles." 96 *Harv. L. Rev.* 781 (1985).

———. "Living in a Constitutional Moment." 46 *Case West. Res. L. Rev.* 845 (1996).

———. "A Note on the Revival of Textualism in Constitutional Theory." 58 *S. Cal. L. Rev.* 683 (1985).

———. *Taking the Constitution Away from the Courts*. Princeton: Princeton University Press, 1999.

Van Alstyne, William. "A Critical Guide to *Marbury v. Madison*." 1969 *Duke L. J.* 1.

———. "Federalism, Congress, the States, and the Tenth Amendment: Adrift in the Cellophane Sea." 1987 *Duke L. J.* 769.

Waldron, Jeremy. Book Review of Bruce Ackerman, 1 *We the People*. 90 *J. Phil.* 149 (1993).

Waluchow, W. J. *Inclusive Legal Positivism*. Oxford: Clarendon Press, 1994.

Walzer, Michael. "Minimal Moralism." In *From the Twilight of Probability: Ethics and Politics* 3, William R. Shea and Antonio Spadafora eds. Canton, Mass.: Science History Publications, 1992.

Warren, C. "Legislative and Judicial Attacks on the Supreme Court of the United States — A History of the Twenty-Fifth Section of the Judiciary Act." 47 *Am. L. Rev.* 1 (1913).

———. *The Supreme Court and Sovereign States*. New York: Da Capo Press, 1972.

———. *The Supreme Court in United States History*. Boston: Little, Brown, 1926.

Wechsler, Herbert. "Toward Neutral Principles of Constitutional Law." 73 *Harv. L. Rev.* 1 (1959).

Wellington, Carl. "The Nature of Judicial Review." 91 *Yale L. J.* 486 (1982).

West, Robin. "Is Progressive Constitutionalism Possible?" 4 *Widener Symposium L.J.* 1 (1999).

Westmoreland, Robert. "Dworkin and Legal Pragmatism." 11 *Oxford J. Leg. Stud.* 174 (1991).

White, James Boyd. "Thinking About Language." 96 *Yale L. J.* 1960 (1987).

――――. *When Words Lose Meaning: Constitutions and Reconstitutions of Language, Character, and Community.* Chicago: University of Chicago Press, 1984.

White, M. *Philosophy, the Federalist, and the Constitution.* New York: Oxford University Press, 1987.

Wilkinson, J., III. *From Brown to Bakke.* New York: Oxford University Press, 1979.

Wilson, E. O. *On Human Nature.* Cambridge: Harvard University Press, 1977.

Wilson, James G. "The Morality of Formalism." 33 *UCLA L. Rev.* 431 (1985).

Wilson, Woodrow. *Constitutional Government In The United States.* New York: Columbia University Press, 1908.

Wittgenstein, Ludwig. *On Certainty,* G. E. M. Anscombe trans. Oxford: Basil Blackwell, 1967.

――――. *Philosophical Investigations,* G.E.M. Anscombe ed. Oxford: Basil Blackwell, 1953.

――――. *Remarks on the Foundations of Mathematics,* G. E. M. Anscombe trans. Oxford: Basil Blackwell, 1964.

――――. *Zettel,* G. E. M. Anscombe trans. Oxford: Basil Blackwell, 1967.

Wolfe, Christopher. *The Rise of Modern Judicial Review.* New York: Basic Books, 1986.

――――. "A Theory of U.S. Constitutional History." 43 *J. Pol.* 292 (1981).

Wright, B., Jr. *American Interpretations of Natural Law: A Study in the History of Political Thought.* New York: Russell and Russell, 1931.

Yarbrough, Jean. "Federalism in the Foundation and Preservation of the American Republic." 6 *Publius: J. Fed.* 43 (1976).

INDEX

Judges: appointing and holding accountable, 246 n.31; autonomy of, 125; conservative, 226; countermajoritarian roles of, 161–62; electing, 8; identifying the need for revolutionary adjudication, 207–8; interpretation of Constitution, 145; majoritarianism and, 246 n.31; pragmatist, 127, 293 n.27; restrained vs. activist, 222–23, 226–27; role in making constitutional law, 144; roles of legislators vs. 145; self-conceptions of, 226–28; theory of constitutional revolutions and, 208–15, 226–28; translation of political culture into constitutional law, 139. See also Judicial discretion

Judgments, 235–36; first- vs. second-order, xii, 237, 239; that conflict with political principles, 83

Judicial activism, 108

Judicial appointments, 259 n.90

Judicial decisions conflicting with Constitution, 207

Judicial discretion, 125, 271 n.58, 324 n.165

Judicial dualism. See Dualism

Judicial independence, 9

Judicial reasoning, theory of, 150–53

Judicial review, 247 n.38; activist vs. passive, xii; activist vs. Thayerian, 164; compatibility with American democracy, 10; countermajoritarian character of, xii–xiii, 160–62; established as only effective form of review, 163; justification of, 235–36; meanings of, 305 n.14; normative dimension of theories of, xiii; and progressive political theory, 239; requirements for justifying, ix; virtue(s) of, 16. See also Revolutionary judicial review

Judicial Review and the National Political Process (Choper), 252 n.31

Judicial revolutions, 120

"Jurisgeneris," 7

Jurisprudence: approaches to testing theories of constitutional, 227; "correct" and "original," 213

Jurisprudential paradigm, standard, x

Justification, 91–93, 212; relationship between fit and, 93–108, 111, 271 n.59

Justificatory and explanatory values, 116

Justificatory principles, 110–11, 130, 271 n.60

Kahn, Paul W., 311 n.57, 334 n.25

Kennedy, Anthony M., 274 n.79, 304 n.5

Korematsu v. United States, 142, 277 n.94

Kuhn, Thomas, 118, 133–34, 156, 333 n.18

Landmark cases, 224–25

Langdellian formalism, 289 n.17

Language: constitutional, 116, 130–31; Court's use of, 193

Law(s): creating, 6, 145; dichotomy between making and applying, 136; discovering, 6; vs. politics, 219; surface vs. deep structure of, 104. See also Integrity, law as

Legal code vs. constitution, 138–39

Legal rule vs. legal principle, 105–6

Legislation: vs. adjudication, 217; congressional, 162

Legislators, role of, 145

Legislature: as appropriate place for "revolutionary" change, 217. See also Congress

Legitimacy, 241 n.1; constitutional, xii, 7–13, 36, 226; and countermajori-